The Ways of Naysaying

Also by Eva Brann

The World of the Imagination: Sum and Substance

What, Then, Is Time?

The Ways of Naysaying

No, Not, Nothing, and Nonbeing

EVA BRANN

ROWMAN & LITTLEFIELD PUBLISHERS, INC.
Lanham • Boulder • New York • Oxford

ROWMAN & LITTLEFIELD PUBLISHERS, INC.

Published in the United States of America
by Rowman & Littlefield Publishers, Inc.
4720 Boston Way, Lanham, Maryland 20706
www.rowmanlittlefield.com

12 Hid's Copse Road
Cumnor Hill, Oxford OX2 9JJ, England

British Library Cataloguing in Publication Information Available

Library of Congress Cataloging-in-Publication Data

Brann, Eva T. H.
    The ways of naysaying : no, not, nothing, and nonbeing / Eva Brann.
        p.   cm.
    Includes bibliographical references and index.
    ISBN 0-7425-1228-2 (alk. paper) — ISBN 0-7425-1229-0 (pbk.: alk. paper)
    1. Negation (Logic)   2. Nonbeing.   3. Nothing (Philosophy)   I. Title.

BC199.N4 B73   2000
160—dc21   00-062638

Printed in the United States of America

∞ ™ The paper used in this publication meets the minimum requirements of
American National Standard for Information Sciences—Permanence of Paper for
Printed Library Materials, ANSI/NISO Z39.48–1992.

To my college and my colleagues

Contents

Preface

Purpose and Plan

Imagination, Time, and Naysaying are three closely entwined capabilities of our inwardness, and I have come to think of *The World of the Imagination* (1991), *What, Then, Is Time?* (1999), and now *The Ways of Naysaying* as a trilogy of the human center. All models of the inner human being are, as far as I know, spatial metaphors.[1] So I have had before me all along a figure of the soul—a working hypothesis, nothing like a theory—as having a front, a middle, and a background.

The front is where a world that impinges on us as it wills, an adventitious world, confronts us: at the organs of our external senses. We can shut off at our pleasure (and sometimes at our peril) the representational or distance senses, sight and hearing, and it is this ability that contributes most to our notion of having an inside and an outside, a soul and a body. At the other end of our conscious being there is thinking. Thinking too sometimes seems like a discretionary activity; although we may shut down its deliberate employment, it is behind and beneath everything we are and do, as its prop and ground. Even our—invariably purposeful—irrationality is worlds apart from the arational intelligence of animals and nonrational intelligibility of inanimate nature. The human difference is revealed, of course, in the term "rational" itself, which means, from way back, reason manifested in speech. Naysaying originates in this most ultimate and dominating rear of our psychic territory; perhaps it is coeval with thinking itself.

In between sensing and thinking I imagine a large middle space, where we contain representations and entertain experiences—the products, it may be, of sense by thought—that belong to us in the most intimately and intensely personal way. Among these are that subtly reactive receptivity we call feeling, the psychic stir seeking expression we call emotion, and the not always unwelcome suffering we call passion. These affective capacities at the heart of our inwardness are deeply involved with the more representational capabilities of having images and sensing time, which are sometimes their instigator and sometimes their crucible:

> for pain must enter into its glorified life of memory before it can turn into compassion.[2]

But they are not my subjects—partly from a sense that they want quite a lot of leaving alone.

Imagination and time, on the other hand, are sturdily inexhaustible subjects to think about. And both are found, when subjected to analysis, to be even more deeply implicated with negation than with feeling.[3] Imagining makes a presence of an absence; an image is the presence, internal or external, of what is *not* here and now confronting the senses, and it can therefore be said to be a mixture of Nonbeing and Being. The image is *not* the original, and then again it claims to be just that:

> So, either by thy picture or my love,
> Thyself away are present still with me.[4]

Time is similarly constituted; it is the image pulled apart by passage, so to speak. The past is what is no more, the future is what is not yet, the now is evanescent; and yet the past, at least, seems ineradicably fixed. Temporality has the thought-structure of becoming: Nonbeing and Being in one.[5]

Imagination and time are related to the brink of identity through memory, which is the presence of what has gone absent through passage. As there are external images, so there are external bearers of memory—scenes and artifacts whose outer film lets through their inward freight:

> Transparent things through which the past shines![6]

But even before the world becomes fraught with the past, there is internal memory, the imagination in its longitudinal mode, the origin of our sense of time. As the imagination in general makes present what is *not* before us by reason of nonexistence or withdrawal, so memory peculiarly holds what is *not* with us by reason of having gone by. But of course, these two absences mingle:

> When all this all doth passe from age to age,
>
> . . .
>
> When Love doth change his seat from heart to heart,
>
> . . .
>
> Absence my presence is, strangenesse my grace.[7]

Therefore, if we want to understand something of imagination, memory, and time, we must mount an inquiry into what it means to say that something is not what it claims to be or is not there or is nonexistent or is affected by Nonbeing. And that is what I am after in *Ways of Naysaying*.

Thinking about negations is different from thinking about imagination and time—less dependent on introspective observation, more turned to logic and language. There is, to be sure, an infantile naysaying of instinct and gesture that occurs awhile before the first, willful, *no* of speech arises. But once there is speech, words are of the essence of negation, for most of it is nay-*saying*. Words, spoken long before reflection and analysis, alert us to the *not* of denial and the *non-* that is not mere rejection. We could, it is thinkable, be aware of our internal images and passages without having language for them because they are inner presentations—*re*-presentations, in fact. But whether we would know about negation—*that* we are capable of it and *how*—without speech is doubtful to me. Hence within my scheme, *no, not, non-* are deeper than imagination and time, in the sense that the former underlie the latter and are revealed in their analysis.

So while the first impetus to the study of naysaying was from the desire to understand these central human capacities of imagination and time, the inquiry soon developed many larger questions.

For "names stretch into what is not here."[8] They bring what is absent into presence. But sentences also *negate* and consign to Nonbeing or Nonexistence what is proposed. The words that utter thought do not re-present their objects (that is, they do not bring onto the inner scene what is absent or nonexistent by means of similitude) as do the images of the imagination, but they *intend* them. The mysteries and conundrums of intention—denotation and reference, sense and meaning—are satisfactorily settled by no one (all my reading tells me) and are happily not within the task of this book. But I do touch on some of the questions raised by the *unsaying* of words and sentences that negation effects—piggybacking these problems onto the prior enigma of speech itself.

Here are the sorts of question that arise: Is negation at bottom a significant activity of thought, or is it a merely formal symbolic operator of logic? Whichever of these it be, is it true that "it does not introduce anything in reality but only in conceptuality *(in ratione)*, for negation belongs to reason, not to nature"?[9] Or is it perhaps the case that, although naysaying, the *not* of subjective judgment, belongs to reason and its utterance, there is also an objective *non-* that signifies a kind of knowable being, the Nonbeing of the realm of intelligibles, or the nonexistence of the world of nature? Then it would be a question not only "whether intuitive cognition of a nonexistent object is possible?"[10] but, above all, whether Nonbeing is somehow manifest in the world. And there are *many* more subordinate problems.

But my underlying purpose in this book is to see whether it might not be possible to discover what all the ways of naysaying have in common, in order to throw some further light not only on imagination and time but on the denials of thought itself. I have taken to heart the warning that it is a pathologically bad craving to want a word to have one ultimate meaning, worse to look for one meaning over many words, and worst to assume that such a meaning may apply to a something beyond the realm of language. But consider, on the other side, the phenomenal persistence with which that little root *ne* enters into nearly *all* the words of negation in *all* the languages whose texts turn up in this book—English, of course, and Greek, Latin, German, and French (always, I might say here, in translation); to prove the point, those words of negation are collected in the introduction. The history of our languages must, used cautiously, count for something and allow at least the surmise that one human propensity is at work here and perhaps one objective condition. And consider too that this craving to look for one truth behind many appearances may be simply ineradicable, being nothing less than the philosophical impulse.[11]

∞   ∞   ∞

The marshaling of the ways of naysaying seems to fall naturally into six chapters.

Chapter One. Among the earliest gestures and words of the human young is *No!*, the *no* of rejection and rebellion. This chapter is about the willful *no* from infants to adults, from humans to fallen angels, from demonic possession to contentious disputation.

Chapter Two. The negation that enters into the sentences of language is signified by *not*. *Not* is the negation of logic and raises many issues: What *is* logical negation? What are the effects of *not* in different locations in a sentence? Why is negation, but not affirmation, an operation? Why does negation seem to be more closely related to falsity than to truth? When does twice *no* mean yes? These and some other by-plays of negation are considered under the adverb *not*.

Chapter Three. If *not* belonged to logic, *Nonexistence* belongs to logicians; it is considered next. Whether nonexistence can pertain to objects and how it can enter into logical propositions became, early in the last century, a great concern to philosophically inclined logicians like Alexius Meinong and Bertrand Russell, and it remains a lively topic. Along with the formal problem of "existential quantification" comes the question concerning all the fictions of the imagination: how is their logical nonexistence to be reconciled with their affective power?

Chapter Four. This chapter is the center of the book, for here comes on the scene the *Non-* of philosophy, a prefix signifying not the brusquely rejecting denial of fact in words but the more forgiving opposition of two elements in the same world. The thought of Nonbeing comes among us as the unbidden effect of Parmenides' injunction against it, and Plato will domesticate that same Nonbeing, bringing it into philosophy as the relational principle of diversity, the Other. In this chapter, then, negation extends its domain from the refusals and denials of will and thought to all there is. Naysaying gains its proper object in Nonbeing.

Chapter Five. Nonbeing is an object of thought, but *Negativity* is for G. W. F. Hegel thought itself or rather the life and motor of thought. Here, then, is set out that negating activity of the Spirit called dialectic, together with its cut-and-dried Kantian counterpart, the negating understanding. And the question is asked: Where does that journey of negativity, the self-development of conceptual thought truly begin: in Being or in Nothing?

Chapter Six. Here finally this *Nothing* comes front and center. It is the absolute antagonist of Being and beings, concrete in its thinglike opposition and perfectly inapprehensible for all that. This *Nothing*, the supreme attainment of the East, is the ultimate anathema to the West. Yet in modernity, expressing one of its deep aspects, arise nihilistic movements, until finally for Martin Heidegger the Nothing makes an epiphany as the manifesting source of Being. The chapter ends with a section on our death, in which we all come to nothing—or perhaps not.

$$\infty \qquad \infty \qquad \infty$$

Are the ways of naysaying, then, a cheerless or a charmless subject? Not at all; they are a peculiarly captivating one, though perhaps not as amenable to visionary musing as is the imagination or to eavesdropping meditation as is time. All the descendants of that little root *ne* taken separately offer a wonderful variety of satisfyingly definable and often decidable problems, while taken together they bring us within sight of the way we are and the way things are. I will say in the conclusion, as concisely and as clearly as I can, what seems to have come into view in the course of studying the ways of negation; I will try to answer the question: What, then, is naysaying? But I want to warn the reader now that there will not be anything very novel. My defense is that reflective inquiry is unlike other investigations, which are usually undertaken for the sake of adding something new to the store of knowledge. In philosophy newness is at best irrelevant to the purpose, which is for us all—the more the merrier—to think through, for the umpteenth time, some everlastingly captivating questions in their old and new guises, so as to gain some clarity, add some complexity, come to some comprehension, and possibly live better thereby. And at worst newness is suspect, because it often betokens willful construction rather than candid discovery. There are, of course, writers who manage to be original in both senses—novel *and* deep-delving, and upon their guidance this book gratefully relies—and it is no perfunctory gratitude.

Thanks are also owed and gladly given to Ann Martin, not only for her knowledgeable manuscript preparation but for logical acumen, and to my colleagues Stewart Umphrey and Peter Kalkavage, the former for looking at the manuscript with his eagle eye for significant detail, the latter for giving it an appreciative reading and then denominating it—surprising me into delighted recognition—as my "cradle-to-grave book."

This book is dedicated to St. John's College, where I learned to think of philosophy as an ample and generous way of life, and to my colleagues who, by a wise resistance to false ambitions, keep this remarkable community of learning intact. It was in my thoughts to accompany the dedication in front with an epigram that happens to be the fundamental dictum pinpointing the crucial constructive function of naysaying (p. 163). But it fits better here, since it requires elucidation by translation:

Omnis determinatio est negatio,

which I render for present purposes:

All determined devotion involves some naysaying.

$$\infty \qquad \infty \qquad \infty$$

The ways of naysaying consist of so many highways and byways that to keep the main route fairly straightforward it seemed good to consign to endnotes not only all the citations and references but also the comments and digressions it was beyond my power to suppress. In effect the notes constitute a kind of counterpoint to the main text, and some of the fun is stashed away there. I would be delighted if readers found their way to them.

The bibliography consists almost entirely of works referenced in the notes, but it includes a very few that said nothing to me but might yield up sense to other readers.

Eva Brann
St. John's College
Annapolis, 2000

NOTES

1. I think of these visual models as the *via negativa* of psychology; just as theology tries to reach God by first imputing to him humanly accessible attributes in order then to deny them, so the study of the soul uses spatial models but subverts them in thought by not meaning them. For spatial models of the soul, see Brann 1991, 618 ff.

2. George Eliot, *Middlemarch*, chapter 78.

3. I feel sure that the affective and the negative element are closely related. Our most pervasive affect is, after all, desire, and desire can be analyzed as the "revelation of an emptiness, the presence of an absence of a reality" (Kojève, 5). That is, of course, also a description of the work of the imagination and the constitution of time, so that

in one analytic aspect these three are identical. In those animals that are likely to have no mental representations there seems to be instinctually focused appetite, but in human beings, so Aristotle thought, an image is needed to call forth desire. "Imagination prepares desire" (*Movement of Animals* 702 a 19). To me this is a great unresolved question: Granted that our evolutionary history relates us to animals basically driven by instinctual appetite, have we, by a revolution tantamount to a new genesis, cast loose and become primarily representational rather than appetitive beings, for whom images and memories are the necessary catalysts of desire or its repelling negative? Probably.

4. Shakespeare, Sonnet 47.

5. For the negative element in the imagination, see Brann 1991, index: "Non-Being" and "Nonexistence and nonexistent objects." For the negative element in time, see Brann 1999, index: "Becoming," "Negation," "Nonbeing," "Nothing." For the affective element in the imagination, see Brann 1991, index: "Emotions." For memory as the condition of the possibility of time, see Brann 1999, index: "Memory."

6. Nabokov, 1–2.

7. Greville, *Caelica*, Sonnet 69.

8. Sokolowski 1978, 29. He goes on to: "Even when they name what is present, they do so with a sense of its capacity to be not present, and it is the thing as exercising this other capacity, the thing as absent, which they name in reports about objects that are not before us. It is the object which is absent but still appreciated 'as presentable' that we name. . . ."

9. Albert the Great in *On Dionysius' "Concerning the Divine Names"* (c. 1250) quoted in MacDonald, 40.

10. Ockham in *Quodlibeta* VI, question vi (25). He answers the question first in the negative: It is a contradiction that there should be an act of seeing without an object that is seen. Then, on the contrary: Vision is one absolute quality distinct from an object, so there is no contradiction in the vision of a nonexistent object. His own conclusion is that God can produce the effect of vision directly without a causative object, but that such seeing cannot happen through merely natural causes. The main point, however, is that what neither exists in effect nor in possibility, like a chimaera, can never be seen. But what *can* be or once *was* in the nature of things *can* be intuitively seen even without its immediate cause. See also Ockham, xxv.

11. Wittgenstein, of whom I am, of course, thinking, expresses the warning very clearly in respect to Augustine's question "What, then, is time?" in the so-called *Blue Books* (27) that are the preliminary notes for the *Philosophical Investigations*. People look for the one exact usage of words like "knowledge" or "time." But that is hopeless: "I want you to remember that words have those meanings which we have given them; and we give meanings by explanation."

The difficulty in my particular case, negation-words, is that (1) we don't really know what meanings the primordial users gave the *ne* root; (2) we don't really know whether they *gave* the word a meaning or *found* within themselves or in the world a meaning to which they gave a sound; and (3) I don't know how anyone can explain a word merely by more words without running, not eventually but there and then, into a furiously infinite regress.

In the *Philosophical Investigations* (103), Wittgenstein uses the famous figure of a fly buzzing in a bottle for the pathological efforts people make in relation to understanding the inner states, such as one certainly has to hypothesize if one believes the meanings are antecedent to their verbal expressions. He asks and answers: "What is your aim in philosophy?—To show the fly the way out of the fly-bottle." But what if that fly keeps thinking "it is better to have buzzed and bumped than never to have buzzed at all"?

It seems to me that what Keats calls *Negative Capability*, "that is when man is capable of being in uncertainties, Mysteries, doubts, without any irritable reaching after fact and reason—" (Keats, 71, December 22, 1817), is the disposition suitable to my sort of inquiry: a groping faith in findable truth that yet regards theories as working hypothesis rather than as demonstrable doctrine.

I might mention here that Imagination, Time, and Negativity are topics treated with special interest by writers taking account of the postmodern mode; see, for example, Kearney 1988, Gallagher 1998, Budick and Iser 1996. The preoccupation with negativity in particular revolves around the oppositionality of power relations as well as the social and intellectual functions of naysaying. The most comprehensive treatment of visuality and its naysayers in modern and postmodern writers is Jay's *Downcast Eyes*.

Introduction

The Words of Naysaying

My hope of working out what all the forms of naysaying have in common is encouraged by the fact that almost all the words by means of which it is done have one and the same root: *ne*. That holds true not only for English but for French, German, Latin, and Greek—for those same languages in which the texts to which we may go for help are written.[1]

1. THE ROOT OF NAYSAYING

It would be gratifying if this root itself had a meaning that might throw light on what it is to say *no, not, non-, nothing*. Etymology, the account of the true meaning of words as revealed in their origin, is a bewitching study.[2] It seduces us into thinking that language speaks beyond human beings so that our words signify more than we intend. This belief seems to me true and false in equal parts. It seems to me false that by going back to such original meanings as we can accurately get hold of—false etymologizing is a *jeu d'esprit* that shows the author's wit more than the truth of things—we can have the depth of a matter delivered to us for free. And yet it makes sober sense that our linguistic ancestors, who came on a region of thought in a more direct and simple way than is open to us, should have seen aspects of the world that are now buried for us.[3] If on the stroke of midnight of the year 2000 (just about when I am writing this introduction) all the pages in all the etymological dictionaries had gone blank, we would not, I believe, have lost the bare possibility of thinking our way to the bottom of things, although we were floating on mere unanchored usages, on current denotations and connotations. But a world of suggestiveness would have been lost, and who knows if what is in principle possible—to think without the least learnedness in the original meanings of words—is in human fact achievable. The same holds true in the large for the

1

study of the textual tradition that plays so great a role in these three books: It ought in principle to be possible to think about such universally human experiences as Imagination, Time, and Nonbeing on one's own. But in brute fact, without the thought-evoking study of thoughtful books, one would be soon stymied—at least I would.[4]

With this caution (which is incidentally also a description of the spirit in which I wrote this trilogy), let me return to the root *ne*. In fact no one knows what it means, but there are two suggestive conjectures. One is the notion that the *ne* root is connected to the Latin word for "indeed," *enim*, and that the terms for negation originate, as far back as the Indo-European primal language, in ironic affirmation, as when, upon hearing something implausible, we say with raised eyebrows, "indeed, just so."[5] If this mere conjecture were a fact, it would mean that more original than naysaying is nay-feeling, a disposition to put inner distance between oneself and the other speaker even in the absence of a brutely negative particle.

The second guess connects *no* to the *nose*—a connection, or rather confusion, that in fact occurs in the speech of toddlers. Travelers in Mediterranean parts, from southern Italy to Turkey, but especially in Greece, are often bewildered by the almost imperceptible upward jerk of the head that effects Mediterranean naysaying. One interpretation of this gesture is that it represents a turning up of the nose, and that saying no, the verbal counterpart of nose raising, is named after our only permanently protruding organ; nose wrinkling might produce another etymological connection, and so might snorting through the nose.[6] Those whinnying horses, Gulliver's worshipful Houyhnhnms, who cannot imagine that anyone might say "the thing which was not" (that is to say, tell lies), might be found to be the aboriginal nihilists, since all their speech is neighing.[7]

If this origin of the *ne* sound has truth in it, then negation begins in aversion (and that is in fact the naysaying with which this book starts, chapter 1). So much the more remarkable is the way that leads from the gesture of impulsive physical refusal to that most abstractly formal and undefined symbol which stands for the truth-functional operation of negation (chapter 2).

2. THE TERMS OF NAYSAYING

Let me now run through the chief words that rule those ways of naysaying taken up in this book: *no, not, non-, nothing,* and *negativity.*

No is the briefest and most basic negative particle, though it is actually a word compounded of the root *ne* and *a* ("ever"), "not ever." It is an adverb, a so-called sentence adverb, that fixes the "quality" of the proposition in advance: "No, I will not." It is an adjective: "A point is that which has no part" (Euclid). It enters into a pronoun, *none*: "But you like none, none you, for constant heart" (Shakespeare). It is an exclamation: "Oh no!" It is a noun: "The Noes have it." And it can function as a complete sentence: "No. Period." Of these, the sentential function is, I would guess, the most frequent and certainly the most brisk in ordinary speech. There is also the form "nay" used in the title of this book.[8]

Both *not* and *non-*, the brusque adverb that negates propositions and the milder prefix that unsays entities,[9] contain two elements. *Not* is an alteration of Middle English *naught* or *nought*; *non-* goes back to *ne* plus an early Latin form of *unum*, "one"; in *Nonbeing* this prefix has its most august use, but there is also "nonentity" and "nonsense."

There are several negating prefixes with *ne* as root that come into English by various routes: *in-, un-, a-*. They have subtly different meanings and contexts of use, sensed but not necessarily understood by English speakers: nonrational, arational, irrational, unreasonable. In fact these prefixes afford lessons in the varieties of negation.[10] In the chapters to come they will be specified.

Nothing, "no-thing," might be called the most radically negative of terms because in it is canceled every entity. It is parallel to *nought* and *naught* (which consist of *no* plus Old English *wiht*, "thing"). *Naught*, charmingly, yields "naughty" (I leave it to parents' imagination how that came about); Heidegger will make a verb from the German counterpart of *naught*: *to naught*, "to effect nothingness". In English the word is also used for zero or *null*, which derives from the Latin word for "not any." That leads into the Latinate set of naysaying terms.

Negation is a name from the Latin verb for saying no, *negare*; it is the most widely used word in the literature on naysaying. *Negativity*, a term that will head a chapter in this book, does not even turn up in all dictionaries; it is a technical term signifying the conceptual energy of negation.

Nihil, from *ni-hilum*, "not a smidgen," is the Latin word for *Nothing*, adopted by the Nihilist movement.

And then there is a whole slew of words that incorporate the *ne* root and have trickled into English by all sorts of paths, such as annul, annihilate, deny, denigrate, abnegate, and the like. I mention these to show how absolutely pervasive the *ne* root is.

∞   ∞   ∞

People feel pressure to get hold of a word that will encompass and circumscribe negation; the word that presents itself is *opposition*. And they have good cause to rest content with this convenient term. The dictionaries encourage definitions of negation in terms of opposition, the logic books present the relation between a proposition and its various negations in a "square of opposition", the experiences of life reveal the negative as oppositional, but above all the word "opposition" is etymologically forthcoming, unlike the essentially opaque *ne* of negation.

Still, that approach to understanding what it means to say *no* won't do. The least difficulty is that while almost every sort of opposition can be framed—by a human intention—negatively, there are naysayings that seem to precede or go beyond opposition; for example, the *nihil absolutum*, the relationless Nothing or the *nihil originarium,* and the originary Nothing can be, somehow, spoken of, but not in terms of opposition. The real trouble is that to refer all our naysaying to the ground of opposition is to answer all the questions before they have been asked. For an "opposition" means a *position* that confronts or is up against another. Both sides of a pair of opposites are firmly grounded in the place of the *positive.* Thus the party of the positive has taken control of the negative, and negation takes its place within the territory of the positive. Hence to say *no* is always to repel the given; to say *not* is always to negate a prior affirmative; to speak of *Nonbeing* is always to point to difference within Being; to speak of *Nothing* is always to imply a prior Something—all of which may, upon reflection, prove to be true: *Upon reflection* and by way of conclusion, not by an implicit assumption!

NOTES

1. It is a curious fact that in Greek, in which the first great texts on Western negation were written, it is not the word for no *(ou)* but for yes *(nai)* that shows the *n* root. A possible explanation is given in the text. A second negation particle, *me, may* be related to *ne* (Jesperson 1924, 335). Nonetheless the *n* root turns up everywhere in Greek: in the alpha-privative *(an)* and in words like *nepenthes,* "sorrowless," and *nepias,* "wordless," i.e. "infantine." See Frisk I, 1, under "a, *alpha.*"

2. *Etymos* means "true," and particularly the "true sense of a word," especially as opposed to *alethea,* "true things." A foreshadowing of this distinction may already be found in Hesiod's *Theogony* (27–28) when the Muses say to him:

> We know how to speak many falsehoods that resemble true [words] *(etymoisin)*
> And we know, when we wish, how to utter true [things] *(alethea).*

Curtius, 53 ff. and 486 ff. (chap. 14, "Etymology as a Form of Thought") traces etymologizing, which plays a great role in antiquity, especially in Plato, and again in modern times in Heidegger, through the Middle Ages. Isidor of Seville, whose *Book of Etymologies* (A.D. 622–633) was the basis of medieval etymologizing, says that it leads to the origin and the "force" of things. For, he argues, if you know the descent of a word, you understand its force much more quickly; every word is more clearly grasped if you know its etymology.

3. I am bypassing here *the* great question concerning the absolute origin of language: whether the very first words uttered by a human being already expressed, as ours do, a thought, a universal that goes beyond the particular indicated.

4. Again I am circumventing in this simple but for my purposes sufficient way the

huge debate that preoccupied especially the Continental philosophers of the twentieth century: whether the thought of the past is of the essence to thinking deeply in the present, and, if so, how and to what degree past thought can be recovered. There is one respect, however, in which there cannot be much doubt about the necessity for knowing the development of meanings—in the professionally reflective disciplines, above all in academically learned philosophy. For there, unless the "intentional history" of terms is receptively entered into, talk about earlier philosophers becomes a sort of cackle, emitted by human chanticleers crowing from the top of the compacted midden-heap of unappropriated significance.

5. Walde and Hoffmann, 2:151.

6. Morris et al. call the Greek gesture "the head toss" (162 ff.) and tabulate its distribution in the Mediterranean region. They trace its origin, following Darwin, to the upward or sideways motion infants make when refusing food. In heroic Greece the gesture of supplication was to kneel, clasping the person in power by the beard, so a head toss might have effected extrication from the request.

In northern parts, the head shake that goes from side to side is the gesture of refusal; Morris et al. observe that it is the less ambiguous of the two, since the head toss has many other uses, such as beckoning and querying.

Jesperson 1922, 136, is the linguist who makes the direct connection to the nose: "Many little children use *nenenene* (short e) as a natural expression of fretfulness and discomfort. It is perhaps so natural that it need not be learned: there is good reason for the fact that in so many languages words of negation begin with *n* (or *m*). Sometimes the *n* is heard without a vowel: It is only the gesture of 'turning up one's nose' made audible." In Jesperson 1924, 335, the *ne*-root is traced to contracting the muscles of the nose, i.e., nose wrinkling.

The grandfather of all these surmises is Darwin, who understood gestures as the vestiges, preserved as habit, of once serviceable bodily movements. In the paragraphs on affirmation and negation of his *Expression of Emotion in Man and Animals* (chap. 11, 272), he cites with approval the opinion that the *n* or *m* sound of *the negating particle* arises when the voice is exerted with teeth clenched against some offered food, and that this is the origin of the negative particles; I might add that these sounds are in fact nasal.

7. The reference is to Jonathan Swift, *Gulliver's Travels*, part 4, chapter 4; these horses that Gulliver reverences do behave like a species of that contradiction in terms, the contented nihilist: they are rational to the point of unreason, brutally intolerant of alien ways, smug and totally without transcendence in their lives.

8. In earlier English, *yea* and *nay* were used to respond to questions framed affirmatively, *yes* and *no* for negative ones; see the long usage note in the *Variorum* edition of Shakespeare's *Much Ado about Nothing*, 25. This distinction is not without significance; see p. 37.

9. Thomas More's title for his imagined land, "Utopia," offers an excellent illustration of the difference between *not* and *non*-. "Utopia" is from Greek *ou*, "not," and *topos*, "place," and so means *not*-place. More could have formed it from *me* and *topos* to get Metopia, "non-place." But Utopia is a strong-featured land that is *not* at the exact latitude and longitude at which it is placed; to call it a "non-place" would have made it a nonbeing rather than a vivid place at an obscure location; it would have

fudged its existence rather than denied its spatial specificity. For a helpful note on the differences between *ou* and *me,* see More, 385–86, and also chapter 4, n. 37. For the peculiar not-being of imaginary places like More's *Utopia,* see Brann 1991, 714 ff.

10. For the common etymology, see Watkins, 2115; for the different meanings see the usage notes, also found in the *American Heritage Dictionary,* for *un-* (1) and *un-* (2). *Un-* tends to be used in words that have English endings, *in-* when the endings are Latinate, as shown by "irrational" and "unreasonable." I understand "nonrational" to pertain to everything whatsoever in the universe that is other than rational, "arational" to anything that is without reason but bears some specific relation of opposition to rational beings, and "irrational" to a rational being that is behaving mindlessly. These are varieties of negation recognized in logic.

Austin 1956, approaching negation as a linguistic philosopher who believes that the detailed examination of the usages of ordinary language should be the first step in philosophical inquiry, claims to observe that opposites gotten via a negating prefix sometimes diverge, as can be seen by negating them in turn. Thus the opposite of "voluntary" might be "under duress," and the opposite of "involuntary" might be "deliberately," and, he implies, "under duress" and "deliberately" bypass each other as opposites. Not to me, unfortunately. But be that as it may, his point is that we must not "assume that a word must have an opposite or one opposite." Well, first, though every word may not have a verbal opposite (he cites "inadvertent"), it may still have one in thought, gotten at in the same way that Austin gets at the reason why "advertent" isn't needed in the language. And second, since there are several kinds of negation, it is almost bound to be the case that many words have multiple opposites; one could try to enumerate them through a usage inventory of the word "opposite," but in the end one would have to think it through, helped but not constrained by the vagaries of usage.

1

Aboriginal Naysaying: Willful *No*

No, that diminutive but independent vocable, begins its great role early in human life and never loses it. For not only can it head a negative sentence, announcing its judgment, or answer a question, implying its negated content, it can, and mostly does, in the beginning of speech, express an assertion of the resistant will—sometimes just that and nothing more. The adult antiphony to the toddler's incessant *no* is another *no*, that of preventive command, and the great commandments of later life continue to be prohibitions: Nine of the Ten Commandments are in the negative.[1]

Therefore I will begin with *no* as it is an expression of the will. By will, I mean here nothing more than willingness, inclination, readiness—whatever is meant in the immortal line of that lilting linguist, Mr. Alfred Doolittle:

I'm willing to tell you. I'm wanting to tell you. I'm waiting to tell you,[2]

except that in this chapter the willing bears a negative sign: unwillingness, disinclination, resistance. The last thing I want is to get involved here in the definition of the will or the conundrums of the free will.[3] All I want to postulate here about the will is that it usually, though not always, shows up as determinate desire, wanting or rejecting something in a focused and active way. There is, as one might expect, a vigorous difference of opinion about the relation of willing to knowing. Some people think that truth exercises its compulsion without involving the will, and others that every affirmation and denial is an act of the will. To René Descartes, this question is of great importance because he wishes to assert that error is entirely due to our infinite will exceeding our limited knowledge and choosing to say yes or no to judgments that the understanding has not clearly apprehended. He says, "For by the understanding I neither assert nor deny anything but apprehend the idea of things as to which I can form a judgment." Now the faculty of the will consists only

7

in choosing to affirm or deny, pursue or shun anything, so it is for him the will that accepts or rejects cognitive propositions.[4]

Again without entering into the deep motives behind this assignment of the yeas and nays of asserted judgments to the will (of which Descartes's argument itself may well be an example), I assume in this chapter that it is sometimes true that our judgments are conscious or unconscious choices of calculating will or unacknowledged desire. In subsequent chapters, I shall assume without any more argument that there *are* volitionally neutral judgments and not just those made in the inferences of logic (whose axioms may well be powerfully willful) but also those made in the ardent pursuit of truth (which seems able to arouse a desire that is minimally willful and receptive rather than active).

So in this chapter, *no* will appear as the willful rejection observed (1) in very young children and then, by a natural and easy transition, (2) in demons and devils and other naysayers, and finally (3) in answering questions willfully rather than truthfully.

1. THE TERRIBLE TWOS

For newborn babies being in the world is too much; most of their reactions are avoidances, wordless naysayings to the obtruding universe.[5] But by the second month they begin to take pleasure in their new surroundings and signs of positive interest become more common than indicators of negative feelings. In displaying these polar reactions, these little animals of our own species mirror the rest of nature, animate and inanimate. All animals, be they human infants or adults of any species, wordlessly, though not soundlessly, take what they want and repel what they don't want, and in these serviceable movements may well be the origin of our gestures of acceptance and rejection. They seem to be bits of a Nature, which, in the large, has always appeared to human beings to be a complex of pairs of opposite elements or forces, one of which was usually discernibly positive and the other negative. Thus

> The earth the air the water and the fire
> Then gan to range themselves in huge array,
> And with contrary forces to conspire
> Each against other by all means they may.

So Empedocles says of the powers that organize the cosmos:

> Sometimes by Love everything comes together in one,
> And sometimes again each thing is borne asunder in the strife of Hate.

So also modern physicists speak of particles and antiparticles, of matter and antimatter. And they think of magnetic forces and electric charges as discernibly positive and negative, albeit they are only opposites.[6]

My point here is only that in the world of animals and of mere bodies pairs of opposites are pervasive and that *we* tend to interpret them in terms of yea and nay. But how can there be positive and negative in the world, before there is human will and human speech? Is a *merely* somatic negativity intelligible? It is an open question (p. 214). And so back to babies.

(a) The infant who arches back from the offered bottle turns into a talking toddler. And now something truly wonderful happens, something too little remarked and too little understood: Children acquire some words, some two-word phrases, and then *no*. Not only do they, between two and three, turn into terrors of negativity. They do it speakingly and willfully and even reflexively; a two-year-old of my acquaintance whom I was minding (in both senses of the word) said to me after a long wrangle: "I want not to want . . ."

They say excited *no* both for the pleasure of articulating and for the joy of resisting. They say excited *no* to everything and guilelessly contradict their naysaying in the action: "Do you want some of my jelly sandwich?" "No." Gets on my lap and takes it away from me.[7] What is more, this *no* precedes *yes*, as brief and easy a vocable as any, for quite a while.

What is the meaning of this primordial *no* to everything? Current baby books don't even index the phenomenon of naysaying, but they speak in passing of a first bid for independence and a balking at being forever bossed.[8] That certainly fits with the children's preference for taking what they want over accepting what is offered, and for appropriating the word of prohibition they hear so often.

These are amateur surmises. It *is* a documented observation that the particle *no* occurs very early in children's speech, sometime in the second year, quite a while before sentences are negated by *not*.[9] Typical expressions are: "No singing song," "No the sun shining," "No play that," "No fall!" "No want stand head," "No Mom sharpen it." It is never quite clear whether the *no* is meant as a sentential adverb, as in, "No, don't play with that," or in an adjectival sense, as in "There is no sun shining," or as an imperative such as "No falling!" Probably these distinctions aren't there for the child, who is simply letting that negative particle he hears all day long function as an all-purpose naysayer. One additional use that I have observed might be called veridical; point to a picture of a duck and say "Here's an elephant," and you'll hear an indignant "No effant."[10] There is at this time also a plentiful use of the plain *no* of rejection, which into the terrible twos often becomes "No-no-no-no!"— illuminating, incidentally, a portion of a line uttered by the terrible royal child Lear: "No, no, no, no! . . ."[11]

In the next period, the negation passes *into* the sentence: "I can't catch you," "I don't want it." What seems significant is that internal negation ap-

pears to coincide with the first use of the personal pronouns *I* and *you*.[12] And
that, in turn, means that the child can show particularized affection. Now too
is the beginning of imagining, pretending, and lying, which require respectively a readiness to see what is not present, a desire to be what one is not,
and the will to say "the thing that is not." A father once said to me, "He told
me he didn't do it. He was lying. Now he's joined the human race." He had
hit the nail on the head. Only an animal having the speech that utters thought
can practice nonsomatic deceit: can lie, can know one thing and say another—
and that is our species.

This tumultuous time when the *no* of rejection is gradually supplanted by
the *not* of negation, when reasonableness slowly succeeds rebellion, seems to
me epoch-making in a human life. It is matched only by one other natural
crisis of growth, to which it in fact bears a remarkable resemblance: adoles-
cence, a time when, under the aegis of emerging erotic feeling, sheer rebellion,
heightened imagination, ardent role-playing, a new secretiveness and new loy-
alties—and the first (and sometimes the last) glimmer of philosophical profun-
dity, particularly of the negative sort—are mixed into a coruscating psychic
chaos that once again puts parents to the test.

(b) There is, unfortunately, only one school of thought that accords the naysaying of young children the importance it deserves—Freudian psychoanalytic theory. I say "unfortunately" because the valuable observations all come
interpreted in the questionable theoretical framework of Freud's influential
five-page essay "Negation."[13] Here is its wider thesis:

> A negative judgment is the intellectual substitute for repression; the "No" in
> which it is expressed is the hall-mark of repression, a certificate of origin, as it
> were, like "Made in Germany."

The more specific thesis is that

> the subject-matter of a repressed image or thought can make its way into con-
> sciousness on condition that it is *denied*. Negation is a way of taking account of
> what is repressed; indeed it is actually a removal of the repression, though not,
> of course, an acceptance of what is repressed.

Hence the intellectual function is distinct from the affective process, and the
very conscious articulation of the matter helps to keep intact the repression,
that is, the banishment of unacceptable impulses from consciousness, even if
analysis succeeds in establishing complete intellectual acceptance.

The study of the origin of judgment, the final intellectual action that decides
the choice of motor action, that leads from the "procrastination of thinking"
to acting,

affords us, perhaps for the first time, an insight into the derivation of an intellectual function from the interplay of primary impulses.

For judging has systematically developed its polarity of affirmation and negation out of two groups of opposing instincts:

Affirmation, as being a substitute for union, belongs to Eros; while negation, the derivative expulsion, belongs to the instinct of destruction.

The function of judging requires that thought achieve "a first degree of independence" from repression and the polar instincts, and this comes about with "the creation of the symbol of negation."

This view of negation, Freud says, "harmonizes very well with the fact that in analysis we never discover a 'No' in the unconscious." He does not explain, but he seems to me to mean that just because the unconscious is all-assertive (I avoid saying "positive"), negation is the device for undoing the repression of its contents—at a distance.

Judgment is ultimately concerned with two kinds of decision. One concerns acceptance or rejection, and its prototype, expressed in terms of the oldest, the oral impulse, goes like this: "I want this inside me" or "I want this kept outside me." The other decision is about existence and nonexistence, and again refers to internal and external. For what is not really existent is imagined. This contrast between what is subjective and what is objective thus arises only when the faculty for reproducing absent objects as images comes into play. The first testing of reality is therefore not an attempt to discover an object corresponding to the image "but *to rediscover* such an object; to convince oneself that it is still there." It is from these claims that the investigation into the *no* of babies takes off.

But it is impossible to leave this remarkable and, I think, unique *psychological* account of negation without a comment. The issue can be stated in Freud's own terms like this: Granted the whole theory of the unconscious, including the theory of repression as a negative verbal acknowledgment of an affect, has he shown that if repression is negation, then all negation is repression? It seems to me that Freud's own answer is implicitly no. For he says:

By the help of the symbol of negation, the thinking-process frees itself from the limitations of repression and enriches itself with the subject-matter without which it could not work efficiently.

Whence comes the symbol and the subject-matter?

To put the issue in more general terms: Granted that *no* is originally purely impulsive, must that mean that negation never escapes its origin in our affective constitution? Doesn't there come a time in a child's development, signaled by the incorporation of the *no* as a *not* in a sentence, in what the Greeks call a *logos*, a fully articulated thought, when a third use of negation besides that of articulating rejection and nonexistence comes on the scene: denial of truth or untruth? Of this third use Freud says not a word, though it seems to me most intimately related to Freud's "symbol of negation." So the psychoanalytic theory does not tell whence comes mature negation and possible truth telling; these may not have a naturalistic genesis.

Again, back to babies: René Spitz in the 1950s and 1960s did a great deal of research on the genesis of *no* and *yes*, which he presented in a Freudian framework.[14] Spitz takes the fact that the newborn baby, although it displays lots of diffuse aversive behavior, shows no organized expression of negation to be "the observational duplicate" of Freud's postulate that there is no *no* in the unconscious.[15] During the first six months there is one activity that is relatively goal directed, and that is *rooting*, a kind of scanning motion in search of the breast. It has no negative, aversive counterpart, for when the baby has had enough it simply drops off to sleep. Spitz regards this phase as preparatory to the protojudgment of "take in or keep out," which comes into its own when rooting behavior turns into its opposite, a motion of refusal.[16] These motions are semantic precursors of words, primal words. It was Freud's observation that such words often have opposite meanings (for example, Latin *sacer*: sacred and accursed). Spitz thinks that the protogestures may be showing the same trait, only successively; later on, in the second year, the opposites come together in the familiar phenomenon of children's saying *no* in imitation of the dominating adult, the "aggressor," while doing *yes* in pursuit of their own desires. By the time the child reaches fifteen months, focused refusal has developed into

> headshaking "No," a semantic gesture, at the level of object relations at which semantic communication with the help of verbal symbols is initiated by the acquisition of the symbol of negation.

This new *no* is now used to refuse intentionally what is to stay outside and also to acknowledge nonexistence. Spitz sees the earliest genesis of this judgment of nonexistence in the scanning—without finding—of the nipple by "rooting," which implies that it might even precede the judgment of refusal. Noticing nonexistence presupposes memory images, so one might speculate that mental imagery may be at the bottom of all negation (p. 217).

The *no* of refusal is first used against the mother, who thus becomes an object to the child, a separate being. And then it is used by the child to set off *itself* as a discrete being; thus at about eighteen months, just when semantic *no* appears, the child begins to speak of itself in the third person.

> The volitional use of the semantic content of negation in the semantic "No" gesture is beyond doubt the most spectacular intellectual and semantic achievement in early childhood.[17]

Words to designate things and people appear earlier, but *no* "is probably the first conquest of the gestural and verbal symbol of an abstract concept." The social consequences of this achievement are enormous: Instead of the muscular discharge of libidinal and aggressive drives there can now be discussion. *"Thus, social intercourse in humans can begin."* But meanwhile, in the terrible twos, there is also the *no* that is a mere manifesto of independence. It shows a cleavage in the child's ego, for while the child is saying *no*, it is, as was observed, often doing what the adult demands. The naysaying does not concern the objective issue but the ownership of the will: "I have a will of my own and even when it is the same as yours, it is different because it is my own. I am doing this because *I* want it and I am not doing what *you* want!"

We can, I think, profit from the careful observation in this account of the phased progress of naysaying without committing ourselves to the theory behind it. *That* these little creatures with huge wills come to achieve selfhood is a miraculous fact; the *route* by which they do it is well described; but *how* it happens that a being hitherto only lovable comes one day to demand our respect—that we do not know. But this much is clear: Along with the will and from the same source, from naysaying, comes thoughtfulness. So it is not just romantic sentimentality when a poet apostrophizes a child:

> Thou, whose exterior semblance doth belie
> Thy Soul's immensity
> Thou best Philosopher, . . .[18]

It remains, however, to be said that just about where the developmental *no* of the terrible twos leaves off, the "naughty" *no* of the rest of childhood begins.

2. DEVILS AND DEMONS

In the last section the *no* that is a normal phase in the growth of children was considered; now comes the naysaying that belongs to the very nature of certain beings or descends on others as a sort of possession. This is the permanently oppositional, implacable *no*, born of a perverse will or some other inner force for evil (or for good).

(a) By an old tradition there is in the world a personification and even an incarnation of evil itself. His name is "Satan," the Hebrew word for adversary, or "Devil," the Greek word for a false accuser and reviler (*diabolos*). He is a fallen angel whose name in heaven was Lucifer, the Lightbringer, but was changed after the Fall:

> Satan—so call him now; his former name
> Is heard no more in Heaven.

For he, among the first of archangels, from envy and offended pride at the elevation of the Son of God

>   resolved
>   With all his legions to dislodge, and leave
>   Unworshipped, unobeyed, the throne supreme,
>   Contemptuous; . . .[19]

In the book of Job, he is, although already Satan, yet counted among the Sons of God and welcome in the court of heaven. But it is earth he patrols; to God's "Whence comest thou?" he answers, "From going to and fro in the earth, and from walking up and down in it." So he is permitted, perhaps even commissioned, to try to turn Job against God.[20]

Satan, or the incarnate power of evil, is depicted as entering the body of a serpent from first to last. It is the serpent that tempts Eve into disobeying the earliest commandment given to human beings, the single order that "of the tree of the knowledge of good and evil, thou shalt not eat."

And it is this serpent, well over two and a half millennia later, who deludes himself into thinking that its Nothing equals the power of Being; it is the "beautiful serpent lulled in the blue" who addresses God, imagining that the thirst for the bitter fruits of its tree, which

>   Maddens the children of mud . . .
>   —That thirst which made you gigantic
>   Exalts even onto Being the alien
>   All-potency of Naught![21]

>   *Affole les fils de la fange . . .*
>   *—Cette soif qui te fit géant,*
>   *Jusqu'à l'Être exalte l'étrange*
>   *Toute-Puissance du Néant!*

The human agent of Satan is the Antichrist, who, however many forms he takes, is Christ's antagonist, the perfidious Opposition.[22] Where in Christ "was not yea and nay, but in him was yea," in the Antichrist all is *nay*.

The devil has minions, among them the small devil Mephistopheles, the familial spirit, the perverse demon of the insatiably experience-seeking Faust. This is a light-minded, witty, ironical devil to suit the satiatedly learned doctor who invokes him. He is shamelessly candid about his self-frustrating nature; he is "a part of that force / Which constantly wills evil and constantly effects good." And he defines himself as naysayer: "I am the spirit who constantly says nay!"[23]

(b) Not all personal naysaying demons are, however, destructive. The counterexample is Socrates' enigmatic inner voice, which he called *to daimonion*:

"the divine something." The word from which this appellation derives is *daimon*, a divinity, after Homer usually not one of the Olympians, often a tutelary deity, in nature between the gods and human beings. Socrates' inner divinity does one thing: it says *no*. Its voice stops him from doing certain deeds and from keeping certain company. In Plato's account of the explanation of his life that Socrates gave before the court of Athenians—who will, by a narrow margin, find him guilty of charges that include the introduction of new *daimonia*, new divinities—Socrates tells how, from boyhood on, there was "a certain voice" that only held him back and never urged him toward an action. Among other things, it kept him away from politics.[24]

Socrates' report of his *daimonion* all but imposes an obligation on readers of the Platonic dialogues to puzzle out its meaning. Hegel took it very seriously: It is the particular "genius" of Socrates, the peculiarly personal complement of the universality of his thought. What Hegel leaves out of account is the exclusively naysaying character of the voice. I will try my hand at an understanding of this aspect.[25]

Certainly it seems to be a sort of moral intuition, the equally negative counterpart of his negative dialectic, the probing conversation that cares more ardently to bring home ignorance than to establish positive doctrine. Yet Socrates' talk is full of clear positive opinions and brilliant panoptic visions; to these the *daimonion* is the specific practical complement: In the light of and for the sake of the whole he must refrain from this or that particular deed, much as Hegel says.

But I see another explanation, not incompatible with the foregoing. In a passage of the *Theaetetus,* Socrates says that there will always be bad things, "for of necessity something must be opposed to the good," and since the bad cannot settle among the gods, it must circulate on earth, again "of necessity." We should, he says, try as soon as possible to escape to the other, divine world.[26]

I think that whatever is by force of necessity is for Socrates beyond reason, and it does seem to be true that he, at least, had mounted no inquiry into badness and had no reflected knowledge about it. But for Socrates good action is the direct consequence of having achieved some thoughtful knowledge. So in the absence of such knowledge, there was granted him a special way of doing right in the face of murky situations, especially human badness.

Another way to see the same thing is from the point of view of the will, or rather the lack of such a notion in the writings of the classical Greek philosophers. Neither Socrates, nor the people he talks with, seem to be able to conceive of a human being who chooses the bad knowingly and on purpose, who is bad for the sheer hell of it—in sum, who has a *perverse* will. But the very notion of a will cannot work its way forward until some huge pride spices the pleasures of sinning, and rebellion galvanizes self-indulgence.[27] And such pride is expressed above all in the will to disobey, and disobedience is possible only where there are commandments. Moreover, if the commandments are negative—"thou shalt *not* . . ."—as they indeed are in the Book accepted by the Christian tradition, which brought the will on the human scene, then disobedience will take the same tone: It will be a *no* said to a *no*, a willful double negation that makes sin a positive.[28]

For Socrates there is a power of the soul which is, I think, the antique analogue of the will. It is not, as is the will, a faculty for submitting to or rejecting specific commandments or general rules. It is rather a quality of temperament. When well-conditioned, it is a capacity for indignation at what is beneath the dignity of that human being and for pride that fears the shame of lowness. Its name is *thymos*, and "spiritedness" may be its most inclusive translation. It is central to Socrates' model of the soul as set out by Plato in the *Republic*.[29] There "spiritedness" is first of all the capacity to *resist* the temptation to indecency, whose positive side is aggressive bravery, the soldier's virtue. I would say, therefore, that Socrates' "divine something" is a philosopher's spiritedness, an inborn gift for immediate, surefooted naysaying to moral imbroglios.

(c) Finally, there is a sort of naysaying possession that takes hold of people simply through their disposition. Two examples are Bazarov the Nihilist, who will reappear later, and Bartleby the Inanist, who quietly wills himself into inanition.[30]

This scrivener of Melville's story has a perfectly implacable, gently negative will, so negative that he himself denies that it *is* a will. The principal of a cheerful, snug little legal firm in New York hires a copyist, Bartleby. He is installed at his desk with a screen behind which he gently disappears after each passage of words. For it quickly appears that he is going to refuse certain tasks, uttering the almost invariable formula "I would prefer not to." "You *will* not?" asks the lawyer. "I *prefer* not," retorts Bartleby. He says it more than a dozen times, and before long the whole good-natured office is infected, not with the point-blank "not," but with the insidious pleasant plosiveness of "prefer," which, seeming to fall below insubordination, eludes control and reason with the perfect impugnability of passive resistance. Can't he be a little reasonable? asks the kindly lawyer, and Bartleby answers: "At present I would prefer not to be a little reasonable." Nor does he ever give reasons for his negative preference, except to say that the proffered task or suggestion does not suit him—though he is "not particular." He is indeed not particular; he is universally negative. Eventually he refuses to write at all or to quit the premises, the screened "hermitage" that he has been using as his abode. One day the landlord has the scrivener removed to the Tombs as a vagrant. There he refuses the dinners the lawyer sends in to him and dies of inanition, of sheer evanishment. It is a subtlety in Melville's telling of the story that Bartleby's "I prefer not to" is altered on his last day at the office by the addition of the particle *no*. Thrice he now says it in reply to benevolent offers from the lawyer: "No, I would prefer not to make any change"; "No, I would prefer to be doing something else"; "No, at present I would prefer not to make any change at all."

Those *noes* reveal, I think, one reason why this story so fascinates its readers. Bartleby's "I prefer" is a screen that hides behind a polite pretense of agreeable options (for preference is a choice among positives) his fully determined will to make life leave him alone, and that failing, to become null and void. "I prefer not to" is the mild ripple on the implacable undertow of his naysaying will.

3. WILLFUL ANSWERS

By willful answers I mean wrongheaded answers, on the assumption that normally responses should be in accordance with the demand of the question and not the will of the respondent. *Yes* and *no* are the briefest and probably the most frequent of replies because the type of inquiry, called a "yes/no question" in the literature of erotetics (the study of questions) and a "dialectical question" by Aristotle, is so basic.[31] Questions of this type—there are many others—are often mere requests to affirm or deny facts or surmises, to be straightforwardly and spontaneously answered: "Is this chapter nearly finished?" Such questions are interesting mostly because they assume the normal division of replies into positive and negative.

(a) Other questions request the performance of a favor or an assumption of responsibility: "Will you do this for me?" or the—actually illogical—demand "Did you or did you not . . . ? Answer yes or no." Under the pressure of an unwelcome petition or the constraint of a probing cross-examination, replies become less spontaneous and more willful. In fact here, with one small false particle, an insincere *yes* and an uncandid *no*, lying often begins, and lying is willful speech, or rather a willful use of speech.

These questions and the answers they elicit are more than interesting; they are engrossing. For they display the fact that when one animal species became human by acquiring speech it did not thereby become inevitably more transparent than the rest of inexpressive animaldom. Speech is utterance, that is, an "outering" of inward thought, and so there is a presumption of candor, of intended translucence.[32] But a successful willfully false *no* (and defensive denials are probably the most frequent simple lies) is testimony that our inwardness is a lair and speech can serve as its cover. Or by another metaphor, a lying *no* is like a twist of the Ring of Gyges,[33] which makes the wearer invisible—only in lying it is not the outer shapes but the inner consciousness that goes out of sight—sometimes to the liar himself. Hence effective lying is, at least at first, not only a useful escape route but a satisfaction, the experience of being impenetrably safe from exposure, safe within oneself. It may be a child's first experience of mental privacy.

A human community obviously has much to gain by breaking the will to lie, as has a human being, by keeping the natural bond of thought and speech intact (which is most of what is meant by integrity). But while this is not an inquiry into the morality of lying,[34] and the logic of lies will be discussed later (p. 95), it seems to me that there is one more yes-no answer to be taken up here, an ethically fraught and formally murky answer, which is not always precisely willful nor exactly a lie—unless we accept the notion of "the lie in the soul", the willing retention of ignorance.

(b) Thus we come to the dialectical question in its original sense, the question that requests not deeds or confessions but a focus on speculative truth. Dialectic is inquiry by questioning: An understanding is ventured and the guiding partner asks a series of questions that have "yes-no" answers; usually the initial opinion is shown to be insufficient or self-contradictory.[35] But under the guidance of Socrates, who, as represented in the Platonic dialogues, is the model partner of such conversations, the outcomes are by no means merely negative. Often great positive discoveries are made on the way, and sometimes the recognition of a perplexity is itself a revelation. The disputational, refutational tone of dialectic so emphasized by Aristotle is seldom evident in Socrates' questioning; in fact he will rarely tolerate contentiousness, "eristic," in himself or in others.[36] Eristic is argument carried on under the aegis of the will to win; it breaks the nexus between a question and its intrinsic response.

Precisely because so much of his conversation consists of his asking the question and his partners responding with simple yesses and noes, everything depends on the disposition of those who participate. They should be willing and wanting and waiting to answer, but they should not be willful. They should not answer to please, or to gain their point, or to get it over with. They are expected to search within themselves for the response that engages the question, to follow the question's request, and to utter it candidly.

$$\infty \qquad \infty \qquad \infty$$

This dialectic requires a *yes*, and a *no* that is free from all willing except the willing desire for finding truth.[37] We will find the formal conditions for such objective yea-and-naysaying in logic.

NOTES

1. Exodus 20:3–17. Burke, 297, surmises that the (historical) origin of the negative was in moral commandments like the Decalogue, not in semantic situations.

2. Bernard Shaw, *Pygmalion*, act 2.

3. Arendt, vol. 2, *Willing*, is a thoughtful review of the will in Western philosophy.

4. Descartes, Fourth Meditation, "Of the True and the False." The quotation includes Descartes's addition to the first French translation. Descartes evidently thinks that where knowledge is clear and distinct the will assents most perfectly: "I should be

entirely free without ever being indifferent." He insists on this view against Hobbes's thirteenth objection, which says that we give at least inner assent to credible argument whether we will or no.

Kant, in the *Critique of Judgment,* shows that aesthetic judgment, the judgment that "this is beautiful," is also "disinterested," meaning not related to gratification (para. 2–3).

5. Maurer and Maurer, 213–214.

6. The first quotation is from Edmund Spenser, "A Hymne in Honour of Love," 78 ff.; the second is from *On Nature*, Diehls 1:316.

7. Piaget, 163 ff., says that "the child is insensible to [self-] contradiction" until seven to eight years old. But his analysis holds for classificatory concepts and causal explanations; children of four certainly know that if they say *no* to an offer of a goody, they can't then just take it. Piaget ascribes children's frequent self-contradiction to (1) amnesia (which also affects adults), i.e., they simply forget the previous assertion, and (2) condensation (which is peculiar to children), i.e., they overdetermine the concept with confusing heterogeneous incidentals.

The child who wanted not to want was Peter Heinz, who died the year this was written, on March 26, 2000, at age forty-five.

8. Even the legendary Dr. Spock, 1968, devotes only one paragraph to this most remarkable phenomenon: "Contrariness," para. 506.

9. Klima and Bellugi-Klima, 450, 455. The three children observed for this project were from eighteen to twenty-seven months old but shared the same level of speech development. Since this was a strictly syntactic investigation, no semantic conclusions were drawn.

10. Brown, 117 ff., cites three distinct types of negations in children (the first two of which actually derive from Freud's essay "Negation," see p. 10): (1) nonexistence, when the referent is not now there; (2) rejection, when the referent is opposed by the child; (3) denial, when an assertion is said not to be the case. Once children progress to intra-sentential negation, like "no more noise," nonexistence here and now seems to precede both rejection and denial in their speech, and remains preponderant in the early stage. Would it go too far to conjecture that speaking in sentences has a positive effect on children's temper and also engenders a contemplative interest in absence?

11. Shakespeare, *King Lear* 5.3.8:

> No, no, no, no! Come let's away to prison:
> We two alone will sing like birds i' the cage.

12. Klima and Bellugi-Klima, 456–457. Children now use auxiliary verbs, but *only* in negative sentences: "I don't like him"; ibid., 457.

13. Freud, "Negation" (1925). This essay states boldly the method of affirmation through denial that has in the last decades led to critiques of Freud's science as unfalsifiable: "'You ask who this person in the dream can have been. It was *not* my mother.' We emend this: so it *was* his mother" (213). Although arguments from global self-contradiction always seem a little sophomoric to me, it is, with respect to this essay, hard to get away from the fact that Freud is in every instance negating his analysand's negation, so that his method is wide open to a secondary analysis, as it were.

The quotations are, in order, from 214, 213–214, 216, 216, 215, 214.

Kristeva, chap. 2, "Negativity: Rejection," 107–164, displays the infelicitous influence of Freud combined with Hegelian vocabulary on French intellectuals with respect to intelligibility. Try understanding this text, as opposed to lapping it up.

14. Spitz, *No and Yes*, 1957, and *The First Year of Life*, 1965. Freud's essay is particularly acknowledged in Spitz 1957, 86 ff.; 1965, 188 ff.

15. I have used "avoidance" above as in Maurer and Maurer, 213, to refer to the uncoordinated reactions of newborns. Spitz, 1957, 93, however, uses the term for the next stage, the beginning of a *no* gesture in a definite refusal of the nipple, which occurs after the sixth month.

16. "Yes" takes a very secondary place in the psychoanalytic context because "affirmation is the essential attribute of instinct." No ideational content is required to elicit appetition. The motor antecedent of semantic (affirmative) head-nodding may be an approach to the nipple observed in babies old enough to hold up their heads (three months). Rooting, on the other hand, is innate (Spitz 1957, 104, 108–109; the quotation is from 94).

17. Spitz 1957, 99. The discussion below in my text quotes from 99, 131, 140.

18. William Wordsworth, "Ode: Intimations of Immortality from Recollection of Early Childhood" (1802–4, sec. 8).

Even older children retain an interest in the negation through which they entered the world of imaginative thought, as in betokened by the number of first-rate children's books that deal with the fading of existence into nothing. For example, Frank Tashlin's *The Bear That Wasn't*, whose title is proof that people who claim you can't use the verb "to be" as a predicate in English are wrong, though Tashlin means it in both ways: the bear that wasn't there any more and the bear that wasn't a bear any more from being talked out of his bear qualities; also Madeleine L'Engle's *A Wind in the Door*, in which the "Enemies" are negating, annihilating the sky; and above all, and incomparably, Michael Ende's *The Endless Story*, in which the Land of the Imagination is slowly being obliterated by the lack of it.

19. Milton, *Paradise Lost* V 658 ff. Milton says that the heavenly name of Satan was blotted out at his fall, so that Lucifer is his postlapsarian name (I 136 ff.). The origin of "Lucifer" seems to be Isaiah 14:12: "How art thou fallen from Heaven, O Lucifer."

20. Job 1:6–12.

21. First quotation, Genesis 2:16; second quotation Valéry, *Ebauche d'un serpent*" ("Outline of a Serpent," end). The classic history of the Devil is by Carus 1900.

The nothingness of the Satanic serpent is imagined, of course, on the analogy of the nothingness of evil as seen in human sin. Ricoeur, 14 ff., has studied the symbolism of sin as Nothing among the Hebrews, who had no explicit contrary notion of Being. The nothing and vanity of sin are, he says, blended with the nothing of idols and false gods: "Ye are of nothing, and your work of nought" (Isaiah 41:24). What is nothing to God is "real non-being" to man, and the choice between good and evil is equivalent to the choice between God and Nothing (74).

Here can be seen in germ the difficulty that the "real non-being" of the devil poses for those philosophical theologians who follow the Plotinian tradition of identifying badness with a radical deficiency in Being. Plotinus sets this view out plainly in *Ennead* 1.8, "Concerning What Are and Whence Come Bad Things." Since all that *is*, is good, the source of badness is in the shapeless, measureless, needy, poverty-stricken material *(hyle)* that underlies all shape-giving form. *It* is the beingness *(ousia)*, the badness, of bad things. Its character is that of an *eidolon*, literally an "idol," a phantasm, in comparison with the *eidos*, the form of Being (3); it is a shadow being, a false being, a being defined by opposition to Being (6)—not Nothing simply, but Being defined by lack. Particular bad things come from the mingling of form with its material. It seems pretty clear that the Neoplatonic principle of shapelessness is not a good candidate for personification as devil. See O'Brien, 171 ff., for the relation of matter to evil.

Thomas, however, while subscribing to the notion of deficiency of Being as the nature of evil, follows Aristotle in regarding matter as a potentiality for good rather than the cause of bad (*Summa*, question 49, article 1). So when he treats of devils and demons (questions 63–64), he has no difficulty with their being angels, that is, immaterial intellectual beings, because matter is, in any case, not the source of evil. The evil of voluntary natures in general differs, to be sure, from the bad of natural things; it arises from a defect of the will (question 49, Reply to Objection 3)—devils are not *naturally* evil. The angels sinned by choosing freely their own good rather than the rule of the divine will. Happily, it is not part of this book to understand how the will is determined, and the object of this note is really to plead that bad, evil, and their personal representatives are, speaking philosophically and theologically, not at home within the blank silhouette of Nothing and Nonbeing, but belong instead in the shadow realm of almost-being, deficiency, and privation, and so not in this book.

Yet there is a text of particular interest for later parts of this book, Anselm's "On the Fall of the Devil," a little dialogue between a pupil and his teacher that begins by dealing with the devil's peculiar will: It is not an evil will, for the will is a being and all beings are good. But it is an inordinate will, one whose object exceeds God's gift to the angels (III–IV, 138–139). This object of the will is the evil called injustice. It is nothing, a mere privation of good (IX–X, 145–146; XX, 164). Anselm asks how speech can signify Nothing, continuing an inquiry started by Augustine in *On the Teacher* II. "Nothing" as a word does, he answers, somehow signify Nothing and Evil, mainly by a "destroying" or negating signification (XI, 149).

What strikes me in Anselm's treatment is his continually referring to evil as "nothing," which is only a hair's breadth away from convertibility: Nothingness is evil. That would be a sort of devil's *via negativa* to Nothing, i.e., Nothing conceived in terms of evil, an approach that acknowledged or unacknowledged, underlies the West's *horror nihili.*

22. For a history of the Antichrist, see McGinn 1994. The quotation just below is from 2 Corinthians 1:19.

23. The quotations are from Goethe, *Faust*, pt. 1, 1336–1337, 1338. The "Prologue in Heaven" of *Faust* is a parody of the Job passage cited above, so Faust's Mephistopheles is as much sent as invoked. The very interesting article "Mephistopheles" in the famous eleventh edition of the *Encyclopedia Britannica* (1911) says that the Mephistophilis (*sic*) of Marlowe's *Tragical History of Dr. Faustus* and of the medieval Faust legend is a clairvoyant's alter ego, and akin to Socrates' "demon"; see the next note.

24. The chief references are Plato, *Apology* 31 d, 40 a (where the *daimonion* is called "the sign from the god"), and *Phaedrus* 242 b, *Theaetetus* 151 a, *Euthedemus* 272 e, *Alcibiades* 105 d (where it is called "the god"), and *Theages* 128 d ff. (which,

though the longest, is probably not by Plato). Friedländer, 2:36 ff., canvasses the treatment of Socrates' *daimonion* in later ancient writers. They sometimes ranked it in their demonologies as a personal demon in a sense close to ours.

25. Hegel, "Philosophy of Socrates," *History of Philosophy*, vol. 2, pt. I, sec. 1, chap. 2, B2. The reason Hegel does not acknowledge the purely negative functions of the *daimonion* is that he relies on Xenophon, who in the *Memorabilia* (*Memoirs of Socrates*) several times refers to the sign as telling Socrates both what to do and what not to do (first at I 1, 4).

Kierkegaard writes on the *daimonion* in his dissertation on irony: He regards it as a phenomenon transitional between reliance on an external oracle as guide to ethical action and fully free individual subjectivity; it belongs to a phase whose moral decision is internal but still in need of a semisensory representation (190–191).

26. Plato, *Theaetetus* 176 a, a favorite reference for Plotinus.

27. Arendt, *Willing*, 15 ff., discusses the absence of both the word and the notion of a will in Greek philosophy. She notes that Aristotle did coin a word, *proairesis*, the "fore-choice" that precedes action. But I must add that this word denotes an activity, not a faculty; there is a virtue that approximates the will: "self-control" *(egkrateia)*, the ability to follow the dictates of reason (*Nichomachean Ethics* 1102 b 15, 1145 a 15 ff.).

To the notions like *Will* and *Evil* that antique thinkers refused to conceive and dwell on can be added also *Nothing*, which disappears from rational Western philosophy with the school of Parmenides (Rosen 1988, 153) if not with Parmenides himself, soon after its first occurrence. But see note 21 on Nothing in theology.

A passage in Plato's *Meno* (77 c) exemplifies the readiness with which all Socrates' partners agree to the proposition that the good is what everyone really wants. Meno—a corrupt man—at first balks at saying that everyone wants the good and not the bad, but as soon as Socrates changes his own term "good" to "profitable" Meno begins to agree that no one desires the bad, the unprofitable.

The first description I know of a purely perverse will in action is Augustine's account in the *Confessions* (II 4) of the sin of his childhood, the stealing of some pears that he neither needed nor wanted: "I did not will to enjoy what I had coveted by theft, but only the theft and the sin itself." It is Augustine, the Roman Christian, who first established the will in theology and philosophy (Arendt, *Willing*, 84–110). I surmise that he came on it first in its naysaying, rebelliously self-involved form, as the will that insists more on its willing than its object.

28. There is, of course, also a healthy naysaying, the resistance to temptation (expressed in the slogan "Just Say No" of the antidrug campaign) and to tyranny (expressed in posters saying "No to . . .).

Bertolt Brecht's play *The Naysayer* is the complement to a play called *The Yeasayer*, which is identical except for the ending; both are adaptations based on a Japanese Noh play, *Taniko*. They were "didactic" plays intended for the education of the players only and not to be performed before an audience: A group of Shintoist Buddhist students go on some sort of pilgrimage across the mountains. It is the "Great Usage" of the journey that if a member of the troop gets sick he has to be hurled into the valley, but he also must be asked to agree—as everyone has hitherto done. In the *Naysayer* the boy who gets sick says *no* to the request, thus making it necessary for the whole group to return. Braving the possible scorn of their community, the students institute a new and more rational law, "with open eyes, none more craven than his neighbor."

29. See Plato, *Republic* 439 e ff., where the spirited part of the soul is introduced as a mediating middle between the desiring and the reasoning part and is described as a fierce power of resistance to lust and a capacity for self-rebuke allied with reason. Platonic *thymos* is thus a *faculty* not so different from the *virtue* Aristotle calls *egkrateia* (note 27).

30. See Hardwick, 218.

31. Aristotle *Topics* 158 a 14 ff., *On Interpretation* 20 b 22 ff. Yes-no questions are discussed in Belnap and Steel, passim; in Hiż, passim; in Lyons 2:753 ff.; for a classification and ranking of questions, see Brann 1992.

32. The German verb *sich äussern*, "to express oneself" on something, literally "to outer oneself," makes the point even better.

On lying, see Bok 1978; on secrets, Bok 1983, where the relation of lying to privacy is taken into account.

A topic of great fascination is omitted in this book: how it is possible to conceal things from oneself, as for example, in "going into denial." Let me say only that from Plato through Freud into contemporary writers, no one seems to have found a way to explain self-deception except by supposing some sort of vertical duality that is, a hierarchy of control, in the psychic organization. Even the internal affirmation and denial of the silent inner "dialogue of the soul with itself" (Plato *Sophist* 263 e) seems to demand a similar self-opposition, only in the lateral dimension. For self-deception, see Bok 1983, 59–72; Barnes 1997.

33. The Ring of Gyges appears in the *Republic* 359 d. Such a ring is what infants lack. When they engage in preverbal pretense, their deceptions are perfectly patent and therefore *somehow* innocent. See Eck, 12 ff., on children's preverbal and verbal lying.

34. See Brann 1993, "Telling Lies," for various reasons not to lie. The classical argument occurs, of course, in Kant's moral writings; he condemns lying absolutely as effecting the self-destruction of thought and speech, and with it human dignity. He mentions especially the case of unavoidable answers to yes-no questions; even under the severest examination, where an innocent life might be at stake (if, for example, the hiding place of an innocent victim is demanded), lying is proscribed (in Bok 1978, 268).

35. See Aristotle, *On Rhetoric*, ed. Kennedy, 25 ff., for a delineation of Aristotle's understanding of dialectic, which is much narrower and more technical than Plato's; it is essentially disputation.

36. For example, in the *Phaedo* Socrates allows himself just one moment's mood, but no more, of loving victory more than wisdom, namely, in letting himself be persuaded by his own arguments concerning the immortality of the soul (91 a). In the *Meno* he shows how a smart aristocrat like Meno cannot produce a yes or no as genuinely serious as that of a little boy, a household slave. In the *Gorgias* he is even driven to speech-making by the angry polemical levity of Callicles. Even that most serious of interlocutors, young Theaetetus, is questioned in Socrates' spirit by the visiting dialectician: "Are you assenting, then, because you recognize this to be the case, or did some impulse sweep you along to a speedy assent because the account has accustomed you to it?" (*Sophist* 236 d). But usually his partners respond to him with deep attention, and their yesses and noes are not to be taken as mere chiming.

37. People sometimes feel put out that the same man who requires a genuine, spontaneous yes or no from his interlocutors should himself engage in *irony*, the deception that comes from withholding one's thought, in Socrates' case, from pretending intellectual inability. As Hegel and Kierkegaard were both fascinated by Socrates' *daimonion*, so they are by his irony (note 25, ibid., B 1). Hegel contrasts it with the irony of the contemporary Romantics, which is the negation of all determinations by a sovereign subjectivity that hovers above all questions, as really being done with them. Socratic irony, on the other hand, a sound irony, has two aspects. One is his playful conversational manner; the other is his "tragic irony." This latter begins with his inner reflection insofar as it is directed against the intellectual and ethical conventions of the day; his claim of ignorance is in this sense no pretense at all, for it is true that these reflections yield no doctrine. But in this very lack he is wiser than the others, and so he pretends ignorance in order to (1) get out of their way—hence his dialectical playfulness—as they themselves begin to reflect and (2) make them express their own principles. Each such principle is then allowed to develop its own dialectical negation under Socrates' doctrineless questioning. Thus Socratic irony is an expression of the negativity of dialectic (p. 156).

Kierkegaard devotes most of his *Concept of Irony* to a study of the major Platonic dialogues with a view to extracting from them the nature of Socrates' irony. He concludes, in express contrast to Hegel, that Socratic irony, though the first of its kind, was even then "infinite absolute negativity." Socrates de-realized all the established actuality of his age, thus becoming lighter and lighter and ever more negatively free (287–288). In his complete negativity toward existence "he hovered in ironic satisfaction above all the determinations of substantial life" (240). Kierkegaard has discovered in Socratic irony his own understanding: Irony is infinite, absolute negativity—a boundless, relationless nonpositivity.

In his comedy *The Clouds*, Aristophanes introduces a Socrates who hangs in a basket from the roof of his thinkery and invokes the Clouds, formless Forms, as deities. Even that suspended Socrates is more like the Socrates of the Platonic dialogues than is Kierkegaard's negatingly hovering Socrates.

2

The Negation of Speech: Logical *Not*

We now turn from *no* to *not*. Even the sounds of these two negating particles express their different use: the drawn-out wail of no-o-o against the plosive decisiveness of no-t. Where the naysaying of willful rejection is (or can be) prolonged and passionate, the naysaying of logic is brisk and objective (albeit logicians are not always so).[1] For it is not a thing or state of affairs that is being repelled but a texture of words and meanings that is being negated: a sentence of our language, or the mere proposition it conveys, is being turned into an asserted statement by being denied.

By and large the negations of logic take place in symbols and are found in books. They are not so much naysayings as naywritings. Consequently, when you come across the assertion sign before a proposition—which is often itself not in words but in symbols—there is no real person actually doing any affirming: The author of a logic book is not meant to be the assertor. To be sure, for reflective logicians, what might be called the framing question for negations looms quite large: Is there an initiating language act for negation, such as a question or a prior affirmation? If we reserve the word "denial" for the *act* of negation, the question becomes: Whatever else happens in a logical sequence, is every negation a denial, an implied response? These questions will be taken up below, but this is the place to mention that Frege, who thought deeply about negation, held that every negation is the answer to a question, and, moreover, that every question had as a "content," a "thought." This thought can be entertained before it is judged true or false, affirmed or denied, asserted or negated. Thoughts are impervious to negation (or any other act of judgment).[2] This possibility—that there are thought contents to be merely entertained—is full of consequences to be discussed later (p. 30).

Before asking the immediate question, I should state that the negation about to be considered is sentential and that the sentences to be considered are declarative in form, indicative in mood, and indeterminate in quantity. In other words, I omit reference to the kind of logic called modal, in which possibility and necessity are considered, and to the quantity of propositions, that is, the quantifying adjectives "all," "some," and "none," attention to which is necessary for the study of inference. All that is at issue here is the *quality* of the proposition. In traditional terms, propositions are said to have *positive* or *negative* quality.

Here then is the first question.

1. WHAT IS NEGATION?

Rational negation is a subspecies of *opposition*. But before inquiring into negation as a particular condition, I shall say a brief word about it as an activity, for negation refers to both an initial action and the sentential consequence that casts loose from it.

(a) Negating is a kind of discerning or distinguishing. When we make distinctions, we do it within a setting, a context that obscurely prefigures the whole we are so neatly distinguishing into oppositions, "This is *not* that," as that rambunctiously logical Wife of Bath observes:

> Men may conseille a womman to be oon,
> But conseillyng is no commandement.[3]

Such distinctions are antecedent to the positive predicating judgments that tell what the "this" which is not "that" actually is. A grand and deliberate form of distinction making is the "way of division" *(diairesis)* found first in Platonic dialogues. Here the thing sought is discovered by surveying the universe, dividing its layout into a "left" and a "right" side, and rejecting the one by negation while focusing on the other so as to hunt down the object within it by forcing it into ever narrower branchings (thus generating the ancestor of a logical "decision tree"). The end is a collection of positive terms amounting to a well-grounded or at least a highly specified definition.[4]

(b) But back to opposition. Both the Greek and the Latin terms *(antikeimenon, oppositio)* signify "what lies or is set before another."[5] This is not an innocuous beginning. It betokens that opposition is conceived by the observant speaker of these languages to be a relation of the fixed to the facing, of something that is there first and something that confronts it. There are at least three questions concerning logical negation that, if they are to be answered at all, must be answered not within the negations of logic but over the larger class of opposition: (1) Do oppositions belong to the intellect only, so that human thinking is the sole source of discernment and human speech is the source of divisions, or is the confronting world itself already determinately riven? (2) Is the nonbeing that seems to be denoted by some not-saying in some way—difficult to comprehend positively—built into the world or are all distinctions into a *this* and a *that*, a positive one and its coequally positive other? (3) In view of the lopsided confrontation of the parts betokened by the term *op-position* itself, does priority attach to the articulated affirmative? Only slight attempts at grappling with the first two of these perplexities will be made, but the third is treated at more length, being somewhat more peculiarly logical in character.

There are words to describe what relates opposing parts: polar, antithetical, incompatible, discrepant, contrastive. But in the realm of human reasoning opposition itself seems to be both as pervasive and as ultimate a notion as there is, for whatever else it may be, it is, as was said, the first consequence of that discerning thinking which arguably precedes everything else.[6] Hence it is impossible to give a definition of opposition that is not circular.

(c) It is, therefore, more feasible to list the types of opposition. Here the tradition was set by Aristotle, who clearly attaches the greatest importance to this topic. He sets out three types of opposition of particular interest to us in this section: contrariety (exemplified by black and white), privation (exemplified by being blind and being sighted), and contradiction (exemplified by the state of sitting and not sitting).[7]

He distinguishes sharply between contraries and privations as they appear in things: Contraries (such as black and white) are by and large not necessary attributes of their subjects and usually have intermediate states such as gray, while privations, such as blindness, are specific to some positive condition and can only occur in what is by nature sighted. It is worth noting that Aristotle here views these oppositions as pertaining to *terms* whose oppositional character is determined by the *beings* in which they occur. Seen merely logically, contraries and privations are quite close. Since each can have intermediates, either meets the logical test for contrariety: Both members of each type of opposition can't be true at the same time, but both can be false (p. 36).[8]

Aristotle says that contradiction is the *primary* opposition, for it is sheer, unintermediated opposition. But it is—and this may be crucial—an opposition of *statements*, not of terms (and so, of things). To be sure, the asserted propositions are indeed also about things. But Aristotle insists that

> what underlies the affirmation and negation is *not* the affirmation or negation; . . . for what underlies is in no way a sentence. These things are, however, said to oppose each other as do affirmation and negation.[9]

I think it is safe to say that for Aristotle contradiction, opposition, properly so-called, belongs to thinking and speaking, though among beings "contrariety is a kind of difference and difference is otherness."

This claim holds even for that great axiom of thought, speech, *and* being first fully enunciated by Aristotle, the so-called Law of Contradiction. Aristotle had said, clearly with reference to opposition in speech, that "opposites do not accept being present *(hyparchein)* at the same time." He is echoing his own formulation of the law: "It is impossible for the same [attribute] to be present and not present at the same time. . . ."[10] This axiom, which, as I said, holds for Being *and* for speaking, is the most assured and most unprovable of all principles (though its denial is in effect refuted as soon as the antagonist tries to say even *one* significant thing). Aristotle proceeds to imagine what our world would be like if the principle did not hold: no set essential being and so all attributes merely accidental, all predications equally true and so no distinctions, all assertions true (or false) and so no judgment, no determinate right or wrong and so no significant speech.

How can I claim that the primary opposition belongs only to thought and speech when its law is asserted of Being as well? Opposition in speech distinguishes parts of logical space, that, the law says, must lie, speaking figuratively, outside of each other; the same law declares that the real features which these opposing parts represent must not inhabit or occupy the same real place at the same real time.[11] Whereas, however, the contradictory members of a primary opposition each take up a distinct part of the space representing logical speech, in the world of real beings there is no place for the negative member—there is no not-black in nature, though there is white and gray. If a being is *spoken of* as not black, it *is* some other color. Denial, the act of negation, is always *contrary* with respect to its real ground, never contradictory—meaning that the world is full of variety but contains no real negatives. For contrariety, which lives within an articulated spectrum of possibilities and alternatives, implies a wholly positive world of determinate opposites, a world within which balanced distinctions function, while contradiction assumes no responsibility for determining the negated opposite: It is *simply the "not"* of its kind—the most unreal, purely *logical,* of oppositions.[12] So the axiom stated for Being is in fact a Law of Contrariety.

Since there is no intermediate term in contradiction, Aristotle assumes the bipolarity of assertion and negation and its rule: that every statement has one and only one contradictory opposite, the "Law of Excluded Middle." Again the thought and speech of contradiction is grounded in the nature of beings: They cannot both be and not be, or have a property and not have it at the same time or in the same way. And since that is so, a statement about beings is either true of false, and "true" and "false" determine statements opposite in logical quality.[13]

It may be well and truly said that Aristotle fixed the ways to think of negation even into current times.[14] But he in turn lived, first, with a language that from the earliest texts abounds in "polar expressions," starting with that lovable little pair of particles *men:de*, cumbrously translated as "on the one hand: on the other hand," and including the ubiquitous "not just in word but also in deed." Homer seems sometimes to engage in these antitheses (which need not be mutually exclusive) for the sheer joy of the balance.[15] And second, Aristotle had a philosophical tradition behind him that was deeply engaged not only with naysaying and nonbeing (see chapter 4) but with discovering the real opposites that govern the world. Aristotle himself seems to have written a treatise on contraries *(enantia)*, and he lists and critiques other tables of opposites.[16]

In modern languages too opposition is deeply ingrained. In linguistics, which has a terminology that might seem to shadow philosophical distinctions but is actually far more differentiated, many polarities besides the analogues to logical contrariety and contradiction are observed.[17]

(d) Enough for present purposes has been said about the source of logical negation in the oppositions found in language, in beings, and in thought. But I want to include here a proposed logic in which negation figures differently. Dewey desires a logic of inquiry, which would jettison the Aristotelian tradition as resting on a defined ontology. Quality, the old term for the positive or negative *character* of propositions, is to be replaced by the name of an *operation* they perform: "*re*qualifying the original indeterminate situation." Affirmative propositions signify the evidential agreement of their subject matters as they support each other and point in the same direction. Negative propositions, on the other hand, represent subject matters to be eliminated because they are irrelevant to the evidence by which a material problem is solved. Consequently the situation is *re*qualified, transformed, and clarified from an indeterminate to a determinate one.

Thus affirmation and negation are not qualities of, or operations on, propositions but rather operations on the situation of a scientific inquiry. I think Dewey means by the "situation" primarily the attitude of the researcher; the negative proposition represents the rejection and ruling out of factors that inconveniently confine the situation. Dewey takes this operational understanding so far as to define the asserted proposition as the deferred culmination of the organic practical interaction, by way of selection/rejection, of the researcher with the material studied. In this process, negation is merely the excluding side of selection. In the traditional scheme, affirmation is conceptually prior to negation; in Dewey's operation logic they are correlative in concept and in time. It follows that the negative proposition is not merely a mention of an omission or lack, not just a record of defective being or "ontological inferiority," but an instruction for change *to be effected* on existing conditions by the operations set forth in it.

It seems to me that Dewey has not so much redefined negation as shown how researchers use negative propositions for making those distinctions that lead to discoveries in which existence plays a large role—those of empirical science. In other words, he has reflected formal logic back onto the distinction-making *activity* with which I began.[18]

(e) Has the question "What is negation?" been answered? Yes, to some extent. Negation arises from the human desire and ability to make distinctions;

it is (most likely) grounded in the oppositions and polarities that belong to beings (of which the first, the opposition of oppositions, is surely that of thinking itself to its object, be it ideal or real). Thinking makes (or finds) at least three kinds of oppositions. Two of these, privation and contrariety, belong to the terms that enter a proposition to describe beings, to record the fact that some beings are in various degrees deprived of properties that properly belong to them and that they have other attributes, accidentally and over a spectrum of degrees. The oppositions by way of terms are responsible for negations that will later be called "internal" to the proposition: "the eagle is blind (not properly sighted)," "the sky is dull (neither bright nor dark)." The third opposition, contradiction, belongs to the statement itself and is signified by negating the copula—for that position is regarded as negating the whole—or by making the negation precede the proposition: "This person is-not a logician" or "It is not the case that this person is a logician."[19] Contradiction is, I repeat, considered by Aristotle to be the primary case of negation. It shows itself as the disjoining of subject from predicate in a sentence and as the division of subject from attribute in a statement. It is the primary act of distinction, in which the negation is pure as negation because it is unalloyed by any kind of a positive consequence. That, in sum, is classical negation.

(f) Frege appeared at the beginning of this section, and to him we must now return, for he mounts a deep critique of the classical view.[20] Questions and negative statements have, he says, something in common. They both have a "content," a "thought," a sense to be grasped by all who hear them. Such a question content can receive a negative answer; similarly a negative statement is the negation of such a thought content. The thought itself *remains integral*; negation does not touch it and it is *not* the dissolution (or, as above, the disjunction) of the thought into component parts: A thought is impervious to negation. Even a false thought is not affected by negation. Thoughts cannot be torn apart, for what are the elements, the objects into which they would be separated? Things, parts of images, sentence parts?

Consequently there are not two judgments, affirmative and negative. In fact we have no criterion for distinguishing these, for a negative particle may occur anywhere in a sentence without making it indubitably negative: "Consider the sentences 'Christ is immortal,' 'Christ lives for ever,' 'Christ is not immortal,' 'Christ does not live for ever,' " and try to say which sentence states a negative judgment.

Thus, since there is no criterion for distinguishing negative from affirmative judgments, the principle of economy demands that we drop the terms. Instead of an affirmative assertion and another, negative one that is inseparably (and confusingly) attached to the world "false," we now have just an assertion and a negative particle. Every thought has a contradictory or an opposite, and we acknowledge its falsity simply by admitting the truth of its contradictory. "If we *can* make do with one way of judging, then we must."

Frege's understanding of the reasons why classical negation was so long accepted reveals most clearly what is at issue.

> Perhaps the act of negating, which maintains a questionable existence as the polar opposite of [affirmative] judging, is a chimerical construction, formed by a fusing of the act of judging with the negation.

This construction comes about first because of the admirable but hopeless desire to define the essentially indefinable judgment in terms of "positive" and "negative." But more significantly it is the result of false arrogation of power in matters of judgment: the notion that "the judging subject sets up the connexion or order of the parts in the act of judging and thereby brings the judgment into existence. Here the act of grasping a thought and acknowledgment of its truth are not kept separate." Yet the grasping of a thought and the judging of its truth are *not* the same: years of labor may intervene between them.

But the "grasping" of a thought is, in fact, not a "production" of the thought, that is, of setting its parts in order. For the thought was there, with its parts in order and its truth, *before* it was grasped. No more than a traveler makes the mountain he crosses does a judging subject *make* the thought he acknowledges as true. Thus, just as if someone has made the error of thinking it within his power to produce by his act of judging what he then affirms as true, so he will credit himself with the power of destroying it. Negation is, then, the breaking up of the interconnection built up in the original judgment, and affirmation and negation look like polar opposites. And since we find the negative particle that signals our negation often united with the predicate, we think that we have negated not the whole sentence but just this part. Yet we are again misled by our own language. "On the contrary: it is by combining the negative syllable with a part of the sentence that we do negate the content of the whole sentence." For the thought is one and indivisible.

What is so very remarkable in Frege's revision of classical negation is that, in the interests of economy, modesty, and the neutrality of thought, he is willing to forego all the following: (1) the possibly inherent involvement in the declaration that "this is [not] so" of content and assertion, of the way things are said to be [or not to be] with *our affirmation* [or denial]; (2) the possibility of accounting for the nonsubjective, communicable character of a thought through the *intelligible nature* of its object; (3) the possible mirroring in a sentence, by means of an opposition other than contradiction, of different *real oppositions* found among beings, such as contraries; (4) the possibility of asking what negation might be with the hope of receiving a *significant answer*. It seems too high a price to pay.

2. WHERE IS A SENTENCE NEGATED?

No one can fail to notice that a simple declarative sentence, your basic utterance, can be negated in a number of ways. Thinking about the ways of negation as expressed in speech profitably starts with the position of the negating particle that turns a sentence into an asserted statement:

> Rosencrantz. Do you think Death could possibly be a boat?
> Guildenstern. No, no, no. . . . Death is the ultimate negative. Not-being.
>   You can't not be on a boat.
> Rosencrantz. I've frequently not been on boats.
> Guildenstern. No, no, no—what you've been is not on boats.[21]

But perhaps the qualification "in speech" is superfluous—perhaps negation occurs only in speech; one might argue that a negation is an *ens rationis*, a being of reason that *can* occur only in thought and its articulation in language. For my part, I think, as I have already intimated, that there is lack, privation, and otherness right in the world and so there is a worldly counterpart of negation, but were it true—and it is worth a lot of thought—that only speech shows negation, then where it occurs in the basic unit of fully realized thinking, the sentence, is even more suggestive.

I take the basic sentence and statement pattern to be the one that turns up in books on logic, the tripartite "S is P," where "S" stands for the grammatical and the logical subject (the thing put forth for consideration), "is" for a grammatical or logical copula (the connecting center) and "P" for the grammatical predicate or the logical property (the feature attributed to the subject). It is rightly a topic of suspicious questioning that the grammar and the logic of this form coincide. We must ask, Is it a blessing from above that our articulated thought mirrors the way things are, or a snare and a delusion forcing us to construe the world in the image of our linguistic constitution? It seems to me that our only recourse is (1) *to investigate* what languages other than our own Indo-European ones do, in particular, to know whether, even if their units of stateable sense were not tripartite or if they did not have sentences at all (though I've never heard of *such* a language), their speakers did not in fact *think* in tripartite terms[22] or (2) *to imagine* what a language utterly different from ours might be like.

I am sure investigations of the first kind abound, though one would have to be fiendishly clever to discover the thoughts *behind* an alien language, since unutterable thoughts (which some people even claim don't exist) are apprehensible, if at all, only through introspection. The second task, to imagine a language with a different, especially a smaller, number of constituents, seems somewhat easier, because our own language appears to include sentences of fewer than three elements. In moments of Parmenidean depth, people produce two-word predicateless sentences like "Being is," but the intention is to push language to its limits: to speak without making distinctions (p. 137). Other, more normal sentences (even more normal in ancient languages than in English) omit the copula—*nomen omen*, "a name is a sign of fate"—but we understand them as gnomic rhetoric, a way of condensing grammatical subject and predicate to approach the succinct unity of the original apprehension. Next, the speech of children just coming out of infancy abounds in one-word, subject-only sentences, for example, "Effant!" which we, however, construe as "That's an elephant." And that brings us to the no-word language of pointed looking, for if intuitive thought is unitary, so much the more is the thing itself. If you direct someone by a look to observe an open door, what both of you see is an open door, not "that a door is open," though that is how you will eventually speak of it. Moreover, you might go on to say that it has the keys still stuck in it and that it has numerous other attributes. So the sample cases within my linguistic experience all seem to lead back to the tripartite sentence, and so does every imaginary sentence. That things come apart in this way when discerning thinking dwells on them and speech articulates them was one of Aristotle's particular preoccupations, and the skeleton sentence "S is P" is his formulation. I will accept it here and will now proceed to the various placements of its denials.

1. S is-not P. In the traditional understanding, since the copula holds the sentence together, the copula is the place to break it asunder, to effect its brusque, its direct denial. Thus a negation affixed to any other part leaves the sentence actually affirmative: "It is important to note that a proposition is affirmative or negative by reason of the *copula* and the copula alone."[23] That rule (which few logicians actually observe) holds in whichever of its three functions "is" appears; whether it announces identity (S is S) or existence (S *is*) or predication (S is P), it is still a copula, though in the existence case it is usually understood as a predicate-verb. "Being is" takes "is" as having more force than a mere binder, and so "exists" is substituted (sometimes misleadingly, p. 129). Of course, many sentences absorb the copula-function into a verb-action: We can say either "this book is boring" or "this book bores [me]." These sentences are rhetorically different but logically the same; when we deny the second, something like the copula even reappears: "This book does-not bore [me]." Whatever the function of the copula may be, its negation strikes at the heart of the sentence. It is called "internal negation."

2. S is not-P. This placement of the negating particle has two branches, S is not-P and S is non-P. The first of these can be thought of as establishing a "complement class" to P, the class of all properties outside P.[24] Whatever S is,

it is now outside P. But in logical contexts it is outside P *within* the universe that pertains to P, not just anywhere.

The second branch uses not the adverb "not" but the prefix "non-": S is non-P. This "privative predicate" is a softer negation; it does not only empha-size that S is not, but suggests that it is something other. The class not-P was merely negative, but non-P suggests worlds wider than not-P, in fact infinitely wider; "S is non-P" is the form called the "infinite judgment" in older logic books. Thus it emphasizes otherness rather than flatly determinate negation. These two ways of denying the predicate are behind the distinction between contradiction and contrariety.[25] Both of these negations are still "internal."

Between "not" and "non-," the former briskly determinate and the latter more flabbily suggestive, it is "non-" that plays a large role—not in logic (where it has no formal place) but in ontology, the study of Being. So it makes sense that of the two corresponding Greek particles, *ou* and *me*, the latter should disappear when logic comes to the fore in Aristotle's writing, and Non-being is no longer a great ontic principle.[26] In fact, the case of "Nonbeing" shows what "non-" is good for: the negation of "intension" rather than "ex-tension." The intension of a class is its defining concept while the extension is its members;[27] what Nonbeing negates is not all the beings but the form of Being itself.

3. Not (S is P). This is the negation to which the future would belong, though it had been in use by ancient logicians.[28] Here the whole proposition is negated, permitting it to be written as an opaque, atomic *p* for the purposes of the propositional calculus (p. 43). This negation is called external. Frege says:

> It is incorrect to say: "Because the negative syllable is combined with part of a sentence [for example the predicate], the sense of the whole sentence is not negated."[29]

It is because of what Frege says that internal negation can be taken outside. Once this is done, *p* regains its initial positivity; it could be false, but it is not negative. This propositional negation is a logical formulation that is, *pace* Frege, *derivative* from the original thought activity of negation, which works internally, that is, with the terms of the proposition.

[4] Not-S is P. This is arguably not a thinkable proposition because it is about nothing (or, if not-S is taken as denoting the complement class of S, almost everything). It certainly induces confusion: When the Cyclops, who has just been blinded by Odysseus, asks his name, the clever hero says, "No-body is my name." So the giant calls his troglodyte neighbors to aid. When they come by to ask who has done him harm, he cries out, "My friends, No-body is killing me with guile and force." So these great friends leave, saying

that if nobody is doing him any harm, he is probably just sick and had better pray.[30]

Later on the question "Can we can think and speak of nonexistent objects?" will come forward (chapter 3). This type of negation is a foretaste of that problem. Socrates says quite unequivocally, in the course of a conversation on how we can think something false, that "one who has an opinion about nothing does not have an opinion at all."[31] And common speech unconsciously mirrors this view. We often say, "I don't think anyone's coming" rather than "I think nobody's coming."

"Not-S is P" is very different from "No S is P." The latter does not deny that S is, but that any S is P. It expresses a logical quantity—universality—rolled into an internal negation that it has pulled out of the proposition.[32]

The following statements illustrate the negations just listed:

0.   "Thought is logical": Positive.

1.   "Thought is-not logical": Breaks coupling of thought and logicality, the simplest negation.

2a. "Thought is not-logical": Puts thought in the complement class of logical things, those that are flatly not logical or outright illogical. This is the sheer contradictory of the positive.

2b. "Thought is non-logical": Holds open the possibility that thought might be, for instance, intuitive or anything else. This is a contrary to the positive.

3.   "It is not the case that thought is logical": The whole proposition is externally denied *as* a proposition, not through its terms; it remains positive.

[4] "Non-thought is logical": Paradoxical, for its says that the null class of Thought is reason bound: a no-brainer is logical.

[5] "No thought is logical": Every thought is other than logical, equivalent to the normal understanding of 1 and 2a.

To return to the opening question: Clearly a sentence can be negated anywhere, inside or out—even (in banter) at the end: "I kid you not." And, Frege claims, the sentence (and its proposition) are in all cases *meant* to be negated, although, as I said, textbooks sometimes state that a sentence is not made into a negative statement by the negation of any term but only by negating the copula. If this textbook restriction were accepted, negation would be only and always the unsaying of the coupling. But it is achievable in other ways: by saying that the predicate is not or is otherwise or by unsaying the whole sentence.

Each of these positions seems to me to signify a different course of negating thought. In "S is-not P" we put subject and predicate in thought into the same universe of things that exist and then disjoin the subject from this particular

attribute in our mind. In "S is not-P" we think out what S *is* and conclude that
it has the property P but in its negative or privative version, and in so thinking
we conceive a *negative* property, not-P, or for "S is non-P" an *other* property,
non-P. In "not (S is P)" we have done our thinking about P's relation to S, and
having concluded that it is the opposite of "S is P" we *state* "not-*p*," which
is the expression in which negation will become a mere symbol of opposition
(p. 44).

That completes the object of the exercise in this section: to see how the way
a sentence is negated expresses the various ways of negating thought.

3. WHETHER THE POSITIVE IS PRIOR TO THE NEGATIVE?

For small children and little devils, negation comes before affirmation. But
in the thinking and speaking that adults practice normally, it is normally the
opposite.

(a) That it is not senseless to ask about the posteriority of negation in general is further shown by the human fact that there are people of unquestionable
seriousness—a seriousness on the face of it the greater for its refusal to "be
positive" in the approved American way—who affirm Nothing or nothingness,
be it in despair or with serenity. Their views will be taken up in the last chapter, on Nihilism. Meanwhile the argument brought against them from their
own language, that is to say, the logical argument, has to be advanced with
the realization that the self-corroboration of speech does not resonate in the
anechoic chambers of nihilistic intention. For if the argument from speech
says that to negate what appears to be and to affirm its nothingness is yet to
negate or posit *something*, an object, they will say either that speech cannot
render their intention and therefore cannot nullify it; or they will find a way
of speaking that, like the scorpion which is said to sting itself to death when
encircled by fire, does itself in under the pressure of the speaker's comprehension—such as self-contradiction and paradox.

Thus the question here raised is not that greatest one, whether Something
or Nothing is ultimate, but the lesser one, whether in human speaking denial
is always derivative and in human speech negation is always secondary. I distinguish here between denial as a human disposition and negation as a logical
function.

Denial as a general disposition does not so much assert nothingness as it
denigrates the worth and value of what exists; it may be a sort of half-cocked
rebellion against existence—existential hate, so to speak. A little devil like
Mephistopheles evinces it: "I am the spirit that ever negates! *(verneint).*"[33]
The logical activity of negation, on the other hand, is just the dispassionate
assertion of a negated proposition. Even as speech acts, denial and negation

are distinguishable to some purpose, as may be discerned in the following example.

Suppose you are suspected of a misdeed. I ask, in an encouraging way, "You didn't do it, did you?" The proposition in question here is "You did not do it" or not-*p*. You, wanting to affirm your innocence, should say, "Yes" to not-*p* or "Yes, I didn't do it." But English speakers would all say, "*No*, I did not do it." The reason is, I think, that the adverbs *no* and *not* play different roles here. "No" is a particle of denial; it means "I disaffirm," "I deny," while "not" is a sentential function that negates the proposition (p. 43).[34]

Although denial and negation are often used exchangeably in logic textbooks, the priority question is better thought through when they are kept distinct. Whether existential or ontological denial can come before affirmation is what might be called a meta-metaphysical question. Next, whether in judgments of truth something must be affirmed before anything can be denied is ultimately a metaphysical question. But whether logical negation is posterior or equal to its logical pole (which has no noun-name)—that is a far more restricted and determinable problem, a meta-logical problem.

(b) In fact, to my knowledge, there is no argument for the priority of logical negation. For internal negation, the kind that stands within a sentence, such an argument would fly in the face of the fact that no term can be negated that is not posited, that negation is indefeasibly qualifying—primarily of the copula. There might, of course, be an inherently negative predicate, but in a sentence of logic it will play a positive role, whatever it means in philosophy: "That's nothing" would qualify as a positive sentence in the textbooks.

Once we look only at the opaque, externally negated propositions of propositional logic, the posteriority of negation becomes even clearer. To be sure, Wittgenstein will present a theory that makes propositions inherently bipolar,[35] but the terminology of logic books says otherwise. Their tacit assumption is that *p*, the atomic proposition, is posited, as it were, as the base line, before the logical processes begin. And that is why, I think, positing has no name in logic while negation names an operation of logic. But it might be better to say that the mental action that puts *p* on the scene is different from the function of negation which has *p* for an argument: Negation simply flips whatever truth-value was assigned to *p*. (In logical truth tables both T and F are in turn assigned to every *p*, though in the real world someone might know whether any given *p* was in fact true or false.) So negation is posterior, but only in the way that a function might be thought of as posterior to its range, that is, as a relation is posterior to its terms.[36]

The difference in the mental action of positing and negating is confirmed by a symmetrical terminological absence: As the term for the opposite of negation is missing, so the opposite of assertion is missing. Some symbolic systems use an assertion sign which signifies that the *p* in question is postulated or proved, but they have no sign for mere unasserted *p*, the unclaimed proposition thought, advanced in a way analogous to a nautical command in older times, which would first be given as an alerting description of the operation to be performed and then driven home with a "Make it so!" The mental action of assertion follows on the necessarily prior act of unasserted positing. To be sure, these ways of thinking of negation embody a philosophically weighty decision, one which is in logical contexts usually ascribed to Frege: that there *are* unasserted propositions because there are "thoughts" that are neither true nor false, as-yet-unjudging acts of grasping a sense.[37]

So it seems that at the outset, where the logical terminology is settled, positing precedes negation as an argument does a function that is applied to it.[38] But as soon as the system gets going, positive and negative become equi-valent, in the sense that *p* and not-*p* behave with perfect symmetry, each being simply the other's opposite in truth-value, whatever *p* is. Hence the logical equi-valence of positive and negative is tied to a certain understanding of truth and falsity, which will be considered in the next section.

(c) Let me begin then by mentioning first an answer to the question posed above that comes both from ancient philosophy and from modern cognitive science, though in different form: Negation is secondary because it takes longer to understand.

Thus Boethius says that when negation is used to distinguish something, the positive should be mentioned first,

> as in "Of numbers some are prime, others non-prime"—because if the negation is said first there will be a delay in a person's understanding of the thing we are presenting.[39]

The reason is that the positive gives the simple name of a natural being, a species, for "every species is an ordering of being," while the negative does not name another species but destroys the first one: "non-prime." So Boethius's reason for the delay is in the relation of affirmation to particular being.[40]

"Latency," the experimentally observed time lag in the verification of sentences, shows that "sentences containing inherently negative terms tend to take longer to verify than sentences containing their affirmative counterparts." Thus "the circle is absent" takes longer to verify than "the circle is present." The effect may come from the necessity of extracting the negation in "absent" and then finding the truth-value of the proposition "the circle is not-present." This explanation of course assumes the priority of the positive, since it regards negation as a truth-value changing operator. Since, however, cognitive science tends to work on some physicalist hypothesis, for example, that understanding depends on the computations of the nervous system, this priority does actually amount to an explanation: We are wired to think affirmatively.[41]

Natural being and neural wiring are very different hypotheses, and very differently arrived at, but they are both hypotheses. To regard the one or the other as more satisfying to the intellect is the distinguishing mark of two great modes of thought and probably of two kinds of life. Be that (for the moment) as it may, the evidence for the speedier accessibility of affirmation is the same for both—and that is the point here. Viewed from a psychological vantage point (here that of temporally conditioned thinking), a negation appears to be an elaboration upon a basic thought. One might, in the mode of cognitive psychology, look for an evolutionary advantage in that fact.

(d) From a philosophical point of view, negation is generally regarded as secondary for just the reasons that Boethius gives to account for the time delay in comprehension: Being is original, Nonbeing is Being qualified: "we even say that Nonbeing *is* Non-being" because it is a negation of beinghood. And this primacy is reflected in our knowledge: "The knowledge of 'that which [anything] is' is the knowledge of an affirmation."[42] This judgment of the priority of the affirmative over the negative makes its way through the writings of philosophers and philosophical logicians; the grounds may be very different, but the ordering is the same.

Three reasons are given in the Aristotelian tradition, the tradition of the *logos* that expresses faithfully the distinctions and combinations of thinking. The tradition begins with an assumption: The word structure is a sign of the thought and the thought is a sign of the thing. Therefore: First, affirmation in *enunciations* is prior to negation because it is simpler, since negation adds a particle. Second, affirmation in *thought* is prior to negation because negation signifies division, which is intellectually posterior to composition (for division is only of already composite things, as corruption is only of things already generated). And third, affirmation in a *thing* signifies that "it is [something]," which is prior to the negation that "it is not [something]," since being and having something comes before being deprived of it. One might add to this list Aristotle's association of a kind of nonbeing with falsity, insofar as a false proposition severs the subject from its property in speech, as well as Thomas's explicit formulation of Aristotle's meaning: Negation belongs to the mind, not to things.[43] Moreover it is easier to focus on presence than on absence.

Later philosopher-logicians also put negation second, in fresh and subtle versions. Bernard Bosanquet, to whom this is clearly a matter of living importance, answers the disputed question "whether Affirmation is prior to Negation" in this way: Negation is not as such a denial of affirmative judgment; it does not presuppose a particular affirmative *judgment* to be denied. But it does presuppose *some* general affirmation, namely, that of a world having a positive content judged to be real. Such an immediate affirmation of reality is the condition of the possibility of anything following from the "removal," that is the negation, of a "suggested idea." Such negation will follow soon upon the consciousness of a real, positive world, and so it is true that in the beginning of knowledge negation is a degree more remote from reality than affirmation and that this "ideality" always clings to it. For an affirmation can be to some degree given as a fact, while a negation always presupposes a *suggested* affirmative relation, the "suggested idea" just mentioned: A negation is not given but made. Yet because a negative judgment betokens an interest in reality, it gains objective value. In short, the positive judgment itself cannot take place before the distinction between a mere idea and a fact of reality is recognized. "And with this distinction the idea of negation *is* given." So one might even say that any judgment *presupposes* the idea of a negative relation.

The circularity we have now arrived at tells us that affirmation presupposes the idea of a negative relation in general, while negation presupposes not an affirmative judgment but the idea of a corresponding affirmative relation—at least in the beginning of knowledge. As we go on the two are found to be more on a level, involving each other. In its primary shape, however, "negation is the exclusion of a suggested qualification of reality." As Bradley, who follows Bosanquet in his view of negation, puts it: "I have to turn my experience into a disjunctive totality of elements which, according to the conditions, explicitly imply and negate each other."[44] Here negation is essentially discernment of the facts of reality.

This account of negation, which has turned from the division of beings to the disjunction of real facts, is intelligible, even very sensible, on its own, but I should alert the reader here to the fact that it has been abstracted from an "idealist" system that endeavors to ground the relation (here merely assumed) between thought and reality.

The answers to the question of this section so far considered begin with the given trinity of thought, language, world. I should now report a project, much more radical in conception, to show the genesis of negation as a second moment in the constitution of consciousness itself.

(e) So here is an attempt to understand the posteriority of negation not just as a fact of our reason but as a factor in the very genesis of consciousness. Fichte[45] finds negation as falling out from the second of his "foundational tenets," *Grundsätze*. The German word *Satz*, in English "sentence" or "tenet," is, conveniently, from *setzen*, "positing," which will be Fichte's key word. It means an original act of making something so. These positings are the way consciousness begins; they mark the coming into being of self-consciousness, of the "I" as a self.

Fichte's way is deliberately circular. He begins with an empirical fact, the universal acceptance of the logical law of identity, A equals A. Then, by an "abstractive reflection," he reasons thus: In the logical law, the term A is not materially posited; the law really says only "*if* A, then A." But what *is* posited is the relation of identity, and that is what the "I" contributes. Thus there is an identity relation, the necessary connection between two terms, and it, at least, is *in* the I and posited by the I. But this relation within consciousness *must* have its own material, that is, content-laden, terms, and there are no others than the positing agency itself, the I. Thus we arrive at "I am I" as *the* first and founding tenet of self-consciousness. We have reasoned our way from a fact *(Tatsache)* to an act *(Tathandlung)*, for this first positing is the deed *(Tat)* of self-positing. This result is neither a proof nor a derivation, Fichte insists. Perhaps it is some sort of induction, but whatever it is, it is a course of thought. By yet one further abstraction (the Fichtean system is a riot of abstractive thought), namely, by looking at the logical law of identity not as standing for acts of judgment but just as the mode of action of the human spirit, we get the category of reality. For anything that is posited as being *itself* has essence or reality, according to Fichte.

Now comes a second fundamental tenet.[46] It is dependent on the first for its terms, its matter, but its relation or form is independent. The second empirical fact accepted by everyone is that "not-A does not equal A." (This rule is not one of the traditional Laws of Thought, like that of Contradiction or Excluded Middle; it might be understood as a law of opposition, whose analogy in propositional logic would be "if p is true, not-p is false.") Again by abstractive reflection Fichte gets to the counterpart in consciousness: The I—which has been gained as a content through the positing of the first relation—now engages in the act of positing its opposite, the not-I. Fichte says it is shallow to think of this second moment in the genesis of self-consciousness as a mere abstraction from the I's representations: It is the I's discovery of itself as that subject which is opposed to the object it represents to itself. But no such object can teach me that *I* am the originator of the opposing relation, that knowledge has to come from my self. By a second, downward abstraction, he gets as a law of logic the accepted fact with which the derivation began. He calls this, quite rightly, not the law of [dead] opposition *(Gegensatz)* but of active "oppositing" *(Gegensetzen)*. And again abstracting from the proper activity of the oppositing judgment, which is to infer negation from opposition, he gets the *category of negation.* This derivation of negation as a moment in the genesis of the self is quite a feat, but to believe it you have to accept the possibility of finding, and the feasibility of positing, an "absolutely first, simply unconditioned foundational tenet of human knowledge."

∞   ∞   ∞

The reader of these arguments for the posteriority of negation might be tempted to say, "But all that is lost labor; the answer was a foregone conclusion when the question was posed *in words.*" The use of syntactical evidence, the interpretation of response-time observations, the *logos* understood as connecting and dividing subject beings and predicate beings, the enunciation of suggested ideal alternatives to reality, the laws of logic as clues to the constitution of consciousness—all these approaches and devices have as their point of departure the tripartite declarative sentence of the human speech most familiar to us, to which *not* or *non-* are unavoidably qualifying additions.

But is that fact an objection to such inquiries? No, it should rather be construed as an insight, which is being specified. Wherever there is (developed) human speech, meaning the temporally extended and articulated, audible or visible mediation between a thinking, feeling being and its world, the human sentence in its thought-conveying mode is declarative. That is to say, it clarifies the world—or the thinking being itself—by the light of thought. How this miracle is possible was not the question here, but rather whether and why the declarative sentence is initially positive and why, consequently, negation is secondary. The various answers given were indeed all reflections on the original positivity of declarative speech and on the reasons why *nay*-saying comes after saying. That is, after all, what reflection does: to go out wherein it went, but now laden with clarifying specifications.

This book is framed by thoughts about speechless denials (chapters 1 and 6); of the kinds of nay-*saying* that come in between, the primary negation of logic, the *not*, is the most speech bound and therefore most revealing of the nature of negation.

4. HOW IS NEGATION RELATED TO FALSITY?

The question is put in terms of negation and falsity, but of course, true and false, positive and negative, are coordinates. The question is really, Why are there coordinated pairs in the oldest, and what matters more, in the most elementary, most natural logic, and why are there two such pairs, and why are they in turn coordinated with each other: True and Positive, False and Negative? I mean to imply that the standard sentential two-valued logic is in vital respects also first. Not that our natural speech, even where perfectly rational, is always in terms of positive or negative. We dither and deviate all the time, but when we think of ourselves as decisive and correctly discriminating we notice our speech becoming declaratively positive or negative.[47]

(a) It makes sense to begin with the vocabulary induced by bivalent logic:

1. True:false. We take any statement seriously made to be declarative of truth or to be false. In logic every statement has a truth-value, T or F.
2. Asserted:unasserted. We either speak as engaged with the truth of our statement, or we utter when the cogs of truth telling are disengaged, for example, where we have an as-yet-unseated thought that we are merely considering, or when we feel the need to vent by mere exhalations of the voice. In some logical notations there is a special sign to convey: "This proposition is asserted," meaning it is either primitive or proved.

3. Affirm:deny. Mere propositions turn into statements by being affirmed or denied by us, and we thereby take responsibility for their truthfulness.
4. [Positing]:negating. There is, significantly, no special word commonly in use for the opposite of negation; negating itself is the denial of whatever truth-value a first proposition has. Thus negative propositions are usually not defined as having any particular relation to falsity.

That last fact, and the related one, that while people affirm, logicians assert and statements are "posited," makes it problematic where "true" and "false" first appear—whether in the world, in speaking or in the statements themselves. That is the object of inquiry now.

(b) This question is most starkly posed not in the classical logic of the first three sections, in which the negation was primarily internal to the proposition, but in the propositional calculus, as set out by Alfred North Whitehead and Bertrand Russell in *Principia Mathematica*.[48] In symbolic logic we do not enter the propositions as we did in section 2, but take them as primitive, symbolized by p or q, etc. In this treatment of propositions logic gets away from philosophy in this way: The inner necessity linking terms in propositions (which was taken somehow to capture the inner connections of thought or of Being) is bypassed now in favor of working out the relations that obtain among simply opaque propositional items that have no patent content. Of course, the philosophical consequences are that much more subversive.

The chief relation transparent propositions have is entailment. One proposition is entailed by or follows from another by an inner necessity, one residing in the *terms* and their relation within the proposition. Thus "If God is the one and only maximal being, he must exist" is an entailment implication that we affirm or deny according to our understanding and acceptance of these terms and their logical relations.

But the new implication of the *propositional* calculus links two propositions that may be brutely diverse. Russell called it "material implication" because the propositions are related as mere matter of fact and may have no discernible connection. (Russell observed that the propositions of mathematics, for example of Euclid's *Elements*, while each separately stating an entailment, were linked to each other by material implication,[49] and this was no doubt a main motive for developing it.)

This is the textbook definition of material implication: "p implies q" means "not-p or q."[50] It is not as strange as it may seem at first. It says, to begin with, that unless p is negated, as a matter of fact q follows.—It does, to be sure, not say that it *must* follow, for how would one assert that without getting inside the proposition?[51] But otherwise it has a ghostly familiarity; ordinarily, we say that "B follows from A" means that we can expect B whenever A is the case. Since "or" is taken inclusively, that is, as meaning "not-p or q or both" (while ordinarily we take the either-or relation to mean the one or the other but *not* both) there are other, stranger things it also says.

To see this it is useful to look at the other approach to defining this implication, which is through a truth table. Although to think it out is a true elementary education in the propositional calculus, I have relegated it to a note,[52] since for my purposes the simpler truth table for the operation of negation will serve. I introduced material implication only to drive home the points that on this level propositions are now closed off so that negation is always external, that negation is prior to implication since it helps to define it, and that truth tables are also a way to define a function (for both implication and negation are called "functions" with propositions as arguments).

Here is the truth table for negation, the simplest tabulation around which the others are built:

p	not-p
T	F
F	T

It is plain enough that negation is here displayed as being the flipping function. Start with a true proposition, and its negative will be false; start with a false proposition and its negative will be true. It is also apparent that the bipolarity of True and False is built into the table, and that truth and falsity are antecedent to negation, since they define it. Moreover negation, "the contradictory function," is primarily associated with falsity in a way only hinted at in the table by the convention that lists T first, so that negation is first applied to a true proposition to yield a false one. But that isn't a *mere* convention; logicians invariably present *p* as the original position. Thus in *Principia Mathematica* the symbol for the negation of any proposition *p* is given with the words that it represents the proposition "not-*p*" or "*p is false*." One might explain this otherwise ungrounded priority of the positive by the fact that, as I said above, all the negation has been got out of the internal structure of the elementary propositions we are here dealing with. So of course they are in themselves positive. For if negation is a function *on* the proposition *p*, it can't be *in* it. Wittgenstein will also say that elementary propositions are essentially positive, but with much more reason given.

Almost all textbooks treat truth and falsity as properties that propositions—or better, statements—just happen to have; and which are, as it happens, related to negation:

> The peculiarity of *statements* which sets them apart from other linguistic forms is that they admit truth and falsity, and may hence be significantly affirmed or denied. To deny a statement is to affirm another statement known as the *negation* or *contradictory* of the first.[53]

Truth and falsity do, somehow, seem to be intimately related to the character of each statement, while negation can function over true as well as false statements. But what really is the relation of the pair true and false to negation? (It is plain by now why negation has no specially named positive: being-*p* is not a function, as I just pointed out.) Why is elementary logic so thoroughly bipolar?

(c) Wittgenstein in his *Tractatus* gave a lot of thought to this matter. His answers have lucidity, and even though he retracted them, they are worth thinking through.[54]

It is not that *Principia Mathematica* has nothing to say about truth. Truth, it says, derives from the universe of complex objects having various qualities and standing in various relations and each capable of being perceived as one object. A judgment concerning this complexity—that the object is composed of, say, two parts having a relation to each other—is derived from perception by mere attention and is called a judgment of perception. "Since an object of perception cannot be nothing" such a judgment must be true (unless the judgment only *appears* to be perceptual, which leads to error). "In fact, we define *truth* . . . as consisting in the fact that there is a complex *corresponding* to the discursive thought which is the judgment." Falsehood is then the absence of a precisely corresponding complex object.[55]

Truth beyond this particularistic beginning comes on different levels, depending on the order of the judgment. For example, judgments made about judgments are of a higher order. Herein lies *Principia*'s resolution of the Cretan Liar paradox (p. 53). For if the Cretan includes himself in the assertion that all Cretans are liars he is mixing orders of judgment and truth: His judgment of himself as judge cannot be included among his judgments of every other Cretan.

Here truth is straightforwardly defined as correspondence. Most logicians still adhere to some version of truth as *adaequatio intellectus et rei*—the equalization of thought and thing (even now when people plying philosophy eschew it)—because they need their formalism to be about the world at the lower end to give a start-up meaning to T, F and not-.[56] Thus it is a primitive assumption that there is a world that can correspond truly to our statements and that falsity is gotten either by a negative capability for original error that we have or by negating an originally positive statement. Here truth is first; negation is a function; falsity can come pre-logically as error or derivatively by negation. It is a pretty unsatisfactory layout, and it is to this muddle that Wittgenstein addresses himself.

The world, he says, is the totality of facts, not things. Facts are states of affairs, meaning the connection of things, though the occurrence of a thing in a state of affairs is "prejudged" within the thing, so things are "fittingly," that is, internally, related to their contexts or configurations (1–2.012). Thus the world with which Wittgenstein begins is not that of the *Principia* in which judgments reach corresponding complexes derived from a unitary perception by paying attention. The "world" of the *Tractatus* is already logical, a world in "logical space" within which it divides into the facts that make it up. These facts correlate with the symbolic proposition, though he says elsewhere that "*I correlate* [my italics] the facts" to the proposition;[57] this latter expression sounds more like what is said, imperially, in *Principia*, where the world must correspond to us and our statements. Note that the old Latin formula speaks not of a correspondence or correlation of proposition *to* thing but of an "equalization of thought *and* thing"; I think really to understand Wittgenstein would be to be able to say whether in the end he actually leaves the world as it is or transforms it quite thoroughly—but that is not the present project.[58]

The facts are correlated to the proposition by being divided (as they already lie in logical space) "into those of like sense and those of opposite sense." Now the proposition itself also has a sense. "Sense" here has two aspects: sense as meaning and sense as affirmation and negation. The proposition has a content which pertains to the "how" of the facts and also a double direction (as in "directed numbers") which pertains to the "that," the truth or falsity of the fact. The remarkable observation here is that a proposition when asserted is absolutely no different than when denied, for it already possesses either of these possibilities as part of its sense (4.022, 4.064, 4.0641).

Here the analogy of proposition to picture comes in handy (4.01). If we realize it in space, sense 1. of the proposition is what the picture shows and sense 2. is what we can do with it. For example "He is a good person" can be represented by a man with a halo, and "he is not a good person" by turning the picture upside down, like "thumbs down."

Three consequences are immediate: (1) Negation is not an object or an extra property stuck onto a proposition but is already part of its sense. "The propositions *p* and not-*p* have opposite sense, but there corresponds to them one and the same reality." The fact that *p* and not-*p* can say the same thing shows that nothing in reality corresponds to "not-" (5.44).[59] (2) There are no (inherently) "negative facts", since we can't depict a no-thing; there are only our denials; and (3) there are no unasserted propositions, since the picture automatically has a position and thus one of the senses 2. holds for the proposition (2.06). I might inject here that this aspect of the theory gives me most pause: That negative facts and merely contemplated propositions *should* be possible is probably a precondition of taking fiction seriously (p. 102).

It is worth going a bit more graphically into the process of making statements here described, because that will bring out the clarification of the relation of truth to falsity, positive to negative and of these pairs to each other for the sake of which the *Tractatus* was brought in.

It all begins with a discrimination exercised by us over a logical space wherein things are seated within their place in their proper relational configurations, a discrimination of the otherness of what is false. So prototruth is in the world of fact. Now comes a proposition. Its negative and positive capability can also be pictured in this way: In its negative sense it is like a solid body that restricts all movement into a certain place; in its positive sense it has an empty place in the solid body where the object can fit in (4.463). These are pictures of the sense[s] 2., of the inherent bipolarity of every proposition. It shows negation from the beginning related to the negated proposition, for it is that hole which the negating proposition is blocking (4.0641). So to understand a proposition is to see the logical space (3.4) and to discriminate what the facts would have to be like to make a proposition, whose sense 1. is always the same, true or false.

Truth, then, or falsity, is the consonance or correlation of a propositional picture with reality (2.21), where reality *(Wirklichkeit)* is the existence or nonexistence of facts (2; 2.06)—a nonexistent fact being one that is pushed out of the world picture by the fact that exists.[60] In this correspondence is truth in the primary sense, and it comes in the duality true-false because of the way logical space divides and we discriminate the facts. In the sense of propositions lies the polarity positive-negative, the latter of which is expressed in the sign not- when the facts fail to correspond to p. Truth-values, T and F, are secondary to and derived from negation: "The sense of a truth function of p is a function of the sense of p" (5.2341). Thus T and F are not properties of propositions (6.111) any more than are positive and negative. The truth-values of the truth tables capture the relations of T and F to p and not-p more than they define the latter. Thus it would be right to adjust the ordinary layout of a truth table for negation (p. 44) to show that the sense polarity of propositions, P and N, not T and F, leads off:[61]

$$
\begin{array}{c|cc}
p & & \\
\hline
P & T & F \\
N & F & T \\
\end{array}
$$

Wittgenstein has answered the questions: "How do Truth and Falsity come to be obverses?" and "How is negation related to them and to truth-values?" There remains a last big question: Why are propositions bipolar? Is there a way to show that they must be such as to answer to the duality discernible in facts? Wittgenstein is at pains to show "that nothing in reality corresponds to the sign not-" (4.0621), so the warrant for the bipolarity of propositions is not to be found among the facts, nor even in the use propositions are put to, which is to represent the existence and nonexistence of states of affairs (4.1). Through the proposition picture we have some way of seeing that there *are* negative propositions. But can we make it plausible or even show that each proposition has *only one* negative?

Wittgenstein thinks so. First:

The negating proposition determines a logical place *other* than that determined by the negated statement.

The negating proposition determines a logical place with the help of the logical place of the negated proposition, by describing it as lying outside the latter. (4.0641)

And in addition:

And thus we can say: . . . Two propositions are opposed to one another if they have nothing in common with one another, and: Every proposition has only one negative, because there is only one proposition that lies wholly outside it. (5.513)

There are more and less formal tests for "having nothing in common."[62] One informal test is pictorial. Let *p* be represented by a point in logical space. Then not-*p* is represented by the rest of that space. Could *this* same *p* exist in a second space as well, so that there would be a second non-*p*? Not to the representational imagination. The spatial metaphor displays the character of the logical space we live in: It admits only one proposition totally outside another. A more formal proof is given in a note.[63]

(d) It is in itself a satisfaction to have raked up and gotten one lucid solution to questions seldom regarded. But now a remarkable break with traditional philosophy is revealed in addition: For these philosophical logicians *truth comes from the world, and negation is in propositions.* For traditional philosophers it is just the other way around: *Negation is in the world of appearances and in the beings of the intellect, and truth is in the propositions.* It is a cause of considerable wonder to come on an intellectual revolution in this way. Aristotle (who, recall, regards only contradiction as a purely logical negation) says it strikingly:

For to say that what is, is not and what is not, is, is the false while to say that what is, is and what is not, is not, is the truthful.

And:

For the false and the truthful are not in things, the good, for example, being truthful and the bad just false, but in thinking.[64]

The claim that a correspondence theory of truth is not to be found in Aristotle's texts, made by Heidegger, is at least suggested by these passages.[65] For I take such a theory to be inherently somewhat ambivalent about the last locus of truth: Is it to be found in the *Principia*'s universe of perceptually accessible objects or in Wittgenstein's logically discriminable facts? Are these objects or facts to be called true, or at least truth congruent, or is truth merely relational, just the fit, however achieved, of sentence and thing? Aristotle, on the other hand, is clear where truth is when we think and then speak truthfully or falsely: It is in our discerning in thought and articulating in speech the presences and absences, endowments and privations, of beings. Indeed, earlier thinkers constitute the world directly from Being and Nonbeing, the subjects of chapter four. Under this view of what speech is about it can be what Heidegger claims it for when he denies it the correspondence relation: a showing or making manifest of Being or beings and Nonbeing and privations.

Of course Aristotle, the first formulator of the theory of logical negation, also treats of the relation that negation and affirmation have to falsity and truth. In fact, according to Heidegger, he is the first to make manifest one quandary anyone who begins to think about these pairs will run into: that on the face of it, affirmation seems to have a special relation to truth and denial to falsity—for we affirm the true and deny the false—while it is plain that negative statements can also be true and positive statements false.[66] This difficulty arises for logical statements, which have built in the polarity that permits any truth to be told positively or negatively, as well as in dialogical and dialectical speech, which is responsive to antecedent statements. But it seems to me to vanish in what one might call primary speech—when we first say in a positing vein what *is*.

I have let Aristotle speak for a world very different from the one in which the propositional calculus of Russell and Wittgenstein is at home. For Aristotle negation (I mean negation in an objective form, contrariety interpreted as Nonbeing and its effects) is in the world and falsity (I mean the not always unintentional failure of speech to reveal beings) is in statements. Is this a difference that makes a difference? Well, I think whether negation is in the world or in speech is one of the numerous but interrelated marks by which a classical world (wherever and whenever it takes place) is distinguished from a modern world. For a world that has negation built in responds to receptive thought since it *reveals* its own distinctions, while a solidly positive one demands constructive reason since oppositions need to be *made*. And these *are* well-known marks distinguishing the two complementarily distinct epochs of the West.

5. DOUBLE NEGATION

One way to immerse oneself in the deep question of the priority of the positive is to consider double negation. Why do two successive applications of negation to a proposition return it to its original positive, while no compounding of the positive with itself ever makes it more positive or more securely affirmed?—It is, after all, a *Dunce* who says:

> "The proof is complete,
> If only I've stated it thrice."[67]

This is a question the more interesting because in common speech double negation does often have just that effect of strengthening an assertion: "I don't get no respect" is meant as a strongly negative complaint. In fact, even in the most literate English, negation could be doubled and even quadrupled with only a strengthening effect. Thus Chaucer:

> He *nevere* yet *no* vileinye *ne* sayde
> In al his lyfe, unto *no* maner wight.

That double negation is not an immediate experience can be ascertained by this little thought experiment. If someone had a debt of five dollars and you offered two sorts of debt relief: either to contribute five dollars or to multiply the debt by minus one, how many people wouldn't take the fiver, at least right off?

What kind of thinking goes into a double negation, not the reiteration of a negative (as when we say "that's a no-no") but the operation of the negative on a negation?

In a logical setting, the return to the positive by double negation is an immediate effect of the Law of Excluded Middle, which says that between affirmation and negation there is no middle ground: "Let your yea be yea, and your nay, nay," in the words of the New Testament. In informal speech and real life, to be sure, modal qualifications like "maybe" tend to fudge the stark opposition mandated by the Law and consequently to fudge the double negative as well.

"Will you or won't you, then?"	(First speaker asserts Law of Excluded Middle)
"It's not a matter of either-or."	(Second speaker rejects it, or at least its application to this case)
"But will you?"	
"I'm not unwilling."	(Double negation)
"Then you will?"	(Falsely hopeful inference)
"Well, maybe."	(Admissible dithering, by rejection of Law)

In the propositional calculus of Whitehead and Russell double negation is a formal theorem that is *proved* from the Law of Excluded Middle.[68] In another approach it is *defined* in terms of a truth table. Its elements are a proposition p, the operation of negation (" $-$ ")[69] and two "truth-values," T and F.

p	$-p$	$-(-p)$
T	F	T
F	T	F

This table simply says that each application of the negation operator flips the truth-value, so that whatever truth-value p has to begin with, there being only two, that it will have after double negation. Of course, the Law of Excluded Middle, stated for truth,[70] is really built into the truth table. This definition is crisp but not very illuminating.

For it leaves the question posed above: What motion of the mind is double negation? It is a canceling of a cancellation, or a recovery. But it is unlike the "sublation," the saving *and* elevating negativity of Hegelian dialectic, which will be the subject of chapter five. For it returns thinking exactly to its original position, being a simple second application of the mental operation of negation to an original negation. So whatever negation was, it is just that compounded. One might ask whether the second application operates on the previous negation or on the whole negated thing or sentence—do we think (not-not)p or not(not-p)? It seems to me that we do either, depending on the occasion: Sometimes, often in a mood of mere routine, we recall only our denial and reverse that without much attention to the original issue, as an official revokes the cancellation of a permit. But when we have a real interest in the matter, we think back to the original denial, like the refusal of a favor (not-p), and try to undo that: not (not-p).

Sometimes we even use double negation in preference to original positivity to show that we have gone through a reflection. This is the rhetorical figure called "litotes." An example is: "It is not unwise to think twice," which means: "It is *very* wise to think twice; I've tried thinking only once and reflected on the consequences."[71]

But for all its rhetorical force, simple double negation (or the mere undoing of an omission) only gets us back where we were and where any number of reiterations of the positive placed us and leaves us.[72] For nothing comes from nothing by mere logical negation. That requires an act of creation. The original command of the Creation was not and could not have been "Let darkness cease!" but "Let there be light!" But for human beings, for whom Creation is not an option, undoing the undone in speech (or action) requires a pregiven positive as a place of reference and return. For the negation of a positive is hard enough to apprehend, and the negation of a negative would be pretty nearly impossible to conceive if this negative were not in turn the negation of some positive assertion (or some action or thing)[73] whose thought image the first cancellation preserves. Thus Frege says, "Wrapping up a thought in a double negation does not alter its truth value."[74] In the theological tradition, on which this book on naysaying in the West often draws, the positive is the original position and our capacity to double the negative testifies to that primordial fact.

And yet—one might ask what our thinking and our world would be like if double negation only strengthened the original, and the negative were as immune to cancellation by iteration as is the positive.[75] Well, we would have to hurl ourselves over to the positive if we changed our minds—if we even *could* change our minds—without reflective recantation, without reconsideration of the negation to be taken back. In our various habitats, too, chasms would open up. In the world of finance all loan giving would cease, since no one would understand the cancellation of debt. In arithmetic we would never have come upon the idea of operations with negative numbers. In reasoning, the Law of Excluded Middle, congenitally related to double negation as it is, would have to go, and with it all determinate classification in real life. And from the moral world would vanish the hope of redemption from sin. This is the stuff of high fantasy fiction.

6. NEGATIVE SELF-REFERENCE

The "Law of (non-)Contradiction" when properly stated is qualified by time: You cannot say that something is the case and is not the case at the same time. Therefore people contradict or appear to contradict themselves in three ways:

(1) If they say now one thing and then another, contradictory, thing about the same matter, they may plead that affairs have changed or they have changed their mind over time.

(2) They may say things apparently flatly opposite about the same matter at the same time. The most blind and the most illuminated speech belongs to this class: the simply inadvertent or willful unsaying of one's own position and the deepest and most truthful apprehension of the way things may well be—in themselves unamenable to clear, univocal articulation. The most famous ancient exponent of such self-contradictory wisdom was Heraclitus, known as "the Obscure" for sayings that are flatly self-contradictory, such as: "We step and do not step into the same river; we are and we are not." Such contradictions are instigators of thought. Thus Socrates, an admirer of Heraclitus, says that the beginning of reflection, "the winch of the soul" from Becoming to Being, is when we see that our fourth finger embodies a contradiction since we must say that it is larger and smaller at once—larger than the pinkie and smaller than the middle finger.[76] It is hardly possible to give a catalogue of the serious roles that paradox, the concise self-contradictory statement, has played in philosophical and theological inquiries and even in physics into modern times.[77]

(3) It is the third kind of self-contradiction that is particularly relevant to understanding the power of negation. This is the *inherently* self-contradictory assertion. Here it is no longer the case that someone says two contradictory things simultaneously or says that they are simultaneously true of the same thing. Now one and the same sentence both affirms and denies some claim in one fell swoop.

(a) These are the self-referring paradoxes. They play some role in logic and philosophy insofar as they point toward the deeper questions of reflexivity or self-reference. The best known scandal of self-reference is the Russell paradox: Think of the class whose membership includes just those classes that are not members of themselves; is this class a member of itself? If yes, then no; if no, then yes.[78] But especially in postmodern philosophy questions of reflexivity, especially where the self of the self-reference is a human self, have become acute: How humans can know themselves, how speech can speak about speaking, how thought can think about thinking, has always been a source of perplexity. But when the preoccupation shifts from Being to text, and from theory in the contemplative sense to theory in the critical sense, discourse becomes predominantly self-referential and the problems of reflexivity are exploited to subvert rationality.[79] However, it is not such great matters I want to touch on here but one small-gauged, albeit very famous paradox, the Cretan Liar. For it displays neatly the power of negation:

> A Cretan says: "Either all Cretans always lie or some or none.
> I say all Cretans always lie."[80]

On the flat plane of a mere propositional expression, the paradox is insoluble: If this Cretan is telling the truth, then his statement is false because he, for one, has told the truth. But if he is telling a lie, then his statement is true because he, along with all the others, has told a lie. So in whatever spirit he speaks, he produces self-contradiction. One can also look at this event as if it were an extended process: The Cretan in speaking truly falsifies his statement and so he speaks falsely; but in speaking falsely he verifies it and so is speaking truly—and so on, flip-flop, flip-flop.[81]

Now a real-life Cretan could not generate such a paradox. For one thing, it's not a human possibility always to lie. It requires knowing the truth about everything and always deliberately falsifying it. No one could or would speak so; as Kant pointed out and everyone knows anyhow: lies destroy speech.[82] So there could be no sane Cretan who actually said this. But maybe that's a might-and-main solution, though practical enough.

One could imagine a superior Cretan who, for a lucid moment, raised himself beyond his type, and spoke, as we often do, of his congenital flaw from beyond its bondage. (But of course, again, no one who had such an exceptional moment would say such a thing, for so wise a person would, first of all, know that he was involving himself in paradox just by uttering his discovery, and would, secondly, never imagine that he really knows every intention of every fellow islander; yet the paradox depends on the totality of the statement: all . . . always.)

Or one could try to look at the fact of the matter, and if one decided (against all likelihood) that all Cretans do always lie, then the talking Cretan is a liar by a law of his island nature and *can't* tell the truth; hence his paradox can't come about, since it depends on our hypothetical "If this Cretan is telling the truth," and that can't happen. Of course, the whole condition for such a paradox is that reality should not step in, for in real life trivial paradoxes don't get said in the first place or get practically exploded, as I've just done. But to see what language all on its own is capable of, one has to pursue the paradox nonpractically and nonpragmatically, that is, without attention to the actual behavior of actual speakers.

Seen in this way the trickery of The Liar, which really lies in this, that it deliberately conflates falsity with falsehood, acquires a new depth. Speaking falsely means "lying" insofar as the Cretan speaks but "being wrong" insofar as his statement is evaluated. If one attends to the fact that "telling the truth" is ambiguous and means both "not lying" and "saying what is the case," the self-reference of the paradox comes out; In this case the speaker's intention does invade the truth content of his sentence. In ordinary statements, the speaker's truthfulness or his lying intention doesn't affect the truth of the proposition, which is independent of the teller.[83] But in the paradox, the Cretan's intention is what makes the proposition itself, thoroughly universal as it pretends to be (and so inclusive of the speaker and his every utterance), true or false.

The Cretan Liar paradox is chafingly puzzling because it is at once perspicuous and obscure, like the "Strange Loops" found in Escher drawings.[84] But it becomes deeply thought provoking when it induces wonder about our ability to produce language that is well formed and not nonsensical but also not "apophantic," as Aristotle would say, that is, not declarative, not good for showing forth a matter.

Although such simultaneous self-contradictions are out of the context of working reality, they may thus well mirror an ineradicable negative capability of our thinking: that of enmeshing itself in infinities of indecision, a kind of neurosis of the intellect, a loss of rational control compounded of self-reference and self-contradiction. A sound mind seems to crave periodic positivity, the settling of thought in definite affirmation or determinate denial.[85]

(b) Then what in our minds makes possible the kind of self-reference that is negative in the sense of being nonpositing? It has to have something to do with the discrepancy between the range of thinking and of saying. Just as we sometimes search unsuccessfully for the verbal articulation of a thought we are sure we have, so we sometimes say well-formed sentences that we do not understand.

Take these two sentences: "I sometimes lie"; "I always tell the truth." They have, I imagine, about an equal public effect on the speaker's credibility. Now exchange "sometimes" for "always" in the liar's sentence. It rolls just as trippingly off the tongue, but now it is a stripped-down version of the Liar (which was, I think significantly, not recognized as a paradox by its originator), not quite as interesting but equally corrupting to speech. We are saying sentences but not speaking thoughts. Look at what is happening to someone who says "I always lie" in an alternation so tight as to be practically simultaneous:

He is telling truth, so this *statement* turns false, so *he* is telling a lie.
He is telling a lie, so his *statement* turns true, so *he* is telling truth.

One might call this the backlash of thoughtless language; it turns on its abuser. It does not happen to the speaker who says "I always tell the truth." Rhetorical effects apart, that statement may be wasted breath, but it is not a vicious circle, because if the speaker intends truth, it's true and if he means to lie it's false. Unlike the liar, this self-certified truth teller doesn't make his proposition flip into its contradictory opposites just by asserting it, so he's immune from the liar's fate, who is frustrated whether he intends to come clean or to deny his fault.

What causes that backlash effect? I think it is the highly unintended consequence of the intrusion of the speaker's veracity-intention, which usually stays *behind* the speaker's statement, *into* the statement to change its truth-value—but not only that. Not all self-reference, after all, leads to self-cancellation. For example, "I always tell the truth" can be said by someone intending to lie: That intention falsifies the statement in accordance with the would-be liar's intention, and there it ends. But see what happens when a liar says "I always lie." Let me replace "to lie" with its definition as the deliberate negation of truth-telling:

Intention: The unseen "I" means *not* to tell the truth.
Statement: "I am *not* a truth teller."
Effect: The statement is made true.
Consequence: "I" has told the truth *against* original intention.

If "I" starts with the opposite intention, to tell the truth, the negative statement will be falsified and make the "I" not a truth teller, again against the veracity intention.

What is happening is that there is just the wrong number of negations in each case, or better, the right number to frustrate the speaker's intention. If he starts out intending *not* to tell the truth, he negates his already negative statement so as to give it a positive truth-value, so he frustrates his own intention by a double negative. If he intends positively to tell the truth, the negative statement remains that way and he's not a truth teller, contra his intention.

In sum, we can *say* sentences that systematically frustrate our veracity intention, but we can't thoughtfully *speak* them. And language so used takes its revenge. Such self-reference is a *negative force*.

7. NEGATIVE NUMBERS AND ZERO

We turn now from the most self-involved to the most self-less of negations. And a first question is: Are negative numbers negations of something? The question arises because of their name and because of their marking symbol, the minus sign (as in $-a$), looks like a negation sign, and above all because this sign behaves in some respects as does logical negation: compounding minus and minus, like the double negation of logic, gives a positive (p. 000).

(a) But what is the negative number negating? Logically $-a$ should mean all numbers other than a. Instead $-a$ means a number symmetrical with a around an origin. To be sure, the whole realm of numbers in the nether world below zero or on the left, the sinister side of the origin, might be thought of by students not yet resigned to formalisms as being infected by negativity. Negative numbers are, after all, naively and intuitively understood as debts, regressions and losses, and the O-point as being out of debt but without assets. In that understanding negative numbers are not ordinary negations of their positives but more like privations: degrees of one and the same characteristic along a single-dimensional spectrum, going from positive through neutral to negative—great pleasure decreasing to indifference going over into negative pleasure, or pain.

The reason, then, why a negative number $-a$ is not the negation of its positive is that it is not everything that a is not (which a logical negation is) but a's mirror image in a realm called conventionally negative (as if something were being negated) but really not any less original or more derivative than its positive, from which any of its members is separated by a double distance from O. This O, the point around which the counting numbers (the "natural" numbers beginning with 1) are reflected into their negatives, is really the O of Origin, not the 0 of Zero, for zero may indeed be understood as the negation of not any one number but of all numbers (p. 58).

All the above is a way of saying that when the numbers are signed, when negative signs are adjoined to the natural numbers, the *whole* system dramatically changes its character; positive numbers are in a different world from the natural integers with which we count.[86] They are now *directed* quantities, metaphorically above or below an O-point which is needed so that -1 and $+1$ will have the same equal "distance" from the origin as have all the other numbers from each other. When they are laid out horizontally in a geometric line they designate nonmetaphorical distances. All these developments are true revolutions in the understanding of number,[87] and it is no wonder that the ancient mathematicians, who certainly knew that since the natural numbers are not closed under subtraction, they could end up willy-nilly in numbers less than nothing, simply refused to give them legitimacy. For they regarded a number *(arithmos)* as being composed of units *(monades)* and a unit "as that by virtue of which each of the *beings* is called one."[88] Such a monad has an almost sacred positivity and its negation would yield arithmetic chaos. They were preserving a natural, integral world, one which the moderns were willing to leave behind.

(b) It was Kant who, in his remarkable little essay discussed below (p. 159), "An Attempt to Introduce Negative Numbers into Philosophy" (1763), first gave a philosophical interpretation to negative numbers. These numbers were still strange enough in 1673 to elicit from John Wallis this observation:

> But it is also Impossible, that any Quantity . . . can be *Negative*. Since that it is not possible that any *Magnitude* can be *Less than Nothing*, or any *Number Fewer than None*.
>
> Yet is not that Supposition (of Negative Quantities,) either Unuseful or Absurd, when rightly understood. And though, as to bare Algebraick Notation, it import a Quantity less than nothing: Yet, when it comes to Physical Application, it denotes as Real a Quantity as if the Sign were $+$; but to be interpreted in a contrary sense.[89]

What Kant does is to give the logical interpretation of the "contrary sense": negative numbers are the contraries, not the contradictories, of positive numbers. The meaning is exactly what I was trying to catch above: Contrarily opposed terms lie along the same spectrum of meaning, like pleasure and pain; they do not obey the Law of Excluded Middle—there is not only either pleasure or pain, but a (fleeting) middle state, pleasurelessness or painlessness, to which O is analogous. Thus signed numbers are good for representing "real opposition" in the world; things are not simply canceled by being affected in contrary ways (as they are by becoming contradictory predicates) but merely modified in one or the other direction. The acceptance of numerical contrariety is a major step in our ability to apply exact measurements to the continua of the real world, and not only to distances and forces: Kant contemplated such measurements even of our natural psyche. Pleasure and "negative" pleasure are among the many examples he mentions.[90] So negative numbers are far more interesting as the contrary degrees of their positives than as contradictories, flat denials.

(c) Zero, on the other hand, is more interesting as a sort of contradictory of number. Zero is an altogether difficult notion, as is signaled by the fact that diverse understandings abound:

(1) In ordinary talk, zero means zilch, nada, nothing. (2) In the system of natural numbers it is (in modern treatments) often the first and least. (3) In the line of signed numbers it is the point of reflection. (4) If zero is the magnitude of a distance along the numbered line, so that the terminal points coincide, it will betoken identity of location. (5) In the Arabic system of numerals, our system, it is a numeral, a place holder, marking the start of each successive power of ten and of each decade following.[91] It is as a numeral that zero arrives

in Europe. (6) In some notations, 0 stands for the null or empty class or set[92] from which zero is logically derived. (7) In philosophical reflection zero is the contradictory negation of number in general.

Zero comes into Western mathematics indirectly from India, the land where nothingness becomes sensible, and the name may be—albeit remotely— derived from the Sanskrit word for void, *sunya*.[93] Useful as it is as a numeral, it is as a number that it shows its strange and wonderful characteristics. The two main formal rules for operating with zero are quite intuitively apprehensi- ble: "$a + 0 = a$" corresponds to our sense that adding (or subtracting, if we are in the signed numbers) nothing leaves us where we were, and "$a \times 0 = 0$" corresponds to taking nothing a number of times, which produces nothing. ("$a \div 0$" is a forbidden operation, but students have fun with thinking of it as infinity because they think of the quantity as being divided into infinitely many near nothings.) No other number behaves quite this way, not even 1, which is curious enough.[94] Being nothing is really different from being any other quantity, and this fact seems to corroborate the common sense that zero is nothing and outside all the somethings (1); yet it is also a number among numbers and so a nothing of a very determinate sort: to get 0 on an examina- tion is different from handing in nothing (2). Zero as the first natural number is usually presented as the initial generating object which, as part of the natu- ral number sequence, is perfectly primitive: "God made the integers, all the rest is the work of man" is the famous quotation under whose aegis zero has been placed. That explanation is plainly implausible—zero is not a primitive notion and it is theologically doubtful that God is its maker, for he makes *something* out of nothing, not nothing itself.[95] But the motivation for including zero is very plausible: It is both prospective, since zero will eventually be needed, and it also has an eye to the logical derivation of numbers from classes; such derivations start with the null class which is ready and waiting in the theory of classes, and it will yield 0.[96]

(d) All the understandings (1–7) listed above are matter for thought, but it is the last that answers the big question: What is the logical relation of zero to the other numbers? I don't mean of particular numbers; they happen to be such that the distance between each number and zero is given by the (signed) number itself. I mean: How does the peculiarity of zero express itself? This is the question Russell answers boldly:

> a zero magnitude is the denial of the defining concept of a kind of magnitudes, not the denial of any particular magnitude or of all of them.

Russell is emending, or rather extending, a definition or criterion given by Alexius Meinong—the same who will dominate the next chapter—who in turn refers to Kant.[97] Meinong's definition of zero (really an indirect one, since it is magnitude he is defining primarily) goes: "That is or has magnitude, which allows the interpolation of terms between itself and its contradictory opposite," that is, zero. Russell wants to be able to speak of "the pure zero of magnitude" (which is definable neither in terms of the number 0 nor of the null class of logic, though it is connected to them). This zero is a definite magnitude (and reachable by magnitudes) which remains of the same *kind*, though no quantity whose magnitude *is* zero can *exist*.[98] Although first approached in terms of continuous magnitude, "Zero seems to be definable by some general characteristic, without any reference to any special peculiarity of the kind of quantity to which it belongs."

There are two great difficulties in delineating zero. One is to define it in such a way that one definition of zero will cover all the zeros of various types of magnitudes. That objective is achieved by Russell's emendation, which excludes reference to the specific kind of magnitude involved.

The other, more complex difficulty makes Russell "face the problem as to the nature of negation": Meinong's "contradictory opposite" was faulty because in logic that term means every individual not belonging to a given class; thus zero would be everything but the magnitude(s) under consideration, and that will not do.

So Russell considers the meaning of "no pleasure." It does not signify something other than pleasure (as when, Russell says, "our friends assure us that it is no pleasure to tell us our faults"). Nor is no pleasure just nothing, which would be like a zero that belonged to no magnitude at all. "No pleasure" must be one of the magnitudes of pleasure, one less than all the others of its kind. But this zero magnitude is also not quite "not pleasure," the *logical* denial of pleasure:

> On the contrary, *no pleasure* is essentially a quantitative concept, having a curious and intimate relation to logical denial, just as 0 has a very intimate relation to the null-class. The relation is this, that there is no *quantity* whose *magnitude* is zero, so that the class of 0 quantities is the null-class. The zero of any kind of magnitude is incapable of that relation to existence or to particulars, of which other magnitudes are capable.[99]

Thus it is not the *concrete quantity* of anything that can be assigned a magnitude of 0. Zero cannot apply to existents. Hence it is the *kind* that is denied by zero, each zero denying its own *kind* rather than their *individual* magnitudes. One might say that zero denies a higher type than quantities. Thus, owning zero books does not mean owning everything that is not a book or owning all books but the zero book, but owning nothing of a bookish kind.

The negation that is characteristic of zero is, then, analogous to but not *identical* with logical contradiction (understood extensionally), because it is the denial of the (intensional) kind rather than its quantitative individuals. "This," says Russell, referring to the last sentence of the quotation above, "is

a synthetic proposition, to be accepted only on account of its self-evidence."
What is evident to Russell is that by means of zero nonexistence intrudes into
the realm of number and other quantities not as the negation of any individual
quantity but as the contradictory of each specific kind of magnitude. Zero is
always the same, takes on all comers of all kinds and yet negates them specifically, and it can do that because the individual quantities within these kinds
have simultaneously met with nonexistence.

∞   ∞   ∞

And so nonexistence has come on the scene. It will be the preoccupation of
the next chapter, for it is the spook of naysaying.

NOTES

1. It is a memorable fact for me that I once had a colleague who nursed a personal
and sustained passion against zero and negative numbers, a type of negation discussed
later on (p. 56).

2. Frege 1919, 117 ff. Frege was in this anticipated by Aristotle, *On Interpretation*
17 a 1 ff.: Every sentence has meaning, but only those are statements that can be true
or false.

3. See Sokolowski 1979, 640, for the fundamental importance of distinguishing.
The quotation is from Chaucer, "The Wife of Bath's Prologue" 66–67; *oon* means
"single."

4. See, for example, *Phaedrus* 266 b, and above all *Sophist* 235 c; also *Plato's
Sophist*, Brann, Kalkavage, and Salem, 5–9. This way of discernment becomes, when
jigged, the "method of classification."

Here is the place to mention that Plato's Socrates also employed and probably discovered other negative ways, the ways of *refutation* and of *dialectic* in general. A Socratic refutation shows the absurd consequences of laying down what is not well
thought out. A good example is *Republic* 331 c ff., where Polemarchus says that justice
is returning what you receive to hold in trust, and Socrates shows what will happen
under this definition if your creditor has gone insane. Socratic negative refutation was
regarded as the model for mathematical *reductio ad absurdum* proofs, which are themselves a negative form of *analysis* (Heath, 1925 I 140). Since mathematical analysis is
a method of laying down as known what is unknown and reasoning through its consequences to something known, it is clearly a stricter version of Socratic dialectic, which
starts with assumptions made in confessed ignorance and by questions works its way
to something to hang on to, even if it is only a more determinate perplexity.

The ways of laying down the false (refutation and *reductio*) and of laying down the
unknown have this in common with the way of *division:* In all three cases we are working in the dark, or left, or other, or sinister side of the universe of discourse, in that
half (or much more than half) in which things not so, not known, or not attended to
have their place. This is the way that I think of as the scrambling philosophy—by
which, to adapt Jane Austen's words, human beings, without professions of refined
nonsense, scramble themselves into a little clarification (*Emma*, chap. 3): Rather than

transfixing with exactitude the heart of things we make tentative circumscribing approaches. It is the way I trust.

For Aristotle's treatment of negative proofs, see *Prior Analytics* 41 a 21 ff.; 62 b 15 ff.

5. *Antikeisthai*, "to lie over against," is in fact used as the passive of *antitithenai*, "to set over against," and "to oppose" is the exact translation of the latter.

6. See Inwood, 205–208: "Opposition."

7. Aristotle actually lists four or more oppositions. I have omitted relative opposition (i.e., double and of what it is the double). For medieval logicians this list is traditional; see Kretzmann and Stump, passim. Here are the main references: *Categories* 11 b 15 ff. defines opposition and lists the kinds with explanations. *Topics* 109 b 17 ff.; 113 b 15 ff., 135 b 7 ff. tells how to use oppositions in argument. *Metaphysics* 1018 a 20 ff., 1055 a 33 ff. gives clues to the ontological significance of opposition; 1055 b 2 says that contradiction is primary; 1055 b 38 says that opposites cannot both be true at the same time.

Aristotle is responsible for the "Square of Opposition" in which quality and quantity are exhaustively combined and the inferential relations of the resultant propositions are displayed. For the record:

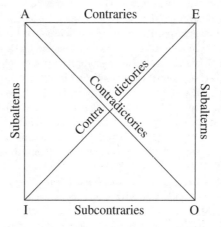

A: All thought is logical.   E: No thought is logical
I: Some thought is logical.   O: Some thought is not logical.

While A and E cannot both be true, they can both be false. From the point of view of logical quantity this means that *some* thought *might* be logical. But from the point of view of real-world opposites, it suggests the possibility of nonlogical, perhaps intuitive thought.

8. *Categories* 12 a 26 ff. So I don't quite see why he says at *Metaphysics* 1055 b 4 that "privation is a kind of contradiction," for he notes immediately a chief difference: Contradiction has no intermediates while privation sometimes does.

9. *Categories* 12 b 6 ff. He has said the same thing about privation, 12 a 35 ff. The quotation below about contrariety and otherness is from *Metaphysics* 1004 a 22. This

last passage, together with 1055 a 38 – b 3, in fact encourages the surmise that contradiction belongs entirely to speech and contrariety primarily to beings.

In 1004 a 20–22 Aristotle says that otherness (*heterotes*) includes difference (*dia-
phora*) and difference includes contrariety (*enantiotes*). Difference shows up only
within a genus, that is, within Being, and contrariety is the greatest such difference.

In 1055 a 38 ff. he lists the "opposite statements" (*antikeimenai phaseis*, 1011 b
14): contradiction (*antiphasis*), privation (*steresis*, which is included in contradiction,
see note 8), and contrariety. As mentioned in the text, contradiction is the primary
opposition because it is the starkest; it has no mean.

I understand these two passages together to say that while contradiction, as its
name implies, functions in the realm of speech, contrariety, as a kind of otherness,
belongs first to beings, though it is an opposition of speech as well.

10. Opposition of speech: *Metaphysics* 1055 b 38 f.; Law of Contradiction: 1005 b
19 ff., 1061 b 36 ff.; consequences of denying the law: 1007 a 22 ff. In propositional
logic *the* great ontological law becomes just another logical theorem (note 68).

11. On the way the Law of Contradiction fares in Hegelian dialectic, see p. 163. But
I want to point out here an apparent oddity: The Aristotelian law is time-qualified but
pertains to fixed, identifiable *moments* of time, while Hegelian dialectic is pretemporal
but pertains to fluid conceptual *passages*. These passages do terminate in new conceptual moments, which have, however, already developed past the level of brute self-
contradiction. From this perspective the temporal universe of the Aristotelian Law of
Contradiction is not even tangent to the atemporal sphere of Hegelian dialectic, and
therefore Hegel's dialectic cannot be said to abrogate Aristotle's law.

12. Bradley, 123–124: "Denial or contradiction is not the same thing as assertion
of the contrary; but in the end it can rest on nothing else. The contrary, however, which
denial asserts is never explicit. In 'A is not B' the discrepant ground is wholly unspeci-
fied. . . . Sokrates may be not sick because he is well, or because there is now no such
thing as Sokrates." Bradley wants to banish contradiction from logic because it has no
positive ground; it tells only what is not but gives us no illumination about the negative.

13. *Categories* 17 b 23 ff., 18 a 28 ff.; see also *Metaphysics* 1007 b 19 ff. An attempt to prove the bipolarity of propositions *within* logic is sketched later (p. 47). For
the relation of truth and falsity to positive and negative, see p. 42.

14. For example, Miller and Johnson-Laird, 262 f., writing as cognitive scientists
nearly a millennium and a half after Aristotle, find that the oppositions of logic still
work basically in the same framework. In studying the language of negation and its
perceptual correlatives they note that sensory, common negations regularly occur
within "contrastive sets." Such sets contain words that have the same superordinate
term but are incompatible with each other, i.e., they are subclasses of the same class.
The contrast can be direct: poodle vs. collie. Or it can be indirect: poodle vs. cat; this
happens if one or both are "hyponyms" of the same contrastive set: dog vs. cat.

15. Lloyd, 90 ff., gives lists of nearly idiomatic Greek oppositional pairs from
Homer on, but he also points out that dualistic classifications, both exhaustive and par-
tial, abound in present-day societies, 88 f. Here is Lloyd's example of Homeric polar
exuberance: When a loyal servant thinks Odysseus' son Telemachus is taking foolish
chances, he says: "Some one among the immortals has damaged the good sense in
him—or some one among men" (*Odyssey* XIV 128 f.); the men appear there only for

balance. (I think, however, that Homer never indulges in mere patterns and that one more reading will reveal what was being intimated.)

16. *Metaphysics* 1004 a 3 ff., b 28 ff.

17. Lyons 1970, 271–287, "Opposition and Contrast." "Gradable" and "ungradable" roughly correspond to contrary and contradictory opposites (272). Among the many kinds of opposition Lyons distinguishes there is "directional" opposition (e.g., east–west, left–right), which is important to negative numbers and "real" opposition as set out by Kant (p. 57).

18. Dewey, 181–198. "Affirmation and Negation: Judgment as Requalification." After the general redescription of negative propositions, Dewey shows how the Square of Opposition (note 7) is affected. For example, a relation of contrariety (A–E) sets the limits of the determinations proper to the inquiry: All marine vertebrates are cold-blooded or none are. A relation of contradiction (A–O) "affords the crowning proof of the functional or operative import of affirmative-negative propositions" (197). For while in the static traditional logic, contradictory assertions stop inquiry, since there is no ground for deciding which one of two contradictories is invalid, in the new logic they are not the final word. The reason is that in scientific inquiry the old quantifier "some" (which occurs in the O contradictory of A) is too vague. The negation needs to be specified in terms of determinate singulars and then represents an incomplete empirical state of inquiry: The contradictory "Some properties of light are not wave-like" is the formulation of a scientific inquiry, not an end.

19. The Greek and Latin word order is "not-is," hence the medieval rule that "negation governs what follows it" (Kretzmann and Stump, 298).

20. Frege 1919, 117 ff.; quotations in the order cited: 125, 131, 128, 126–127, 131.

21. Tom Stoppard, *Rosencrantz and Guildenstern Are Dead*. The ancestor of the exercise in this section is Aristotle, *Prior Analytics* 51 b 37 ff.

22. If the universalist claims of Chomsky's Universal Grammar are right and all human languages are generated from the same innate rules, this question would at first seem to be more or less answered, independently of empirical research (see Lyons 1970, 123 ff.). For this grammar begins with "phrase structures" in which the basic tripartite sentence is expressed: A noun phrase plus a verb phrase, where the latter may in turn consist of a verb and a noun phrase. In the spoken language the verb might be the copula *is*.

But of course, the question pertinent to "S is P" is not thus answered because it concerns the copula not as just any verb, but specifically as a form of "to be": Is Being at the true center of every sentence even if it is obscured by a predicative verb? To be sure, most thoughts can be forced into the logical form: "I think logically" can be made into "My thought is logical" by nominalizing the verb, but is that a return to the primordial meaning or an unnatural twist? I am altogether unsure whether there can be a linguistic, that is to say, an empirical answer to this question. Thus Curme, 28–29, says that originally sentences were "apposite," meaning they had the form S-P, without copula (such as is now used in newspaper headlines). Then, before Indo-European split into different languages, the predicative verb (e.g. "think," "sing," etc.) became established in cases where the subject was acting or was acted upon. But if the predicate was a noun, the form "S is P" could come into use because *is* had by then lost any predicative meaning. Yet from the very beginning of recorded speech "S is P" was associated with formal and accurate speech, and hence it is "employed in the calm flow of thought in declarative sentences," but is not so prevalent in emotive speech (29).

How would we ever know whether or not the "apposite" sentence had in the early speakers' minds some unexpressed bond of common being within it, or whether or not the later speaker's copula was an expression of a mind ready to engage in Aristotelian reflections on the relation of predication to being? Who can tell the latent thoughts of the millennia-since dead? Or for that matter, of the presently living? That is why, if I heard of some small and wonderful tribe who indubitably lived without the copula, nothing much would seem to me, at least, to follow very immediately for "S is P" as the fundamental sentence form. I accept it because people whose thought is congenial to me have built on it structures that are of great interest, and because I have corroborated by introspection that it *is* my most basic declarative mode of internal speech, closer to thinking than the bipartite sentence consisting of a subject and a predicative verb: The briefest way to put the reason why is that thinking speech brings its objects to a standstill even as it goes about discerning them through their properties. The declarative *is* expresses at once that transfixing done by thought and the expansion with which the object of thought responds.

I owe to my colleague Cordell Yee a very pertinent reference: Graham 1989, appendix 2, "The Relation of Chinese Thought to Language," 389 ff., especially "Being," 406 ff., "Chinese concepts comparable with Being," 408 ff., and "Modern translations of Western ontology into Chinese," 412 ff. Graham concludes that "Classical Chinese syntax is close to symbolic logic: it has an existential quantifier *(yu)* which forbids mistaking existence for a predicate and is distinct from the copulae (which come to include a special copula for identity), and it has no copula linking subject to predicative adjective and no common symbol for them all" (412). Thus a "fully successful Chinese translation [of sentences in Western ontology and logic] would require not merely the coinage of the predicable *ts'un-tsai* for 'exist,' but its extension to cover the copulative use of 'be' " (414).

But here's the point: "One is hindered but not finally trapped by the initial choices among similarities and differences behind the formulation of one's language; . . . Whenever a logical distinction is marked in Language A but not in Language B, one must expect confusions of thought in B which can be analysed but not reproduced in A. It is not that the distinction is relative to language, real for A but not for B. On the contrary, thinkers in B can learn the distinction from A (as Latin scholasticism learned the existential/copulative distinction from the Arabs), or discover it out of the resources of B itself (as Aristotle had already done)" (414). Graham is entitled to say this because it is what he himself has just done in his investigation of Chinese equivalents to "to be."

It is, therefore, finally not what we first and last *say* that bears on the question of linguistic universality but what we manage on occasion to *entertain* and *describe*.

23. Maritain, 110.

24. Two complementary classes divide a given universe between them and are mutually exclusive by definition (Langer, 145; thus is solved, albeit by fiat, the problem of section 4: What makes us think that *p* has only one negation?). If the universe of discourse is all-inclusive, the negative complement class is infinite, but usually the uni-

verse that the complement completes is restricted; the dichotomy from the examples below, "logical:not-logical," might be restricted to the universe of characteristics pertaining to mere thought, in which case "not-logical" would not, for example, include "emotional."

Lewis Carroll, 1896, 172, has a lot of fun with logicians who insist on distinguishing "S is-not P" from "S is not-P" because of a "perfectly *morbid* dread of negative Attributes," arising from the large size of the negative complement class. Is, he asks, the class of the men you would *not* like to be seen with really so much larger than the class of men you *would* like to be seen with? Well, that's friendly, but he's wrong nonetheless. The position of the negating particle is not "merely a matter of *taste*," and the two forms don't have the same meaning; see Aristotle, *Prior Analytics* 51 b 6 ff.

25. The logical test of contradictories is that they *cannot* both be true, and of contraries that they *may* both be false. "Thought is logical" and "Thought is illogical" cannot both be true, but "Thought is logical" and "Thought is intuitive" can both be false—it may be yet some other thing. Another way to put this is that you can reverse a contradiction by negation, but not a contrariety. Contradiction is more logical and total, contrariety is more realistic and specific.

26. Cohen, 85 ff., has a lovely disquisition on *ou*, *me*, and the alpha-privative, which betoken, respectively, simple Negation, Otherness, and the *Un*-limited or *In*-finite (see p. 142).

27. See Stebbing, 27 ff., for the different vocabularies used for making this distinction in subtly different ways, for example, "connotation and denotation." Although I have not attended much to quantity here (see note 32), the terms of the sentence form and these illustrations are clearly all meant extensionally.

28. Kneale 1962, 147: The Stoics insisted that a statement (*axioma*) should be negated as a whole.

29. Frege 1919, 131.

30. Homer *Odyssey* IX, 408.

31. Plato *Theaetetus* 189 a, also *Republic* 478 b. Augustine, however, implicitly corrects Socrates in *On the Teacher* II: His son Adeodatus is wondering what it means to have "nothing" as subject of a sentence when they have agreed that a sign is not a sign unless it signifies something. Augustine's solution is that a certain affection of the mind, the one that follows on *not* finding a thing, yet also *finding* that it does not exist, is what "nothing" here signifies. In other words, he gives not a logical but a psychological explanation.

32. I am again omitting here the consideration of "quantity" (all, some, none), lest I turn the section into a poorly presented logic lesson. The relations that simple propositions have by reason of their quantity and their quality (affirmative, negative) together is set out in textbooks as the "square of opposition" (note 7). For the hierarchy of negations quantity gives rise to, see Zwarts, 170 ff. The notion that truth and falsity, as related to positive and negative states of affairs, give a proposition its "quality" occurs, I believe for the first time, in Plato's *Sophist* 263 a.

33. Goethe, *Faust* I, 1338.

34. "No" as a speech act is said to be "illocutionary"; it expresses the speaker's attitude (Lyons 1970, 770). In Russian, Japanese, and other languages, the illocutionary adverb refers not to the proposition but to the first speaker's implied opinion. Thus to

the question "You didn't do it, did you [not]?" a Russian might answer "Yes, I didn't" (see Lyons, 777).

35. And even for him the polarity of a proposition is determined by a world that occurs to us first as one of positive facts. To be sure, Wittgenstein's world picture leaves the origin of negation effectively in limbo, since negations are neither inherent in the factual world nor a potently real part of propositions; see also Rosen 1980, 141).

36. That *p* is the original position is shown by the double application of the negative function which returns to the positive, while the double function on not-*p* has no real sense (p. 51).

37. See Frege 1919, 119.

38. A highly technical article by Ladusaw 1996, 127 ff., argues that the asymmetry of propositional logic makes it incapable of dealing with the double negation ("negative concord") of common language except by consigning it to illogicality: (1) In that logic there is no affirming operator because the affirmative is taken as the default position. Moreover, the negating function can take a negated proposition as its argument: not(not-*p*). This double negation invariably returns to the positive default proposition. Such an operator is termed "endocentric." (2) "Exocentric" negation, on the other hand, does not have this effect. That is the [infelicitously named] negation that is internal to the sentence, where terms rather than propositions are negated. An internally negated sentence is not a possible argument for an exocentric negation because that kind of negation, term negation, doesn't take propositions as arguments. For such affirmations and negations are elements of judgments rather than operators, and they have symmetry; neither has priority. They qualify sentences in language rather than by formulas of symbols. (3) Therefore they *can* deal with ordinary double negation. We can see that if we think of them in this way: There is only one qualifying mode, which may be positive or negative, and only one noniterative negating judgment, which is reinforced by being doubly marked: "I don't know nothing" is not a double negation but a reinforced negation, behaving symmetrically with any reinforced affirmation: "I *do* get *lots* of respect."

The reason this argument is interesting in this context is that it seems to turn one's expectations on their head. We would expect logic to subvert the hierarchies of philosophy and natural language. Instead the subverting equi-valence of affirmation and negation is located in common speech. How did that come about? The answer is, I think, in the difference between what might be called the running use and the grounded use of language. The first is good for the business of life, where we simply want to enforce our meaning or to hear the right answer to our questions or to give the fair judgment, be it positive or negative. But when we want to touch the base of our being by means of speech, its ultimate priorities and hierarchies appear.

39. Boethius, 23.

40. Once it is discovered that "all determination is negation" this argument pretty much lapses, because the first focus can no longer be on individual substance but is instead on the whole determinable field.

41. See Johnson-Laird 1983, 211 for negation, 450 for the neural hypothesis. Maritain, 111, terms the claim that negative judgments presuppose positive ones—which is the one involved in the explanations of cognitive science—a *purely psychological* one;

negative and positive judgments are really in the same class. Of course, the other side might say that the psychological priority is nothing but the temporal expression of the fact that thinking always gets hold first of what is or exists.

42. First quotation: Aristotle, *Metaphysics* 1003 b 11; Being *(to on)* is the neuter participle of the verb to be; beinghood *(ousia)* is a noun formed on its feminine participle (or possibly on the neuter stem: *ontsia* = *ousia*). Second quotation: *Posterior Analytics* 79 a 28; "that which [any thing] is" renders *to ti estin*, literally "the 'what it is.' "

43. The set of reasons comes from Thomas Aquinas and Cajetan, 64, on 17 a 9 of *On Interpretation*. Thomas's claim that negation belongs to the mind is in the *Commentary on the* Metaphysics, vol. I, 219, no. 540, on *Metaphysics* 1003. I think he comes to say this in the following way. Aristotle certainly chides Plato for giving negations independent being as forms (e.g., *Metaphysics* 990 b 15). Much later he speaks of nonbeing as associated with falsity, just as being is with truth. This sense of being and nonbeing is not the mainline meaning, but arises from the fact that affirmation is (primarily) the combination of a subject with the predicate that belongs to it, while negation is their separation, the one signifying a true and proper being, the other producing a falsity, a sort of merely mental [non]being (*Metaphysics* 1027 b 26 ff.).

44. Bosanquet, 1:279–281; Bradley, 2:665. Bradley, 2:662–667; when he accepted Bosanquet's view of negation he revised the second edition accordingly: Negation is grounded in reality rather than based on a prior affirmative judgment. Thus he explains double negation (1:158 ff.) by the fact that every denial must have a positive ground, and the second negation has as its (real) ground the property denied by the first. To show that "not (A is-not B)," we must show that A *is* B; in other words, we appeal to the positive reality. Thus double negation gets back to the positive not via an iterated application of a negating function but by a direct return to the fact.

Wilson, 1:249 ff., agrees that negative and affirmative forms of proposition involve each other. Nonetheless they are irreducibly distinct and not properly coordinate, since the affirmative is prior. He takes the unusual step of actually offering a proof that a negative proposition cannot be reduced to a positive one: The attempt to do so begins by attaching the negation to the predicate, for in traditional logic propositions that are not negated through the copula are taken to be positive. Since the predicate P is to be thought of as a universal, not-P should also be a universal. Positive universals are distinguished from each other by their own positive nature, by what they *are*, namely P or Q. How are negative universals distinguished? Only, if at all, through what they are *not*, namely P or Q. Thus "S is not-P" remains irreducibly different from a positive proposition, for the test of its distinction from other propositions is not the same as it would be were it really positive, namely through its *own* proper nature. Moreover, it depends on "S is P," the positive, for its meaning. So "S is not-P" is neither positive nor underived.

45. Fichte, pt. I, para. 1.

46. Fichte, pt. I, para. 2. A third and ultimate law, through which the first two are further explicated, is a law of divisibility (para. 3): "A taken partially equals not-A" and the converse. It means that everything posited is equal to its opposite in some mark and everything equal is opposed to its equal in some mark: "We have united the antiposited *(entgegengesetzt)* I and not-I through the concept of divisibility." For they are

similar in one mark as antiposited, and opposed in one mark as equal. In its abstracted logical form this yields the law of ground; for such a mark is called the ground—in the case of equals for differentiating, in the case of opposites for relating. The category so derived is that of determination, for here the I and the not-I delimit and determine each other.

47. There are many other logics than the elementary ones here discussed: Besides the modal logics dealing with the possibility and necessity of statements, there are many deviant logics dealing with the matter of classical logic in ways different from its standards. Some reject the Law of Excluded Middle, some allow referring expressions that are nondenoting, some use more than two truth-values. Some of these are closer to natural language than standard logic, but they are not more *elementary*, and in that sense are not merely chronologically posterior. Here I mean by "elementary," as in the text, what we first come on when we get down to the brass tacks of rationality.

48. Whitehead and Russell 1913, material implication, the "Implicative Function," 7; truth defined, 43; elementary propositions and material implication defined, 93 f.

49. Russell 1903, 14, speaks of implication as impossible to define, because when you have worked out the truth table for what you understand "*p* implies *q*" to mean it is the same as the definition "not-*p* or *q*," and this equivalence means material implication—a circle. In *Principia* implication is not understood independently of the definition.

On the same page Russell illustrates material implication as it applies to Euclid's propositions taken as constants, independently of their content: proposition 5 follows from proposition 4 means that if prop. 5 is false, so is prop. 4.

50. I use the textbook expression because in *Principia* itself, implication is simultaneously defined by the formula and by true and false. It helps to separate the two, although they come to the same thing.

51. Stebbing, 225: "to say that '*p* entails *q*' is to say that it *could* not be the case that *p* is true and *q* false. To say that '*p* materially implies *q*' is to say that it is *not as a matter of fact* the case that *p* is true and *q* false." This difference is exemplified, he says, by the relation between "This is red" and "This is colored" on the one hand, and "Socrates is a triangle" and "2 plus 2 equals 4" on the other. (There is also a type called "strict implication" in which material implication is adjusted to be a necessary relation. For negation in such systems see Stelzner, 87 ff.)

52. Truth table for "*p* implies *q*":

p	q	p implies q		
T	T	T	:	The obvious case: Both are true, so q is true.
T	F	F	:	The chief case: what the definition leads us to expect.
F	T	T	:	The idle case: If q is already true it doesn't matter what p is. This is "both not-p and q."
F	F	T	:	The strange case: Though neither p nor q is true, their implication holds.

The chief case renders the crux of the propositional definition, though put in a back-to-front way: that q doesn't in fact fail when p holds. The first three lines of the truth table thus say that "*p* implies *q*" is always true except when q has failed.

The strange last case can be understood by considering that it is no stranger than the obvious case, for if the connection of p and q is not through their inner sense, why shouldn't their negations be connected as their affirmations were? The question is why the truth table (which is after all a definition) is set out in this way, and one answer is: To make implication so defined equivalent to "not-p or q"; thus you can see right away that "not(not-p) or not-q," the case when both are false, has to be just as true as the original. What this fact displays is that in material implication there is not, as there is in traditional implication, some sort of descent or fallout, but it is a relation of two coequal propositions.

The two last lines together yield what is sometimes called a paradox, though it is merely a strange fact: A false proposition truly implies both a false and a true proposition. Put succinctly though inaccurately: From a falsity anything follows. This statement is, to be sure, quite false in traditional logic (but perhaps not quite so false in common sense: "If you believe that, you'll believe anything"). But in material implication it is, instead of false, idle. It lacks what Russell calls "the practical feasibility of inference" as opposed to implication. For to infer that q follows from p, p must be posited, that is, asserted. But it can't be, since it is false, so nothing follows inferentially (Stebbing, 195). Implication is not inference or entailment, as one can see by looking at the table itself: The conclusion, the truth or falsity of q, comes *before* the truth or falsity of the implication.

Langer, chaps. XI and XII, are a thoughtful introduction to the propositional calculus and *Principia Mathematica*.

53. Quine 1950, 9.

54. The statements of the *Tractatus* (Wittgenstein 1921) bearing specifically on negation and truth and falsity are scattered and will be cited in the text as they come up.

There is one aspect of the *Tractatus* which Anscombe, 28, calls "fantastically untrue," namely the argued rejection of an inquiry into the way world, pictured fact, language and thought are related. Later consideration made Wittgenstein retract central dogmas of the *Tractatus*; among these are the very ones bearing on negation. In the *Philosophical Investigations*, 53, he implicitly renounces the whole theory set out in this text and says that " 'p' is true $= p$" and " 'p' is false $=$ not-p" is a matter of use: "And to say that a proposition can be true or false amounts to saying: we call something a proposition when *in our language* we apply the calculus of truth functions to it." We sound as if the proposition engaged the concept of truth, as with a cogwheel, but in fact true and false do not 'fit' the concept of proposition but just belong to it as parts of the language game.

Another part of the exposition rejected later is the notion of the picture proposition, that a picture is a model of reality and a proposition is like a picture. This was an old theory when he used it in the *Tractatus*. It goes back to antiquity, but a really close example is Lavoisier's uses of it in explaining his preoccupation with nomenclature and his incessant neologizing: "physical science must consist of three things; the series of facts which are the objects of science, the ideas which represent these facts [i.e., pictures], and the words by which these ideas are expressed" (author's preface, xiv). This quotation could almost come from the *Tractatus*. While the theory seems naive and in the long run untenable, it is lucid and illuminating at least in showing a way that the bipolarity of the proposition might be explained (see Anscombe, 77–78).

55. Whitehead and Russell, 41 ff. A judgment then has a plurality of objects that come together in the proposition the judgment asserts (44).

56. See in Pitcher 1964: Austin, 21, for example, sees nothing wrong with it except that it might be misleading, and Dummett, ibid., 106, admits that even those who don't accept correspondence believe that there is something in reality "in virtue of which" statements are true or false; he prefers to go to a use theory of the terms.

57. Quoted in Mounce, 36. The passage, from *Notebooks*, 98, is contemporary with the genesis of the *Tractatus*.

58. A harmless explanation of the locution "correlating the facts with the proposition" is, of course, that it is the propositions that are being tested. Yet in ordinary, nonscientific life we don't often have propositions which we look to test for truth, but we try to fit them to the facts as we go. There is something coercive in this way of talking (although it is perfectly appropriate to the *Tractatus*'s understanding of fact): "The truth conditions determine the scope that is allowed the facts by the proposition" (4.463).

59. The fact that *p* can be false and not-*p* true, so that both *p* and not-*p* can in different contexts be true, shows that negation has nothing in reality corresponding to it; neither does double negation, for that operation simply disappears (4.0621, 4.0641, 5.254). At 2.06 Wittgenstein calls the existence and nonexistence of a state of affairs a positive or negative fact, but this *has* to be a misnomer, if only because there are no negative facts, only positive facts that make other, would-be facts impossible; see Anscombe, 30. Rosen 1980, 141, tacitly corrects to "negating facts."

60. Anscombe, 64.

61. Anscombe, 53, 64.

62. One formal but opaque test is given by Anscombe, 61 ff. My colleague Stewart Umphrey suggested the pictorial proof.

63. The proof is again by Stewart Umphrey. We suppose that some proposition *p* has two contradictories or negations, not-*p*(1) and not-*p*(2). Now, from what it is to be the contradictory or negation of some proposition it follows that, necessarily, if '*p*' is false, then 'not-*p*(1)' is true and 'not-*p*(2)' is true, hence 'not-*p*(1) and not-*p*(2)' is true. But, from the supposition that not-*p*(1) and not-*p*(2) are different propositions it follows that they have different senses, hence different truth conditions (according to Wittgenstein and Anscombe). Therefore it is possible that, if '*p*' is false, then 'not-*p*(2)' is true whereas 'not-*p*(1)' is false. Let this possibility obtain. Then 'not-*p*(1) and not-*p*(2)' is false. But it's also true, which is absurd. Clearly, the premise to reject is our supposition that *p* has two different contradictories or negations.

So on this somewhat technical note we have completed the answer to the remaining question: How can we begin to see why every proposition *has* a negation and has only *one*?

64. *Metaphysics* 1011 b 26, 1027 b 26: Aristotle, however, also admits, since Being is not univocal, a use of Being as truth and Nonbeing as falsity (1027 b 19, 1051 b 3; p.   ).

65. Heidegger, *Logik*, 132, translates "truthful" *(alethes)* as "uncovering" *(entdeckend)* and "false" *(pseudos)* as "covering up" *(verdeckend*; see p. 94 for falsity and falsehood in Greek). This version is in aid of his insistence that for Aristotle speech does not "correspond" to its object but shows and manifest beings (128, 142). The

noun Truth *(aletheia)* does not actually occur in any of the passages dealing with declarative speech, and Heidegger uses this fact to claim that "Statement is not the place of Truth, but Truth the place of Statement" (135). For a statement can be true *or* false. Truth in a higher sense, the "Unconcealed", is later spoken of by Heidegger as a determination of Being for Aristotle (191 ff.), but this is interpretative and beyond my present point.

66. Heidegger displays the close relation that logical negation and affirmation have to truth and falsity for Aristotle in a tabulation of Aristotelian terms: combining—dividing; "uncovering"—"covering up"; affirming—denying. What Heidegger's interpretation further brings out is a respect in which Aristotle is close to Wittgenstein. The *logos*, like the proposition, is positive and negative at once, and is so in conjunction with its meaning. In the following statement, "The board is not black," "the 'not' which is supposed to separate and deny does not, after all, take the statement to pieces but is itself possible as an element of the expression only through the fact that being black is related to, is connected with, the blackboard" *(Logik, 141).*

67. Lewis Carroll, *The Hunting of the Snark,* Fit the Fifth. A double positive *might* sometimes give a negative: I read somewhere about a teacher who was holding forth to the class about how you can't say "I don't get no respect." Comes a voice from the back: "Yeah, yeah." I am told by my colleague Stewart Umphrey that the voice was actually Wittgenstein's.

68. Here as a sample is a version in words of half of a proof adapted from *Principia Mathematica,* by Wilder, 217, 3.4.1:

A. To prove that p implies not(not-p)   Law of Double Negation.
  1. p or not-p Law of Excluded Middle.
  2. not-p or not(not-p)   Substituting not-p for p.
  3. (not-p or q) means (p implies q)   Definition of implication.
  4. (not-p or not(not-p)) means   Substituting not(not-p) for q.
     p implies (not(not-p))
  Therefore p implies not(not-p).   By 2.
B. To prove the converse, that not(not-p) implies p, takes a little longer, see Wilder, 217, 3.4.2–3.

In the propositional calculus—where everything is strange (though nothing is marvelous)—the Law of Excluded Middle (p or not-p) and the Law of Contradiction (not [p and not-p]) are both theorems and are, moreover, equivalent to each other (Whitehead and Russell, 13, 111, prop. *3.24; Wilder, 219 f.).

In the Intuitionist system of mathematics, only a limited form of the Law of Excluded Middle is admitted; consequently double negation does not always regain the original positive.

69. Quine 1950, 14, gives reasons for using the dash rather than the tilde.

70. As usual, Aristotle states this Law of Thought for affirmation and denial *and* for Being and Nonbeing, and so for truth and falsity, *Metaphysics* 996 b 26 ff.; the law as stated there—"It is necessary that everything be either affirmed or denied"—seems to imply the Law of Excluded Middle.

71. The slanging match, with its alternation of "It is," "It isn't," "It is *so*," contains no double negation because no one is actually responding to the other's negation.

72. In the text I've dealt only with negations of whole propositions, but in formal,

as opposed to casual, speech (note 38), double negation works wherever the negation operates within the proposition, be it on the predicate or the copula: "He is good," "He is a no-good," "No, he is not a no-good." The last statement might be read as a case of litotes because it is somewhat more emphatic than the original positive. There is, once again, no logical sign to mark a positive proposition (as there is to mark a positive number) because positivity is tacitly regarded as the base line.

I am indebted to my colleague William Pastille for a note on double negation touching the example just cited. The actual thought in double negation (as distinct from the formalism) is, he surmises, the negation of an "indefinite name." (Aristotle coined this term for predicates like "no good" or "not-good," more accurately "non-good," because they are highly nonspecific, *On Interpretation* 16 a 29, 19 b 8.) So while the logical proposition goes: "He is not (not (good))," our thought is: "He is not (not-good)." But the indefinite name "not-good" excludes nothing definite from the subject. Therefore its negation cannot reverse it and return to a definite positive base. Hence double negations are useless for determining what truly is the case.

73. I have included actions and things in parentheses, because some statements *are* actions, and some acts of distinction and restoration can be construed as concrete double negatives.

74. Frege 1919, 135.

75. Mounce, 112, raises just this question.

76. Heraclitus fragment: 49a in Diehls. Socrates: Plato, *Republic* 523 c ff. It is reported that Socrates, given Heraclitus' writings by Euripides, said, "What I can make out is the real thing, and I think what I can't make out is so as well, but it requires someone like a Delian diver." (Diehls 145, 5; divers from Delos were known for going deep, and also the word *delos* means lucid, as obscure is *adelos*.)

77. For example, both Hegel and his critic Kierkegaard make paradox central. Hegel's third dialectic moment is often phrased as a paradox, for example, "the unity of Being and Nothing" (p. 163), while Kierkegaard gives the title the Paradox outright to the incarnate God who is both absolutely like and absolutely unlike man ("The Absolute Paradox," *Philosophical Fragments*). Consider also Zeno's paradoxes of motion, the Twin Paradox of Relativity Theory, and a plethora of other paradoxes. A collection of paradoxes and a discussion of their role in determining the limits of logic and physics is to be found in Barrow, 12–24.

78. Example of a set including itself: the class of all classes; ordinary collections don't include themselves. The class that includes all those classes that are not members of themselves can't include itself because then it would *be* a member of itself, and it can't exclude itself because then, now being a class that is not a member of itself, it *ought* to include itself.

79. Récanati, 290, points out exactly this fact: that the Cretan enters into paradox simply by *speaking*. Of course he can't actually *think* it either, while being of one unitary mind. People, however, are often of two minds—in real life.

80. The Cretan's stipulation, that either all Cretans lie or some or none, is necessary to make the paradox continue when the Cretan is lying. For if he lies in the absence of the stipulation it follows only that *some* Cretans are liars and that his statement is half-true.

81. Leiber 1993 has collected various versions of The Cretan Liar. Martin 1978 is

a collection of attempts to solve the paradox by logical means. Kneale 1962, 652 ff., reviews attempts from Cantor on. The Cretan Liar paradox is attributed to Epimenides, a Cretan poet and wonderworker of the sixth century B.C.: "The Cretans [are] ever liars, bad beasts, lazy bellies" (Diehls, 32). Paul of Tarsus quotes him in Titus 1:12. There seems to be no paradox intended by the one or understood by the other. The Cretan reputation for lying must be very old; when Homer's Odysseus tells lying stories about himself, he regularly presents himself as a Cretan—and people don't entirely believe him.

82. Lawson 1985 examines postmodern writers who are particularly engaged with destructive reflexivity: Nietzsche, Heidegger, Derrida.

83. This assertion, that a proposition has objective, noncontextual meaning and truth is, of course, just what is rejected in the postmodern vein because reality is considered as itself shaped or even constituted by language.

84. Hofstadter, 10. A "Strange Loop" is a movement ascending (or descending) through a hierarchy in which you find yourself unaccountably on the level on which you started. Hofstadter's book is shot through with references to Epimenides' paradox.

85. Heiss 1932, 81 ff., has an illuminating discussion of the philosophical implications of The Liar and other self-referring paradoxes. He distinguishes positive and negative "self-applications." The perfect example of the positive type is double negation which returns to positivity and terminates. The amended Liar is the purest example of negative self-application because it simply subverts its subject by infinite alternation (64, 85).

86. Waismann, 42.

87. See Klein, 211 ff.

88. Euclid, bk. VII, definitions 1 and 2 (Heath 1925, 277 ff.).

89. In Smith 1929, 46. For a brief history of negative numbers, see Smith 1923, 257 ff.

90. Of course, such measurements assume the introduction of the reals, which make it possible to let the points of a line continuum correspond to the real number system.

91. That is, $10^1 = 10 \ldots 20 \ldots$; $10^2 = 100 \ldots 110$, etc. Between 0 and 1, it does, in the decimal system, the same for the negative powers of 10: $10^{-1} = 1/10 = 0.1$, $10^{-2} = 1/100 = 0.01$.

92. Classes have rules of operation for the null class, here called 0, that correspond *in form* to those given in the text below for numbers. For classes, the "logical sum" $a + 0 = a$ means that the class of all the elements belonging to a plus those belonging also or only to 0 is just a, for 0 adds nothing. The "logical product" $a \times 0 = 0$ is the class of all those elements that a and 0 have in common, their overlap or "intersection," which is just the class 0, for there are *no* a-elements in 0.

Note that one can interpret $a + 0 = a$ as saying that every class includes one and the same null class, *the* null class. This seems absurd, but unavoidable when classes are taken extensionally, i.e., as quantitatively different collections of elements, and not intensionally, as qualitatively different concepts. Extensionally all classes with no members are the same: 0. One reason why the null class is admitted at all is that elements are often defined whose existence or nonexistence is unproved, and 0 accommodates these. (Hausdorff, 13, cites as an example the natural numbers that are solutions to $x^n + y^n = z^n$ for $n > 2$. Fermat's Last Theorem conjectured that none exist, but it was proved only in 1994.) See Russell's discussion of the symbolic necessity of the null class and of the problems associated with the idea of nothing (1903, 73 ff.).

93. See Smith 1923, 71 ff. A most poignant account of a Western experience of and recoil before Indian Nothingness is to be found in E. M. Forster, *A Passage to India* (p. 172).

94. Of course, such division, if conceivable at all, is not by nothing $= 0$ but by an evanescently small quantity caught in the act of vanishing—an infinitesimal. The rules for operating with 1 are really interesting to compare with those dealing with 0: $a + 1$ produces the successor, the next number, for the unit is the element of increase; $a \times 1$ yields the identical a, for taking the unit a number of times reproduces the number; $a \div 1$ also yields the identical a because a has just that number of unit parts. Thus while in addition the unit causes progress, zero causes stasis, while in multiplication the unit preserves identity, zero causes disappearance; and while in division the unit again preserves identity, zero is inoperative. Zero and one are alike in being exceptions among integers, but almost opposite in their effects.

95. The quotation is Kronecker's, cited by Kleene, 19, in support of regarding the number sequence 0, 1, 2, 3, . . . as primitive. Including 0 has the following effects: The set of the first *four* numbers has 3 as its largest number; the "least" number has no unit at all; the negative numbers, once introduced, will not be in one-to-one correspondence with the positives. Besides, Kronecker was not, in any case, speaking of 0.

96. Russell 1903, 128, gives a succinct derivation of this sort, here truncated: (1) 0 is the class of classes whose only member is the null class. (2) A number is the class of all classes similar to any one of themselves. (Similarity is defined in terms of a correlation of elements from class to class, so phrased as to include the null class.) (3) 1 is the class of all classes that are not null and are such that, if x belongs to the class, the class without x is the null class. There follow stipulations for generating successive numbers and for getting every finite number by induction.

97. See Russell 1903, chap. 22, "Zero," 187, for his own "specification" (since zero is properly speaking indefinable); 168 for Meinong's.

98. Russell 1903, 159, distinguishes between the more abstract "magnitude" and the more concrete "quantity." A quantity, such as pleasure, may become equal to zero and cease to exist, but it retains its kind and magnitude: no pleasure.

99. Russell 1903, 187.

3

Nonfact and Fiction:
Logical *Nonexistence*

"Nonexistence" means existence denied, and that is not so easy a notion. For existence pertains primarily to definite, usually concrete things, to individual objects or facts, to such beings as—we usually say—"exist" in a certain place at a certain time. But of course, not everyone speaks in the same way or so carefully, not even people writing philosophically.[1] The authors most concerned with nonexistence, above all Russell, Meinong, and their followers and critics, do, however, use the term in some such distinctive sense.

If existence is taken as betokening thisness and thereness, then nonexistence is going to have, speaking informally, this problem: It obliges us to speak of *a* nothing. If a nonexistent object were always like a footprint in the sand, we might refer to it by its mold, its negative place. But usually the world closes up without much trace around things that have passed their time and ceased to exist, and often there is not even a world left to hold the mold—think of extinct dodos and never existent unicorns; there is no empty niche left in our "real" world for the former and there never was—some say—one for the latter. What kind of focus allows us then to speak of things that are definitely and determinately nowhere and not now and not ever? What, if anything, is it we are referring to when we say: *This* does not exist?

I shall begin by trying to show that nonexistence is a specifically modern problem arising from the displacement of Being by Existence, and end by reminding the reader of an old medieval but ever lively debate concerning the most intellectually captivating of all the theological proofs in which is at stake the existence of that unique Individual who is not somewhere and sometimes but everywhere and always; this so-called ontological proof of the existence of God rests on making existence a predicate, which is to say, on understanding the sentence "God exists" to say something *about* God, to qualify his

Being, his suchness. Of course, since my interest is in *non*-existence, the question whether nonexistence is a predicate will come to the fore—once again—in this context.

For by then a great symbolic theory will have been established, largely to dispose of the problem of nonexistence, but redefining existence as a precondition and doing it in such a way that whatever it is, it is not a predicate: Russell's Theory of (Definite) Descriptions. This theory will be set out, particularly as it bears on nonexistence. Like all good attempts to dispose of a subset of the problem of Nonbeing, it will serve to sharpen the question, but the theory that is *the* winner in the world of logic will turn out to be something of a loser in the world of fiction.

Russell devised his theory in part as a response to Meinong's Theory of Nonexistent Objects, which is designed, among other things, to do justice to the lively role fictions play in life—unicorns will be, so to speak, the ever handy example. Alexius Meinong's theory, which ascribes a sort of existence to many kinds of nonbeings, offends, as Willard Van Orman Quine says, "the aesthetic sense of us [logicians] who have a taste for desert landscapes . . . [Meinong's] slum is a breeding ground for disorderly elements."[2] But this theory, "whose overpopulated universe is in many ways unlovely" to Quine, is rehabilitated by Parsons; I will sketch out this revamped version because it proves to be useful in saving many a lovely being of poetry and novels, all the nonexistences of fiction—be they deceitful or just captivating.

1. A MODERN PROBLEM: NONEXISTENCE

Let me return now to the intrinsic modernity of the initial problem of nonexistence, which is simple to state and the devil to deal with. When we refer to a nonexistent object, what are we thinking of and what are we talking about? The two theories just alluded to deal with the problem in diametrically opposite ways; they are anathema to one another. One, the less influential one, presupposes that people care enough about enough things that don't exist in the commonsense way to try to save the significance of talk about them. So does the other, Russell's theory, the most influential logical theory of the century just bygone,[3] but at this price: Such propositions are false; it is by giving up their truth that speech about nonexistent objects rises to the demands of logic. What Meinong regards as a fact of mental life, Russell regards as an error of common speech. But both theories are very serious about nonexistence.

Why did this problem become so grave throughout the twentieth century and bodes to continue so? And how did its interesting treatments become the preserve of logicians or logically inclined philosophers?

Here I must embark on a quasi-digression. In his founding paper "On Denoting" Russell says: "A logical theory may be tested by its capacity for dealing with puzzles."[4] Puzzles are, I think, just what philosophy tends to evade. Great philosophy hews its way to the "heart of truth" and lets the chips fall where they may—often for logicians to try to sweep up. Philosophical inquiries deepen *questions*; logicians solve *problems*, which are puzzles of large scope.[5] Moreover, as Whitehead, Russell's coauthor of the *Principia Mathematica*, says: "A Science which hesitates to forget its founders is lost. To this hesitation I ascribe the barrenness of logic."[6] Just the opposite is eminently true of philosophy, which becomes airy when divorced from its originating terms. This chapter therefore cannot help but be an object lesson in the irreconcilable difference—and the unbreakable connection—between these two undertakings. And of course, the question must arise: Why did the question of nonexistence have to land as a problem in logic? And what is gained and what is lost when the question that was asked experientially is set aside while the problem is solved formally, that is, symbolically?

I think Russell and Whitehead say it exactly right: Logic became the venue for nonexistence because logicians were willing to see it as a soluble problem and to kick away all the struts that kept it standing as a high mystery. They were willing to be radically *spare*.[7]

The ancient question, "inquired after of old and now and ever," that propped up old enigmas was "What *is* Being?", and this inquiry is modernized by being diverted into a new one: What do being and existence *mean*?[8] Not that theories of language, such as deal with meaning, intending, referring, denoting, connoting were absent in antiquity or in the middle ages. But these were mostly concerned with the way words reach toward or are about beings of thought and sense—how and what they *intend*.[9] The new philosophical analysis first focused on the rectification of ordinary language, the elimination of undesirable entities, and the symbolic formalization of the propositions asserted in sentences[10] of natural language aside from context and intent—all elements that will turn up in a while.

Along with this intense interest in the logical aspect of language goes a strong presupposition, a faith really, in the empirically verifiable objects and facts of science, or at the least, in so-called reality:

> The sense of reality is vital in logic, and whoever juggles with it by pretending that Hamlet has another kind of reality is doing a disservice to thought. A robust sense of reality is very necessary in framing a correct analysis of propositions about unicorns, golden mountains, round squares, and other such pseudo-objects.
>
> In obedience to the feeling of reality, we shall insist that, in the analysis of propositions, nothing "unreal" is to be admitted.[11]

These two interests—analysis and reality—will, at their intersection, make acute questions of nonexistence and, of course, of existence. What role they play in propositions, how so-called negative existentials (sentences of the form "There is no such thing as . . .") are explicable,[12] whether the words and phrases "unicorn," "golden mountain," "round square" refer to anything or not—these and similar problems are treated seriously because the project of speaking rigorously about reality comes directly up against them.

Among these it is those unicorns that have a special poignancy in the light of logic. Golden mountains merely happen not to exist,[13] round squares are logically impossible, but unicorns are not so afflicted. Their legendary status, that is to say, the acknowledged lack of existence of these elegant and awesome creatures does not seem to impair not merely their significance to us but even the power over us of the sentences in which they appear. In fact, a unicorn might imaginably turn the tables with respect to nonexistence:

> "This is a child" Haigha replied eagerly, coming in front of Alice to introduce her, and spreading out both his hands in an Anglo-Saxon attitude. "We only found it to-day. It's as large as life, and twice as natural!"
>
> "I always thought they were fabulous monsters!" said the Unicorn. "Is it alive?"[14]

What I mean to intimate is that whereas for thinking within logic a "robust sense of reality" may be required, for thinking about fiction a robust sense of unreality might be desirable.

Hence fictional nonexistence is often separated off from other kinds of failure to exist, and receives special treatment, some of which will be laid out below. The immediate task, however, is to say how existence got its modern meaning, or more accurately, what the word "existence," once it had come into wide use, primarily meant and what it was that had to give way to it.

2. NONEXISTENCE VERSUS NONBEING

Existence is a protean term in our language, but it got there fairly late. Shakespeare uses the noun not at all, the verb only a couple of times. Both can mean a whole range of things from the fullest existence of God to the mere existence of a life barely carried on, from fullest actuality to merest maintenance. The central and main meaning of existence is factuality or reality. "To exist" and "to be real" are practically synonymous.[15] "Real" is the adjective from Latin *res*, thing, and since in its early uses, especially in common speech, real existence is opposed to insubstantial appearance, the identification of reality and existence makes some sense.[16] Such a state of affairs is an invitation to intervene with a definition and have done with it. But definitions are at best terminal thoughts and no good to inquiries in progress, so I will let the meaning emerge on its own.

In the logical world, which is dominated by Russell, existence has, as he says in a paper just preceding "On Denoting," two meanings: the one that occurs in philosophy and in daily life lets existence be predicated of an individual, not necessarily but most properly a spatiotemporal entity. This meaning "lies wholly outside Symbolic Logic, which does not care a pin whether its entities exist in this sense or not."[17]—It will turn out, however, that the symbolic theory so central to the problem of nonexistence will in fact be deeply implicated with the "daily life" understanding of existence.

Here is how the fact of common language bears on the meaning given to *non*-existence, a meaning that makes nonexistence a newly acute problem. If existence means being an individual in space and time, nonexistence is naturally understood as its "complement class," the class of all the things that don't exist. And since every thing that exists is a definite, determinable, concrete individual, one might, simple-mindedly, expect whatever does *not* exist to begin by being an entity as well, only a nonexistent, a canceled one. For example, when people complain of being treated as nonpersons they seem to have something of that sort in mind. This is the problem of nonexistence propounded in a more naively experienced way than is usual. For in books the problem comes up in terms of the object of thought: How can we deny anything without proffering to ourselves an object *to* deny, and then what is the status of that object? But in my version the emphasis is on the pull toward concreteness that real existence exerts on nonexistence.

Of course this collection of nonexistents is both a motley and an elusive crew. For on the one hand it includes a vivid collection not only all the canceled entities, like the members of extinct species and deceased human beings and artifacts no longer extant,[18] but also all the entities that never did exist in the ordinary sensible sense, such as unicorns. And on the other hand the class seems to consist of vastly and vaguely overlapping parts. For if I put "non-" before a thing or notion, for example "non-sense," I get—in a carping mood—practically everything in the world, an uncountable amount; a predicate of this sort appears in what used to be called an infinite judgment, one that assigned its subject to the indefinite complement of the positive class. What I am saying is that the lay thinker probably has the feeling that nonexistent objects, entities that bear the prefix "non-," are both very definitely in some world as anti-entities and very indefinitely everywhere and nowhere as non-entities.

Existence and its peculiar way of shaping nonexistence is the end of the story (in the century just gone by), but its prelude is Being and Nonbeing, very differently conceived.[19] This Being enters our awareness through Parmenides (chapter 4). He is enjoined by a goddess who lives in the heart of Truth to utter only "is" and never "is not" and to think only Being and never Nonbeing. Interpreters who introduce into the poem's single-minded insistence on the gravity of "is" the term "exist" are fudging the drama of the initiatory revelation. For Parmenides, Being is what is first and last, not only too all-absorbing to have the differentiations and the transcendental properties later found to be required for ideal being but also too divorced from space and time for real existence. Nonetheless, for all his descendants, all the philosophers of Being, it will retain in some one of its senses the scope and potency it had for its first proponent.

Being is thus an ancient and medieval term that survives into a new world—I am thinking not of the temporal extranea of history, but of the world of thought, particularly Russell's. Being was once the richest thought but is now the poorest concept, neither an idea, nor a universal, nor a particular substance but a mere abstracted latter-day generality, hugely expanded and therefore attenuated to the point of extinction. Thus Russell says:

> *Being* is that which belongs to every conceivable term, to every possible object of thought—in short to everything that can possibly occur in any proposition, true *or false*, and all such *propositions themselves* [my italics]. Being belongs to whatever can be counted. If A be any term that can be counted as one, it is plain that A is something, and therefore that A is. "A is not" must always be either false or meaningless. . . . Numbers, the Homeric gods, relations, chimeras and four-dimensional spaces all have being, for if they were not entities of a kind, we could make no propositions about them. Thus Being is a general attribute of everything, and to mention anything is to show that it is.[20]

This is Being on the way out, and within two years Russell himself will have given it up "in obedience to the feeling of reality" proper to logicians.[21] Now the term existence takes over: "Everything exists." The positive effect of that odd-sounding sentence is first to replace "is" by "exist" as the universal of universals, but the negative intent is to enforce the nonexistence of all that does not exist in the way specified above, as *particular* things.[22] It is therefore meant as an exclusion rather than a reflection on the nature of existence. Whatever does not exist in the strong sense is out of consideration: no nonexistent objects; it's existence or nothing—a deliberately illiberal view of what there is. (One of the consequences, however, of such hard-edged logicistic views is that they call forth as their complement softly sophisticated gropings into human existence, such as existentialism.

So Being is now not even the ghost of a departed thought in these quarters, and the wheel has come full circle: As Parmenides once completely denied existence, so Being is now not a problem worth attending to.[23] But how does this transformation bear on nonexistence, my theme? The answer was broached above, but it is worth noting here that it will be such as to turn the question around: It is the problem of nonexistence that sharpens and constricts the understanding of existence.

So far I have argued that the existents *behind*—as we will see, not *of*—mainstream logic are those of common sense and ordinary speech. But what do people really believe about these matters? No more than politicians, when they announce what "the American people want," know what they are talking about, do I know what people believe; in fact that may in principle not be accurately ascertainable, since the moment we are asked we begin to think and hence to efface our unformulated naive opinions. Still, I will make a guess from self-inspection: I naturally use the word "exist" for some thing somewhere in place and somewhere in time. Thus horses exist and rhinoceroses exist, but unicorns, which are like horses in body and like rhinoceroses in having one horn, don't *exist*.[24] To be sure, we also say: "There *are* no unicorns," but this locution almost proves the point. "There" is a locative whose placing function is weak but not gone.[25] "There is" has an echo of somewhere in the world; recall Gertrude Stein's comment on Oakland, CA: "There's no there there."

And though we ask "Is there a God?" it is also common to ask "Does God exist?" because we are pursuing not impersonal divine Being but an ultimate Individual. (The bearing of existence and nonexistence on the question of God will be considered in the last section.

So accepting the "realism" of the ordinary use of existence, the problem—to recapitulate—shapes up as follows: In saying of anything that it does not exist we do not seem to be thinking and speaking of nothing, both because we are focusing on it somewhat as we would on things that do exist and because we can say false sentences about it, such as "Unicorns are winged horses," when they are, in fact, horned horses, and only Pegasus is a winged horse. Thus we seem to be putting nonexistent objects on the scene. To this perplexity there is an eliminative and a proliferating answer, that of Russell and Meinong respectively. These answers, one a philosophical logician's, the other a logically minded philosopher's, will teach us how to deal with the blessed fact that there are no round squares, the boring fact that there are no golden mountains, and the sobering fact that there are no unicorns. To my mind that theory will be best which is most liberal in defending the right to life of ungenerate unicorns; I think that, as not everything we speak of is in the real world, so not everything we fail to find there is entirely out of it.

3. NONEXISTENCE DEFANGED: RUSSELL'S THEORY OF DESCRIPTIONS

This theory, first advanced in 1905, is the most influential attempt of the just past century to do away with the problems of nonexistence. I could add "through logic" as if there were other ways to approach the problem, but I can't think of any except to embrace it as a perennial question. So this solution is *intrinsically* logical, and the brief exposition that follows will, I hope, show what that means.

Two preliminary points: First, since logic claims to need and want no historical context, I shall feel free to invert the order of presentation, leaving the theory that aroused the logical response for the next section (4). Second, I shall present the theory only as far as it bears on nonexistence, leaving out much that belongs to its complete foundational format.

The theory was first announced in the succinct article "On Denoting"; "Theory of Descriptions" is Russell's own name.[26] Like other influential theories, it is somewhat misnamed. Just as the Theory of Relativity might just as well be called the Theory of the Absolute World, so the theory of descriptions might be called the Theory of Nondescriptions, and (not to pass up a pun the language offers) it does turn out that the theory leaves what would once have been called the subject of a proposition in a severely nondescript state.

Though Russell is overthrowing earlier opinions, among them his own,[27] he starts without context, by giving examples of three cases of denoting: (1) a denoting phrase may not denote anything: "*the* present king of France"; (2) or it may denote one definite object: "*the* present king of England [in 1905]; (3) or it may denote ambiguously: a man. I should say now that the denoting functions will for the most part evaporate and the descriptive phrases will be dissolved in the theory.

Then he introduces a famous distinction. It is that between *acquaintance*, immediate knowledge such as we have of sensory objects in perception and of abstract objects in [intuitive] thought, and *knowledge about*, which we have of things we can only reach by denoting phrases, that is, descriptions. As an example of the latter he gives other people's minds, which we never know by direct presentation but only by description; all real knowledge, however, *starts* by acquaintance.

Russell makes the definite article "the" in its unique, singular sense, the first focus of his inquiry: "like Browning's Grammarian with the enclitic *de*, I would give the doctrine of this word if I were 'dead from the waist down' and not merely in prison."[28] The reasons for this interest in the definite article are in the three puzzles that arise about it: First, in the sentence "Scott was the author of *Waverley*," if "the author of Waverley" is identical with Scott, that is, denotes the same object, then we can substitute Scott for the phrase and get "Scott is Scott," and that is not what anyone meant to say.

It is, however, in the second and third puzzle that our interest lies. So, second, by the Law of Excluded Middle, for every proposition, either "The present King of France is bald" is true or it is false. But the list of baldies does not include him, *nor* does the list of creatures that have hair, so we have an impermissible case.

And third, and most to the point of nonexistence: How can a nonentity either be or not be the subject of a proposition, for example, "the nonexistent present king of France" or the nonexistent fact that occurs in a false proposition? How can a proposition refer to nonexistents or negated facts or fail to refer to them?

Here, finally, is the theory intended to solve these puzzles, not in Russell's first version but in the form that is standard in logic books:[29]

$$(\exists x)(Fx \cdot [(y)(Fy \to y = x)] \cdot Gx$$

First read within the square brackets: $[(y)(Fy \to y = x)]$. This longest part of the formula symbolizes the uniqueness of "the"; it says that any y that has the property F is identical with x, or "there is one and only one x," *the* one.

There remains $(\exists x)(Fx \cdot Gx)$, which says that "there exists an x such that x has the property F and also the property G."

In common language: "There is something that is the king of France, and there is only one king of France, and he is bald."

Now what has this symbolic proposition accomplished?

First: the unintended identity statement is gone, for the expression has no subject (Scott) and predicate (the author of *Waverley*) to *be* identified: Both have been turned into descriptions—Russell claims that referring names too denote as do descriptions—and so they can be treated as properties of a nondescript variable x of which a value may exist.[30]

Second: Put a negative sign ($\sim$) before the whole expression and the proposition is now acknowledged as plain false. It is no longer a maverick proposition about a nonexistent object, one disobeying the Law of Excluded Middle, but just a false proposition. For there is no x, no thing, that has this complex of properties: king of France and bald.

Third: This symbolic proposition is not, as was just said, about a nonentity, so the problem of reference is solved. What it *is* about and what it says of its object is both interesting and problematic. Solutions of problems often *are* problematic: What price was there to pay?

In answer, let us, to begin with, look at "description":

In the true analysis of a proposition, the description is broken up and disappears.[31]

What does Russell mean, in view of all the mention "description" gets? He means that descriptions are removed as far as possible from denoting, from being "constituents" of the proposition, that is, from being *about* something. Instead they have meaning only in the context of the expression: the "the" of a descriptive phrase like "*the* present king of France" is in *no* way definite or demonstrative. Such phrases, which have no meaning in the denotative sense, such *nondenoting* phrases, work only within the propositional function; they are therefore called incomplete symbols.[32]

Consequently, to reiterate the chief gain, it is neither nonsense nor a commitment to the denotation of a nonexistent object to say either that "*The* Unicorn [the unique one] is a horse with a horn" or that *"The* Unicorn [so described] does not exist," provided the sentences are properly paraphrased: "There exists a thing that is a horse and it has a horn and . . . [whatever used to be part of an apparently denoting description]," and "It is false that there exists a thing that is a horse and has a horn, etc." Each of these propositions affirms and denies as a proposition should, but neither has a *subject*, as does any ordinary sentence, a grammatical subject that might represent some fictional or nonexistent object. Not only is the descriptive phrase, the incomplete symbol, by itself meaningless, but the "thing," the x that "satisfies" the expression and turns it into a proposition, is a *mere* entity.

Russell himself emphasizes the difference between the symbolic expression and a sentence. "It is," he says, "a disgrace to the human race that it has chosen to employ the same word 'is' for these two entirely different ideas—a disgrace which a symbolic logical language of course remedies."[33] The two ideas are the subject-predicate relation and the identity relation; the latter is the relation between an object named and an object described, as expressed by the symbolism of the Theory of Descriptions. Russell does not go so far as to proscribe the subject-predicate use of "is," but he certainly supersedes it in the course of his rectification of common language.

The enabling presupposition of the saving remedy is the distinction between knowledge by acquaintance and knowledge by description noted above (p. 82).

> The referend of a demonstrative symbol [i.e., "the . . ."] is the object directly presented which the demonstrative symbol indicates. Thus a symbol cannot be demonstrative unless the speaker using the symbol is acquainted with its denotation. But a descriptive phrase may be used to refer to what is not presented . . . [and in some cases] *could* not be directly presented. An object cannot, for instance, be directly presented as *the one and only object* of a certain sort.[34]

The cases Russell's theory covers first of all are just these: those of the one and only object not demonstratively presented.

One more point: The theory began with the existence of particular spatiotemporal individuals, but it ends up with a meaning of existence, logical existence, that actually excludes these. For either to assert or to deny the existence of what is demonstratively named is now meaningless. As was said, proper names do not really belong in the theory; only descriptions do. The existence quantifier (∃) does not refer to the existence of individuals but to a mere thing, an x, insofar as certain properties belong to it: "It is of propositional functions that you can assert or deny existence."[35]

In the paragraphs just preceding, I have collected the elements of the theory that induce misgivings. There have been numerous critiques dealing with its technical difficulties,[36] but I am thinking of those that leap to the eye of the lay beholder. At what price, as I asked above, does nonexistence make its disappearance?

(1) In general: It is not quite believable that what people really meant to say, had they been thinking straight, is what a propositional function says, and that the expression is a rectification of language rather than a transformation of thought. I am not sure that people *ought* to say what the expression says for them.

In particular: a. The presupposed sharp distinction between "by acquaintance" and "by description" seems much more fuzzy in actual cognitive life. It is doubtful to me that a human being can point or refer to anything without a lot of inchoate, implicit description *contemporaneously* going on, and, what is more, that a human being can hear descriptions without *immediately* supplying a subject to which the descriptive properties not merely *adhere* but from which they seem to arise, in which they *inhere*.

b. It is not plausible to me that descriptions—predicates in ordinary language—are very often paratactic, meaning that they stand atomically separated, connected only by "and." A unicorn is not, I think, a horse, and one-horned, and a symbol of sovereignty, and virginity. I would rather expect that, upon research, these featured properties would turn out to be in an intertwined or in a piggyback relation, a characteristic the ordinary predicate "one-horned horse by its very aspect representing unapproachable sovereignty" preserves. Indeed, the visualizability of a description depends on these involvements being expressed: the long straight horn representing power that emerges from the forehead of the horse is part of a possibly unique being that as a whole symbolizes majesty.

c. The "thing," the x in the propositional function, is too pallidly nonsubstantial to represent what is in my mind when I attribute properties to a subject in an ordinary sentence. As I said in a. above, we do not either in thinking or in speaking drape a bare armature with properties, but we begin at both ends at once: with a being that has inherent properties making it receptive to others. The x of the expression, which is, as it were, a strange kind of neutral substrate, both featureless and individual, is a product of analysis, not a constituent of normal thought, at least not mine.

d. In the same vein, the existential quantifier symbolizes a notion of existence quite remote from the spatiotemporal "there exists" from which it was abstracted and to which it must, in applications, once more return. To exist by means of a satisfied propositional function is just not to exist in the world, and it is the things of the world that are usually in my thoughts. Moreover, I doubt that *quantification*, the quantity of existents such as "at least one," is what people are focused on when they say (if they do): "Unicorns exist." And finally, I would prefer that the question whether existence is a predicate was left open, than have the logical symbolism, which abstracts the word "exists" from the function and makes it a kind of prefix, settle the question in the negative.

(2) With respect to literature: The theory commits us to treating the sentences of fiction as false, while most of us think they have at least a sort of truth, and some of us even believe that they often have more truth than mere fact does. This dilemma and its logical remedies along with the living actuality of imaginative beings are considered in the next two sections.

Now Russell would, I am sure, agree with the gist of all these reservations, since he agreed that logic was distinct in just these ways from ordinary language and that such language has no exact logic. Hence he must have believed—I interpolate—that language says something more or different from logic, albeit inexactly. The question is whether these inexact intimations of language are worthy of being pursued. And they would be if nonexistence turned out to be indispensable to certain indefeasible human interests.

4. NONEXISTENCE ESTABLISHED: MEINONG'S THEORY OF OBJECTS

In the theory about to be summarized, nonexistence is given recognition, but in a curiously backhanded way. Meinong says:

> Those who like paradoxical modes of expression could very well say: "There are objects *[es gibt Gegenstände]* of which it is true that there are no such objects."[37]

Succinctly put:

> some objects do not exist at all.[38]

The reader is to focus on the *objects*. They are on the scene, but not necessarily as entities that *are* in the general sense of having being and even less as things that *exist* in the particular sense of being in space and time. Nonetheless they "are" objects. Meinong's theory concerns objects insofar as their character determines the type of being they have—though in advance of the theory "being" is to be taken in the most noncommittal sense possible. Meinong's German has the advantage of having a colorlessly impersonal phrase, *es gibt*, which he uses in the quotation above so as to keep the paradox from being seriously vicious, while in English the only available locution, "there are," overstates his meaning from the outset.

For what Meinong is *not* saying is that certain nonexistent objects *exist* or some such self-contradictory nonsense. This opinion was attributed to him by Russell, for Russell saw the Theory of Objects in his own terms. He said, critically, that it "regards any grammatically correct denoting phrase as standing for an object." For Russell a "denoting phrase" may denote nothing, for example "the present king of France." But "object" he takes tacitly to mean "existing object." So it looks as if Meinong contended "that the existent present King of France exists, and also does not exist," since he is the existing object referent of a nothing-denoting phrase.[39]

Let me inject here the justification for beginning Meinongian theory with Russellian misapprehensions. These latter are illuminating for the following intertwined reasons: The Theory of Objects and the Theory of Descriptions at first appear—and appeared to Russell—as directly antithetical. But to look into his objections is to see that the terms of the theories in fact talk past each other and that it is really the truths each hopes to save that meet in battle. For example, Russell's reference to grammar in the critique cited is apt: The deliverances of ordinary grammatical language were indeed a guide to Meinong in the sense that speech reveals the object spoken of, while for Russell the grammar of common speech is misleading. Furthermore the same quotation shows that for Russell it is existence or nothing, while for Meinong there are nuances; indeed they will be the best part of his theory. Thus Russell curtly rejected one of Meinong's defenses against his criticism, one that rested on a fine distinction expressed in the sentence: "The round square is existent but does not exist."[40] This is not gobbledygook but subtle sense, as we shall see (p. 92). Here is yet one more, perhaps the most important (though not the last) mutual bypassing of the theories, also evident in the short quotation above: For Russell propositions are to be purified; for Meinong objects are to be established.

Indeed, for all its apparent weirdness, it is Meinong's theory that sticks soberly close to human experience, while Russell's views display a sort of flamboyant extremism, from the era before his discovery of the theory, when everything had Being indiscriminately, through the subsequent reduction of existence to the quantifier of a proposition, so that nonexistence now means merely the negation of the proposition.

Having, then, sidled up to Meinong's theory by a glance toward the matters at stake and the misconstruals to which its terms are vulnerable, I shall try to present as briskly as possible its chief elements—as always, with an eye to nonexistence.[41]

The gist of the theory lies (a) in the notion of *objects* and (b) in their differentiated *ways of being*. With each of these terms is associated an inherited initial principle.

(a) Meinong learned from his teacher, Franz Brentano, of

> a particular affinity and analogy which exists among all mental phenomena, while the physical do not share it. Every mental phenomenon is characterized by what the scholastics of the Middle Ages called the intentional (and also mental) inexistence of an object *(Gegenstand)*, and what we would call . . . a direction

upon an object (by which we are not to understand a reality in this case), or an immanent objectivity.[42]

\
Meinong takes off from the firm assumption "that knowing is impossible without something being known" and that psychological events have the distinctive "character of being directed at something." But he diverges from Brentano in respect to the "inexistence"[43] of intentional objects. Objects at which thought (or feeling) is directed are not always only immanent, that is, lodged in the thinking that intends them as part of it, but have some transcendent, that is, extra-mental character. Here is a sample of how these two ways of regarding an object of thought would be expressed in speech. Immanent: "A golden mountain exists in thought"; transcendent: "There exists a thought about a golden mountain" ("exists" being used loosely here).

So it must become Meinong's task to establish the various objects of mental directedness, the more so if such objects are not merely mental but possess an independent power to modify the thought directed at them.

That thinking has an independent intelligible object is an ancient doctrine. Thus Plato's Socrates gets Theaetetus, a young mathematician, to admit that anyone who has an opinion must have it about some one thing that *is*, and moreover the Platonic dialogues are full of the intelligible Being and beings that thinking should attain. Aristotle makes explicit the receptivity of thought: the (passive) intellect *becomes* all things. At the other, modern end is Kant's claim that the understanding rigorously forms its object.[44] Meinong will grant his objects independence and influence (but not always Being). One sign that we must not consider the object as identical with the thought, that is to say, as merely an idea content, is precisely our ability to think of nonexistent objects. For if these were literally a part of our idea, they would exist "as much as does the idea of which they form a part,"[45] which Meinong finds intolerable; the existence of nonexistent objects is not of that sort. It comes rather from the "logical priority" of the object, from its givenness, its being "pregiven" *(vorgegeben)*—the condition indeed expressed in the ontologically neutral phrase *es gibt* cited above.[46]

Meinong distinguishes two kinds of objects in the larger sense toward which our mind can be directed: objects and objectives. Objects are primary things, objectives are judgments of which the primary objects are constituents. Objectives express facts or states of affairs involving objects. They are themselves objects, the objects of certain cognitive attitudes, but objects of a higher order: "I think that . . ." is an expression introducing one sort of objective.[47] Objectives have a "being" other than many primary objects. Sometimes what I am expressing with quotation marks is put this way: "Objectives have no existence." But, as will be made clearer below, they are not therefore nonexistences.

Before going to the feature of most relevance to nonexistence, the specification of "Being," it is worth noting that Meinong devoted a lot of thought to the position of his Theory of Objects among the disciplines. Does it belong with the psychology of cognition and of affections or is it metaphysics? Not with psychology, because that science, while dealing with objects of thinking and feeling, is not concerned with these objects for their own sake, as is the Theory of Objects; not with metaphysics, because that is the "science of the totality of the actual," while the Theory of Objects deals with all that is given, actual *or not*, "without paying any attention to its Being." The Theory is therefore an independent science parallel to metaphysics.[48] And now comes the payoff for our purposes.

(b) Meinong learned from his student Ernst Mally a fact that "is sufficiently important to be explicitly formulated as the principle of the independence of Being-thus *(Sosein)* from Being *(Sein)*."[49] Meinong had been casting around for a term and its concept that would cover the vast part of the objects of knowledge that he had discovered. For, he claimed,

> the totality of what exists, including what has existed and will exist, is infinitely small in comparison with the Objects of knowledge. This fact easily goes unnoticed, probably because the lively interest in reality which is part of our nature tends to favor that exaggeration which finds the non-real a mere nothing.[50]

Of the objects that do not *exist* in the normal spatiotemporal mode, some *subsist*. Subsistence, traditionally the term for independent Being in the widest sense, is used by Meinong to cut out from the infinity of nonexistents those entities that are "ideal" objects. The states of affairs held in mind called objectives and mathematical objects are chief among them. They have natures that are quite determinate and quite independent of our knowing them.[51] Existence and Subsistence together make up Being, and are not the focus here.

There is left to be named the infinite territory of all the objects that *are not*, for the Not-being *(Nichtsein)* of an object can be as much an objective as its Being. "The term 'Quasibeing' seemed to me for a while to be a completely suitable expression for this rather oddly constituted type of being," a third order, so to speak "adjoined to Existence and Subsistence."

But to attribute even this odd sort of Being to the nonbeings we have in mind runs into this question: "Can Being in principle unopposed by Nonbeing [such as is Quasibeing insofar as it is itself already a sort of Nonbeing] be called Being at all?" Yet there is an experience that speaks for a positive answer: In order to grasp the Nonbeing of an object it is necessary to make an affirmative assumption of its Being; to deny A I must assume the Being of A as somehow given beforehand, although it is a merely "pregiven," an assumed Being, belonging to an object whose Being is denied and is therefore not simply the opposite of Nonbeing.[52] Some new concept is needed that supersedes or stands beyond the sort of being that is defined by its straightforward opposition to a nonbeing.

Here the principle of the independence of Being-so from Being, cited at the beginning, supplies a solution. Being-so, *Sosein*, is a German term for essence. But essence, the properties that make a being what it is supposed to be as being of a kind, is not what is meant here. Being-so is what describes an individual object either exhaustively or sometimes incompletely. It consists of the properties, essential *and* accidental, that are attributed to the object. It is quite separable from the Being that comprises the real existence or ideal subsistence of objects. We can intend objects with properties that cannot belong to entities at all.

The principle of independence immediately furnishes what the translators of the Theory of Objects call "the principle of the indifference of pure Objects to Being." "Indifference . . . to Being" translates *Aussersein*, literally, "Outside-of-being."[53] Being and Nonbeing are equally external to the Being-so of an object, and conversely, the object so understood is external to them.

Everything that we direct our minds to is an object. Of objects some exist, for example, sticks and stones. Some others subsist; for example, lines and circles. Both of these types have Being. But a great many, indeed infinitely more objects are well enough described and focused on by us so that we may make true or false assertions about them. Yet they have no Being; they are Outside-of-being, for example, magical wands and philosopher's stones, and, of course, unicorns. They have no Nonbeing either, for they are outside both Being and its proper opposite.

The principle of the independence of Being-so from Being showed why it is possible for us to talk, as we ordinarily do, about two kinds of nonbeings: nonexistent objects like golden mountains and nonsubsistent objects like the side of a square equal to the area of a given circle. The principle also suggested that some objects are outside of Being—for example, impossibilities like round squares—and, we must add, outside of Nonbeing as well. To me, at least, it seems to follow that objects outside of Being are not nonexistent. And this is a great gain in talking about those objects that have scarcely any existence in the ordinary aggressive sense but have all the charm in the world, the objects of the imagination and phantasy. For to call them nonexistent, as we must in Russell's theory, is much too harsh and contrary to our normal speech behavior and intimate experience. Moreover, these outsider objects have a characteristic friendly to fiction: Unlike existent and subsistent objects, which are, in principle, completely determined and exhaustively describable, objects outside of Being may be quite sparsely described so that we cannot answer questions about them except by using our own imaginations. This is a characteristic called incompleteness (p. 92), one which is obviously relevant to the objects of stories and pictures. So "Meinong's conception exactly fits literary fictions"[54]—it seems.

I would say that Meinong comes near to saving the phenomena of that intentional experience of central interest to this trilogy and to be discussed in the following sections, the experiences of imagining. He is able to accomplish that because his approach is, as he himself says, "quasi-empirical"; he attends very carefully to the phenomena, and doesn't much care whether the objects he finds himself obliged to acknowledge have any immediately discernible use in science or real life.

Findlay calls it a strange fact of philosophy, "that highest iridescence of the human spirit," that issues most hotly debated, by a sudden shift of light lose all their point, and that Meinong, whose theories were highly topical during the breakdown of idealism in the first fifth of the last century, underwent such a fate: His questions were forgotten.[55] But by a reverse shift, Meinong was recalled in the last two fifths, proving that the fires of philosophy are banked, not quenched.

5. MEINONG REVIVED: PARSONS'S ANALYTIC VERSION

Among Meinongian revivals one is especially interesting because the author, Terence Parsons, sets himself the task of presenting a theory that will be in content inconsistent with the Theory of Descriptions, that is, non-Russellian, but whose style will be analytic—axiomatic and symbolic. Here is a brief, nonformal account of what Meinong looks like in Russell territory.[56]

Parsons takes from Meinong the term "nuclear property" (or predicate). Such properties belong to objects in themselves, individually, and form complexes analogous to Meinong's Being-so. They are contrasted with "extranuclear predicates," which do not belong to objects in that mode, such as "exists," "is impossible," "is fictional." Nuclear properties are thus not all essential, nor are extranuclear properties predicates in an incontestable way.[57]

Then Parsons makes a list. On the left-hand side are listed all the objects that exist in the normal, "real" way. On the right-hand side are listed the sets of nuclear properties describing each object. Each object is supposed to be uniquely characterized by its set, which will thus contain at least one property no other object's set has. All the existent objects are considered to be completely described by these nuclear sets. (It is, of course, a fiction of logic that we can practically get hold of *all* existent objects and describe them *completely,* since there may be, for all we know, infinitely many, and, moreover, any object may have indefinitely many properties, depending on how we ascertain a property; but set that little obstacle aside.) Now, how to go on?

Go on by constructing more and more sets of properties that *aren't in the list so far.* Since the first part of the list, containing the existing objects, is assumed to "exhaust the ontology of concrete objects that people like Russell, Quine, Frege, and most of us find acceptable," the new right-hand list can be thought of as describing *nonexistent* objects, of which there will be "a *lot* more."

Two principles summarize the list making: No two objects in the whole list have the same nuclear properties, and for each set there is some object that has just these properties.

A logically "complete" object is a normal object, one concerning which you can always say whether it has a particular nuclear property or not. Nonexistent objects may, on the other hand, be "incomplete," indeterminate. That golden mountain, which is just golden and a mountain, does not respond to questions of location, for example.

We may surely suspect that that is because it doesn't exist; any existent mountain has latitude and longitude. On the other hand, this notorious mountain may be "existent"—recall that that was Meinong's explanation to Russell for why we sometimes, albeit imprecisely, say that nonexistent objects exist. In Parson's terms Meinong's assertion gets a precise meaning: Existence in the strong sense is an extranuclear predicate[58] and this individual mountain does *not* have that property. But there might also be a "watered-down" existence, which is a nuclear property. A (nuclearly) existent golden mountain is one to which existence is *attributed* as a predicate, as when some prospector fervently believes that "thar's gold in them thar mountains—a whole mountain of gold." Nuclear existence belongs to entities we merely entertain, to nonexistent objects.

The motive for Parson's revival of Meinongian nonexistence was to challenge the "Russellian rut," the widespread, normal, positive belief within the philosophical profession that there are no nonexistent objects,[59] since the price paid is high: Some people, at least, do think they are making a genuine reference when they speak of Pegasus and a genuine predication when they say he is winged. Parsons wants to preserve everything that is said in orthodox logic about existent objects—to maintain what Russell praised as a "robust sense of reality" and Meinong decried as "the prejudice in favor of the actual."[60] But then he also wants his theory to take "a more libertine view." It would permit a vision of the unreal but "reduce to" the orthodox theory when applied to real objects. The chief application of this libertine theory will be fictions, and also, oddly enough, theology.

Is this revived Meinong still Meinong? Well, he's a bit of a zombie, since his vivid notions about the objects of thought and the kinds of Being are gone. On the other hand, it has been lucidly shown that his narrower theory of existence and nonexistence does not spawn an unregimentable rabble of unreal objects, that his attribution of a sort of existence to some of these objects is not self-contradictory, and that these objects do not fail to have a definite identity.[61]

What matters more to me, however, is that a question hangs over both the old and the new theories of nonexistence. Is this nonexistence vital enough to account for the life of the imagination as expressed in fictions? Is there not, as I suggested at the beginning of the section, something backhanded, I would almost say, self-countermanding, about it? Yes, there is, and for that reason good faith fiction will have to be looked at in the following sections from two perspectives. One is that of the sober theories struggling to qualify unreality, the other is—well, different.

6. LYING AND FICTION: FORMAL THEORY AND HUMAN EXPERIENCE

There is a way of understanding lies that makes them fictions; there is a way of understanding fictions that makes them lies. We needn't subscribe to either way to see that fictions and lies should be treated in close proximity.

(a) I will say something about lying first, because lies, although often spawned by the murkiest of motives, throw in their intelligible aspect more light on fiction than fiction throws on them. Two preliminary points: To come at fiction from lies is, of course, to focus on verbal fiction.[62] And to consider lies even semiformally is to bypass what most of us, in life as in study, regard as the chief question about them: How, when, and why are they bad? When Meinong comes to treat "The Lie" he says:

> There is an understandable reluctance to be overcome before we can bring our-
> selves to make an investigation of the lie in immediate connection with our state-
> ments directed at art. By adopting that sequence, we are according recognition to
> a certain affinity between a human activity that stands very high and one that
> stands very low. But it is just a part of the mysteriousness of human nature that
> high and low in it can dwell together in such close proximity. Anyway, facts are
> facts.[63]

Meinong's theory of lying follows directly from his Theory of Objects, which allows him to make a distinction between the objective that a liar has in thought, an intelligible judgment, and his attitude toward it, which is that of nonbelief. "What the liar really thinks remains very much an open question," but his objective is not empty "subjectively meaningless" language. This view is put forcefully by Nietzsche when he says that "the appreciation of what is factual . . . has been greatest exactly among liars":[64] The ideal lie, so to speak, is not told by befuddled but by—narrowly—clear-headed people.

It is thus almost universally agreed that what defines a lie and distinguishes it from the fictions of verbal art is the will to deceive, the intention to mislead in words.[65] If fictions are feignings of the imagination, lies are feignings of the will, with these important qualifications: Just as fictions *might* be said to depend on a sort of intended deception, so some lies *do* involve the imagination, while some lies *may not* be deceptions in the ordinary way.

To this last class belongs that much cited "lie in the soul" which Socrates singles out as most hateful, the lie in the soul of which the uttered lie is only an image. The inner lie "might be called the lie that is truly a lie—the ignorance in the soul [concerning beings] of someone subjected to falsity." The words "lie" (meaning verbal deception) and "falsity" (meaning both logical fallacy and fakery) are the same in Greek, *pseudos*, and that nicely supports Socrates' identification of lying and ignorance as the self-subjection to falsity.[66] Socrates is saying, in the extremist way he adopts when truth is at issue, that ignorance (and the error that goes with it) is a sort of *self*-deception—for he names no other culprit. Self-deception is a variant of deception that is notoriously problematic—for how can we be deceiver and deceived at once, in view of the circumstance noted above, that a liar must know something of the truth to lie effectively?[67] What Socrates means is, I think, that we are responsible to ourselves not for knowing truth (which may be beyond human ability) but for turning inertly false opinions into search-inducing perplexities. Self-deception is the antithesis of self-knowledge, which to Socrates is the beginning of virtue. Thus the lie in the soul is a case not of active self-deceit but of passive acceptance, which is, however, not the state a human being *really* longs for.[68] Moreover, if the spoken lie is only a verbal image, a "phantom" *(eidolon)*, extruded from the self-deceived soul, then a good deal of public lying may in turn not be so much actively deceitful as passively clueless.

What the Platonic passage on "the lie in the soul" does in this context is to focus attention on the elements of actual, practical lying I am about to enumerate, without any claim about their necessary psychological order. There is in the prospective liar, first, a thought-objective neutrally held in mind, a mental piece of ignorance (as Socrates says) or of truth (as Nietzsche claims). There is next, depending on the case in point, a passive willingness by the liar to propagate some accepted ignorance or a determined will to instill some known falsehood. Then the deed is done; the lie is uttered. And finally the article of nescience or the untruth is lodged in the mind of the receptive listener. If the first element named were also first in the psychological genesis of the lie one could call it the last moment of innocence. The next stage, which is surely often simultaneous or even earlier than the first, is the stage of intention in the ordinary sense of the word; the liar has a motive in mind, usually something selfish, and intends to deceive to get his way; here is the still reversible inception of culpability. And finally the deed is irrevocably done, the lie is uttered, and seeks its target. It seems to be an assertion the listener is intended to believe, but it may have hidden within it also some pressure for the listener to do something the liar wants done.[69] Lying is a complex act of speech, and *part* of its effectiveness as a lie is that the person meant to be deceived cannot parse out the willed intention from the thought intention, that is, the selfish motive from the neutral "objective" (using Meinong's term for a proposition in thought; p. 88).

The deleterious effects of lying are generally agreed to extend over both the liar and lied to (though affecting them differently, corrupting the moral fabric of the one and blinding the judgment of the other). They are, as I said, not so much the point here as is that morally neutral objective without which lying cannot get a purchase on a matter, so to speak. What is the anatomy of a lie from the point of view of this objective? How do we train our mind on the matter of a lie? Those brutally noble horses, the Houyhnhnms, whom that "gentle yahoo," Gulliver, is privileged to serve, pretend not to comprehend lying (nor doubting or not believing). His master thinks that it would be an abuse of speech, one that undermines its very purpose, "*if anyone said the thing which was not.*" So he really understands perfectly its propositional objective, if not its willful motive: Lying is *intentionally* saying *the thing which is not.*[70] And that can be achieved in a number of versions.

(b) The ways of negating a proposition or the sentence that expresses it seem to me a guide to these versions.[71] There were, recall, naturally three (p. 35). (1) Negate the whole sentence: not (S is P); (2) negate the predicate: (S is not-P); (3) negate the copula: (S is-not P). Three related types of lie can be uttered:

(1) The liar says that not (S is P). This is the false denial of an objective, like an accusation: "Did you cut down the cherry tree?" "No, I did not do it." The children I know have learned to plead not guilty, to lie in this negating fashion first, even before asserting such false positives as: "Did you go to the potty?" "Oh, yes" (with angelic eye batting).

(2) The liar says that (S is not-P). This is the false denial of an object's being-so, and therefore the Houyhnhnm's case of saying the thing which is not, by negating the property that belongs to its objecthood: and then perhaps—again the corresponding false positive—attributing to it the contrary property. The horse's own example is: "I am led to believe a thing *black* when it is *white*, and *short* when it is *long*."

(3) The liar says that (S is-not P). He willfully disjoins subject and predicate altogether—they are not to be in the normal coupling achieved by the copula; the link or medium is in itself denied. Negation has settled in the center of the sentence; subject and predicate are simply not to be put together in the listener's mind. A poignant example comes from the *Iliad*.[72] His goddess-mother has told Achilles early on, not for the first time, that it is his fate to be short-lived. He sits out the battle, angry over an insult offered him by his king. As things come to a climax Patroclus, his intimate, begs him to return to the battle to save the Greeks from being driven into the sea and asks Achilles whether he has heard anything from his mother to keep him away. Achilles answers excitedly: "Patroclus, what have you said! . . . My mistress-mother has *not* declared anything to me from Zeus"— which seems to me to mean: "My mother *is-not* the messenger of death—

don't even connect my mother with such a message." Having declared denial, he goes on to phantasize a scenario that will not come true. I can't frame the false positive that might go with (S is-not P) except as a levering of the whole utterance from fact to fantasy.[73]

So this third form of lie seems to me to be the initial stage of what psychologists call confabulation, the partly unconscious slide into fantasy, the conjuring up of wished-for truths. It is the rejection of the connections of existence in favor of the constructions of the imagination. If—a big if—fictions are indeed well-finished lies, then some lies must be inchoate fictions. Fictions would then be prepared not in "that willing suspension of disbelief for the moment, which constitutes poetic faith,"[74] but rather by a willful suspension of belief, of our ordinary trust that even the painful couplings of existence are preferable to a world built on a false copula. I think, however, that this analysis only holds for what one might call psychogenic fictions: escapes, denials and avoidances, with their stand-in fantasies. I will show my hand by saying that subverting existence seems to me a worthwhile task—but not in this way.

(c) Even those fictions that are the robust productions of lusty poets are, however, similarly accused by Socrates of being shot through with lies.[75] In the earlier books of the dialogue *Republic* he accuses the greatest and most venerable poets, Homer, Hesiod, Aeschylus, of telling terrible falsehoods about the conduct of the gods, whom they represent as scandalous and irrational. And they also show heroes behaving disgracefully. Socrates doesn't so much argue that the truth about the gods and the heroes must be suppressed in his model city for the sake of the children's upbringing as that the poets lie. It is their professional deformation. They deny gods and heroes their proper virtue and dignity and invent horrible or indecently hilarious situations for them. They do it to arouse the pleasurable excitation that representations of human extremities, tragic or comic, violent or laughable, do—as we well know—incite. In adopting a deliberately pedestrian understanding of poetry Socrates may well be purposefully missing the point—but only in order to face poetry with a bald seriousness that its unreflective devotees cannot equal.

In the last book of the *Republic*, Socrates gives much more radical reasons why all works of art, poetry *and* painting, are in their very constitution contemptible—another example of his extremism in pursuit of true Being: For take a bed, he says (recall that it is by now very late at night). There is the Bed that has Being and is divinely made, there are the many beds we sleep in made by a carpenter, and there is the painter's bed, twice removed from *the* Bed and not so good for sleeping in. Here Socrates is probably having fun—not so when it comes to the poets and their truthless, third-hand representations of good and evil.

There's no freshman has ever loved a story who doesn't see what's wrong here: Socrates is perversely representing the poets as telling falsehoods about real beings, while he ought to know perfectly well that the poets speak truths about fictional beings. I think that Socrates would reply (and to reply to such freshmen would be the one reason he might leave his Elysian Fields): "If the gods were really just the invention of the poets—*euphemein!* speak reverently!— so much the more ought they to make them wholly good. As for Truth, it just isn't accessible to a craft that works in the third degree of decline from true Being. Poets and painters are not just liars who knowingly say the thing that is not instead of the thing that *is*, they are (what is far worse) ignoramuses who do not even begin to know the nature of the things which they appear to imitate." I am imagining Socrates as responding recalcitrantly so as to reinforce the radicalness of his understanding.

The issue for him was never the correct imitation *(mimesis)* of a sensory object in the sensory mode, but the truthful presentation of an object in its nonsensory Being. Imitative works of art tend, he thinks, by the very reason of their imitative, re-presentative character, to decline into Nonbeing—in two ways: As copies they are *not,* and are in fact less than, their originals, and as products of makers who have never troubled themselves to catch sight of the Ideas, they are *false* and are, in fact, deceptive copies.

The counterarguments for this view of the arts can go off in opposite directions: There is an old, Neoplatonic correction of Socrates' theory which claims that works of art do *directly* imitate intelligible Being, the Ideas themselves. And then there is the prevailing esthetic theory of more recent modernity which denies that art is in fact imitative and that the copy theory of art is even intelligible. There is, of course, also the straightforward "creative" theory that makes poetry quite unabashedly a doubling of the visible world: "Poetry is a counterfeit creation and makes things that are not, as though they were."[76]

(d) And here I return to nonexistence. For while some logical-minded critics save works of art from Nonbeing—though probably quite unintentionally—by denying that they are mimetic, some literarily inclined logicians are at work worrying—quite insistently—about the kind of nonexistence that the inhabitants, particularly of books, might possess.[77]

Of the many ways logician-critics grapple with the fact that sober sense tells them simultaneously that fictive beings are nonexistent and that people do speak truly and falsely about them, two extreme positions are not very helpful to that robust sense of the unreal lovers of fiction are proud of possessing. One is Russell's simple denial of any kind of existence: "whoever juggles [with the "robust sense of reality" vital to logicians] by pretending that Hamlet has another kind of reality does a disservice to thought."[78] And he proceeds to show how the subject of the (true or false) predicate can be paraphrased away altogether and that propositions about fictions are simply false. The other way of dealing with the problem, often pursued by postmodern critics, needs no such logical subterfuge. The fictional fabric, the text, is thought of as hermeti-

cally sealed from the outside and as self-referential, that is, as being about
nothing but itself as text—concerned only with the literary devices of which
it consists and which are to be knowledgeably appreciated. This approach
solves all the problems and dissolves all significance—or at least what one
might call "first-order significance," meaning the light that the word casts on
the real world.[79] Neither of these kinds of theory need really face the question:
In what realm do fictions live?

Parsons, on the other hand, gives a strong answer to the question by applying his theory to fictions. It is: fictions live in the realm of Meinongian objects.[80] Recall that objects have nuclear predicates: "Sherlock Holmes is a de-
tective who lives at 221B Baker Street." They also have extranuclear
predicates: "Holmes doesn't exist and he is fictional" (p. 91). We normally
accept the extranuclear properties and concentrate our mistrust on the nuclear
predication. Then the theory says that fictional objects have just those nuclear
properties that can be gotten out of the text: Sherlock Holmes is the object
who has those nuclear properties that Holmes has in the Conan Doyle stories.
We are talking about an *object* here: the object-Holmes has these properties
just if the story-Holmes has those predicates. Some objects in fiction are "native" to these stories: Holmes himself is "created" by the story. Others are
"immigrant": London and Baker Street are, Parsons thinks, real objects that
have been admitted into the story's territory. The theory covers native objects
only.[81]

In interpreting a fiction it is often necessary to draw out the inexplicit but
reliably true circumstances that the literal text entails. The logical counterpart
of this expanded story is called "the maximal account," the collection of all
the mental extrapolations the reader can legitimately make. These are, practically speaking, neither all the logical entailments (some of which are just
vapid), nor just the most obvious ones; exactly how the maximal account is
established is an unsettled problem. But on the hypothesis that we do keep
some such account as we read, it is clear that fictional objects will be typically
very incomplete. This incompleteness is usually not what is called "radical,"
meaning that the object, say a person, is in principle not responsive to our
question "Are you p or not-p?" because any human being has the unitary
property of not-having-p-and-not-having-non-p, say "commensurability."
Fictional people, on the other hand, are just incompletely described, and we
are in ignorance of the name of Sherlock Holmes's mother only because
Conan Doyle didn't tell us; he does tell us about Mycroft, Holmes's brother.[82]
This kind of incompleteness is, I think, the chief incitement to the active use
of the imagination that verbally fictional objects possess.

There are numerous other theories concerning the mode of being of fictions.[83] One of these, that of Lamarque, means to straddle the logician's distrust of the existence of fictions and the humanist critic's faith—under severe
postmodernist attack—that fictions are of indispensable value in helping us to
engage with issues that matter in the real world. The theory concedes to the

"eliminationist" logicians that when we, speaking from the external perspective of the real world, name a fictional character, we can refer only to the
sense, that is, the description and predicates of the character established by
the text, not to particular persons. But as critics, we are allowed enough
"imaginative involvement" to refer to the character as if the person were actual, as if we were in the story and had the internal perspective of a fellow
character for whom the name had a *denotation,* a definite reference. Or at least
we can pretend to be on the inside.[84] Thus nonexistence becomes perspectival:
Within the novel the characters exist and without they become objects by pretense.

Pretense and make-believe are the chief explanatory principles in the non-
objective mode. The question this approach poses is not how the behavior of
nonexistent objects is to be explained but how they manage to come on the
scene to begin with, what *we* cognitively do to cooperate in fiction making.[85] A
strong make-believe theory has been advanced by Currie, who regards making
believe as one of our fundamental "propositional attitudes"—in the same
class as are beliefs and desires. Make-believe, he claims, is a well-known notion, affirmed by folk psychology, though people don't usually think of it so
much as a mode of entertaining propositions as a way of picturing mental images. But that is a mistake: "What distinguishes the reading of fiction from
the reading of nonfiction is not the activity of the imagination but the attitude
we adopt toward the content of what we read: make-believe in the one case,
belief in the other."

So both the author's intention and the reader's attitude are what characterizes fiction, and the burden of its enigmas is thrown on the "stubbornly irre-
ducible" notion of make-believe. Fictional objects have been replaced by
propositions entertained in that mode.

∞   ∞   ∞

(e) The theories here outlined may mark out the limits of respectability. But
how can they satisfy a reader—and our name is still legion—who lives by and
through the fictions of the imagination? So let me try a little disreputableness,
as Quine would say—after having stated what seems to me unsatisfying about
the theories proposed.

I will begin with one of the last-mentioned theories, that the making and
receiving of a fiction is a form of pretending. It seems right to me that initially
a certain consciously willing receptivity is part of the adult experience of fiction, but I would not call it "adopting an attitude," and certainly not a propositional attitude. Logician-critics like to speak of adopting attitudes—mostly
Anglo-Saxon attitudes. In this case the pretending attitude must mean that we
self-consciously behave to ourselves as if we believed assertions that we know
are not meant to be true. But it seems to me that being absorbed into a fiction,
living in its landscapes and with its people, is not well described as a form of

pretense—not on the reader's or viewer's part and so much the less on the poet's or painter's part.

It is rather a temporary form of self-and-reality forgetfulness, often attended with a sense of heightened truth, in which the sentences of the work are the instigators of a lot of nonpropositional experience. Children, to be sure, play "Let's pretend," but that is usually when the game requires that roles be assigned, and I'd bet that the mover of the pretense doesn't often assign, say, the submissive role to herself; in participating in a novel, on the other hand, we may well surrender ourselves to the experiences of the underdog.

Next, the external-internal theory seems to me to have the advantage of noticing that participation in fiction *is* somewhat split-minded. As commenting critics we stay outside the world of a book and talk *about* it, savoring it as connoisseurs; as actual readers we join that world—in a manner of speaking, for we are not, after all, inside the book in the sense of being a fellow citizen of the realm, together with the other fictions.

What it is like to be inside a fiction is a question children's books are most apt to have the courage to ask and the imagination to answer, books like Michael Ende's *Endless Story,* which not only includes within itself the rite of passage from the world of reality to the world of the imagination but even teaches that the soundness of the latter is the condition for the health of the former. But neither this tale nor any scholarly theory I know of really explains how we get on a denoting basis with fictions. Therefore, while it seems true enough that we sometimes talk about a book and sometimes as if we were within it, the latter mode remains an enigma.

Now I'll go back to Russell and Socrates who, curiously enough, ask, at least in one important respect, to be mentioned in the same breath, since both say that fictions are *false.* For Russell this is just flatly the case: no x exists such as to make a fictive description true of anything, so that propositions of this sort are simply false. Socrates says that poets lie insofar as what they say about gods and heroes doesn't apply to them, and so their accounts are also simply false. What Russell says he means, flatly and irremediably, and therefore he must be flatly and irremediably wrong: It cannot be the case that what is said about and within fictions is false—unless one maintains that logically accurate speech has *no* correspondence with humanly normal speech. For we say both that it is true and that it is true to life that Natasha Rostov marries Pierre Bezuhov, and we want to keep on saying just that.

What Socrates says he means, at first, only contingently: poets might be made to tell the truth. But later on in the *Republic* he means something much less remediable: poetry and painting are in their nature twice removed from truth. On the other hand, the Platonic dialogues are shot through with poetry that appears at significant junctures and is contributed by Socrates himself: the myths that round out the argument and give it its cosmic place. So it ought not to be surprising that the understanding of poetry which underlies so philosophical a use of it can also be made useful for the salvation of truth-in-fiction. This will be the very same theory that above showed poetry to be inferior to philosophy, the mimetic theory itself.[86]

But first I want to review the most immediately promising of all the theories considered above: Meinong's nonexistent objects, particularly in Parsons's application to fiction. It seems to me nonetheless unsatisfying in three particulars.

1. Incompleteness. On the face of it, one of the reassuring aspects of that theory is that it allows a sharp distinction between real and fictional objects. What exists, in the logically acceptable way, that is, spatiotemporally, is complete; in principle it either possesses any property you can think of asking about or it doesn't. Not so fictions; there are a lot of properties in respect to which they are indeterminate. But in really real life, I think, completeness is not an invariable feature of objects, and I am not even thinking of such hard-edged indeterminacies as those that the electrons of quantum physics display under observation. As our biological nature is elusive (as anyone who has gone to a doctor with a nonstandard ailment knows), so our souls are in part opaque even to ourselves. Why else would it be so hard to follow the Socratic injunction to "Know Thyself"? And if there are others who think they can read us, personally or professionally, like an open book, they are often reading into us psychic schemata out of some other book. So it is by no means obvious that the existent objects called human beings are really logically complete; they may even be "radically" incomplete (p. 98).

On the other hand, fictions are less incomplete than the theory allows. Fictions cast loose from the literal text and even from the "maximal account," the clearly articulable "presuppositional implications" and entailments of that text. For example, from the fact that we find Natasha as Pierre's wife in the first part of the epilogue, the peace-time part of *War and Peace*, that glory of novelistic fiction, we can indeed infer that there was an institution of marriage in the Russia of 1820. But there are multitudes of nontrivial questions we can answer about her although the answer is not presupposed or entailed by the text—yet the text tells us, as surely as if it said so. For example: Has Natasha Rostov a high-bridged nose? Never, though Tolstoy is silent on the matter. He does say that she has broadened out after marriage, so she's a little dumpy, but does she have thick ankles? Unthinkable. She's given up singing, we're told, except for special occasions; is her voice still that former soprano of "virginal purity"? No, it's a little more like a contralto. In a memorable moment, in days of her girlhood, this young Frenchified aristocrat showed in the untaught knowledge of the peasant dance that she has the inimitable, unteachable Russian spirit; is it still in her? If anyone is to find out, it'll be the children in the nursery.

The assurance that the above is not an arbitrary or antic exercise comes from the fact that many a companionable, semiserious argument can arise among friends about the beyond- and afterlife of fictional characters, and what one can argue about with others is never entirely "subjective." In fact, some authors themselves enter with pleased promptitude into these imaginative posttextual completions of their creatures; Tolstoy, I'm sure, would have been among them. Moreover, such curious speculations have always been regarded as possible; Sir Thomas Browne willingly reraises an old sophistic topic in his *Urne-Burial*, comfortably supposing that "What Song the *Syrens* sang, or what name *Achilles* assumed when he hid himself among women, though puzzling Questions are not beyond all conjecture."[87]

2. If the mark of incompleteness doesn't sufficiently stamp fictional objects, what about nonexistence itself? And again, the line between spatio-temporal existence and nonexistence is not quite so distinctly etched as the Theory of Nonexistent Objects would have it; for example, the boundary between life and death is sometimes physically fuzzy and often indeterminate for the composite human being:

> they lost their pride
> And died as men before their bodies died.

But even leaving such ultimate matters aside, a case can be made that nonexistent beings and places attain for us the force of actuality[88] in their vividness, move us as models and attractors, outlive us by millennia, and in a word, impinge on us as if existence were home to them as well. Think only what Achilles was to Alexander or the City on the Hill to the American founding. It may be that totally reality-tethered reason is not quite up to the beings of fiction and that a certain levitation of mind—levity, if you must—is required to let them live. The neat explanation of fictions as bundles of nuclear properties tied on the back of a nonexistent object, on an insubstantial x, may be adequate to some rather flat genre productions, but not to those great fictional beings that are not composed from the outside in but from the inside out—whose descriptive properties are dictated by their inner being.

3. Nonetheless, let it be granted that fictions don't exist in reality as do, say, flesh-and-blood people, in body, space, and time, the naive belief entertained by children often and by adults occasionally notwithstanding. But perhaps there is a realm *between* that reality and nonexistence. What Socrates makes an accusation against fictions, that they are imitations, may turn out to be their saving grace. As imitations, copies, *images*, they have, not by mere definition but by the reader's strong sense of them, *originals*. As we read—at least, many of us—we naturally form images in the visual and auditory imagination, and it is these we view and think about, both while we are absorbed in the text and afterwards. So in a primary sense *this* is the imaginative world in which we invest belief. And yet we take this world with its people and places as a similitude, as an image of something and an emanation from somewhere

beyond the text. To the question "of what, from where?" a first answer might be "of the figures in the author's imagination."

But that cannot be the end of it, since the poets themselves have from Homer on felt themselves to be intermediaries: "Tell me, O Muse, of the man. . . ." So there remains the ultimate enigma: Whence come these images, from what world of originals? It is disreputable enough to raise the question, and it would be foolhardy to attempt an answer. In any case the point here is that as images, fictions live in a quasi-space and a quasi-time ("Once upon a time in the land of . . ."), and therefore they might well be said to have their being outside of the realm defined by existence and nonexistence (though by a supererogatory grace image-fictions do sometimes in fact obtain existence, either by being intentionally imitated or by being serendipitously instantiated). Fictions inhabit a realm to which the compounded terms Being-and-Nonbeing, Presence-and-Absence, apply. An image is an object that both *is* and *is not* what it re-presents; it makes vividly present what is in very truth absent. Nonexistent objects are, for all the ingenious attempts to give them the status required to preserve ordinary talk about fiction, *not* existent when push comes to shove, and thus *negations* of existence. But images, as formations *melding* Being and Nonbeing, as objects in which are merged the presence and absence of the being they represent, seem to me *somehow* actual.[89] What these intimations leave behind is a critical residue: As explanations of fictions, nonexistent objects seem to be conceptions that inquiring reason requires us to catch but that imaginative experience does not oblige us to keep. For fictions attain an actuality of which nonexistents are incapable.

7. IS NONEXISTENCE A PREDICATE? FINAL QUESTIONS

What makes nonexistence so problematic? It is that on the one hand it seems to be the logical complement of existence and therefore within the universe of discourse, and on the other it is precisely outside everything that can be denoted. Another way to put the difficulty is this: If existence is a predicate, then so is nonexistence, and if a predicate adds a property to a subject's description, then so does nonexistence.[90] So a final question has to be "Is existence a predicate?" and if the answer is yes, then "What property does nonexistence add to a subject?"

The claim that existence is indeed a property appears to come to the fore as theologically crucial in Anselm's so-called ontological proof of the existence of God. Descartes, giving a concise though unsubtle version of the proof, supports the claim, while Kant denies it in order to dispose of the proof. In this past century, as a consequence of Russell's ejection of existence from inside the propositional function, the question regained vitality as a logical rather than a theological issue; indeed, when Parsons takes up the ontological proof, his purpose is to try out the neo-Meinongian theory of objects on God.[91]

(a) Kant's rejection of existence as a predicate seems to me the most interesting of the antipredicate arguments because he has so clear a conception of what existence and nonexistence in fact are. In a famous sentence from the *Critique of Pure Reason* he says that "A hundred actual thalers do not contain the least bit more than a hundred possible ones." Existence adds nothing to the complete descriptive concept of the object, and presumably, nonexistence can take nothing away. For existence is not a "real" predicate, an actual determination of the subject; it is a merely "logical" predicate that has no content. What those who treat existence as a real predicate have done is to attribute *reality* to the subject to begin with and then to repeat it as *existence* in the predicate as if that did anything but repeat the assumption.[92] What existence is in truth is a *position*, and what position is Kant had set out in his earlier essay on the only possible proof of God's existence (p. 176). It is a "completely simple" concept and is "identical with that of Being in general." Something can be posited relatively, and then the Being is just that of our usual copula "is," which relates predicates to subjects in many possible ways. "But if it is not merely this relation but the thing in and for itself that is being contemplated, then this Being is no more or less than Existence *(Dasein)*." There is no way to develop this concept further except to note that it is not to be confused with those relations that mark things and can describe possible but not real beings.[93]

Thus (1) its existence is divorced from the attributes of the thing, and (2) it is made entirely a matter of human positing. The only way to get to existence is to go beyond the concept of the thing to perception in the context of empirical laws. Objects of pure thought are therefore outside any proof of existence. Here is set aside the very argument Descartes had mounted: that there manifestly is "a Supreme Being, to whose essence alone existence pertains" because he, Descartes, has within himself ideas of infinity and perfection that could not possibly proceed from himself alone.[94] Kant's understanding of existence will not allow even one unique transcendent being whose essence includes existence. In fact in this removal of existence from the nature of any being Kant is so radical as to do more than foreshadow Russell—in the essay he actually speaks his language:

> It is thus not a completely correct expression to say: A sea-unicorn [narwhal] is an existent animal, but the reverse: to a certain existent sea-animal belong the predicates which I think of as being together in a unicorn.

There follows an observation on the occasional incorrectness of ordinary language, more accommodating in spirit, yet Russellian in its import.

(b) Now back to the other side. All the arguments, theological or secular, anonymously given or attributed, might or do take their departure from Anselm's ontological proof of God's existence. The proof is "ontological," that is to say, it depends on "an account of Being," insofar as it elicits God's existence from the nature of his Being, or rather, from our thought of it.

This most astounding feat of reason, which continues to ensnare intellectually even those young students who are indifferent to it theologically, is very brief—three short chapters, and as Hartshorne points out, in gist three sentences.[95] Anselm argues as follows: At first he seems to say, as did Descartes in that form of his argument cited above, that existence is a perfection, lacking which God would not be the maximally perfect being we conceive him to be. The common and obvious objection to this claim is that stated by Kant: Existence is not one among other predicates or attributes, whether they are perfections or not; existent objects are not a special kind of object (while true predicates do indeed distinguish kinds). I will say below whether the Kantian, the common argument seems to me true.

But Anselm has a second argument, much subtler than the first. There are two presuppositions that underlie either argument: (1) "It is one thing for an object to be in the understanding, and another to understand that the object exists" (we see here the prototype of the Meinongian object, p. 88). (2) God is in our understanding as maximal, as "a being than which nothing greater can be conceived"; the attributes that God has are whatever it is better to be than not to be, and they are such as can have a maximum (hence they are not, for instance, magnitudes of mathematics). The distinction made in the first presupposition is in the major tradition of the West allied to the duality of essence and existence, the distinction of *what* from *that*. The second assumption seems to me to be justified by Anselm's announcement that he does not understand so as to have faith but he has faith so that he may understand; for part of that antecedent faith must be some intimations of the grandeur of God.

Here, then, is the second argument itself: It is possible to conceive a being that *cannot* be conceived *not* to exist, and this being is greater than one that *can* be conceived *not* to exist. So if that being than which nothing greater can be conceived can in addition be conceived not to exist, it is not the being originally conceived, for it is less than the being which was conceived as having to exist. So the two conceptions contradict each other and the first must prevail—if it is indeed God who is being conceived.

The gist is this: The being whose nonexistence is *in*conceivable is even greater than the one that is equally great in other respects but whose nonexistence *is* conceivable. Or, even more briefly: of two existent beings, the one that does not exist contingently is the greater. Thus we have contingency and noncontingency at issue as predicates, and *not* primarily existence. God is proved to exist because the *possibility* of his nonexistence is inconceivable, or, even briefer, his nonexistence is unthinkable and impossible.

An existence proof in theology cannot be like such a proof in mathematics, where we often demonstrate the existence of an object or relation by exhibiting, that is, constructing it. What Anselm has shown us is not directly God existing, but that we must *conceive* him as existing—if we are willing to conceive him at all and moreover willing to conceive him as a maximum of conceivability. In other words: Neither Anselm nor anyone can directly demonstrate existence, but only *that* we must believe in it and *why*.

What, however, does unthinkable nonexistence mean? I think that to try to wrap one's mind around this ghostly pile of negatives is to come under the vexing spell of Anselm's argument. We are familiar enough with things whose existence is impossible (like round squares or perfect happiness) or whose nonexistence is only too possible (like gold mountains or unicorns). But to think that an object of thought so conceived that nothing greater than it is conceivable cannot be nonexistent—that requires a riot of negative takes: a being which by reason of *not* being exceeded by anything *cannot* be conceived as *not* existing.

So what is required of us in *Proslogion* III is this: (1) We are able to exercise a sort of borderline intuition, a negative intuition, to envision a negatively delineated maximal being—negatively delineated because that absolves us from facing God as a positive, definite bound. (2) We now attach to this semi-intuited being shape, a deliberate logical condition, a mental disposition: our *in*capacity to conceive its nonexistence—being careful not to collapse the two negatives into a brute premature positive, namely the necessary conception of existence, or worse, the conception of a necessary existence; thus the proof continues to be about how *our* conceptual capacity reaches God; Anselm's Latin puts the possibility with the thought, not with the object: *potest cogitari non esse*. (3) We then compare the above conception with a second one, that of a being whose nonexistence we *can* conceive, and find that the first is greater, since the mind refused the thought of its possible nonexistence and so removed a negative attribute, a diminution: contingency. (4) Hence the second conception of a maximal being irreconcilably contradicts the first one and must be rejected as being the lesser. (5) Therefore, now phrasing the conclusion positively, the God who is conceived as exceeding everything is a being, and the only being, that *must* exist.

If we are persuaded that the being we had in mind is such that we cannot conceive of its possible nonexistence, then we seem to have proved that God must exist *without the presupposition that his existence belongs* to our conception of him, that is to say, *to his essence*. It appears to have been accomplished through the middle term of noncontingency: What cannot not exist must (1) of necessity (2) exist, where existence plays, in Hartshorne's words, a "qualitatively neutral" role.

However that question is settled, the proof is a brilliant play with negation and nonexistence: The impossibility of thinking a nonexistence is turned into the necessity of thinking a being as existent. By a bastard kind of thinking—the type characteristic of negation—we manage to state what it is impossible to intend in thought. And that intention of ours also happens to be a nonexistent object—a definite no-thing—which we hold in mind. And suddenly these—the thought and what it intends—flip into positives: the necessity of thinking an existent God. Whoever is disposed to ponder the mind's dealings with logical naysaying should ponder Anselm's intricate version of the *via negativa*.

Leaving behind the unique case of God's existence, be it proved from his essence or his necessity, there remains the general secular question whether existence is a predicate: Is a being made more than it was by also achieving existence and correspondingly less by falling into nonexistence? "More or less than it was" must not be taken to mean "increased or diminished by the mere addition of being there or by being posited as being there," which would be the logical error of transition into a different genus *(metabasis eis allo genos)*: We asked about the descriptive nature of a thing and got an answer in terms of its position in the world. What I am inquiring about is whether an existing thing is intrinsically different from a nonexisting thing.—Or is it perhaps even doubly different because it differs once from the thing that neither has nor doesn't have existence—which as far as I can see can only be a subsistence, an object of thought (or a ghost)—and in addition must be measured by a double distance from the thing that has negative existence?

It seems to me such reckonings are not as absurd as they might at first seem. I think that beings, and certainly human beings, *are* intrinsically qualified by existence: When they come into existence they not only gain in the vivacity of the impressions they can make on other existences and in the increased completeness of their incidental features. They also gain the negative capacity for nonexistence, that is, for that specific individual nonbeing called mortality, which accounts in life for being insufficiently there and in death for not being there at all—though once dead, mortals achieve as well the nonexistence attributed to fictional objects, especially at memorial services. All in all, I think existence does impinge on the essence of beings, albeit in a way difficult to discern by reason, though manifest enough to our sensibility.

∞   ∞   ∞

In the beginning of this chapter I pointed out that the problem of Nonexistence is a modern one, which arose when Nonexistence, Not-being-here-and-now, had superseded Nonbeing, the relative opposite of Being simply. It is time now to recall this Nonbeing and the questions it once spawned, questions that are sometimes dormant but never dead.

NOTES

1. See Parsons, 6 n. 7.
2. Quine 1953, 4.

3. Linsky, ix; Parsons, 4.

4. Russell 1905c, 109 f.

5. See "The Second Power of Questions" in Brann 1992, 174; also 402.

6. I found this quotation on the front page of Stebbing.

7. Some authors go overboard: They don't so much rethink as dismiss nonexistence. Thus Ogden and Richards, 291 ff.: Negative facts, that is, denials of facts refer, as they say, to complex referents belonging to an "order," such as the order of historical events. One may then say that there are no nonexistent events or negative facts, but merely cases of referents incorrectly assigned to orders other than the one to which they have been allocated by their referring symbol. For example, a historian might mistakenly say: "Charles I died in his bed." This referring symbol places its referent in *"another order than that of historical events."* Later historians find the "place" assigned to this referent filled by another referent: "Charles I died on the scaffold."

The authors consider negative facts as an eradicable species of original sin whose elimination will return us to the peaceable kingdom (295). This defining away of sin, however, invites questions such as these: To what order, then, does the now misnamed referent belong?—for it *is* said to belong to *"another order."* Is there an order of displaced referents? If there is, has nonexistence not been hidden away rather than eliminated? If there isn't, what does it mean in such cases to be a referent, the terminus of a reference?

8. See Rosen 1980, 104.

9. The chief such theory is the one revived by Franz Brentano, the teacher of Meinong who made use of it in his theory (p. 87).

10. A sentence is the linguistic body of the proposition that can be abstracted from it. Different sentences may express the same proposition, which remains identical across different rhetorical versions and different languages. A statement is often defined as an asserted proposition. It is, of course, a matter of dispute whether translations can *in fact* preserve propositions; propositions may be elusively *ideal* entities.

11. Russell 1919, 170.

12. The term "negative existentials" is Cartwright's, 629.

13. The debt language analysis owes to Hume's understanding of existence is obliquely acknowledged by that golden mountain, which as an example of a factually nonexistent but not logically impossible object turns up in almost all texts on the issue at hand. To be sure, the mountain occurs in *An Enquiry Concerning Human Understanding* (sec. 2), whereas the explicit discussion of existence comes in the *Treatise of Human Nature* (bk. I, pt. II, vi). Here Hume says that the idea of this object's existence is the *same* with the idea of the object and makes no addition to it—at least an *initiating* thought for the logical treatment of existence.

14. Carroll 1865, "The Lion and the Unicorn," 287.

15. The *Oxford English Dictionary* entry finds this late appearance of the verb "to exist" remarkable; the term does not yet occur in Cooper's Latin-English dictionary of 1565.

Stebbing, 160: "We use the *expression* 'are unreal' to express the *denial of existence*, not to assert a *special mode of existence*. In an analogous manner, we use the expression 'are real' to assert an *affirmation of existence*."

16. *Res*, thing, has interesting specifications. *Res* is one of the medieval transcen-

dentals, the concepts that apply to all entities *as* beings. Thomas Aquinas makes explicit a distinction between *res rationis* and *res realis*, a thing existing in the mind only and one existing outside, often corporeally, a really real thing in the common understanding. *Res* is not always included in the medieval list (which consists, minimally, of *unum, verum, bonum*) on the plea that "thing" is reducible to "entity" (Latin for "beingness") and adds nothing to being (see Lotz 240; Wallace 91 f.).

I wonder if "thing," especially "real thing," took off into ordinary language as a focus for all that matters just because it was pushed off the list of transcendentals—the more so since that particular concrete individual for which "thing" is now often used as a term had no proper name in the philosophical tradition from which the notion comes; Aristotle coined *tode ti*, "this some[thing]."

Part of Kant's second Copernican revolution is the flipping of the meaning of "thing." What was before the stably intelligible or the solidly immattered entity opposed to mere appearance now becomes the empty conceptual structure within which appearance turns into an object of experience: The concept that "represents a priori this empirical content of appearances is the concept of a *thing* in general" (Kant 1781, 748). And reality is now just one of the abstract categories entering into the thing structure.

17. Russell 1905a, 98. The theory of existence I have set out for the Theory of Descriptions differs from the one discernible from Symbolic Logic (note 27). The foundational paper here referred to was first published in July 1905; "On Denoting" in October. A little earlier he had written that "for my part, inspection would lead to the conclusion that . . . only those objects exist which have to particular parts of space and time the relation of *occupying* them" (Russell 1904, 29).

Parsons points out that individual, spatiotemporal existence indeed enters the Theory of Descriptions, but as an independent assumption (3 n. 3). The assumption behind the theory that peeks through here is the famous distinction Russell made between knowledge by acquaintance and knowledge by description. The former requires things to be directly present to the sense. See p. 84 for further explication of the connection.

Incidentally, the distinction is not original with Russell but comes from John Grote's *Exploratio Philosophica* (London 1865, 60): "Our knowledge may be contemplated in either of two ways. . . . That is, we may either use language thus: we *know* a thing, a man, etc.; or we may use it thus: we know such and such things *about* the thing, the man, etc." Grote calls the first *acquaintance*; it is knowledge by presentation to the senses or representation by a picture, while the other is more intellectual and comes through propositions that embody concepts. Both German and French distinguish the two types: *kennen* and *connaître* versus *wissen* and *savoir*. I found this Grote quotation in James, 147.

Quine criticizes the restriction of existence to objects actualized in space-time: "If Pegasus existed he would indeed be in space and time, but only because the word 'Pegasus' has spatio-temporal connotation and not because 'exist' has spatio-temporal connotations." He says that philosophers who limit the word "existence" to actuality—Quine uses actuality as a synonym of reality—do this in order to preserve an illusion of ontological agreement with "us who repudiate the rest of his bloated universe" (Quine 1953, 3 n. 1). He is referring to Meinong, who will restrict existence to actual, i.e., spatiotemporal objects but will introduce nonexistent objects that have other sorts of being (p. 88). Quine's own ontological commitment is to the empirical sciences and the mathematics involved in the observation of nature, and it is therefore on a level of sophistication beyond the ordinary scope and meaning of existence.

18. Of course, existence so understood is time- and place-affected: Mr. Russell existed from 1872 to 1970 and existed last near Penrhyndeudraeth, but not before and after or ever in Annapolis. Logicians can correct for this affliction by stating that "to exist" means to exist at some time and somewhere.

19. One mark of the difference is that Nonbeing is not countable (p. 141), but non-existences are definitely conceived as having countable plurality. The opposite holds for beings and existents: intelligible beings might be considered as not countable (and ipso facto not addible), since they are each radically unique and countables have to be of the same kind, while *res reales*, real things, are the most countable of entities.

Therefore, when Russell says in the passage quoted just below in the text that "Being belongs to whatever can be counted" he is using a hybrid notion of Being, one that assumes that whatever is one, *unum*, is countable. Or perhaps a better way to put it is that existents are, at this point in Russell's thinking, a subset of all the beings, while Being itself, as a class intension, is a pale reflection of Existence. He soon relinquished these confused conceptions.

20. Russell 1903, 449.

(a) Since Russell here includes mathematicals in Being, this is a good occasion to point out how geometry is traditionally located in at least one tradition, the Platonic one. There the figures of geometry are placed *between* pure Being and real, i.e., sensory, existence, and are apprehended in the quasi-space of the imagination. This is the tradition still carried on by Kant (albeit in a framework in which Being in itself has become unknowable and its attributes have been reduced to categorical functions, while real existence is shaped by the human subject). He establishes two forms of sensibility, located within the subject "between" understanding and sense; one of these forms is spatial and serves for the inscription of geometry and the other is temporal and makes arithmetic possible (Brann 1991, 594 f.; 1999, 72 f.).

(b) Mathematicians do talk of existence, as in "existence proofs." These are called "problems" in elementary mathematics and require a construction, in which the mathematical—most perspicuously, the geometric—object is directly presented to the imagination. Euclid's *Elements* begins with such a construction, that of an equilateral triangle (bk. I, 1). Indirect proofs, called *reductio ad absurdum* proofs, rely on the Law of Excluded Middle (which says "Either A or not-A; there is no middle possibility); these proofs show that it is impossible that the negation of the theorem be true. They are not much good for the *presentation* of an object to intuition, and the ancients dislike them because they are unperspicuous, while a school of modern mathematicians eschews them from distrust of the Law of Excluded Middle. There are also *non*existence proofs. Euclid ends his *Elements* with a beautifully brief proof that no regular solids other than the five he has just constructed exist (bk. XIII, 18; the five are cube, pyramid, octahedron, icosahedron, dodecahedron).

(c) I think one might safely say that mathematical existence, while not existence in the ordinary meaning of a sensory individual, is not merely conceptual or ideal being either, since imaginative space and psychic motion are arguably involved. Even mathematical nonexistents can become the focus of searching attention, for example the side of the figure that squares the circle before its nonexistence became provable.

Hallucinations, too, must be said to come within the realm of Russell's Being:

> Is this a dagger, which I see before me,
> The handle toward my hand? Come let me clutch thee:
> I have thee not, and yet I see thee still. (*Macbeth* 2.1.46 ff.)

This extruded mental image is an entity in Russell's wide sense.

21. Russell 1919, 170. Russell's older view was still maintained by G. E. Moore in 1910–1911. Speaking of centaurs, he says: "To imagine a centaur is certainly not the same as imagining *nothing*. . . . I certainly do imagine *something* when I imagine one; and what *is* 'something,' it would seem, must *be*—there *is* such a thing as what I imagine" (Moore 1953, 212–213; Stebbing, 159). Meinong's specification of Being, which makes a full-blown theory of this view, will be set out below.

The view that there is Being, albeit of a tenuous kind, beyond existence seems to have a certain relation to Frege's famous distinction between sense *(Sinn)* and reference *(Bedeutung)*. "Reference" is not far from what Russell calls "denotation," the capacity of a word, a name, to point at or "designate" a thing (though for Frege not necessarily a *perceptible* existent). Of "sense," Frege says that it is "expressed" by a word or phrase; it is sense that is cognitively interesting, since it says something about the thing, as does a Russellian description. Beings comprise everything about which something can be said, but only existents have proper reference. Indeed, there is a whole list of coordinate couples that belong to a family of understandings: Denotation and connotation, reference and sense, knowledge by acquaintance and by description, denotation and description, and even extension and intension (Kneale 1962, 496; Stebbing 27 ff.; p. 000). Very remotely behind them all is the distinction between *esse* and *essentia* (see note 23).

22. The sentence quoted is Parson's version of the "orthodox mainstream," that is, the Russellian view (1980, 1). See also Stebbing, 158 ff.

23. Since I have followed the scheme of looking at Being from its sublime inception to its emptied end in the total triumph of existence, it makes sense to ask if there is a discernible moment where they hold each other in balance, so to speak. If there is such a one, it must be found in the conceptions of Thomas Aquinas.

The most-read ancient philosophers—who knows what people ordinarily thought—live in a world, I boldly state, without existents. It is not that they and those to whom they were forever preaching against preoccupation with mere appearance did not know about the hard particularity of material things. It is rather that they did not have or apparently want the word existence. Plato contrasts the stable intelligibility of Being with the elusive mutability of the appearances, which are an amalgam of Being and Nonbeing called Becoming. Aristotle places Being in the substances, in ultimate particulars, but not insofar as they are in space and time but rather insofar as they are immattered "essence" (Witt, 121; "essence" is not the happiest but the most common rendering of Aristotle's *ti en einai*, "what [the entity] was [meant] to be").

Thomas adopts the doctrine of the two meanings of *est*, "is": the substantial (*what* anything is) and the accidental (*whether* it is). Take the complete sentence *Socrates est*. In the substantial sense it expresses the proposition that Socrates lives the life of his species, has fully actualized his essence, is what he was meant to be. In the accidental sense the proposition truly affirms that Socrates is *in fact*, as a matter of truth, actualized. This latter *est* is accidental because it is not part of the essence of a being that something true be said of it, for knowledge follows its object and not the reverse. It is true of Socrates that he exists, but it adds nothing to his essence, in fact makes no comment on it, to say so. (Note that the above distinction differs from another one treated by Thomas, that between an essence and its existence, the act by which essence achieves existence-being.)

Now when truth-*est* and substance-*est* have been distinguished, it is possible to say that something truthfully *is* in a respect in which it has no substantial being. For instance, that a certain man is blind is true if there is such a man, but blindness is not an essential predicate, nor part of our essence at all, since it is a privation, a lack. So here we have an intimation of the cleavage of truth in propositions from the essence of beings and, in general, the divorce of speech from substance that will characterize the symbolic propositions of Russell's theory. The chief sources for Thomas are his *Commentary on the Twelve Books of Aristotle's* Metaphysics (on book V) and *On the Sentences of Peter of Lombard*. The material is brought together and explicated in Weidemann, 161 ff.

24. The real rhinoceros is indeed one of the animals behind the envisioning of the unicorn, see Shepard, 213 ff. What is wonderful and not entirely off the point is how masters of visual art manage to represent an animal that exists but that they know only by description, so that it is not only recognizable but more like the animal than the real specimen itself; an example is Dürer's woodcut of a monstrous armor-plated rhinoceros of 1515.

25. See Jesperson 1924, 155, who, however, emphasizes the weakness of the locative function.

26. "On Denoting" was first published in *Mind* 14 (October 1905): 479–493. It is reprinted in Russell, 1905c, 103–119. Explications are to be found in Russell 1919, Stebbing 1931, Linsky 1967, Parsons 1980, Grayling 1982, Crittenden 1991. Of these, Stebbing (chapter 9) is much the most attentive to the presuppositions and the consequences of the formalism. "Theory of Descriptions" occurs, for instance, in Russell 1919, 180.

27. I am referring not only to Russell's earlier view that everything *is* but also to an understanding of logical existence set out in 1905a, 98 f., where existence in symbolic logic (b) is distinguished from ordinary existence (a) in this way: "To say that A exists [in sense (b)] is to say that A is a class that has at least one member. Thus whatever is not a class (e.g., Socrates) does not exist in this sense; and among classes there is just one which does not exist, namely the class having no members, the null-class. In this sense, the class of numbers (e.g.) exists . . . but in sense (a) the class and its numbers alike do not exist: they do not stand out in a part of space and time." In the new theory the thing denoted by a proper name, e.g., Socrates, does exist, but as a special case.

28. "On Denoting," 106 f. The quotation is from Russell 1919, 167. He wrote this *Introduction to Mathematical Philosophy* while imprisoned for his pacifist activities during World War I. Robert Browning says in that triumphal march, "The Grammarian's Funeral," that his hero

> Gave us the doctrine of the enclitic *De*
> Dead from the waist down.
>
> .   .   .
>
> This man decided not to Live but Know.—

As a longtime teacher of Greek to freshmen, I can assure the reader that enclitic *de*, signifying motion toward, possesses rousing vitality still.

29. See particularly Grayling, 112.

The part of the expression that follows (∃x) is a "propositional function" that turns into a proposition when x is assigned a value. (∃x) is an "existential quantifier" which says that "an x exists" and therewith asserts the proposition.

30. Russell says that only "logically proper names denote directly something in the world" and thus enter into the proposition as a "constituent," as something it is *about* (see Stebbing, 166 n. 1, for an analysis of "about"). Most names are actually coded descriptions. Quine shows how the description effect can always be fabricated. Pegasus certainly appears to be a proper name in the sentence "Pegasus is." But if we want to avoid its being a constituent, a denoted thing-in-the-world, we turn the name into a description: "the thing that is-Pegasus" or "that pegasizes" (Quine 1953, 7–8). To me this procedure is completely mysterious; it sounds like the ascription of some sort of name-essence. The notion that names (and nouns) do more than refer, that they in fact also describe what they designate, is old. A spoof of it is to be found in Plato's *Cratylus*, where Socrates invents absurd descriptive etymologies for the gods' names; Greek poetry is full of such *nomen-omen* play. But what does the description signify when the name means nothing?

Having apparently eliminated descriptive names, Quine develops Russell's theory to its ultimate conclusion: "To be assumed as an entity is, purely and simply, to be reckoned as the value of a variable" (Quine 1953, 13). Our faith in the subject-predicate structure of ordinary language, which tells us that a property belongs to the entity named by the subject is to be relinquished, and only those entities are to exist to which we commit ourselves by admitting them as values (entities of science, it turns out). Of course, we *could* admit nonexistent objects (Parsons, 37; Crittenden, 13 ff., did not our sense of reality deter us.

31. Russell 1918, 247–248.

32. For Russell's "incomplete symbols" and for the disappearance of the subject, see Stebbing, 152 ff. For "the" in the plural, that is, for members of classes, see Russell, 1919, 181 ff.; for the way to deal with "*the* unicorns" of legend, that is, with unicorns as a type of class in the Russellian vein, see Stebbing, 162: "If there *were* any unicorns, they would be individual objects of precisely the same type as *horses*."

33. Russell 1919, 172.

34. Stebbing, 152. The relation of this epistemological presupposition to Russell's Theory of Descriptions is clearly set out by Stebbing, 150 ff.

35. Russell, in *The Monist* 1919, 196, as quoted by Stebbing, where a discussion of logical existence is to be found, 160 f.

36. Some major critiques of the Theory of Descriptions are Strawson 1950; Linsky 1967; Donellan 1974; Parsons 1980; Crittenden 1991. An acute philosophical criticism of existence and nonexistence in analysis is to be found in Rosen 1980, 98 ff. and especially 129 ff.

Strawson's critique, to which Russell himself responded (Russell 1957), is the one most often cited, being early and less technical. Its point of departure is the claim that Russell fails to distinguish between the *meaning* of a sentence, which gives "*general directions* for its use in making true or false assertions" (30), and the assertion or *state-*

ment that the sentence may then be used to make on a particular in occasion, when it refers to an object. Hence Russell thought that anyone uttering the sentence is in fact making either a true or a false assertion. But the sentence can be used in a context where it is neither true nor false. Thus, since for him meaning is identified with reference, Russell is off to a wrong start. The gist of Russell's reply was: I understand the distinction very well, but logic is about asserted propositions, not the sentences of common language, for as you yourself say at the end of your paper: "ordinary language has no exact logic," and exactitude is the remedy for confusion.

It strikes me as interesting that "contextuality," which is a buzzword of the present, was incipient in logicians' thinking (quite apart from Wittgenstein) in the first half of the last century; in Russell's theory descriptions have meaning only in the context of the propositional function.

37. Meinong 1904, 83. "The Theory of Objects" is a very accessible, brief exposition of the theory and its position among the disciplines.

38. Umphrey 1988, 169.

39. Russell 1905c, 107. Before "On Denoting" Russell was very appreciative of Meinong, and at all times respectful; see Russell 1904, 1905b.

On Russell's critique of Meinong, including reviews of misunderstandings: Linsky, 14 f.; Grossman, 158 f.; Parsons, 38 ff.; Lambert, 34. Meinong, in turn, made one especially telling criticism of Russell (analyzed by Findlay 1963, 54 f., 345; Grossman, 115 f.). Russell's belief that logical equivalences are identities (p. 84), he says, is justified in a spare symbolic system but is not philosophically adequate. "Ghosts do not exist" in the analytic context means that there is no actual thing that is a ghost. But when "someone thinks about ghosts and denies their existence" the thought is quite different: it is not that there are no instances but that the thought of the being of a ghost is unacceptable."

40. Russell 1907, 93.

41. For a more extensive bibliography of works on Meinong, see Crittenden, p. 5 n. 4. Unlike Russell, who is succinct and spare, Meinong is prolix and a multiplier of (non)-entities. For clean-shaven Russell, Occam's Razor came to be *the* implement of intellectual virtue; Meinong (photographs show) maintained a very full beard. To read Russell, technical help is welcome; to read Meinong one needs directions to the high spots and critical summations. In his tireless and candid revisions and qualifications, Meinong seems to me comparable to Husserl (Brann 1999, 128).

42. Brentano 1874. Omitted here is a footnote on the scholastic use of "objectively," which meant "ideally"—just the opposite of real existence outside the mind. Brentano later adopted a much restricted doctrine of objects: Only concrete individual things in their reality qualify (Chisholm, 5). Meinong, as we will see, found modes of being between mental inexistence and external reality.

43. Inexistence is synonymous with nonexistence, but perhaps not quite. Could there be a hint of "unrelated to existence," that is, out of the realm of existence and nonexistence?

44. Plato *Theaetetus* 189 a, for example; Aristotle *On the Soul* 430 a 14; Kant *Critique of Pure Reason* B 74 ff.

45. Findlay 1963, 18.

46. See Meinong 1910, xxix and chap. III; Chisholm, 6 f.

47. Parsons, 45 and n. 9, distinguishes objectives from propositions: both true and false propositions exist (recall that in logic existence is said of the symbolic proposition itself), but objectives, which never *exist*, do, when factual, *subsist*, a term explained below.

48. Meinong 1904, 88, 108–109.

49. Meinong 1904, 82.

50. Meinong 1904, 79.

51. Findlay 1963, 113 ff.

52. Everything in this paragraph and those following refers to Meinong 1904, 83–86. See also Meinong 1910, para. 2.

53. Meinong 1904, 86. The more attractive "Beyond-being" is too close to the term for the highest principle in Plato's *Republic*, the Good, which is said to be "beyond Being" (509 b), and to other theological terms; see chapter 6, notes 12, 21.

54. Crittenden, 64.

55. Findlay 1963, 347, 322.

56. Parsons 1980, 9 f. It might seem a little absurd to speak of a theory whose very point is to be formal in informal terms, were it not for the saving grace that Parsons himself begins with an "Initial Sketch" of this sort (17 ff.).

57. Parsons, 17 ff. See Findlay 1963, 176, and Lambert, 22, for Meinong's nuclear *(konstitutorisch)* and extranuclear *(ausserkonstitutorisch)* properties. A difficulty in addition to the feasibility of enumerating real-life properties is that of their logical conjunction. In logical conjunction the elements combined remain unaffected, but in life, where the whole often enlarges the parts, two features may not be simply addible. For example, a person who is separately good and clever is a lesser being than one who is good-and-clever, in whom the moral and intellectual virtues are in thorough communication. Logic cannot take account of such conjunctive effects (see Parsons, 21: logical closure).

58. Parsons, 43 f.; he doesn't pretend to know whether there *are* nonexistent objects with the nuclear existence predicate.

59. Parsons, 1 ff. My colleague Stewart Umphrey allowed me to read the chapter "Ways of Negation" of a manuscript provisionally entitled *Complexity*. In it he decertifies, with close and elegant reasoning, Kant's transcendental irrealism, the claim that there are no entities but those open to our inspection, i.e., to experience. He gives an inventory of all the "profundities" that are diminished or lost to us if Kant's dialectic prevails. Among these are Meinongian nonexistent objects. He salvages them by showing that Kant's dialectical attack on beings of reason is itself so infected with distinctions made from a transcendent point of view that we need not accept it as devastatingly certain. So at least the critical block to the wondering perplexity that causes us to contemplate such objects in the first place is breached.

60. Russell 1919, 170; Meinong 1904, 78.

61. Quine 1953, 4, intimated that a Meinongian creature, for example, a "possible fat man in the doorway," could not be either identified with or distinguished from a "possible bald man in the doorway." In Parsons's list they are each identifiable as well as distinct, since their set of nuclear properties is different (Parsons, 27).

62. Brann 1991, "Logic: The Being of Images," 387 ff., addresses itself largely to visual fictions.

63. Meinong 1910, para. 17, 86 ff. I am wholeheartedly of the same opinion, and here wish to declare myself to be what I term to myself an "occasional Kantian." I think that Kant says the deepest thing to be said about lying when he asserts that "the lie is the casting away and, as it were, the annihilation of a human being's dignity" (*Metaphysics of Morals: Doctrine of Virtue,* para. 9, 429 ff.). It is a doctrine that applies to what I think of as knife's-edge occasions when my own integrity and that of my world is at stake. But Kant's extremist prohibition against *all* lying seems to me unlivable and on the old principle that "the corruption of the best is the worst" should be softened before the whole doctrine is either applied in rigidly ugly ways or is simply thrown out: "White lies" that save us and others embarrassment are the lubricants of life, and lies that ensure safety are, it seems to me, the strain that decency is permitted to place on perfect rectitude; two kinds of lies are not allowed and require restitution: lying for gain or reputation and lying to oneself. So much for the record.

I want to point out, on the side, that Socrates and Kant don't share much, but they are one in their extremism for truth.

64. *Will to Power,* no. 378.

65. There are, of course, kinds of nonverbal deceptions galore; see Brann 1991, 401, 665, for the visual sort.

66. Plato *Republic* 382 b. The context shows that Socrates really *is* playing on both senses of *pseudos*: deliberate deceit and falsity in the sense of erroneousness and lack of genuine being.

67. There is, as one would expect, a large literature on self-deception; see Barnes 1997; add Gardiner, 35 ff.; Bok 1983, 59 ff.; and above all, Sartre, 87: "Bad Faith and Falsehood" (chap. 2, 1). Sartre states the gist of the problem thus: "We shall willingly grant that bad faith is a lie to oneself, on condition that we distinguish the lie to oneself from lying in general. Lying is a negative attitude, we will agree to that. But this negation does not bear on consciousness itself; it aims only at the transcendent [i.e., what is beyond the mere facts pertaining to us—our possibilities and projects]. The essence of the lie implies in fact that the liar actually is in complete possession of the truth which he is hiding. A man does not lie about what he is ignorant of; he does not lie when he spreads an error of which he himself is the dupe; he does not lie when he is mistaken. . . . [Here follows an existential analysis of lying.]

"The situation cannot be the same . . . for a lie to oneself. . . . Thus the duality of the deceiver and the deceived does not exist here. . . . It follows first that the one to whom the lie is told and the one who lies are one and the same person, which means that I must know in my capacity as deceiver the truth which is hidden from me in my capacity as deceived."

Note that Sartre strongly denies the Socratic identification of the inner lie with ignorance. Consequently he is faced with the perennial problem of self-deception: How to account for the duality of consciousness? It seems that neither the existential analysis (Sartre, 88) nor the psychoanalysis (90 ff.) nor the logical analysis (Barnes 1997, 131 ff.) do more than put the intractable problem in their own terms.

68. Socrates' view of the inner lie counterbalances a prevalent contemporary view of traditional opinion. This view makes a virtue of suspicion: Such opinions must always be suspected of bolstering the dominance of the class of people that holds them. Socrates, on the other hand, thinks that ultimately no one wants to be possessed by

error and that unexamined opinions are held more from a fatal sort of complacency than from greed for power. So although it is the Platonic Socrates who establishes a tripartite scheme for the soul—reason, spiritedness, appetite—he uses neither of the latter two to explain the psychic duality of self-deception, which for him is mainly, if not totally, an intra-cognitive occurrence, a kind of cognitive passivity. It is a Socratic tenet that the intellect has its own passions.

69. I am trying to delineate what is called the "illocutionary" aspect of the liar's utterance, the speech act he is performing, whether it is to tell hearers truly or falsely what the case is or to get them to do things or to express his feelings, etc. (Searle, 166). On the specific harm lies do to the mind of the victim, see Fried 438 ff., and in general Bok 1978, which has an appendix of excerpts on lying from Augustine to Warnock (250 ff., 176).

70. Swift, pt. 4, "Voyage to the Country of the Houyhnhnms," chap. iv. The language is reminiscent of Plato's *Sophist* (260 c): "For to opine or think the things that *are not*—this is, I suppose, the false." By "intentionally" I mean, following what was said above, a disposition ranging from merest acquiescence to strongest purposefulness. It is my belief that the deceitful creature Gulliver so much admires understands the *motive* of a lie as well.

Here is a telling example of the role intention, as opposed to content, plays in lying: An inmate of Bedlam says to his doctor in a tone of sweet reasonableness: "Of course I'm not Napoleon!" But he is lying through his teeth.

71. Brann 1997, "Telling Lies," 320.

72. Homer *Iliad* I 352 ff., XVI 36 ff.

73. For the negated copula in traditional logic, see p. 33. For the relation of falsity to existence, see p. 48.

74. Coleridge 1817, chap. 14.

75. *Republic*, bk. III; second round, bk. X. It will be readily agreed that metaphor is a mainstay of poetry. Now there is a contemporary theory that a metaphor is correctly to be analyzed as a species of lie. Its originator, Donald Davidson, might not be amused to be called a follower of Socrates in respect to the nature of poetry, but so he is; see Nogales, 101–123, for a meticulous analysis and critique of his theory. Its gist is that metaphors are understood in terms of use, and they are used like lies, to make people see things as they are literally not:

> What light through yonder window breaks?
> It is the east, and Juliet is the sun. (*Romeo and Juliet* 2.2.3)

In a reductionist mood one might call Socrates' complaint against all of poetry mere literalism, as Davidson is a literalist in the understanding of metaphor.

One argument against identifying metaphors with lies is that to subject oneself to the actual lie of the metaphor one must first interpret it *as* metaphor: The deceitful proposition of "Juliet is the sun" is not that Juliet is the sun but that she has sunlike qualities—which *may* be false; the literal proposition would deceive no one. Hence being a metaphor is here distinct from and prior to being a lie; see Nogales, 108 ff. Socrates might argue in turn that there are large-scale metaphors—myths—that will be taken literally and *do* deceive people.

76. Panofsky 1924 gives a survey of "Idea" in art from Plato to Dürer. Thus he omits Schopenhauer 1819, bk. III, para. 45, the boldest proponent of the notion that art

conveys knowledge of the Platonic Ideas. The quotation is from Donne 1622, 488, Easter Day Sermon at St. Paul's. The passage begins: "How weak a thing is poetry!"

Goodman 1976, 6 ff., tries to make a strong analytic case against imitation, beginning with the claim that "the copy theory of representation, then, is stopped at the start by inability to specify what is to be copied." Of course, one might wonder whether our inability to specify something with satisfactory rigor in theory does, necessarily, keep it from occurring in fact.

77. I relegate to a footnote the observation I am not alone in making, that the logician uses literature as a source of *examples*, and that the "objects" so brusquely extracted have about the same relation to their fictional character as the subjects of a psychological study have to human beings or the specimens in the laboratory have to animals: Their analysis is surely instructive, but usually not adequate to revealing the *being* of the object of inquiry; see Knight, 435.

78. Russell 1919, 170.

79. The two theories, though the first is logical and the second literary-critical, have a strong inner relation. Russell consigns the existence of the x that replaces the subject to the context of the proposition; literary contextualism is just what the critics of the second theory in fact preach. The critic's theory seems like the adaptation to a whole literary text of the analytic notion that names of fictions don't denote and need to be dissolved into descriptions. But perhaps that is not saying more than that both of these are the opinions of mature modernity achieving in time their various formulations.

An argument that self-referential readings can have revelatory value if the practices of language themselves reveal human reality is given by Harrison, 38 ff.

80. Parsons, chaps. 3, 7.

81. Baker Street is immigrant, but no. 221B is native, as I, like so many others, have ascertained by going there; it doesn't exist.

Parsons's theory is not, he says, a "possible worlds" theory. Parsons's objects have their properties "*according to* a story," not *in* a possible world (Parsons, 56; see, for example, Plantinga, 47). "Possible worlds" are logically constructed consistent alternatives to *the* actual world. The reason Parsons eschews, at least to begin with, the accounts that establish possible worlds is that such accounts typically require completeness (every detail is determined), and that they do not admit impossibilities. Nonexistent objects are almost always incomplete and sometimes impossible (Parsons, 182). Critiques of an earlier possible world theory of fiction, that by Lewis 1978, are given by Currie, 62 ff., and Lamarque 1996, 56 ff.

Parsons considers all sorts of subtleties as the theory progresses: How to tell what objects occur in a fiction and what is (intra-fictionally) true of them, how to accommodate nonnative objects, how to treat intra-fictional watered-down extranuclear properties, and quite a few others. Among these is the confounding question how I can tell that I am not a nonexistent object in a particularly complex tale or perhaps in someone's dream (Parsons, 218; Crittenden, 156), as Alice is accused of being:

"Well, it's no use *your* talking about waking him," said Tweedledum, "when you're only one of the things in his dream. You know very well you're not real."

"I *am* real," said Alice, and began to cry. (*Through the Looking Glass,* chap. 4)

Here Alice begins to engage in a fruitless argument with Tweedledum (who's wrong in the first place in saying that a thing in a dream can't awake you). Parsons's and Crittenden's argument is aggravated by the fact that human beings, logicians notwithstanding, are just as incomplete as fictions and dream figures—at least I think I am (p. 101).

It is an old, old problem: The Chinese sage awoke to ask himself whether he was a butterfly dreaming it was a man or a man dreaming he was a butterfly. I think the question whether I am an independent substance with essential and accidental predicates (to name one extreme) or a nonexistent object with nuclear properties written out for me by an Author is not trivial, though not for this book either:

> We are such stuff
> As dreams are made on, and our little life
> Is rounded with a sleep.

Incompleteness is, I think, the most interesting issue concerning fictions.

82. I offer the geometric inhabitants, the triangles, polygons, etc., of Edwin Abbott's dimensional romance *Flatland* in evidence of some pretty complete fictional objects. We do know that Holmes's grandmother's maiden name was Vernet ("The Greek Interpreter"). On incompleteness in fictional objects, see Parsons, 183–185; Crittenden, 138 ff.

83. For a bibliography, see Howell 1998, 662 f.; Lamarque 1998, 666 f.

84. Lamarque 1996, 31 ff. Knight, 438 ff., argues that the "inside view" is a philosophical fiction and *un*imaginable because "Every story is over before it begins," that is, its inhabitants are fixed figures, not evolving people (Michael Roemer in Knight, 439). I think insider status is not unattainable. To be sure, the story is prewritten. (I wouldn't even look at a so-called interactive, choose-your-own-adventure story, for why should I do the author's work? For that, there's daydreaming.) But the Greek poets knew that the fact that there is fate at work does not diminish—and indeed enhances—the characters' freedom of action. For before the end, no one in the tale knows how fateful the fate really is. The prewritten text is the character's fate, but that never keeps the engaged reader from making continual mental intromissions while reading or from imaging alternatives thereafter.

85. The chief reference is Currie, 18–21. Crittenden, 45 ff., gives a review of these pretense and make-believe theories. Crittenden himself advances a language use theory: A fictional object is "*just* what corresponds to accepted linguistic practice and is nothing metaphysically over and above it; it is not independent of language or thought and is an object only in the sense that references and predictions (and truth-valued claims and the like) are accepted about it" (97).

86. There has been a revival of interest in mimesis going on for some time now. The classic study of realism, understood as "the interpretation of reality through literary representation or 'imitation,' " was that of Auerbach 1946, 489. There intervened a scholarly lapse of interest in, and even acknowledgment of, the mimetic aspect of literature and the visual arts as well as of the mimetic imagination—in recognition, of course, of the long-term decline of interest in these elements of art among mainstream artists. The revival mentioned is evidenced in an overview collection (Gebauer 1992), and in journal issues dedicated to mimesis and imagination (e.g., *Renascence* and

Logos; see Schwartz 1985 and Mikolajczak 1997, both Catholic publications for whose writers imitation has theological significance).

87. (a) "Hydrotaphia," 149. To be sure, it is reported that the proponent of these particular puzzles was a very disingenuous Roman, the emperor Tiberius. On the other hand, in a recent seminar, my freshmen took up with gusto and seriousness the question "what song the Sirens sang" to beguile Odysseus, as, bound to the mast, he was rowed past them (*Odyssey* XII 166 ff.). We thought we could tell: It was a song arousing the wrong sort of *nostalgia*—the Greek word means "return-ache"—nostalgia for the glories of Troy rather than the arms of Penelope.

(b) Eco's *Six Walks in the Fictional Woods* is a subtle and clever book about just the questions I am broaching in these paragraphs. He speaks of the text "as a lazy machine that expects a lot of collaboration from the reader" (28). This reader is "the model reader—a sort of ideal type whom the text not only foresees as a collaborator but also tries to create" (9); this model reader is intra-textual, basically "a set of textual instructions" (16), but the instructions are to us, the "empirical readers." So on those occasions when we are ready to play by the rules of the game, we become realizations of the model reader, who participates on two levels. There is a naive model reader, usually the first-time-through reader, who wants to know how the story ends, and there is also a "model reader of the second level, who wonders what sort of reader that story would like him or her to become and who wants to discover precisely how the model author [the fictional instructor, symmetrical to the model reader] goes about serving as a guide for the reader" (27).

I think this view of interpretation as work applies better to the sort of texts Eco loves, like Nerval's *Sylvie*, "one of the greatest books ever written," texts that contain remarks driving the reader to event plotting and time lining, than it does to the epics and novels I love, like *War and Peace*. The latter, thought written with endless art, are sparing of artifice, and invite a somewhat more direct second-level reading: a sort of delighted noticing which can't well be called work and is yet nothing like a game. In these books the "ghostly existence" (16) of Eco's reader fades into nonexistence. The author so rarely utters instructional asides that it is hard to distinguish the internal model reader from the just-plain-attentive real reader. These books aren't "lazy machines" at all: The reader is all there because the story is all there. By that I mean that there is enough textual evidence to enable attentive "empirical" readers to complete the incomplete objects of the text with enough plausibility to regale their well-disposed friends with their delightful discoveries.

Eco has yet another germane notion: "Fictional worlds *are* parasites of the actual one." This seems to be in effect an admission of a mimetic theory of fiction: We "concentrate on a finite, enclosed world, very similar to ours but ontologically poorer." Yet it is also true that, although the fiction is in one sense a "small world," it is in another sense greater than the real world, since it adds objects to the world of experience: "a fictional universe doesn't end with the story itself but extends indefinitely" (85). To me the chief question is whence they come, those additions, those images, that call on "our competence of the actual world" to be recognized as types, but that are as tokens quite novel (Brann 1991, 439 ff.).

Finally, Eco reverses the parasitism. We have a "tendency to construct life as a novel" (129); we may "interpret life as fiction" (131). I would rather keep the reality of life and the actuality of fiction distinct and say that our indefeasibly real lives are informed by the images of fiction, which stand *behind and by us*, as models and companions—and so, strangely enough, assume the role of originals from which we, on occasion, derive the shape of our life.

88. The lines are from W. H. Auden, "The Shield of Achilles." The word "actuality" is very often used as simply synonymous with reality, with existence or the fact that obtains; for example, Plantinga, 46 ff., distinguishes our "actual" world from possible worlds in this way; see also note 17. But I am using "actual" with a meaning more derivative from the traditional Aristotelian sense: Actuality is the vibrant stasis in which an object is what it was meant to be; it has come into its own and is effective as such, apart from space, time and body, which are not part of its form or essence. Thus "Hermes is in the stone" potentially (*Metaphysics* 1017 b 7) but when he has been actualized as a statue, he has the only incidentally material form of the god. (For the exclusion of matter from essence, see Witt, 126 ff., 191 ff.; for the "actuality" of fictions see Brann 1991, pt. 3, chap. 3). In speaking of fictions as having actuality, I mean actuality for us, the readers or viewers; the textual being of fictions in themselves is in a different mode—but then again, some of us entertain the wild surmise of a realm in which successful fictions actually live.

89. For the temporal mode of fictions, see Brann 1999, 187 f.; for the merged ontology of images, see Brann 1991, 389 ff.

90. Thus Wittgenstein says, "The existence of atomic facts we call a positive fact, their non-existence a negative fact" (Kneale 1936, 40).

91. "Is Existence a Predicate?" is the title of articles by Moore 1936, Kneale 1936, and Pears and Thompson 1963. Parsons's chief point is that the difference between the being of a nonexistent object and the existence that is bestowed by the extranuclear predicate is not weighty enough for anyone to care whether God is a fiction or an existent. As theology this would be hopelessly jejune.

92. See *Critique of Pure Reason* B 627 for the quotation; the argument goes from 625 to 630. The distinction between real and logical predicates (echoing that of nuclear and extra-nuclear predicates) turns up in most of the writing on the question; so does the argument that reality is already assumed in the subject when existence is predicated of it; it is given the name of "referential tautology" (Pears and Thompson, 98).

93. Kant 1763b, First Reflection, secs. 1–2. Heidegger, 1927a, para. 7–8 and passim, discusses at length Kant's concept of existence as position, since it is of major importance to the development of his own notion of existence.

94. Descartes 1641, Meditations III and V. The argument as modified in his *Reply to Objections V* no. 4 is more in line with Anselm's second proof; see p. 105 and Hartshorne, 166.

95. The text here considered is *Proslogion*, chaps. 2, 4. The points to follow owe much to the sympathetic treatment of Hartshorne, 33 ff. This book includes in its second part a review of the anticipations of the proof by Plato, Aristotle, Philo, and subsequent critics beginning with Gaunilo and Thomas through Hume, Kant, and more recent commentators; Descartes (who may or may not have read Anselm) and Hegel (who had) are on the appreciative side. Excerpts of the older critical texts are printed in Anselm c. 1070a, ix ff.

A short dictionary is in order: "the understanding" renders *intellectus*; "conceive"

renders *cogitare*; "exist" renders *esse*. (See Anselm 1070b for the Latin text.) Translators are not to be blamed for these deviations from Anselm's terms because absolute
literalness lands you in all sorts of extraneous trouble. Particularly the standard translation of *esse* as "to exist" rather than "to be" seems to be warranted by the uniqueness,
the individuality of God; his mode of being is at least analogous to the "particular"
meaning of existence (p. 80).

4

Thinking the Unsayable: Philosophical *Nonbeing*

1. NONBEING LAUNCHED: PARMENIDES' POEM

Parmenides learned from the goddess who dwells in the house of truth that "Being is" and that he must not embark on the way of Nonbeing. As far as I know, Nonbeing had not established itself in anyone's thought—at least in the West—before Parmenides' deity warned him off this path of inquiry; nor has it ever vacated its place in thought since. Her repeated prohibitions and injunctions against this Unthinkable and Unsayable seem to have done for this philosophical offense what inveighings against sin have so often accomplished in the moral sphere—they have launched it on its career as a well-formulated and ever attractive presence.

In this chapter I shall try to show how this Nonbeing makes its first appearance and gathers its first meaning. It is a great, even a solemn moment in our common life of thought—this revelation of Being as the sole truth and the unbidden emergence of its opposing coordinate, Nonbeing—and hard to represent accurately and yet without loss of significance. But one must try, for "with Parmenides begins philosophizing proper," thinking for the sake of Truth.[1]

(a) Nonbeing will appear on the scene as an *unintended consequence*. Those who want to think about the way things are almost always ponder these questions: What is most original, most encompassing, most excellent? What is *first*?[2] Being is a chief candidate for being first, and the strange and wonderful thing is that the man—Parmenides—who came on it and put it on the map of thought, so to speak, discovered it not only as the *first* but as the *only* thought. In conveying this truth to us, however, he becomes enmeshed, one might say with deliberate unintentionality, in a second, a derivative thought: *Non*-being, which he thus puts on the scene of thought.

Not for a moment can I believe that no one thought of Being and Nonbeing before Parmenides. Xenophanes, that delicately lusty and long-lived sage, who was said to have been Parmenides' teacher, may have, somehow, conceived of negated Being. Heraclitus, who appears in the history of philosophy as Parmenides' counterpart, had so strong a grip on the Law of (non-)Contradiction, which says that A and non-A cannot both exist or be asserted at the same time, so deep an understanding of the force of negation, that he could dramatically breach it: "We walk into and do not walk into the same river; we are and we are not."[3] What is more, in Nepal, Gautama, the future Buddha, had found, it is said, the contrary way of extinction, Nirvana, in 534 B.C., half a generation before Parmenides was even born.[4]

But it is not of those who composed their insights for the record that I am thinking. It seems to me so unlikely as to be beyond belief that the thought of Being, the sheer "Isness" on which our existence floats, and the contrary thought of Nonbeing, the possibility of a vacant world, should not have wafted, ghostlike, across the consciousness of many a thoughtful human being aeons before anyone ever gave them an appellation. For if it were not so, how could anyone have heard in turn what Parmenides heard from his goddess or experienced its portentousness as he intends? Philosophy itself seems to be a series of reprises, and so it is at least likely that its beginning is not the first beginning of thought.[5] The pathos of a first occurrence is, it seems to me, not lessened but heightened by the dateless aboriginality of human thinking.

Of those, however, who composed their thoughts memorably and appear as figures in that time preservative we call the philosophical tradition, Parmenides is the first, and the one who enunciates the first thought, and he is thus the founder of "First Philosophy," which deals with what is first in itself and in thought.[6] As Aristotle will put it: "And indeed, what is searched for of old and now and ever, and is ever perplexing, is 'What is Being'?" (*Metaphysics* 1028 b 3–5).

This is the thought object (for want of a less burdened word) that Parmenides brings on the scene, and he brings it on as the *only* thought. And yet, as I said, with it comes, an unwanted shadow, Nonbeing.

Is Parmenides then a philosopher, the first philosopher? Yes and no. He is enjoined to enter a way of inquiry whose object is Being and its "signs." But his is not the way of a *lover* of wisdom (the literal meaning of "philosopher"), but of an *initiate* into truth. Thinkers who come before Socrates are referred to by the modern term Presocratics, as a token of the pivotal place Socrates holds in philosophy.[7] Now a particular feature of *this* Presocratic, Parmenides, is just that his way of inquiry begins as he is sequestered from the world and that he takes its departure *from* Being, whereas Socrates sets out from the midst of life and pursues a way of inquiry *to* Being, and so makes *philosophia* that way of life whose once and future aim is Being.[8]

But it is Parmenides who makes this reversal possible for Socrates. For Parmenides, who was not at first, in his early youth, a searcher but a finder, not an aspirant to wisdom but an initiate into Truth, appeared in venerable old age in Athens—either in spirit or in person, it hardly matters—to engage in a searching but inconclusive conversation with young Socrates, a boy, I imagine, then the age of a very young college freshman. This is quite a different Parmenides from the young initiate alight with Truth that I am about to describe. He is a master dialectician. "Dialectician" is a word with many meanings and a great future. Old Parmenides inducts, one might say trains, young Socrates in this art, which is not the highway of the goddess (*hodos* in Greek), but the more constrained, plodding path by way of argument which we, like the Greeks and Plato in particular, call a method (*methodos*).[9] Plato reconstructs—whether from mundane fact or mythical truth is undecidable and, as I said, of small interest—a conversation during which Socrates hears Parmenides in disputation with himself, in the "yes and no," "is and isn't" way of argument. With the generous candor of mind that belongs naturally to those who truly ply "ontology," the account of Being, he puts his own now elaborated theory of the uniqueness and unity of Being at issue by running through its facets both positively and negatively.

I conjecture that for Parmenides repeated raptures, youthful moments of revelatory thought, eventually gave way to a lifetime of pondering on the bald paradoxes of the initial truth. Certainly his companions and pupils followed a method of disputation, though not as evenhandedly as the old man himself. What is noteworthy is that for them negating speech far outweighed positive speech for, as young Socrates shrewdly observes to Parmenides of his pupil Zeno: "*You* say in your poems that the All is one . . . while *he* says that it is *not* many" (*Parmenides* 128 b). Thus Parmenides not only sets Nonbeing on its path but also invents refuting argument. His own goddess urges him to "judge by reason the much contested refutation (*elegchon*) that has been pronounced by me" (Fr. 7, 5), though she herself actually argues and refutes scarcely at all. So one might say that the first pupil of the Goddess of Truth exemplifies an ever repeated course: that truth comes before the search and its revelation before inquiry, and "thus" before "not-thus."

(b) Two themes will dominate the poetry of Parmenides: *ways* and *women*. Parmenides wrote one poem, unmistakably a rival to Homer's *Odyssey*, and, like it, composed in the dactylic hexameter of heroic epic.[10] It was evidently not much longer than just one of the shorter books of the *Odyssey*—in those days fiction was wordier than philosophy. Like the *Odyssey*, Parmenides' poem tells of a journey homeward, sole and singular, on the byways of the world "outside the trodden paths" of men (Fr. 1, 27). But everything else about Parmenides' way is, I think purposefully, distinguished from the Homeric hero's return.[11] Both have known the world: "He saw the towns of many men and knew their mind," says Homer of Odysseus (*Odyssey* I, 3). "They put me on the much speaking way which bears through all the towns the human being that knows," says Parmenides of his horses (Fr. 1, 3).[12] But Odysseus is a mature, battle-wise, canny, and cautious man; Parmenides is a bold, impetuous boy (perhaps no older than Socrates would be when he was to meet Parmenides in his old age).[13] Odysseus circuitously sails the oceans, a man missing and lost, to its extremes and enters Hades, the all-but-invisible underworld where he learns many tales of myth; Parmenides rides straight over earthly ways to the blazing center of the world, the "untrembling heart of trustworthy Truth" (Fr. 1, 29) to learn the one tale of truth.

Here is the subtle but serious beginning of that "ancient difference between philosophy and poetry" which Plato recalls and continues in his *Republic* (607 b 5). It pits Parmenides' truth-telling Deity against Homer's storytelling Muse.[14]

Parmenides is carried on his way, outside the path of men though it is (Fr. 1, 27), in blazing grandeur, in a whirl of light and sound. The glowing axles of his chariot whistle like the pipes of Pan—the god whose name means the "All"[15]—and this same sound also issues from the "pipes," the sockets of the gates, that are pushed back for him. The proem in which Parmenides celebrates the memory of his journeys—there were, attention to grammar tells us, more than one[16]—abounds in carryings, conveyings, escortings. It is, in so small a compass, a veritable thesaurus of Greek words for way, path, road, trail. So also the Greek prefix for "much" and "many" *(poly)* abounds, as it does in the *Odyssey*.[17] The proem is all movement and sensation and incantatory repetition—and begins as if it were all yet present to him:

> The mares that are bearing me, as far as ever my spirit would reach,
> They conducted me, as they went, leading me into the much speaking
> 　way
> Of the Deity, which bears the knowing human through all the towns.
> On that way was I borne, for on it the much discerning mares were
> 　bearing me,
> Straining at the chariot, and the Maidens led the way. (Fr. 1, 1–5)

So he comes, conducted by the Maidens of the Sun, to "the portals of the roads of night and day," which the Maidens coax their guardian, Justice, the "Show-er" *(Dike,* whose name in probably connected to "showing," *deixis)* into throwing open to make a "gaping gap" through which Parmenides' chariot is driven. This is a crucial moment in his initiation, preceding the spoken revelations of his deity.[18] What the showing divinity has done is to obliterate the distinction between night and day, light and dark. This duality will stand in the poem as the emblem of human error; the belief that both, equally and separately, pervade the world will signify the "two-headed" notion that the world admits oppositions (Fr. 9, 1 ff.). When Parmenides enters the "untrembling heart" of Truth, the gates of difference have already been thrown open. The illumination at the heart is not of the heavens but of the mind.

Now the goddess receives him, taking his right hand with hers:

O Youth, consort of immortal charioteers,
Who reach our house with the mares that bear you—
Welcome. (Fr. 1, 24–26)

Here the rushing drive, full of sensory excitement and multitudinousness, comes to an end in utter singleness and simplicity, and in a way, in silence. For the goddess puts a taboo on all ways but one and on all words but one.

If we regard this rapturous process, the part of the poem that is Parmenides' own, as a mere "literary device," we lose the inherent inner conflict of the poem, the very one that issues in the establishment of Nonbeing.[19] More of this below.

Now to the women. All beings that figure in the proem except the boy himself are female: the mares, the Maidens, Justice, Right, Necessity, Fate, and, above all, the unknown goddess herself who speaks to Parmenides.[20] Here too Parmenides is the rival of Odysseus, whose journey is also from female to female: a deity, Calypso—She-who-covers; a witch, Circe—She-who-encircles; a maiden—Nausikaa who wants him for a husband; a wife—Penelope who is his equal in cunning deceit. But above all, there is his goddess Athena who, having left him to his own devices on his sea journey, receives him, as he returns to his own island, with words of fond praise for his lying deceptions (*Odyssey* XIII, 291).

But where Odysseus' women are splendidly devious and secretive, even up to his Olympian goddess Athena, Parmenides' deities are nobly truthful and open. Thus Odysseus spends seven years with the "Coverer," Calypso, while the Sun Maidens whose "consort" Parmenides is *uncover* themselves for him, "pushing" their covering veils *(kalyptras)* from their heads as they come into the light, just as they persuade the Show-er to "push" back the portals.

In *The White Goddess*, his quirky homage to the "lost rudiments of the poetic magic" of the Moon Muse, Robert Graves says that "the early Greek philosophers, who were strongly opposed to magical poetry as threatening their new religion of logic," substituted male Apollo for the elemental, maternal goddess and imposed him on the world as the last word in spiritual illumination (vi). Well, not so for Parmenides. The divinities of rational illumination, of transparent truth, of initiation into the central mystery of thought, though not at all primevally and darkly feminine, are certainly female. Why?

In the first line of his poem, Parmenides speaks of the reach of his spirit, *thymos*. This word, to which Socrates will in the *Republic* firmly assign a middle position between articulate reason and passive desire, is the element of courage, "heart" in the sense of spirited resistance and pride; in Parmindes' day it still had more the sense of "heart" as the seat of passionate love. So Parmenides' contemporary, Sappho, in the throes of passion confesses to her goddess Aphrodite "what she so much wants to come about in her raging heart" *(mainolai thymoi)*.[21] We may therefore think that the youth Parmenides is driven to the heart of truth by a sort of passionate love, and that is what the female-saturated ambiance and all the passive being borne along betoken.

Having welcomed her youth to "our house,"[22] the goddess begins to tell truth—but not before she has promised that she will tell him something very strange: After her trustworthy truth she will tell him also the untrustworthy opinion of humans.

(c) The grand experience that dominates Parmenides' thought is *the way of "Is."* Though Nonbeing is what this chapter is after, its base is Being, and it is the way that sweeps Parmenides to Being that is also, unwittingly—or at least incidentally—the way to Nonbeing:

> Come, *I* will speak, and *you* hear and convey my tale (*mythos*),[23]
> What ways of inquiry alone there are for thinking—
> The one [says]: "Is," and that "Is not" is not to be [or: that Not-to-be is
>   not possible].
> This is the road of conviction, for it follows truth.
> The other [says]: "Is not," and that Not-to-be must be [or: it is fated that
>   "Is" not be].
> This path I show forth to you as all-unlearnable,
> For neither would you know Nonbeing, since it is unattainable,
> Nor could you show it forth. (Fr. 2)

This is the gist of the goddess's teaching. In her very first words she charges Parmenides with the mission of conveying it. After his boisterous way inward, to the heart, he hears of two ways of inquiry, both of which he is evidently to bring back out, but neither of which is really amenable to articulate speech, not to say to proclamation, though one even less so than the other. The goddess acknowledges this fact by—at least at first—not *speaking* it or asking him to speak of it; instead she uses the word "show forth" or "point out."[24]

Parmenides will, of course, fulfill his charge in writing the poem we read. He will never acknowledge any other, human teacher, but neither will he claim to speak out of himself. What does he mean by this? I think he means, or it means, that human originality, in the sense of inventiveness or creativity, has no part in finding truth; indeed philosophical originality is a contradiction in terms. Heraclitus, Parmenides' philosophical counterpart who acknowledges the coexistence of opposites, says something similar in spirit when he bids people hear his truth "not listening to *me* but to the *logos*," the cosmic collecting and distinguishing power.[25] Truth is neither personal nor is it quite impersonal; therefore it comes through a deity. Parmenides is the sole and single initiate into a mystery that he is charged not with keeping secret but with announcing. The Truth is to be a *public* cult.

Something follows for the way of reading the poem, particularly fragments 2 and 3. There is not a line about to be discussed in this section that has not been debated. The reason is partly that Parmenides writes curiously oscillating sentences—some can be read in more than one way, as my translation indicates. It is partly also that the attempt to say the admittedly, nay expressly, unsayable makes for genuine enigmas. But one not inconsiderable part of the debate stems from an unwillingness to believe what one's eyes are seeing on the page—that the goddess is really saying the strange, scandalously absolute things that the unglossed words do say. A part again of this reluctance derives from a latter-day perspective, a view that is disciplined but also constrained by post-Parmenidean categories. I think we had better believe that the poem says what it says and try with all mental might and main to transport ourselves into his frame of mind—not that of a primitive from another world but of a first speaker in *our* tradition. I say "try"—for every attempt to become very positive, in particular to pursue Parmenides with the logic that is developed to police thoughts, ends in making the poem more incomprehensible, and every attempt to make its words amenable to acceptable modes of reasoning makes them more recalcitrant to insight.[26]

The only way that the goddess allows for inquiry is, then, the way of "Is." What does "Is" mean? Some reflection on the Greek verb *esti* is necessary. In Greek it is possible to say this one word as a sentence. We, speaking English, are driven to provide a subject, "It," and then we must ask: *What* is?

The impersonal pronoun "it" does not just fill a formal need. This "conceptual neuter" is the "spirit-like, ghostlike, invisible, uncanny," it is the "great neuter" of nature.[27] So an English speaker is, as I said, almost driven to ask "What is?" "What is the 'it' that is?"

Moreover, if *ésti* has an accent, as written here, it can mean "It is possible . . ." or "X exists . . ." Or it can be the concurring answer to a question: "Yes, that's it, it's true." Accents were placed on Greek words long after Parmenides wrote,[28] so it is up to the reader to assign the meaning.

I do not think "It exists" or "X exists" in the primary philosophical sense of asserting the existence of a particular thing or fact, concretely or provably there in space and time, is ever Parmenides' meaning. If it were, he would be one of those Presocratics called "Physicists" because of their search for the primary material of the sensible world and its motions of birth and growth and change. But, as we shall see, his goddess is so fierce about separating him from that deaf and blind and dazed and judgmentless tribe (Fr. 6, 7) who affirm that what is has the characteristics of material and its motions that *ésti* cannot mean *exists* in that sense. She gives the contrary "signs" (*semata*, Fr. 8, 2), mostly negative: What is, is unborn and imperishable, unbegun and unceasing, and consequently without the phases of time, that is, without past and future. Hence it is in some sense timeless. And it is also not spatial. Parmenides has broached an ontological "negative way" which precedes the theological *via negativa* by a millennium.

In this poem—and for a long time after—to be is not the same as to exist, and to exist is certainly *not* to be (p. 79). Nor can the goddess be telling

Parmenides to say or to concur with something true, for *esti* itself is the truth; there is no "it" that is to be affirmed.[29]

A third sense of accented *ésti* may in fact occur:

> For it is not possible for this to be said or thought: [or: Not to be said or
>   thought is this:]
> That [it] is not. (Fr. 8, 9)

And sometimes, since the goddess's usages tend to be iridescent, several readings, as many as three, make sense. Thus, since there is both a true and an unlearnable way:

> The one [says] that "Is," (1) and that "*Is not*" is not to be,
>   (2) and that Not-to-be *is not*;
>   (3) and that Not-to-be *is not possible*. (Fr. 2, 3)[30]

The play of meanings here brings out the oscillation of "Is not" as subject and as predicate verb in the goddess's showing forth: She denies it as a being in reading (1) and as assertible in reading (2). Moreover, the ambivalence also reveals the futility of trying to utter a mere negation of Nonbeing, for just to negate it is immediately also to assert something stronger, its impossibility, as in (3).

I think, however, that we should take *esti* as basically unaccented and, at least to begin with, read the lines accordingly. And so, as I said, we naturally ask not only "*What* is?" but also "What is *what*?" The answer is that the subject of the verb *might* here be something ghostlike, uncanny and stupendous—but I don't think so. So also the verb itself *might* be a prospective copula through which this enormity is connected to its qualities, the above mentioned signs—but again, I think not, for these signs are mostly negations. Plain *esti* is not here connecting a subject to a set of real predicates. It does in fact occasionally have a subject in the poem, but that subject is some nominal form of the verb "to be" or "not to be," for example, "To-be is" (Fr. 6, 1), "nonbeings are not" (Fr. 7, 1), or the fragment translated above. We often use phrases like "sing a song," where the object is the action of the verb made into a thing accomplished.[31] Parmenides sometimes does something symmetrical with the verb "to be" at the front end of a sentence: He turns the verbal sense into a subject. But I don't think that Being or its negation is thereby established as a thing of thought or nature for him. On the contrary, mere verbal "Is" remains the truest kind of showing forth, and the nounlike forms merely display the inability, or rather unwillingness, of the goddess's speech to get outside the meaning of that little word which courses through human speech surrounded by subject and predicate. Parmenides' poem is a rebuff before the fact to those who will claim that Indo-European languages are indefeasibly subject- and predicate-ridden.

For this is what Parmenides is bidden to convey: the sheer *Isness* of which we always get hold when we think beyond multiplicity, a steadfast vibrancy that fills up the All (Fr. 8, 24) and which it is apparently almost inexpressibly rewarding to accept as Truth.

The common declarative tripartite sentence—This is that—is an implicit expression of three distinctions: between the thinker and the thought (since some thinking person is having and uttering a thought); between the thought and what it is about (since the sentence states a thought-proposition about an object); and between the object and its properties (since the sentence predicates a property of its subject). At the very beginning, before these elements have ever been formally established, the goddess wants to prevent them from being distinguished. One might say that the history of distinguishing thought begins with a divine attempt to prevent it from proceeding. Thus the goddess says two sentences intended to collapse all the distinctions fundamental to reasoning:

> For it is the same—to think and to be (Fr. 3).
> It is the same—to think and the thought that "Is." (Fr. 8, 34)[32]

The first fragment, read straightforwardly, seems to say that thinking (which the goddess elsewhere couples with speaking) and Being are not to be distinguished. Thus collapses the distinction between the human thinker and what he thinks and speaks about. The second line, from a subsequent fragment, might be understood at least to imply that thinking and thought are not distinct. I am tempted to say, anachronistically, that the activity of thinking and its articulated thought-object, the accomplished thought that "intends" what is, are the same.[33] Thus collapses the distinction between thinker and thought.

The third, most obvious, distinction expressed in the common declarative sentence containing the copula "is" is most aggressively prevented by the goddess. For what is permissible to thought has no distinction-making features. "Isness" is not a subject that has predicates nor a substrate—not immaterial and certainly not material—that carries qualities. The goddess does all she can to prevent that way of speaking by using what comes to be in theology the *via negativa* to God; the way of negation leads to a Being whose qualities are beyond human articulation—only the goddess's denial of distinguishing qualities is not (as is that of the theologians) a mental makeshift for humanly inexpressible attributes, but the truth itself: Her Being *has no* qualities but being itself, and the negative attributes, its "signs," express nonattributes.

I have already mentioned that "Is" does not exist in time. It is "*now,* all at once" (Fr. 8, 5). I think "now" does not mean either the "standing now" of

God's eternity nor the everlastingness of sempiternity, but rather the timeless-ness of that which is without source (*anarchon,* Fr. 8, 27), without birth, with-out growth, without end—a tenseless presence:

> Neither ever was, nor will be, since [it] is now all at once (Fr. 8, 5)[34]

Consequently those qualifications anything might undergo by reason of being temporal do not belong to "Is."

Most distinguishable features that occur to human observation as predicates are, however, space-dependent. Space is *the* scene of differences, not only of differences in location and locomotion but also of shape and color. "Is" is neither within the envelope of a place proper to it nor does it extend through space, as the goddess does her best, this time with positive but somehow self-canceling descriptions, to make her pupil understand. She says:

> Look how things absent are firmly present to the mind;[35]
> For you will not cut off Being from holding onto Being. (Fr. 4, 1–2)

That thought can bring the absent to presence is a common human experience:

> If the dull substance of my flesh were thought,
> Injurious distance should not stop my way;
> For then, despite of space, I would be brought,
> From limits far remote, where thou dost stay. (Shakespeare, Sonnet 44)

But the goddess of Truth is, as it were, taking the later poet at his word: Since thought and Being are one and the same, they interpenetrate each other and are both together everywhere. Not "I here . . . it there," but both together, though not anywhere in space. To be sure, she says of the "All" that it holds itself together; it is *syneches,* the word used later for spatial continuity (Fr. 8, 25):

> Therefore the All is held together. For Being draws near to Being. (Fr. 8,
>   25)

But she surely does not mean spatial continuity, that curious feature which holds, say, a length, together by dividing it about a point. She means an undi-vided all-at-onceness, the perfect distanceless transparence, as one might say, of Being that is thought and thought that is Being. (A latter-day analogy is self-consciousness, of which we do not imagine that it contains a distance be-tween self and consciousness.) It is the goddess of Justice, the "Shower," who not only opens the portals for Parmenides but in doing so floods the world with truth. And with her work Necessity and Fate (Fr. 8, 14, 30, 37), who hold the whole stable, enchained by bonds, totally symmetrical, or better self-congruent:

> From all quarters it is like the bulk of a well-rounded sphere
> From the middle in all ways equally matched. (Fr. 8, 43–44)

And again, though the figure and its terms are spatial, the intention is to countermand the simile: The limits and bounds are not external to Being but internal to it, since there is neither nothing nor something beyond them; the center is everywhere just as thought is, and so is the edge, and the perfection of the sphere is in fact the absence of an identifiable center or circumference:

> For, being from everywhere equal to itself, it falls evenly in with its
> bounds. (Fr. 8, 49)

The nonspatial nature of Being is, then, a necessary concomitant of its identity with thinking.[36] Not only must true thought have the changeless steadfastness of Being, but Being must, reciprocally, have the luminous self-transparency of awareness. Being must be a plenum lacking nothing, and thought must be ubiquitous without opacity or dispersion.

My main purpose in this section has been to enter just enough into the meaning of "Is" to make sense of the "Is not" that trails it as its unwelcome but unshakable doppelgänger. However enigmatic "Is" may be—the more enigmatic the more it is spoken of—this much is clear: "Is" cannot be conveyed, as Parmenides is bidden to do, without continual recourse to negative speech, both to describe the "Is" itself and to distinguish its truth from the untrustworthiness of the forbidden way of inquiry, the way of "Is not."

(d) So far I have engaged in scene-setting preliminaries; now comes the crux: *Nonbeing,* the way of "Is not." All along, in enjoining the way of inquiry that is a road following truth, the way of "Is," the goddess has conjoined an injunction against a straight but unlearnable path, as if uttering a taboo: For this way is unknowable, unshowable, unsayable (Fr. 2, 7–8; 6, 4; 8, 7–8).

Unsayable—but she herself does speak it and show it forth, and evidently know it. And she makes sure that her youth at least knows *of* this way of "Is not," for she bids him more than once to consider it (Fr. 6, 2).

She always does it doubly: First she proclaims "Is" and negates "Is not," and then, immediately, she warns him off "Is not" and the negation of "Is." It is, I think, her way of alerting him to the priority of the positive way: It is a deep fact of logical speech that affirmative can be piled on affirmative without affecting what will be called the logical quality of a proposition, but a second negation returns you to the positive (p. 49). I think she uses the double negation in her assertion of the path of truth to show her pupil that one can indeed utter "not" and *return* to the road of truth provided one utters it *twice*; the self-canceling property of double negation is a sort of saving grace which allows her to utter negations without hopelessly infecting this way of inquiry with negativity: not Is-not.

In her second preventative utterance, she simply forbids the denial of "Is," for this denial does put him who pursues it on the "*unturning* path" to the unattainable. However, in the negative part of her warning to stay off the way of "Is not," she herself is drawn into a possibly perilous formulation of the *false* path: Not-to-be must be (Fr. 2, 5)

For now she has *named* the notion, if for the moment only in an oscillating verbal form. Soon her naming will go entirely beyond negated speech to negative Being. For two lines later appears, for the first time in the West, as far as I know, the noun-participle Nonbeing, with its own neuter article *(to me on)*, the unshakable shadow of the Being that has not even yet been named in her speech *(to eon*, Fr. 4, 2).

What she has declared "unthinkable" and "unnamable" (Fr. 8, 17) she has herself named; she has done exactly what mortals usually do, who insist on naming and so giving status to oppositions (Fr. 8, 15, 53 ff.). This naming is a *krisis*, a "decision," that goes from "Is not," which could be shrugged off as merely a *sentence* employing the negative particle "not" of ordinary, received human speech, to Nonbeing, which is a sort of *thought* somehow achieved by a negating prefix.[37] What is more, it is not a previously given but a deliberately invented word, and its use is not an act of condescension to the talk of mankind, but a divine contribution to the speech of truth. Perhaps the goddess has said too much.

Why did she have to? Why was the negative eventually articulated as a noun and progressively more concretely: from the infinitive "Not-to-be" to the participial "Nonbeing" to the adjectival "Nothing" (Frs. 6, 2; 8, 7 ff.) and even the plural "nonbeings" (Fr. 7, 1),[38] in which the negative all but achieves thinghood? When bidden to choose "Is" over "Is not," young Parmenides, like the hero Heracles, had come on a road of forking ways. The forks are apparently coordinate, but in truth incomparable. The way of "Is" is an affirmation that will steep him, absorb him—speaking in a latter-day mode—in unconceptualized Being, undetermining thought, in the pure experience of Isness. The way of "Is not" is, on the other hand, a path of articulated opposition. The "crisis" therefore shows that thinking has an element of preference, of choice, in it and that the goddess is a teacher of intellectual *virtue* who urges her pupil to be willingly receptive to the persuasion of truth (Fr. 2, 4).[39]

In articulating Nonbeing, the goddess shifts her lesson. The early injunction was: not to say "Is not," because it can be neither shown forth nor said nor thought. It *could* of course be said, and she has said it, but it could not be pointed out or thought: Here now the goddess *is* condescending to use the language of mortals who often utter, with "echoing tongue" (Fr. 7, 4), words without intending anything.

Hence I do not think that the unthinkableness of "Is not" is in any way specified, that she is teaching, for example, lessons about the untenableness of negative facts or the use of the Law of Contradiction.[40] "Is not" cannot be thought for this one unarguable reason: because the plenitude of "Is" leaves nothing outside its bounds or any vacancy within its sphere (Fr. 8, 30 ff.; 44 ff.). But now by her own doing young Parmenides does have an "object" for thought: Nonbeing as a proscribed entity.

So again, why does she depart from Isness to enter on the forbidden way of Nonbeing? Because she has received a mortal and spoken to him, giving first negative commands and then examples of forbidden negative speech, and finally the names of the negative thing that is taboo. So in the very "untrembling heart of Truth" is spoken the word to shake it: Nonbeing, which is brought to the youth's attention so that he might shut off his thought from its way (Fr. 7, 2). But we all know that this is an effort beyond human power, as in that story of the man who was promised a fortune if he would but refrain for a whole day from thinking of a white elephant. And the goddess knows it too, for this initiation, she keeps telling him, is not an end but a beginning. She has put him on that *true* way of *inquiry* which, once he has left her house to return to the world of mortals, he must recall as the road that leads past the portals of night and day. But she has also acquainted him with a *second* way necessary for the cities of mortals, the way of opposition. The ways do not differ in the use of negation, only in what is negated, Nonbeing on the first way, Being on the second. Parmenides brings back the knowledge that *both together*, not equal in standing but mutually indispensable, are the mortal mode of inquiry which we call *dialectic*. So much for her justified use of negating speech. But with respect to Nonbeing the goddess loses her gamble. It is never again out of thinking minds.

(e) Indeed, the goddess herself introduces a *third* way, a composite way.[41] It is that of the "unchoosing *(akrita)* tribe" of deaf and blind and dazed mortals. The choosing they fail to do is between "to be and not to be"; they are "two-headed" (Fr. 6, 4 ff.). They have established "two forms" in their intentions and have named them, though one of them they ought not to have named (Fr. 8, 59); the privative term is of course meant.

Almost everyone is puzzled by this second part of the poem, usually called "the Way of Seeming." The goddess herself announces her intention right away; her initiate is to find out not only the "untrembling heart of convincing Truth" but also the "opinions *(doxas)* of mortals in which there is no true trust." And then she adds a riddling description, saying that he is nevertheless to learn "how the things that seem *(dokounta)* must be *dokimos*, penetrating all things throughout the All" (Fr. 1, 31–32).

I have left the word *dokimos* in Greek first to show that it is cognate with "opinions" and "the things that seem," and then because, though much hangs on the meaning, it is hard to ascertain; *dokimos* ordinarily means "genuinely, truly" but in a pinch it could be heard as "seemingly, *not* truly." When she makes a hiatus in the poem by announcing that she is stopping her "trustworthy account *(logos)* and thought about truth," she says that he must now hear and learn the "deceitful order *(kosmon)*" of her words (Fr. 8, 50 ff.). She does in fact present a—very strange—cosmology. Is *it* the "deceitful cosmos" of her words, and are these the opinions of mortals that pervade the All, opinions that are ambivalent with respect to truth and falsity? Is the goddess's third way (1) a serious try at this-worldly truth telling, (2) an ironic recital of mortal fantasies, or (3) an outright falsehood?[42] I know of no persuasive answer to these questions. But I do think that one may discern what the goddess finds to blame in the way of mortals.

It is just their willingness to make and live with *oppositions.* It is not that they contradict themselves. On the contrary, when they allow both "Is *and* Is not" rather than following the goddess's call to a choice between "Is *or* Is not" (Fr. 8, 16), they are accepting a world of differences, such that not one and the same thing both is and is not, but that this thing is not that thing.[43] It follows, incidentally, that the Law of Contradiction is *not* (as is sometimes asserted) proclaimed in this poem. For that law requires the very possibility of a being and its negation or a proposition and its negative, and these possibilities the goddess denies. The law says that A and not-A cannot coexist (if they are things) or be asserted (if they are propositions) *at the same time.* Thus time can overcome the prohibitions of this law, and it implicitly says that either condition is possible.[44] In the world of the goddess the law of contradiction is moot because the negative term is rejected as impossible.

No, the goddess blames mortals for their "two-headedness," their propensity, one might say, for taking her "Is" as a copula and compulsively completing it with a predicate: "This is such *and* that is not such but something else."

Why does she nevertheless pursue this composite way of "Is and Is not" for her pupil? Of course she knows that in the world to which he must return to convey her story this two-headedness is a fact, with which she, like a careful teacher, prepares him to cope. This youngster is not inexperienced—the way that brings him to the great gates is called "much speaking" *(polyphemon)*, a word used of the meeting place, the *agora,* where public speeches were made; it is entirely possible that he comes to the goddess from a very young public life, to which he in fact returns later as a trusted statesman. What she adds to his worldly knowledge is, I think, the recognition that the composite way of dialectic, which unites the ways of affirmation and negation, is inherent in ordinary human speech and therefore teachable by mortals to mortals, and that this is the one way by which Parmenides can safely convey the tale he has heard from his divine teacher—provided he recalls her teaching of the first part, that the affirmation of Being must be ultimate. The deficiency of that first part was that though the goddess represented the way of Being as an *inquiry,* it was never that in the house of Truth; it was one blazing insight not suitable for a life-long occupation in the cities of men. With the imparting of the third way she has shown him the scene of his mature activity and has intimated to him how, by making a judicious composite of the first and second way but never forgetting which of these is the only way that reaches truth, he can convey her tale to his fellow mortals in a mode they can, in turn, hear. I am speculating, but perhaps not wildly.

(f) And thus this Nonbeing, named in the house of the goddess so that it might be the better avoided, is indelibly *established* in the realm of humans. But what can be said about this illicitly named nonentity? Very little.

It is not within the sphere of Being, for that is a plenum since "Being draws near to Being" (Fr. 8, 24–25); nor is it without, for Being has no external limit, no determining negation. It is not void, for it is not spatial, nor is it full because it is not Being. It is not a thought, for thought is preempted by Being, nor is it, once named, totally unthought; it is not to be shown forth nor can it be completely withdrawn.

This featurelessness of Nonbeing differs from the privative "signs" that show forth Being, for these are all at least figuratively apprehensible through their opposites, while Nonbeing is fenced in by impossibility on both sides, so to speak, by what it is (!) and what it is not. It is therefore unamenable to the *via negativa*, the approach by negation.

Yet radically null-featured though Nonbeing be, its force sets the poem trembling, in its hundred and fifty lines and in its two parts. For single lines have multivalent readings, as "not" and "non-" are said to be unsayable and unthinkable whilst being continually proposed by speech to thought: Parmenides is bidden to keep his thought off a way of inquiry which is nonetheless set out for him. He is bidden to decide by reason even as the negative thought articulated is proscribed. And finally the way of Truth is conjoined with its counterpoint, the way of Seeming, in an unsettling second act.

These oscillations have their source right in the untrembling heart of Truth, in the house of the goddess who speaks to a mortal who has gone outside the trodden path of men (Fr. 1, 27). In the judgment of the ages, she ought not to be speaking at all: "if everything were . . . absolutely indistinguishable from anything else, there would be nothing to say" (Austin, "Truth," 22). So her very speaking makes truth quake, for it shows forth Being as infused with Nonbeing, that is, with distinctions, or alternately as carrying Nonbeing about as an external shadow. The latter figure applies to those logicians closer to our time who take the world as consisting of unmitigatedly factual existences and who therefore relegate all negation to the penumbra of logical language (p. 45). For them existence is as dense as Being was for Parmenides, and they invite by their existence-totalism a reaction that is the this-worldly analogue—at a remove of two and half millennia—to what is about to happen to Being: As nonexistent objects would in our time be forcibly inserted into spatiotemporal existence (p. 79), so Nonbeing is about to be deliberately diffused over intelligible Being—by one of Parmenides' own philosophical progeny.

2. NONBEING ENFOLDED IN BEING: PLATO'S DIALOGUE

The next step in the ancient story of Nonbeing is then the reversal of its outlaw status and its integration into the community of Beings. It is taken in Athens, the city of reconciliations. Here primeval wildness is domesticated by kind compromise, the self-perpetuating chain of retributive killing is broken by reasoning judgment, the defiling outcast is invited to his protected place of sacral annihilation.[45] Here Nonbeing finds its place.

A Stranger has come to Athens from Elea, Parmenides' town. He is a devoted pupil of his great teacher, whom he calls his father. But what he is about to do he himself thinks might look like parricide (*Sophist* 241 d).[46] He is about to show that Nonbeing *is*, and what it is, and why it must be. But this is not, in fact, the obliteration of his philosophical father at all, but a vast extension—one might say a doubling—of Parmenides' domain, Being.

Two presences at this great event are the more forcefully there for their absence. One is Plato, the concealed author of the dialogue called the *Sophist*, in which a visiting Stranger revises the Parmenidean doctrine; with characteristic generosity Plato assigns the credit for what is, I think, the second most consequence-laden discovery in the life of ontology to an anonymous Eleatic visitor. The other presence is Socrates, who poses the problem and recedes into silence, turning the conversation over to two boys. One of these is another Socrates who does not, however, seem to resemble Socrates in anything but name, while the other is another Socrates not only in his facial features but also in a likeness of nature; his name is Theaetetus.

(a) Socrates' dialogic life span is framed by Parmenidean associations; they are, so to speak, its termini. It matters not at all whether their truth is mythical or factual, but it is at least possible that the dialogue between a very old Parmenides and a very young Socrates that Plato composed had a factual counterpart. Here Socrates learns dialectic and the generosity of self-refutation. Now in Socrates' old age and soon before his death comes another old man from Elea, once again to refute Parmenidean doctrine. It is probable that Socrates sets this course going. Certainly the question he puts, What is a sophist, a statesman, a philosopher, and are they one or two or three kinds? (217 a), will make a critique of Parmenides' proscription of Nonbeing necessary, as we may imagine Socrates well knows. For the Eleatics were, from antiquity on, thought of as having sophistical affinities, partly because as ingenious dialecticians they sometimes argued from words rather than meanings—sophists are, as their name proclaims, "professors of wisdom," who travel the world selling the art of the word divorced from truth—and partly, we may think, because the doctrine that rejects Nonbeing in behalf of truth turns out to make error indiscernible. And so it is hard to imagine that Socrates had not perceived this perplexity and that it is not the sly agenda behind his posing of the question.[47] But then he bows out, perhaps to mark the fact that he has instigated a new phase in the inquiry into Being which is beyond his life's mission.

Like Parmenides' epic poem, Plato's philosophical prose drama is fraught with humanly significant circumstance; neither abstracts its message from persons and settings. Now of the three types Socrates proposes for inquiry, the statesman will become the subject of the dialogue by that name, the sophist is pursued in the present work, but the philosopher has no dialogue of his own. I think that is because sophists and philosophers are identical—the Stranger keeps coming close to saying so (231 a ff., for example)—except for two differences: One is just the fact that a sophist can divorce himself from the place he is in and the people he faces and above all the life-affecting, almost sacral character of dialectic (253 e) to ply his peculiar expertise for reputation and money, while the philosopher never forgets his human circumstances and the seriousness of his enterprise—which is why Parmenides' poem and Plato's dialogues survive while the sophists' speeches and arguments are largely gone.

The other difference is precisely in their relation to Nonbeing (254 a), which will be considered below. But we may conjecture right now that once the typical sophist's affinity for Nonbeing has been brought to light, the philosopher too is sufficiently elucidated—as that rare sophist who acknowledges Nonbeing without taking cover in it.[48] As I said, I cannot imagine that this outcome is not in Socrates' mind as he sets the conversation going, or rather, that Plato would not smile to have us think so.

The discovery of a new, legitimating name for Nonbeing, a name that has shed the dreaded negative—for that is how it will be saved—is then a byproduct of the pursuit of the sophist-type, though it is the high point of the conversation. Here is what the Stranger finds.

(b) The Sophist is an escape artist who will finally seek shelter in the thicket of Nonbeing. But to begin with he is a type who assumes numerous shapes and lineages in the universe of human expertise.[49] He is, above all, a purveyor of "learnables," a whole world of them. So the question arises whether these are the genuine article or fakes, whether he is a teller of truths or of enchanting simulacra of truth—falsehoods. If he is the latter, the sophist is an imitator and possesses in truth only the art of imitation, by which he can mirror or otherwise copy anything and give this image out for the real thing and sell it off (234 c ff.). So if the Stranger can say what an image is, he ought to be able to catch the sophist.

Therefore the Stranger gives an analysis of "image," the first ever to articulate the proper place in the nature of things of this strange structure that plays so overwhelming a role in contemporary life.[50] *An image*, along with all sorts of "seeming," *is a composite of Being and Nonbeing* (240 b–c). An image *is* truly a likeness and is really *not* its original. And the analysis can descend to speech, the domain shared by sophist and true dialectician: False speaking *is* real utterance, but it *is not* saying—saying what is the case (236 e, p.).

But now the Stranger has landed himself in big trouble. The sophist will certainly not stand still to be captured by this characterization (239 e ff.). He will forthwith escape into the thicket of Nonbeing where no one, least of all an Eleatic, can pursue him. There is something savage about these suave talkers—the Stranger says they are to philosophers as wolves are to dogs (231 a)—but they are smart. The sophist has turned the Stranger's very analysis into a hiding place, since Nonbeing is an inaccessible, unnameable region—it is what is not. But if Nonbeing is not, the sophist is not to be captured as a faker and a teller of falsehoods (in Greek the word for fake and false is conveniently the same: *pseudes*.

Meanwhile the Stranger too knows very well that he has given an analysis forbidden by Parmenides. He himself quotes from the ancestral poem, and it is through him that we have these lines:

> This should not ever prevail, that nonbeings are,
> But do you restrain your thought from this way of inquiry.
> (Fr. 7, 1–2; *Sophist* 237 a, repeated at 258 d)

Therefore the time has come to illuminate the "darkness of Nonbeing" (254 a). The sophist must burst the paternal restraint and show how and why Nonbeing *is*. Note, however, that he has chosen for refutation lines that speak of "nonbeings," in the plural. Nonbeing itself, he will assert, has no number (237 d), but a first consequence of admitting it will be the appearance of a multitude of derivative nonbeings (or rather not-beings). So he has picked a fitting passage. I can here imagine Socrates as he is quietly listening, noticing with a smile how subtly the Stranger is shifting from Parmenides' Being, which is One and All, to Socrates' Being, which is one among many forms that are all beings by "participation" in this greater form *(eidos)*.

For, remarkably, the Stranger seems to be perfectly familiar with the Socratic-Platonic forms and the dialectic they invite.[51] But perhaps it is not too surprising, since these forms are "beings to be thought" *(noeta)*, but not in the sense of being thoughts, meaning some thinker's own ideas, or, as we say, "subjective." They are in themselves, by themselves, whether any human reaches them by thinking or not. To a pupil of Parmenides, used to hearing that thinking and Being are the same, it should be, if anything, a lesser effort to accept that there are thinkable beings whose common character is intelligibility.[52] In any case, the Stranger speaks of the forms familiarly, and is friendly to the "friends of the forms" (248 a).

These forms make it possible to collect an infinite variety of appearing things in this world under a finite number of kinds, for these hold still for thought when all the appearances are changing; they are what each mere appearance truly is and what is expressed in unifying speech.[53] The Stranger, however, is not here interested so much in the relation of the forms to the world of the senses, but in a more advanced problem: the relation of the forms to each other. The reason is plain: It is his—somewhat technical—task to introduce Nonbeing into the realm of Being that comprises the forms. That is how Nonbeing is to be domiciled in Athens—as a form.

In preparation the Stranger launches into a dialectic of Being (249 d ff.). He shows that among the "greatest kinds" *(megista gene)* of the beings that comprise Being (which here names the whole intelligible realm) some mix with each other while others do not. For example, Rest and Motion can hardly take part in each other; in fact they are utterly distinct, though both *are*, and so they both mingle with Being (which here names a single form). There are thus three great kinds, related as stated. "Stranger: Then each of them is *other* [first appearance!] than the remaining pair but itself the same as itself" (254 d).

And he shows that neither Being nor Rest nor Motion can *be* the Same or the Other, though they do participate in sameness (that is, self-identity) and otherness. So first the Same and finally the Other are added as a fourth and fifth to the greatest kinds (255 c–d). The Stranger pays particular attention to distinguishing the Other from Being; they are *not* two names for one kind. They must be distinct, for if the Other were identical with Being, there would be some participants in Being such as Rest and Motion that would as beings remain *utterly* distinct, while as participants in a separable Other they can be related, namely as each other's other.

The Other turns out to be a most wonderful form. It runs through all the forms (255 e), making each other than the other—it is the very principle of *bonding diversity*, of *relationality*. For each being is what it *is* by reason of its own selfsame nature, but it is *related* to all the others by mutual otherness—it is bonded to each of them as that other's other.

And now comes the moment. If all forms participate in the Other, then any one form, say Motion, is *other* than Being, and if it is other, it *is not*; it is in that respect a not-being, though also a being, since it partakes of Being as well (256 d). Nonbeing, alias the Other, is a form among forms (258 c) that makes all the beings, including even Being itself into not-beings (257 a).

So here is Nonbeing as a form, one of the greatest, under its new name of "Other." It has not only been saved; it is even in a certain way grander than Being, for "Being is many, while Nonbeing is unlimited in multitude" (256 e). Why is Nonbeing innumerable? It is, as Otherness, "all chopped up—just like knowledge" (257 c)—recall that the dialogue begins with the ever branching divisions of expertise. Of each form it is true that it is what it is (whether that be a unitary nature or a somewhat complex structure), but it is *not* each of the forms and communities of forms that it confronts—of which there are so many as to be incalculable.[54] But what is the nature of that ubiquitous "not"?

Nonbeing makes not-beings. The Stranger is not consistent in his usage, but the more general "non-" is always used for Nonbeing, while the more definite "not-" is used in certain crucial places (like 256 a, c) to negate the beings as each mingles with Nonbeing.[55]

I think the usage signifies two things. First, the Stranger wants to indicate what will turn out to be the most consequence-laden effect of his identification of Nonbeing as Other. The first step in his refutation of Parmenides, right after he quotes the prohibition against thinking that nonbeings are, is to show the silencing effect of taking Nonbeing to mean "Utter-non-being" (237 b), *nihil absolutum*, absolute nothing.[56] It is its naming as the Other that saves it from the utter inability—which Parmenides does indeed assert—to become sayable. Hence when the Other is suffused over beings, it is important that it not behave like Utter-non-being. Theaetetus would indeed probably hear "not-being" as utter denial, as sheer opposition, cancellation of being. Yet he must learn not to take relating *otherness* for abrupt *opposition*. So "not-" used in certain places is an attention getter: Nonbeing both bonds *and* negates among beings, but its negation is not annihilation.

Second, the Stranger is about to return to language, and "not" is the particle used for negating declarative sentences. Recall that this exercise, grand though it was, had as its object catching out the sophist who is an image maker in words (234 c) and who, while uttering falsehoods and giving out knowledge both fake and false, claims that there is no false speech (260 d). The Stranger has, to be sure, achieved far more than the grounding of *false* speech; he has elucidated all *negative* speech.

The crux of his solution is (1) the establishment of Nonbeing as the Other, (2) the demonstration that forms are interwoven and commune or mingle with each other in various determinate combinations (which I have neglected here), and (3) the peculiar universal relational mingling of the Other, which makes each being an other's other.

And now in addition, there is (4) its mingling with opinion and speech:

> If it doesn't mix with these, then it's necessary that all things are true; but if it does mix, then both false opinion and speech come about. For to opine or to speak things that *are not*—this, I suppose, is the false, insofar as it comes about in both thought and speech. (260 b f.)

All of these results work together right away to help the Stranger dispose of a difficulty of negative speech that has occupied philosophically inclined logicians into our times (p. 75)—what it is that is intended in negating sentences: are they about nonexistent objects, and if so, how can they be? The Stranger wants Theaetetus to understand that when he speaks, for example, of something as not-beautiful, it is not simply nothing, but something other than beautiful that he is speaking about. Consequently every well-formed sentence is a connection made between beings, true if it says that things are as they are, false if it says that they are other than they are because the connection is falsely made.

All such speech is thus (1) about something, namely, beings (262 c), (2) positive or negative in that it speaks either of a being or its other, the not-beings, and (3) true or false in connecting beings truly or falsely; I believe this is the first time the logical term "quality" is used of this property (263 b).

Should anyone be inclined to ask why Plato had to take us into the august dialectic of Being to explain falsehood, the answer must be along these lines: Speech is *about* something, and what it is about are the beings of thought. And since that is, of course, what thinking is about, human speech and human thinking are, except for the fact of sensory utterance, identical: "the soul's inner conversation, when it arises without voice, has been given just this title by us—'thinking' " (263 e).

Hence any deliverance of speech will have to be explained by reference to thinking *and* to the intelligible forms. But whereas the universal form of mutuality, the Other, makes a bond of diversity among the forms, when it descends into speech it makes possible not only true negations but also false attributions.[57] Thus worldly otherness, the Other fallen into appearance, is not always benign.

(c) This coda will enumerate the benefits of ranging Nonbeing among Beings. The sophist, that "hard-to-hunt" kind (261 a), is now well and truly caught, but who cares about that type? He may be an irritating imitator (though actual real sophists tend to be rather nice people in the Dialogues), but his capture is really incidental to something greater: the enfolding of Nonbeing within the sphere of Being, so that one may say not only that Nonbeing *is* but also *what* it is, namely The Other, or Otherness. That enfolding and that naming have a number of wonderful consequences:

(1) For those who want to think about the realm of intelligible beings, this dialogue, by letting us range Nonbeing among the forms, makes a whole out of a heap.

(2) In the face of the current explosion of image making and viewing, and of the postmodern theory of images that breaks their connection to an original in favor of an infinite self-mirroring,[58] it might be profitable to recall an analysis that bonds the image, albeit negatively, to the original of which it is a likeness.

(3) "Professors of wisdom" also abound in our time, and the tracking of

the sophist into the lair of Nonbeing is a salutary exercise in understanding the contemporary type.

(4) Nonbeing is the antidote to nihilism, since the enfolding of Nonbeing in Being turns negation, whether of things or in words, away from being an irruption of nothingness to being an intimation of difference.

(5) Since "diversity" is a contemporary social preoccupation and "the Other" a pervasive intellectual interest,[59] it has to be a concern to recall the aboriginal Western analysis of these notions in terms of domesticated Nonbeing.

$$\infty \qquad \infty \qquad \infty$$

In Nonbeing naysaying has found its enabling principle in the realm of Being. Now comes a view of speech and thought as themselves having inherent negativity. As Nonbeing was a source of ontic diversity, so this Negativity will be the source of mental motion.

NOTES

1. Hegel says this about Parmenides in his *Lectures on the History of Philosophy*, vol. I, pt. I, sec. I, chap. 1, C 2.

2. That never seems to end. Thus Peirce says, "The First is that whose being is simply in itself, not referring to anything or lying behind anything." "The Second is precisely that which cannot be without the first. . . . It meets us in such facts as Another, Relation, . . . Negation. . . . The genuine second suffers and yet resists, like dead matter whose existence consists in its inertia" (Peirce, 248–249). It is just this Second that Parmenides' goddess denounces. Later on Peirce refers to the First, along with a Second and a Third, as the triad of ideas that "must carry me far into the heart of those primaeval mysteries" of soul, nature, God (253). Just so is Parmenides carried into the "heart of untrembling Truth", though it is unitary. See Aristotle on First Philosophy, note 6.

3. The reports of Xenophanes on Nonbeing, or rather, Not-being *(ouk on)*, are all secondhand and probably in latter-day language: "being [would come] from not-being, which is impossible" (Diehls, p. 117, l. 22); compare Parmenides' fragment 8, 10. It is Aristotle who reports that Parmenides was said to have been Xenophanes' student *(Metaphysics* 986 b 24). The example of Heraclitus, one of several, is from Diehls, Fr. 49 a.

4. The date of Parmenides is not known but can be figured out in this way: Plato says of him in the dialogue *Parmenides* (127 b) that he came to Athens and conversed with Socrates when Parmenides was a nobly venerable sixty-five and Socrates was "*very* young." Socrates was born in 470 B.C., and guessing that "*very* young" means about sixteen or seventeen, Parmenides would have been born about 518 B.C. I think of both the Parmenides of the poem and the Socrates of the dialogue as in their teens, since in my experience the powers of pure thought are at their highest potency in very young freshmen.

5. Even in published philosophy there is always a time before the first, and the student is astounded to find that many an originator has in fact a precursor, and many a beginning is in fact a reprise. Here are a few examples: The notion that I can doubt everything but the activities of my own mind and so my existence is usually ascribed to Descartes (*Meditations* II), but here is Augustine (*On the Trinity* X 10): Men, he says, have doubted everything. "Yet who ever doubts that he himself lives and remembers and understands and wills and thinks and knows and judges?" Or take the gist of Russell's "Theory of Descriptions," which is quite recognizably stated by Kant (p. 104). Or Hannah Arendt's thesis of the mediocrity of extreme criminality among the Nazis, set out in *Eichmann in Jerusalem: A Report on the Banality of Evil* (1963), which postdates Joseph Conrad's author's note (1920) to *Under Western Eyes*. Speaking of the horrific terrorist in his novel, he says, "What troubled me most in dealing with him was not his monstrosity but his banality." Or, finally, consider the unattributed etymologizing by Heidegger of the Greek word for "truth," *aletheia*, in terms of a negating *a* plus *lethe*, meaning "oblivion," as the "Unconcealed," which became a signature word for him (e.g., *Being and Time* 1927, 33 and passim; the etymology dominates his *Parmenides* 1942), but which was actually fully set forth half a generation before by Nicolai Hartmann in *Plato's Logic of Being* (1909, pt. II 239, note 1); see also chapter 6, notes 26 and 31.

My point is that when even in the recorded, accessible tradition there is less that is new under the sun than the reading of any one author might suggest, how many unrecorded thoughts must have preceded the first that appears on the public scene? And yet for me this meditation enhances rather than abates the sense of awe that attends the reading of a first well-formulated annunciation.

6. Aristotle's term: e.g., *Metaphysics* 1026 a 16, 1061 b; see also *Physics* 194 b 15: the business of First Philosophy is to decide what has being on its own and what is its nature. For Aristotle, philosophy had largely but not altogether lost the literal meaning of truth sought after but not yet attained: "It is right to call philosophy the *knowledge* of truth" (*Metaphysics* 993 b 20).

7. The term is traceable to Schleiermacher (*Ueberweg* 1:28).

8. For example, "the lover of wisdom *(philosophos)* is between the wise man and the ignorant" (*Symposium* 204 b). At the other end, Hegel considers it his mission to let philosophy divest itself of its name—*love* of knowledge—to become *actual* knowledge (Hegel 1807, early in preface).

9. Some chief uses of the term "dialectic" are (1) a mode of testing and refuting by question and answer, said, significantly, to have been invented by Parmenides' companion Zeno (Aristotle reported in Diehls 1:247) and on occasion used by himself (Plato *Sophist* 217 c); (2) philosophical conversation as practiced by Socrates in Platonic dialogues; (3) the "dialectic method" (*dialektike methodos, Republic* 533 c 7) that Socrates sets out for reaching and discerning the forms of Being; (4) logical disputation beginning from accepted opinions, treated at length by Aristotle (*Topics, Rhetoric, Sophistical Refutations*), and which again becomes central for certain humanists, especially Ramus, as an art of discoursing and disputing effectively (Ong, 178 ff.); (5) Hegel's self-movement of the concept and its derivatives, for example, Marxist dialectic of material conditions.

I think that what holds all these senses together is the prepositional prefix *dia*, which betokens on the one hand distinction and its discernment and, on the other, the connecting passage through the difference: Dialectic is the responsive speech of "yes" and "no" as these separate and relate thoughts and things.

10. The fragment and line numbers for Parmenides' poem are pretty standard. Two useful working editions are those by Tarán (1965) and, above all, by Gallop (1984). We have about 150 lines, perhaps one third of the poem. Since by far the longer part of the surviving lines belongs to the part usually headed "Truth," which deals with Being, this surviving proportion may be as high as nine-tenths (Gallop, 27 n. 8), the largest for any Presocratic.

The title of the poem was said by some ancients to have been *On Nature (Peri physeos)*, but this seems unlikely to me, since (1) it was simply what the so-called Physicists named their poems (the "Physicists" were Presocratics who, unlike Parmenides, were interested in the material out of which the world is made, e.g., Empedocles); (2) *physis* really means "coming into being," "growth," and that is what Parmenides deems impossible; (3) the word *physis* occurs only in the "Seeming" part of the poem (Fr. 10, 1 and 5); when the verb *phyo* occurs (Fr. 8, 10; 10, 6), it means "grow," but such growth is denied in fragment 8.

11. The Presocratics combine a huge regard for Homer with frequent disparagement, for example, Xenophanes (Diehls, Fr. 11) and Heraclitus (Diehls, Fr. 42). Their complaint is mostly that Homer is a polytheist whose gods behave badly to boot, but this is mere sniping, compared to Parmenides' implicit but more powerful assault.

12. "Towns" is a debated reading in Fr. 1, 3; so are the alternatives. Fränkel argues for my reading (37 n. 8).

13. The goddess who receives him calls him "Youth," *kouros* (Fr. 1, 24). A *kouros* is a boy who has just begun to shave *(kerein)*.

14. Fr. 1, 22 ff.; *Odyssey* I, 1. Homer appears once in his own poem, in this first line where he asks the Muse to tell *him* of Odysseus. Parmenides, in his poem, will first be speaking in his own voice and reporting the goddess's tale thereafter.

15. Compare Fr. 8, 5: "since the All is altogether *now*." The word for pipe, nave, and socket is *syrinx* (Fr. 1, 6 and 19). See Kingsley, 117 ff., for all sorts of wonderful observations on Parmenides' way with words.

16. Aside from the use of the present tense in the first line, there are two "iterative optatives" (*hikanoi, sperchoiato,* Fr. 1, 1 and 8), which betoken repeated action.

17. *Odos:* way; *keleuthos:* road; *patos:* a trodden path; *hamaxiton:* wagon way; *atarpos:* a path without a turn. *Poly-:* much speaking and much experienced way; much discerning mares; much contended refutation; many signs—and more.

18. I say "deity" because, while later she is called a goddess, when she is first mentioned she is a *daimon,* which is a more solemnly impersonal appellation (Fr. 1, 3).

19. Tarán, 31. Sextus Empericus (Gallop, 95) interpreted the Mares as being Parmenides' irrational impulses and the Sun Maidens as being the senses. This is an extravagance that nevertheless gets the spirit of the poem right.

20. The named deities are female in gender. It does not seem to me that Truth is a separate deity. She is most certainly not the goddess who speaks; Heidegger makes this unjustified identification the basis of his book *Parmenides,* 5, which is not about Parmenides but about *Aletheia.* (For the nasty consequences of this unprofitable feminization of truth, read Nietzsche, *Beyond Good and Evil,* preface: The presupposition that truth is a woman makes fools of philosophers.)

21. *Thymos*: *Republic* 439 c ff.; Sappho: Verse 5 of "Dapple-throned, immortal Aphrodite."

22. The Sun Maidens come forth from the "houses of night" and accompany the youth to "our house"—the route is from the dark plural to bright singular, though the darkness is absorbed into light on the way.

23. Just as is the case for "way," the poem is a compendium of words for "word" and "speaking": *mythos*: tale told; *epos*: spoken word; *logos*: reasoning speech, account; *rhethenta*: things proclaimed.

So also different verbs are used: point out, say, tell, speak, indicate, proclaim. My impression is that Parmenides often means only to achieve iteration without repetition, but that sometimes the words indicate subtle variations in meaning. For example, *mythos* is used with "way" as of an Odyssean story: "the tale of the way" (Fr. 1, 1–2; 8, 1); *logos* is used only twice, by the goddess, once for "reason" (7, 5), once for a summary: "Here I stop my trustworthy account and thought" (Fr. 8, 50).

A puzzling case is *atarpon*, the path without turning (Fr. 2, 6), used by the goddess of the unintelligible way, though later that same false way, that of Being and Nonbeing equally acknowledged, is called a "back-turning road." See note 43.

24. Of the speaking verbs mentioned above, *phrazein*, which first means "point out, impart, show forth" and only later "tell" (Gallop, 31 n. 20), is the most interesting. This is the verb used in Fr. 2, 6 and 8.

25. Diehls, B 50. Whether Heraclitus is older, younger, or of the same age as Parmenides and whether Parmenides responded to him or the reverse or neither is unsettled, see Tarán, 69 ff., Gallop, 33 n. 32. It is usual to think of Heraclitus as the predecessor, but the opposite argument was made by Reinhardt, 221.

26. Aristotle himself does such a job on Parmenides in his *Physics* (I, 3). He is in pursuit of his project of studying motion, for in Parmenides' Sphere of Being motion is excluded. All of Aristotle's logical arguments, mostly directed against Parmenides' false assumption of the univocity of Being, are logically incontrovertible. Yet he himself begins with a false premise: that Parmenides argues sophistically, making false assumptions and illogical deductions (186 a 3). But the Parmenides of the poem does not argue at all, and the argumentative Parmenides does not defend the unity of Being. Various more recent logicistic interpretations will be taken up below.

It is a tribute to the power of the poem that the temptation to have yet another try at penetrating it, to become yet another member of the set that might be called "the pygmies around Parmenides," is irresistible.

27. Grimm's *Wörterbuch* and Spitzer, as cited by Jespersen 1924, 241. Curme, 7, says that the "it" was introduced into English so as to extend the usual subject-verb pattern to impersonal verbs (such as "rains") which had no subject in Gothic, and to prevent confusion with questions requiring "yes" or "no" as an answer, which used to, and in German still do, begin with the main verb.

It is interesting that Greek permits both declarative verb sentences that have no noun *and* noun sentences, the so-called nominal sentences, that have no verb.

28. By the Alexandrian scholar Aristophanes, about three centuries after Parmenides.

29. Gallop lists five meanings of *esti*, the existential, copulative, and veridical (7), and also "is possible," "is available" (42). Of these the first four are discussed in my

text. The last, a somewhat strained meaning, serves mostly to circumvent the more straightforward reading of the much debated fragment 3 ("For it is the same to think as to be") and to translate: "because the same thing is there for (is available to) thinking and being" (57). What, however, can it really mean for something to be there for and to be available to being? And what is that "something"? But see Gallop, 8 and 32, note 22.

Gallop also observes in this connection that Parmenides is not a direct philosophical ancestor of Berkeley, who said that "to be is to be perceived," or of any other sort of idealism (32 n. 23). I would put the reason this way: An idealist thinks that Being is *dependent* on thought. Parmenides is told that the two are *identical*. The goddess is indeed so far from teaching idealism that she reduces all ideas to one, and collapses that one with its object, not so that all Being will be an idea but so that thinking will itself enter the state of Being.

30. Reading 1 is justified by analogy with the first part of the line, where "Is" is clearly mentioned rather than used; the same might therefore be said of "Is not," which thus becomes the subject of the negated infinitive. Reading 2 is justified by analogy with its negative version in line 5, below: "that Not-to-be needs is." Reading 3 simply takes *ésti* as accented. It is worth noting that "It is possible" is an option only when "Is not" is at issue, since "Is" is neither possible nor impossible, but is what will later be called "actual."

31. This construction is called a "cognate accusative."

32. For fragment 3, see note 29. Plotinus has no trouble reading the fragment as I have (*Enneads* V, 1, 8). For other readings of fragment 8, 34 see Gallop, 71. I accept the reading of Diehls, 238, who takes *houneken* = that.

33. This fragment continues (8, 35–36): "For not without Being, in which it [thinking] is expressed, / Will you find thinking." So the main meaning of these lines is surely that Being is the necessary and only content of thought. But an incidental meaning is that thinking, thought, and its intended content are one. "Intention" is the term used by medieval writers, and revived especially in Phenomenology, to denominate the most distinctive feature of thought, its "aboutness"; intentionality designates the fact that thinking produces thought-contents. Parmenides' goddess, once again, seems to anticipate a puzzle about thinking: just how a particular thought is "about" its object, or in what manner the object is contained in the thought. Being is here the necessary content of every thought, and is identical as well with all thinking activity, while conversely, thinking and thought are themselves the aspects of Being.

34. The much vexed question whether Parmenides discovered atemporality must, it seems to me, be answered by asking: What can be the relation of *his* notion of Being to time? So whether the "now" of the lines quoted betokens not atemporality but rather the temporal continuity of the subject (Fränkel, 46 n. 86), or whether the denial of past and future tense both implies and is implied by the immutability of Being (Owen, 276), or whether "now" conveys completeness of Being at any time (Gallop, 14), is to be decided, I think, in accordance with a construal of the notion of Being. For example, Parmenides can hardly be speaking of eternity as conceived by theologians, because that harbors time within it (e.g., Augustine), nor of the atemporality of the Being that stands behind appearance (Plato) or of the apriorities that ground human existence (Kant and Heidegger), because appearances and existences are what he denies.

To me it seems that the goddess introduces into human thought the notion not so much of atemporality (which could be understood as existence in a privative temporal mode, that is to say, being in space but not in time) but of *timeless presence*, by which I mean to describe Being as that which just *is*, which is "Isness."

Who knows whether Plato had Parmenides in mind when he wrote the *Timaeus*? But there do seem to be echoes, and they are in the spirit of the notion just set out: "We say of eternal Beinghood that it was, is, and shall be, whereas in truth of speech the is alone applies to it" (37 e–38 a). There is, incidentally, another echo. Parmenides' goddess sets out, besides the sphere of Being, a world as it appears to humans; she calls it a *diakosmos eikos*, "a likely cosmos." This is just what Timaeus does for Socrates—he tells a "likely story" of a cosmos that is itself a likeness (29 c, d).

By the way, in the poem is to be found what I think is a first appearance of a term that plays a central role in the Platonic dialogues: "by itself" *(kath heauto)* used in the sense of "absolute," relationless (Fr. 8, 29).

35. The Greek noun is *noos (nous)*; the poem contains (1) the verb "to think" *(noein)*, (2) "*a* thought" *(noema)*, the distinguishable object or content of thinking, and (3) "thought" *(noos)*, the agent of thinking. "Mind" is used only because "Thought" would be strange here.

It would be good to know what are the goddess's connotations for this word group, whose history of usages ranges from the most ordinary (having to do with getting the point, making a plan, having a mind-set) to the most exalted (as in "intellectual insight"). For a survey of the group in early Greek philosophy, see von Fritz, 23 ff.

It seems to me that Parmenides intended to express to us—for the first time in human history—what thought is for someone who has left behind the world of dazed humans and entered the true way of inquiry. There one discovers that thinking and thought are no longer distinguishable and that thought and Being in turn are correlative to the point of identity, that thought, like Being, is in a nonspatial sense everywhere and in an unscattered way everything. And also like Being, thought has a proscribed capability, that of being negated.

36. My unsatisfactory attempt to articulate further what Parmenides has himself said probably as well as ever it can be said, has only this in its favor: faith in the signifying grandeur of these moments of revelation and resistance to premature critical analysis. The logicistic discipline applied to the text by a number of scholars could probably not be carried out on the Greek original, which is—I know no better way to say it—too elusively scintillating and too abysmally deep to take well the fixative treatment of rational analysis. To be sure, the goddess herself bids Parmenides decide *(krinein)* and decide by reason *(logoi)* her refutation of the way of "aimless eye and ringing ear" (Fr. 7, 4–5). She presents him with a moment of decision *(krisis)* and says that it is a necessity that the decision be made *(kekritai)*. But the "crisis" here, as she presents it, is a *choice*: "Is or Is not?" (Fr. 8, 15–16). It is not a course of argument he is to engage in but an effort of right-mindedness, not an attempt to apprehend, say, the Law of Contradiction and to apply it, but a commitment to the choice of one designated member of a disjunction.

So to discipline the text it has first to be transfixed, as is a butterfly in a display case; I mean that the translation has to employ philosophically fixed and fairly familiar terms. And then the lines of argument have to be interpolated: The most egregious example of the first practice is the ubiquitous, debonair use of "exist" for *ésti*, of the second, the interpolation of the steps of that inquiry that the goddess merely mentions by its name to Parmenides (e.g., by Barnes 1982, 164 ff., who formalizes the argument).

To be sure, at some point any text has to submit to being taken not so much exactly at its own word as at some accessible version thereof. It seems to be a feature of a great text that it arouses interesting thought in all its transformations and spawns arguments that are incontrovertible in themselves (albeit not really applicable to the unfixed original).

I append here a small selection of terms with which interpreters have tried to domesticate, as it were, Parmenides' insight. Burnet, 180–182, makes Parmenides a "corporeal monist" to whom the world is a finite material spherical plenum (comment: impossible, because of the identity of thought and Being). Curd, 66, makes him a "predicational monist," one who claims that each thing that is has one predicate which it *is* completely and exclusively (comment: there is only *one* Being). Kirk and Raven, 270, make him a "hesitant" incorporeal, since "the incorporeal was still unknown" (comment: evidently it *was* known). Furth, 243, understands Parmenides' Being to be a fusion of existence and being-of-a-certain-sort, deriving from the existential and predicative use of *ésti* (comment: Being has no distinguishable qualities). Tarán, 194, describes Parmenides' "conception of Being" as "a first attempt at the abstract," because it can have no characteristic except existence (comment: Parmenides thinks of Being as completely full). There are many more—a great tribute to Parmenides, though paid for with the professional profanation of his goddess's truth.

37. There are two negating particles in Greek, *ouk*, "not" and *me*, "non-." Their use in various constructions is certainly dictated by grammar, but the grammar might be suspected of encapsulating distinct meanings. Thus *ouk* is decisively definite; it is used when someone is simply saying no, or in plain denials of fact. *Me* is used in more general, indeterminate contexts; it does not simply, flatly nullify its term but clings to it, turning it into an inexpugnably relational (non-)being. We can simply eject what is *not* from our mind, but there is no way to fight ourselves loose from a nonbeing; it is a sort of being. This situation will be exploited in Plato's *Sophist* (p. 142). See Hartmann, 150–151.

A revealing example of what I am saying occurs in fragment 6, 1, where are mentioned "mortals who know not-a-thing *(ouden)*." These people are nescient rather than acquainted with nothingness. Similarly, when *ouk* is used with *eon* it is to effect a double negation—"Not-being is not" (Fr. 8, 46)—which cancels the thought. For "non-thing" *(meden)* as used by Parmenides, see chapter 6, note 1.

38. In Plato's *Sophist* it is said specifically that Nonbeing has no number (see note 54), so the goddess is going far out in assimilating Nonbeing to a plurality of beings. When I ask myself what the role of Nothing is as one among the names for Nonbeing, I see that it serves in contexts where Being is, *per impossibile*, treated as if it were Nature, and the question is asked: How could it ever grow, beginning from nothing? See Fr. 8, 10, where nothing is opposed to something (physical). This Nothing belongs to the vocabulary of Existence, not of Being (p. 169).

39. I can think of no more forceful believer in the willfulness of error (which is only inchoate in the poem) than Descartes, who is, of course, abetted by the Christian inven-

tion of a perverted will (p. 16), see *Meditation* IV; it is not in the will itself that error and sin arise, but in its having a disproportionately wider range than has human understanding. The goddess blames the forcible way of "much-experienced habit" for the state of error (Fr. 7, 3).

40. It has been suggested that Parmenides is learning about the pitfalls of negative facts (Gallop, 9). I think that the nonexistent objects, nonfactual, fictional, or impossible, which have so occupied logicians in this century (p. 76), are not on Parmenides' mind, primarily because they require a distinction between thinking and worldly existence such as the goddess has obliterated. Nor can the Law of (non-)Contradiction be a Parmenidean discovery, for it is presented as rife—and wrong—in the two-headed world of mortals.

41. That this really is a *third* way (a much debated question) is shown, I believe, in the words of fragment 6, 3–4. The goddess warns her pupil off the way of "Is not" which, though it is, of course, the second way, she now calls "the first," so that she may refer to the new way as "yet a next one." For more argument in favor of three ways, see Reinhardt, 46 f.

42. Mourelatos 1970, 313 ff., shows how many-voiced the Way of Seeming is— ironical, self-canceling, dialectical. I think something like this mode also affects the Way of Truth.

43. The question arises whether these strictures are pointedly directed at Heraclitus, the more so since Parmenides seems to have borrowed a word from him: He speaks of a "back-turning road" (*palintropos keleuthos*; Fr. 6, 9), while Heraclitus speaks of a "back-turning union" (*palintropos harmonie*; Diehls, B 51). I think they are not so directed, or at least not very pointedly, because Heraclitus' phrase intends the *simultaneous* union of opposites, while Parmenides' betokens the *alternating* hither-and-thither of mortals, as described in my text.

44. The law, with the temporal qualification, is set out by Aristotle, *Metaphysics* 1005 b 19 ff.; also p. 27.

45. The Furies are gentled and invited to reside in Athens and the maddening guilt of Orestes' matricide is extinguished by Athena in her city in Aeschylus' *Eumenides*. Oedipus, guilty of parricide and incest, is conducted by Theseus to his Attic place of disappearance in Sophocles' *Oedipus at Colonus*.

46. See Plato 1996 by Brann, Kalkavage, and Salem for a translation and interpretation of the *Sophist* that aims to be both faithful and alive.

47. Hegel in his *History of Philosophy* says, as something obvious, that the sophists drew their denial of the possibility of error from Parmenides' view of truth (vol. 1, pt. I, sec. I, chap. I, C 2).

48. See Howland, 22 ff., for Socrates as a sophist in a class by himself.

49. One of the great changes that Parmenides and his followers must have observed in the world around them is the rise of expertise-proud specialists. The *Sophist* gives, among other things, an expertise tree, whose branchings give Plato a chance for a lot of neologic spoofing. Socrates, when he asks in his conversations what something is, is not really interested in a specifying definition; he wants the steadfast gist of the notion. But the Stranger does define. He begins with a universe, that of human expertise, and by division into branches pursues the kinds from superior to subordinate, *general* to *specific*. In this dialogue, accordingly, the greatest of the forms, the *eide* (Latin *species*), are for the first time distinguished as *gene* (Latin *genera*) from the lower *eide*.

The appellation "sophist" seems to have been accepted voluntarily by at least one sophist, Protagoras (Plato, *Protagoras*, 317 b; see *Plato's Sophist*, trans. Brann, Kalkavage and Salem, 5, for a perspicuous diagram of the expertise tree, the "sophist's thicket").

50. The Stranger's analysis is more complex than reported here; for example, he distinguishes, within the imitative art, between "likenesses" and "apparitions," that is, between exact copies and copies that deform the original for the sake of effect (236 a). For images in general, see Brann 1991; for the *Sophist* in particular, ibid., 35 ff.

51. It should, however, be said that the Stranger is familiar with all the schools of thought concerning Being. And his refutation of Parmenides is more extensive than I report here; the Stranger attacks Parmenidean Being itself, namely, with respect to its partlessness, its being One (Fr. 8, 43 ff.; 244 e ff.).

52. Whether the Platonic forms, which are *for* thought and thinkable *(noeta)*, are to be considered as themselves thoughts is a deep perplexity. The Stranger, perhaps mindful of Parmenides' teaching that thinking and Being are the same, says that Being is a power, *dynamis*, a power of doing and being affected (247 e). And he intimates that therefore Being has mind and life and soul (249 a). Heidegger 1924, 579, in fact, goes so far as to say that the *genos* of "Motion" *(kinesis)*, one of the major forms, is "the aprioristic title for *psyche* and *logos*." The difficulty with this identification is that the Stranger also includes Rest among the beings necessary to mind (249 c).

In any case, it does not help to have just one *noeton* think. Each form has its proper nature for itself, but *all* forms share the characteristic of being thinkable. The perplexity is: How does the power of being *for* thought differ from the power of being *a* thought?

I would not raise this question here, did not the introduction of Nonbeing among the forms, which the Stranger is about to accomplish, have the effect of tacitly making the realm of Being more mindlike: the Stranger hints at this when he speaks of Nonbeing as "all chopped up—just like knowledge" (257 c). Since every form is *also* a—relative—nonbeing, Nonbeing will act among the forms, the beings, much as human reason, *logos*, does in speech. Both relate all beings to each other, and both determine each being by its negations. Only the human *logos* has the additional negative capability of being false. The full development of the here inchoate notion that negation is the subjective thought life of objects of thought, comes from Hegel, see chapter 5.

53. For the several functions of the forms, see Brann, "Plato's Theory of Ideas," (1997, 99 ff.).

54. At least it is not calculable without some algorithm for the combinations. It seems to me possible that the Other is actually infinite, that is, if it turns out, upon reflection, to be the form that brings the infinite appearances of the sense world under the realm of Being. It mixes with opinion and speech, at any rate (260 b). Otherness does play this role for Hegel—Nature is conceptualized as the Other of the Concept: "Nature has presented itself as the Idea in the form of *otherness*," Hegel 1830a *(Philosophy of Nature)*, para. 247; also p. 165.

55. For "not" *(ouk)* and "non-" *(me)*, see note 37.

56. See Rosen 1983, 180 ff., for a detailed discussion of *to medamos on*, "Utter-non-being." Also see Heidegger 1924, 558 ff., for the kind of logical opposition induced by the Other.

57. The subject of the negative in the Platonic dialogues is of course much wider than my focus on the Nonbeing of the *Sophist* might indicate. A most serious and honest book by Nicolai Hartmann, *Plato's Logik des Seins* (1909), is very unjustly unavailable in English. Hartmann wrestles hard with the connection of the Socratic-Platonic method of dialectic to what it attains. He maintains that both the inquiry and its termini are shot through with Nonbeing. Dialectic is a *via negativa*, which yields as results the ideas (i.e., forms), and these are entirely delimited by what they are *not*; they are, for example, uncolored, unshaped, untouchable. These negations are eventually perceived as determinations: Nonbeing becomes positive, governing the very character of the ideas. Hartmann's understanding carries a price (which he welcomes): The ideas are "subjective" in two senses, (1) as "the products of the negating dialectic of a human mind," as the "innermost, most proper achievement of the self," and (2) insofar as they are in and of the mind, as "self-acting," as being active, self-perspicuous self-visions of their own truth; Hartmann thinks that this is what the Platonic formula for a form—*itself by itself* (*auto kath' auto*)—expresses (192 ff.). One need not believe this understanding to respect its force.

In tune with it, Socrates, that first philosophical dialectician (whose dialectical perplexities, I here interject, seem to me, unlike the sophistic dialectic, not to be a sort of self-stymieing, willful abiding within the clashing rocks of positive and negative), embraces *not* knowing. Hartmann observes that the emphasis in Socrates' notorious announcement to the Athenian judges at his trial that "I know within myself that I know nothing" (*Apology* 22 d) is not on his ignorance but on his knowledge (79)—and, one might add, on his knowledge of *nothing*. That "nothing" would be, in Hartmann's spirit, the negative power of dialectic, which chisels away at the thing sought, striking off what it is not, until some shape, its form, finally emerges.

It seems to me possible that Plato has the Stranger of the *Sophist* agree to use Socrates' dialogic and dialectic way rather than the presentations he is accustomed to (217 c) not only from courtesy but also because the dialogic mode is itself already on the way to Nonbeing (217).

58. See Brann 1991, 9 f.

59. For an example, see Levinas 1989, "Time and the Other," 42 ff.

5

The Moving Soul of Thought:
Dialectical *Negativity*

Twenty-two hundred years have gone by since Nonbeing had been made at home among the beings in Plato's *Sophist*. The mere passage of centuries is, to be sure, neither here nor there:

> Thus the history of philosophy, in its true meaning, deals not with a past, but with an eternal and veritable present: and, in its results, resembles not a museum of the aberrations of the human intellect, but a Pantheon of Godlike figures. (*Logic* 86[1])

Hence Hegel reaches right back to Parmenides, whose dictum that "'Being alone is and Nothing is not' . . . was the true starting-point of dialectic." Of course, neither the human naysaying nor the logical negation treated in chapters 2–3 had been neglected in those millennia. But, Hegel observes, dialectic had degenerated into

> a subjective see-saw system of ratiocination going hither and thither over to the other side, where the content is missing and the bareness is covered by such acuity as brings forth such ratiocination. (81)

What Hegel looks to in his ancient predecessors is the positive power of the negative, that is, to Nonbeing. He makes an illuminating distinction between the ancients and the moderns in the *Phenomenology of the Spirit*:[2]

> The type of study belonging to ancient times is distinguished from that of modernity thus: The former was the formative development of natural consciousness. Making special trial of every part of its existence and philosophizing about every occurrence, it gave birth to itself as a generality that was active through and

through. In modern times, on the other hand, the individual finds the abstract
form prepared. . . . Now, therefore, the work consists not so much in purifying
the individual from the immediate sensual mode and in making it into a substance
that is thought and is thinking, as rather in the opposite: through the sublating of
the hard-and-fast determinate thought, to actualize the general and to inspirit it.
(preface, 30)

Hegelian negativity stands in just that relation to Platonic Nonbeing. Nonbeing
is a form, an "active generality" such as is obtained in an effort of purifying
refutation recorded in the *Sophist* (230 e). Negativity, on the other hand, is an
animation of fixed thought forms.

You might call it the second coming of the negative in all its potency. I have
entitled the chapter and its first section "Negativity," both because the word
bears in it a sense of activity and because Hegel uses it in the preface to the
Phenomenology; the last, third, section is about the "negative reason" of the
Logic. Negativity and negative reason are the appropriate terms for the dialectical mode particular to each work (p. 000). Between these, I will deal with
the Kantian negation, from which Hegel distinguishes his own dialectic, and
which puts the latter in relief.

1. THE NEGATIVITY OF THE SPIRIT: HEGEL'S *PHENOMENOLOGY*

Negativity and dialectic belong together as do motor and movement, and to
talk of one is to speak of the other.

(a) Negativity and dialectic are an experience of consciousness (32). Dialectic is not a method in the usual sense, a jig to be externally applied so as to
shape any matter (40). It is

the uncanny and enormous[3] might of the negative; it is the energy of thinking, of
the pure I. Death, if we want so to call that inactuality, is what is most frightful,
and to hold fast to what is dead, is what requires the greatest force . . . not that
life which cringes before death and keeps itself pure from devastation is the life
of the Spirit, but that which bears up under it and preserves itself within it. The
Spirit gains its truth only by finding itself in its absolute dismemberment. This
might is not the positive that looks away from the negative, as when we say of
something that it is nothing or is false, and then, having done with it, pass over
to just anything else; it is rather this might only insofar as it looks the negative in
the face and abides with it. This abiding is the magic might that turns the negative
into Being.—It is the same which was above called the Subject. (29–30)

The impassioned tone alone tells us that Hegel is not speaking of a methodical
procedure or logical negation. This passage is about what "was above called
the Subject," about spirit in its negativity—the thinking human being.

Perhaps it is best first to bring together subject, consciousness and spirit, three terms already on the scene. *Subject* here means what it often does since Descartes: the human "I," the being that engages in knowing; what is known is its "object" or a substance. *Consciousness* is here just the subject as it faces an object; it is both the knowing *and* the "objectivity" *(Gegenständlichkeit)* that is the confronting negative of knowing; it comprises the two "moments" of knowledge quite without mediation. *Spirit* is the way and the end (for Spirit is purposive reason) in which this bald opposition is reconciled as increasingly the subject sees itself in the object-substance it faces, and the object is revealed as itself subjectivity; one way to put this is that Spirit alienates itself into an object and repossesses itself as a subject: "The inequality which takes place in Consciousness between the I and the substance that is its object is its contrariety, the *Negative* in general" (32). So negativity might be said to be first of all the capacity of the human being to have a relation of otherness to an object of knowledge.

And, second, it is the power to bring this object back into the subject. One might say that it is the negative taken to the second power which accomplishes this return. Recall that Parmenides' goddess made use of the fact that a double negation returns us to the original position (p. 133). So also Hegel uses double negation to return the negated, extruded object into the subject by a "negation of negation."[4] The second negation, however, does not return us to the original position, but to a new, higher whole—higher because it contains more thought mediations: It is richer in determinations or more "concrete." Hegel somewhere terms such a movement of thought that has gone through the three moments of dialectic a thought circle; he might have said "spiral," for the completed movement has returned to its beginning on a higher level.[5]

These have been very general descriptions of dialectic negativity. Before giving a more differentiated picture—really by way of finding subtly significant synonyms—we must notice one aspect particular to the *Phenomenology of Spirit*, an aspect of negativity that makes it poignantly complex.

No engaged reader of this vivid biography of the Spirit, in which thought is imaged in brilliant figures that represent the stages of its self-recovery, escapes this puzzlement: Who is ultimately doing the thinking here? The subjects, the "figures," that appear on the scene in their progressive march toward their end in that full *self*-consciousness in which subject and substance are completely at one as Spirit, are each engaged in their temporally local dialectic. But the author of this account is also, or even primarily, thinking—*re*-thinking each development, but from a higher, more final perspective, and so he writes at once a biography and an *auto*-biography of the Spirit. Thus from one point of view the author and the gallery of subjects reach the end together—he is the last subject and the first Spirit. For the completeness of the system, the whole in which all thought determinations have become at the same moment inward to the subject and realized in the world so that the truth is *equally* subject and substance—this completeness is the condition of its own full comprehension: "The truth is actual only as system," meaning as the complete internalized whole of thought (12, 21, 24). But from another point of view the author adds one more final moment, insofar as he is making the whole dialectical development the *object* of his thinking. And now the readers too make both the system and the writer who has recollected it *their* object. Hence there are two higher-order negativities. The poignancy in this ratcheting up of subjectivity is that it somewhat removes any but the most engaged reader from the mission of the Spirit's negativity, insofar as it is that mission to undergo the experience of the matter itself and to summon "the seriousness of Concept" that descends into the depth of the matter (12).

(b) And now the time has come to give specificity to dialectical negativity. The attempt to do this is not unlike the attempt to recover the sense of "Is" in Parmenides—both are *experiences* of human reason. Dialectic is only secondarily the account of a thought development; it is primarily the *self-movement* of thought. The best place to watch and experience this self-movement will be in logic, which, Hegel says in the *Phenomenology*, is nothing but the dialectical "method as the structure of the whole erected in its pure essentiality" (40). This means that in the *Logic* the thinking subject is absent and we can watch the concepts exhibit their inner life on their own without the complication, the extra dimension just noted, of the thinking human subject. In logic—if we live it—we experience pure dialectic, the self-movement of concepts.

In the preface to the *Phenomenology,* however, the explanatory terms are (1) in itself, for itself, in-and-for itself, (2) sublated, (3) determinate, (4) mediated (24, 32). Their meaning and connection is as follows. "In itself" is the unselfconscious original position of consciousness. It is for us, not for itself; it is Spirit-substance, not subject—note once again the two levels: in *itself* but for *us*. This consciousness then begins to face itself; it becomes an object to itself. But right away it recognizes itself as Spirit: It takes itself back as a substance that is also a subject. It is now both in itself *and* for itself, it is *in-and-for itself*. It has *sublated* itself as object. "To sublate," *aufheben*, is *the* most characteristic Hegelian term. The perfectly ordinary German word has, conveniently, these three meanings: (1) to raise up, (2) to preserve, (3) to cancel.[6] The subject has canceled or negated the object (*as* object) in recognizing itself in it; it has preserved within itself the features that *determined* the object, that set it off negatively from the subject, and it has raised or elevated the now appropriated object (and itself) to a new stage of conceptual fullness or concreteness. Such a whole, one that has absorbed its opposed object, is said to be *mediated*, the positive result of a mediating negation. This tripartite dialectical movement is also properly called "experience" (Introduction, 73).

The very first figure of consciousness that makes its appearance in this book of spirit-appearances, the *Phenomenology*, may serve as a particular example:

this consciousness as it confronts *this* immediate sense content. But that content, which seems at first so rich, so definite, so independent of the knower, turns out to be emptily universal: "*this*" is anything and everything. We *mean* something highly individual, but we *say* only individuality in general. The object that confronted sense consciousness has turned out to be empty pure Being; it is canceled, and what I am left with is what *I*, for my own part, meant, which was richly specific. (Hegel hears in the verb *meinen*, "to mean," the echo of *mein*, "my own.") The sense object is preserved in *my* intuition, and the subject has had a dialectically elevating experience. This example both exhibits a first stage in thought on earth and connects the *Phenomenology* to the *Logic*, which begins with pure Being.

As I said above, the purest and most direct experience of dialectical negation is to be had in experiencing Hegel's logic, which will be taken up in the last section. But here seems to be the place for an interlude, which does only what Hegel himself cannot keep from doing: It reaches his dialectic by contrast with Kantian negation.

2. THE NEGATIONS OF POSITIVE UNDERSTANDING: KANT

Although much of the preliminary matter of the *Logic* is devoted to a respectful critique of Kant's critical philosophy, Hegel does not dwell on Kantian negation. He dwells rather on the limitations of the mode of "understanding" that characterize Kant's thought. Understanding is that side of logic which "sticks to fixity of characters and their distinctness from each other" (79–80). It abstracts from sensation and feeling; it discerns universals and separates them by their characteristics. It is therefore for Hegel the mode of the first moment of dialectic, when a concept is immediately given. It is, really, what we call rationality, as distinct from reason. Kant's negation is the negation that belongs to understanding. It is therefore the most proper foil to the Hegelian negativity of dialectical reason.

(a) There is a revealing little pre-Critical essay by Kant entitled "An Attempt to Introduce the Concept of Negative Numbers into Philosophy" *(Weltweisheit)*. Here he begins by distinguishing logical from *real negation*: Logical negation is through contradiction, real negation works without contradiction. He says that only the first opposition, that of contradiction, has so far been noticed. "Real opposition," as expounded here, is thus his own discovery.

The result of a contradiction is a negative nothing—an unthinkable nothing *(nihil negativum irrepraesentabile)*. Real opposition, on the other hand, results in something. For in this opposition one tendency counters another and the opposing predicates can simultaneously belong to a thing. A body in motion and also not in motion is not thinkable. A body with an impetus toward one direction that is canceled by a contrary impetus is a body still, a body at rest.

This thinkable nothing is to be called zero = 0. The zero that results from what Kant calls "real repugnance" is not a negative nothing but a *privative* nothing.

He then applies real negation to what he claims is a new interpretation of signed numbers. A negatively signed number signifies that this number when composed with a positive number will cancel the latter to the extent of its own magnitude. What Kant is introducing is the notion of directed numbers, and his illustrations are of wind directions and canceled debts. Such "real opposition," his point is, does not annul the subject but has a perfectly thinkable resultant. He is, it seems, thinking of contrariety[7] (as distinct from contradiction, in which two causes, positive in themselves though contrary in their effects, come together in a subject without detriment to its intelligibility: An object can endure the application of any composite of black and white color (contraries) but it is annulled if given the predicates black and not-black (contradictories).

Kant now applies his notion not only to physical but also to psychical and mental cases. Thus disgust is negative desire and error negative truth. And finally, applying the numerical model, he sets out two conjectural world principles of philosophy ("world wisdom"). The first says that the sum of all natural changes in real opposition is a constant. The second says that the directed sum of all real grounds at work in the universe is zero: "The whole of the world is in itself Nothing, except insofar as it is Something through the will of another, that is, an omnipotent God." *Heraclitus redivivus!*[8]

The object of these strange principles is, Kant says, to invite the reader to think about matters yet dark to himself. In particular he is preoccupied by the question concerning real grounds, that is, by the causes of real opposition. Logical consequence arises simply from the analysis of the logical ground and an application of the Law of Contradiction. For example, human beings err, and this is an analytical consequence of human finitude, the concept of which contains the mark of fallibility. But how, simply *"because something is, something else is canceled (aufgehoben)"*—this is not expressible, certainly not through a judgment—though possibly through a concept; I think Kant means that we cannot have rational inferential knowledge but only intuitive notions of real causality.

It is in itself wonderful to see Kant, of all people, groping, and groping toward the grand solutions of the *Critique of Pure Reason*.[9] But my immediate point is to contrast Kantian negation with Hegelian negativity. For Kant the world is a complex of positives, though oppositely signed; for Hegel negation is an indwelling force not only of thought but also of nature. And this difference is maintained and sharpened in the *Critique*. Two passages are most pertinent, the Table of Nothing (B 348) and the passage on the "ontological argument" of God's existence (B 624).

(b) Kant says that this *Table of Nothing* is of no great importance and is added at the end of the Transcendental Analytic, just before the Dialectic, only to complete the system (346). Of course, it is *very* significant in retrospect. Hegel has high respect for Kant's revival of serious dialectic, but he finds that the antinomies (that is, the antagonisms of the laws of pure reason) that Kant discerns are not organically connected, connected namely by "the recognition that each actual thing involves a coexistence of opposed elements" (*Logic*, 48). Kant fails to see that negation, and even more primordially Nothing, turns up within all beings.

The Table of Nothing shows why Kant cannot think so. The highest concept of transcendental philosophy is that of an Object in general, and the first division specifies it as Something or Nothing. Since it is the thoughts of the understanding (called categories) that give the Object in general its rational constitution, the type of Nothing an object can be depends on its relation to those thought-functions or concepts. Thus (1) if the concept is empty, that is to say, without object, the nothing is a mere *entity of reason*; (2) if the object is conceived but is itself empty (of sensory filler), it is a *privative nothing*; (3) if the mere forms of sense (the intuition) are employed but without a real sensory object, the nothing is called an *imaginary entity*. And if there is an empty object without any concept, we have a *negative nothing*, the pit of nothingness.

From the perspective of a counterpoint to Hegel, we see at once that Nothing is the result simply of four misfirings of the relation between thinking and its object. It is not the case, as for Hegel, that negativity *is* the relation of subject to object, but that the fixed thought possibilities are not fulfilled as is required. Thus it happens that an intellectual being, an *ens rationis*, is a nothing; Kant recognizes no being of thought, and its notion differs from a *negative nothing*, a *nihil negativum*—which Kant calls a monster, an *Unding*—only in that the former is not possible because it is pure fiction, while the latter is impossible because it is self-canceling.

Thus the four Nothings have no business in a soundly conceived, cognitively accessible world: "Now no one can have a determinate notion of a negation without having the opposing affirmation as a basis" (603). For Kant Nothing doesn't amount to much, not even as a problem.

(c) The ontological proof of God says that God's existence is part of his essence, so that just to conceive God is at once to know that he exists (p. 104). Hegel, as we may imagine, is drawn to this proof while Kant utterly rejects it, and in the course of doing so sets out his own doctrine of existence (620 ff.), which in his system can only pertain to spatiotemporal being. What is relevant to this chapter is the doctrine of negation that follows, that of *external negation*.

In brief, Kant argues that Being (which he uses interchangeably with existence) is not a real predicate, meaning a concept that could be added to the other conceptual determinations of a thing to extend its description. It is instead merely the "position" of a thing expressed by the copula "is" in a judgment (626). He means that Being occurs rightly only as the nod that affirms a connection: "Yes, this thing is and is thus, and this predicate belongs to this subject." Thus existence is quite outside the object or predicative speech about it—it is a little addition that *places* the object among existents. Kant is surely paving the way to the existential quantifier of modern logic which goes outside the content of a proposition. And the same goes for negation which is definitively moved outside the proposition. As Being is not an element of things or of the judgments that express their features, so Negation is not a part of these but simply what one might call their unsaying or depositioning, their mental removal.

For Hegel, Existence is distinguished from Being, and both are Thoughts. Existence is much further on in the *Logic* (122) and much more complex. It is, indeed, Being as a full-blown *thing* (124). For a thing is understood as that Being which has absorbed relativity, having multiple connections of mutual dependence with other existents. Thus what for Kant is a thinker's mere positing is for Hegel a moment in the development of fully determinate Being.

3. NEGATIVE REASON: HEGEL'S *LOGIC*

In Hegel's logic[10] we see thought itself exhibiting its dialectical "indwelling tendency outward": It appears first in its implicit immediacy or *in itself*, then in its mediated appearing *to itself*, and finally in its return *in-and-for itself* (79 ff.).

(a) What I mean to emphasize is that in this logic the dialectic of thought can be most purely witnessed, or better (since logic is "thinking of thinking") actually re-performed—Hegel speaks of "letting the matter take over within oneself." In dialectical logic thought is not a mere formalism but a self-actualizing universal, and in it the opposition of subjective and objective (which governed the Preface to the *Phenomenology*) vanishes (19 ff.). The most dramatic way to see the independence of logical content from embodied human subjectivity is to see it as "the exposition of God as he is in his eternal essence before the creation of Nature and finite Spirit."[11]

Hegel uses Aristotle's phrase for the activity of the divine intellect, thought of thought *(noesis noeseos)* or thought thinking itself, to characterize the Idea, which is the fully developed product of this logic (236).

Within the dialectical development it is always the second "moment," the middle movement, that displays the negative in its initial power. In fact, once again, *it* is the dialectical stage proper, when the "finite characterizations" of the posited thought "supersede themselves and pass into their opposites" (81).

(b) The first two thoughts are Being and Nothing. Being is the beginning, "the first pure thought," immediate and undetermined. "It is not to be felt, or perceived by sense, or pictured in imagination: it is only and merely thought, and as such it forms the beginning" (86). But mere Being is a mere abstraction and is totally negative. "Abstraction" here means not a subsequent elimination of all qualities but an original Parmenidean featurelessness. Think Being and no definition or determination suits it. Everything *is* and is *nothing* more and *nothing* else.

Being is therefore Nothing, Nought *(Nichts)*. Nothing is not a predicate of Being; it *is* Being when it shows itself to us, but more significantly, as it is for itself: Being as a thought flips into the thought Nothing by its own negative force, its indwelling power to cancel itself. It is worth repeating that it is not just *our* thinking that attributes this vacancy to Being and finds it to be Nought. It is the thought called Being that is immediately Nothing as well, and we learn this if we let the thought have its way with us (87–88).

As if to signal the difference between Being as *our* thought and Being on its own—or as a moment in God's essence—Hegel places Being as a *second* stage in the *Phenomenology*; recall that there Being arises from the attempt of a sense consciousness to get a conceptual grasp on itself (p. 159). In the *Logic*, however, Being is first, "an absolute, or what is synonymous here, an abstract beginning."[12]

We see the power of negative dialectic at work here in a doubly intense way. Not only is the dialectical self-opposition of Being that flips into Nothing at work in a most starkly immediate way, but the resultant second moment, Nothing, is the most negative thought that is thinkable.

The last two paragraphs above contain two related question-raising assertions. The first is that Being goes *immediately* into Nothing. This ought not to be, since the negative motion is supposed to be mediating: The first thought goes out of itself, supersedes itself. Hegel gives as an example human mortality: a finite being is not vital and *also* mortal, rather it is true that its life, as life, bears in it the germ of death, and that the finite, being radically self-contradictory, involves its own self-suppression (81).

Now Being does not go beyond itself to suppress itself; it is not thoughtfully self-contradictory but is simply and immediately Nothing. Why is the first step of dialectical logic not a mediation? That this initial moment is an anomaly is expressed in the title "Nothing," where we might expect "Nonbeing." Hegel explains that he is here interested in naming a negation that is abstract and immediate (whereas Nonbeing refers to a mediating relation, a negation of Being). He says that Nothing, *Nichts*, could also be expressed as mere notness: "Nought," *Nicht*.[13]

The answer to the question Why do we begin with an anomaly? is that Being is *incapable* of the determinations that are the marks of dialectical negation. Spinoza formulated the principle that "all determination is negation." Hegel applies the converse: All negation is determination.[14] To negate is to say something definite, to posit something new, as in the *Sophist* Nonbeing turns out to be a new kind of Being (p. 140). But this most absolute, most abstract initial thought doesn't have the precondition for specific negation within itself: It flips as a whole.

And so arises a second problem. Being *is* Nothing simply, complete emptiness, paradoxical as it may seem.[15] And Nothing is Being; they are identical. From our point of view the difference is merely what we *mean* but cannot articulate (88). But if that is so, why couldn't the divine system begin with Nothing? Why is not Hegel's system a self-canceling nihilism? The reason cannot lie in the old principle that Nothing cannot be a beginning because "Nothing comes out of Nothing," which pagan philosophers of intelligible Being accept and Christian theologians of divine Creation deny. For it does not fit the present occasion: Here, just as Nothing has come out of Being, so, by the symmetry of the dialectical motion, Being *could* come out of Nothing. I think that what is appearing here instead is a pure, unargued prejudice in favor of Being: Pure Nothing is identical with Being, but not quite: Both pure abstractions are equal, but one is more equal than the other.[16] Hegel is a protagonist of the great tradition of Being that once guided the West but is in his own logic on the brink of being overturned. Nihilism comes next (chapter 6), and Hegel is not uninvolved in its epiphany.

(b) Being and Existence are not the same, modern logicians notwithstanding (p. 129). Existence *(Dasein)*[17] is what the first triad of the logic drives toward. When Being had revealed itself as Nothing, the identity, we must infer, was not so complete after all; it was rather a *unity*. Now "this unity is Becoming." Becoming is Being and Nothing *simultaneously*: what is becoming both is and is not what it was and what it is going to be. Becoming can also be understood as the *passage* from Being into Nothing or Nothing into Being (88) once we are in the realm of time—which arises in Nature, not in logic. Consequently, Becoming acts in spatial Nature, where it appears as time and acts much as negation does in atemporal, nonspatial logic. Time as a negating power is the motor of nature, a restless power that moves space, which is an empty dead exernality, toward self-consciousness or subjectivity.[18]

Becoming is the first concrete thought, one that has internal determinations. We are now well started on the progressive way of dialectic, on which Existence is the next position. Existence is qualified Being, Being that has determinations and so, qualities. Quality itself as a thought category has as one of its subcategories Negation—not the negative force of dialectic but one of its stations.[19] What has quality is determinate; it has definite features. If it is determinate, however, it is by Hegel's principle replete with negation: Whatever is something definite also has *not* a great many qualities. This negation is not the one that appears in propositions, though it underwrites the latter. It is the negation that belongs to a determinate being.

I included this subsequent stage, Existence, only because it is useful in distinguishing Hegel's logic from logician's logic (p. 80). But Otherness *is* a topic in its own right, because of its great predecessor among the Greeks.

(c) Recall that the Other is the name for the Nonbeing discovered by the Stranger in the *Sophist* (p. 141). Otherness is, as it happens, also an advanced category of Hegel's logic; it is, in fact, the "exposition" of the subcategory Negation just set out: Negation is the "form" a determinate being has insofar as it differentiates itself from others; it is the form of "Otherbeing" (*Anderssein*, 91–92).

But otherness also has a far broader role in Hegel's logic, wider but not conceptually very different. In the very first moment, when Being comes on the scene, Hegel says that its various determinations *are* each other's other, and that every further determination—that is, the specification effected in each dialectical moment—is a passage into an other (84): "Being is determined first against an other in general."[20] Otherness therefore turns up throughout the logic, but especially again at its end, when the now completely developed Being, under the title of "Idea," cancels its own ideality and goes forth into Otherbeing *(Anderssein)* to become spatiotemporal Nature (244).[21]

Now this kind of otherness is indeed at work in the *Sophist*, though it is a lesser notion than *the* Other, the form called the *Heteron*. It is a curious and revealing fact of the Platonic dialogue that within it otherness, the this-worldly effect of the Other, is thoroughly exploited *before* that great form itself is discovered, although the Stranger never says at any point in so many words: "Not only has the revelation of Nonbeing as the Other allowed us to capture that purveyor of shams and falsehoods, the sophist, but it has also provided the ontological foundation for a way of dividing the world of expertise (and any other universe of interests) into that classificatory system of positive and negative branchings, into the 'this' and the 'other,' which tabulates for us clearly the specific character of anything, including sophists—and philosophers." Of course, we wouldn't expect him to use such latter-day terms, but we might expect some moment of connection between Otherness as the principle of relative Nonbeing and that art of dividing a field which knows how always to leave aside one branch as the—potentially determinable—negation of the other, and to pursue that other positively. For indeed the Stranger's Other and the Way of Division *(diairesis)* are to each other as a ground to its effect.

The point here is a question: Is the Otherbeing of the *Logic* the same as the Other of the *Sophist*? I think the answer is: The Other is in the dynamically stable realm of forms about what Otherbeing is in the dialectically developing system of thoughts. Recall that the Other is Nonbeing folded into Being and working there as a bond of diversity; yet it is not only a form among forms; it is also an articulating power within the world. Otherbeing is not only a thought category among categories; it is also an overarching force, dialectic itself, by which the ideal develops into the natural. The former courses through beings and appearances, effecting the reciprocal negations of diversity; the latter is the indwelling negativity that moves within each thought as its life, propelling it out of itself and into its negative from which it returns to itself enriched in concreteness even unto nature. So in both its versions Otherness is the saving grace of negation.

∞   ∞   ∞

In the previous chapter and in this one Nonbeing and Negativity have shown themselves to be two great indirect affirmations of the priority of Being and the self-moving life of Thought. At the same time, there were intimations in the beginning of the *Logic* that the thought of Nothing might well stand at the origin of the dialectical development. As the development proceeds, the priority of Nothing and the ultimate negativity of thought is, on occasion and quite surprisingly, expressed with yet more force.[22] The last chapter will, then, be about originary and final Nothing and Negativity. This Nothing will be the bald contradictory of Being, and this Negativity will be the brusque denial of affirmative thought—and so the most absolute naysaying.

NOTES

1. The *Encyclopedia Logic* is cited by paragraph. See Hegel 1830b. The "Moving Soul" in the chapter title is from 81, taken from the German text; see Hegel 1830a. (My quotations will often be translated directly from the German.) The Wallace version, however, includes more material than does the German edition.

In the quotation that follows Hegel might be thinking of such collections of antitheses as Peter Abelard's *Sic et Non*. He regards Plato's *Parmenides* as dialectic in the "grand style" because it shows the finitude of all hard-and-fast terms of understanding; see chapter 4, note 9. The beginning of the resuscitation of dialectic, Hegel says, was made by Kant, who shows in the Dialectic of his *Critique of Pure Reason* that every abstract proposition of the understanding veers around into its opposite (81). Of course, we should observe that it was not Kant's intention himself to provide a critique of the very mode that Hegel rightly regards as Kant's proper element, the *understanding*, but rather to show an inherent dialectic—for Kant a derogatory term meaning a "delusion"—of the supersensible use of *reason*.

2. There is no standard way to cite this work, so reference must be to whole sections. I will put in the page numbers of a much used German edition: Hegel 1807 *(Philosophische Bibliothek)*. Of the several English editions in use, only that of A. V. Miller numbers the paragraphs, but the reader may not have it handy. Hegel's subtitles for the preface, to which alone my final section refers, are not numbered either and are omitted in several versions.

3. *Ungeheuer* means both "uncanny" and "enormous." This particular passage does not, to be sure, mention dialectic, but there is no doubt in my mind that Hegel is describing the three moments of dialectic: (1) the analysis of the understanding yields fixated abstractions, (2) the negativity of the spirit faces this fixity and makes it fluid, and (3) in doing so it achieves a new, positive being. See also *Logic* 80 (Hegel 1830a).

4. See Mure, 135.

5. Because of the reentrant nature of dialectic, Hegelian terms tend to recur on several levels. Thus dialectic is the name for the whole tripartite development of a thought but also for its second moment in particular. *Being* is the title of the whole first part of the *Logic* but also for its very first moment. Negation is the motor of all conceptual thinking but also a category within Being (*Logic* 81, 87, 91).

6. Hegel 1830a, 94; 1830b, 96; Inwood 1992, 283–285.

7. Kant 1763a, sec. III. For Hegel, contrariety (as Stace, 187, rightly translates *Unterschied*) arises fairly late in the *Logic* and is there identified with "positive" and "negative" (119), a more complex notion than the negation belonging with "Otherbeing" (91). The latter is what might be called determinate contradiction, the not-A that is not just indeterminately anything. It lies between a very specific contrary and what will later be an "infinite" negative judgment (p. 34): Thus not-black might be (1) specifically white, (2) any other color, (3) within an infinite range of possibles; determinate contradiction would be the second, middle case.

8. Kant 1763a, sec. III. Recall that for Heraclitus the world is a tensed composite of opposites.

9. For example, "logical versus real grounds" is the straight ancestor of "analytical versus a priori synthetic." "Judgment versus concept" foreshadows "understanding versus reason." Since I will claim just below that for Kant negation is external to the thing, I should point out that in the *Prolegomena* Kant distinguishes between "bound" *(Grenze)* and "limit" *(Schranke)*, where the first is spatially conceived as an external delimitation, while the second betokens the internal negations that mark an object's incompleteness (para. 57).

10. Hegel wrote two *Logics*. One is a briefer outline that is part of the *Encyclopedia of the Philosophical Sciences in Outline* of 1830, here always referred to just by the standard paragraphs. The other is the extensive, independent *Science of Logic*, here occasionally cited, as Hegel 1812a or b, by pages. The first volume of the latter work is entitled "The Objective Logic."

11. Hegel 1812b, 50.

12. Hegel 1812b, 70.

13. Hegel 1812a, 68.

14. Stace 1923, 33. He points out that the converse is not logically necessary.

15. Hegel 1812b, 84. The principle mentioned below, that "Nothing comes out of Nothing," is discussed in this place.

16. It is to be hoped that George Orwell's *1984* (1949), from which this notorious saying is adapted, has not gone out of fashion just because its year is history and so is its nightmare.

Hegel recognizes in the Nothing of Buddhism (p. 174) the first, most abstract stage of his own dialectic, in which Nothing is the most abstract Being (1812b, 91, 1830b, 87). On the beginning of thinking, see Hegel 1830b, 86 (1, 2).

17. The English word "existence" is commonly used for two Hegelian terms: *Dasein*, "Being-there" (Hegel 1830b, 89), and *Existenz* (123). The latter is an advanced moment in the *Logic*, way beyond what is at issue here; it is a highly specified thought just next to "thing" in concreteness. Wallace very carefully translates *Dasein* by "being in space and time" (51) and, as a dialectical moment, by "Being Determinate" (89); but in other versions, "existence" is the usual translation.

18. Hegel 1830a, 258. See Brann 1999, 23 ff. for time in Hegel's Philosophy of Nature.

19. Besides Negation, the Negative is also a category of the *Logic*. Whereas Negation is determinateness, the Negative signifies "essential Otherness: the confrontation of an essence with *its* very own other" (1830b, 119).

20. Hegel 1812b, 79.

21. Also 247 in Hegel 1830a, *Naturphilosophie*.

22. As in the middle part of the *Science of Logic*, Hegel 1812b, 399 *(Reflection)*: This almost impenetrable chapter deals with Essence, in which Being diversifies into an underlying entity and its appearances. Essence thus requires a showing or show *(Schein)*, which is, however, a nothing without essence, as essence is a nothing without it. The reflective (or reflexive) dialectic motion from essence to show and back is therefore from nothing through nothing to nothing. This thought process can be characterized as pure self-involved negativity. Although Being developed qualities by relation to an other, essence develops by a negative relation to its negative, as a negation by means of a negation. I cannot claim that this exposition is totally perspicuous. See also p. 182.

6

The Absolute Opposite: *Nothing*

"Absolute Opposite" is a kind of necessary nonsense. *Nothing* does bear no determinable relation to Something, and that is what "absolute" ought to mean: absolved from all relations, limits, and restrictions. But Nothing also appears to be irrevocably related to Something as its contradictory opposite, for it is a *no*-thing. So an "absolute opposite" is a contradiction in terms, but an unavoidable one. Things become clearer and life becomes more interesting when Nothing is thus kept distinct from Nonbeing. For Nonbeing is not the contradictory but the contrary of Being, a much softer, more malleable, linked, that is, *relative* opposition; or at least it becomes so once it is interpreted as Otherness, not no-being, but other-being (p. 141). Nonbeing so construed absorbs all the possibilities of intelligible speech; what is left to be said for Nothing comes to a kind of blank-minded stutter. *Nihil absolutum*, sheer Nothing, is inarticulate.

And yet there is in the very word Nothing a kind of brusque concreteness that the other negatives set out in this book don't have: *No* is an expression of the will, *negation* a verbal denial, *Nonbeing* the correlate of an intelligible form, *Negativity* the dynamism of thought. *Nothing* alone is the negation of a thing, a *real* thing, to speak redundantly (p. 78). But then again, this so definite-seeming no-thing is totally unlike a thing in being devoid—so common usage intimates—of even the quality we might most expect it to have. Bad things are said to have badness, but Nothing itself does not have the attribute of nothingness; that is almost always said to belong to real somethings or conditions in the world, and it means worthlessness, a fighting word.

> Must I restrain me, through the fear of strife,
> From holding up the nothingness of life?

Sheer Nothing is thus blankly qualityless, it certainly has no essential qualities, and it is blankly incomprehensible:

but absolutely nothing, meerly nothing, is more incomprehensible than any thing, than all things taken together. It is a state (if a man may call it a state) that the Devil himself in the midst of his torments, cannot wish.[1]

1. APPEARANCES OF NOTHING

Perhaps it is a good idea to collect here some of the ways Nothing itself appears in speech that is not deliberately philosophical, speech about life. There Nothing appears in a spectrum of emotional colorations from bright to somber. Here is a poem by Emily Dickinson:

> By homely gift and hindered Words
> The human heart is told
> Of Nothing—
> "Nothing" is the force
> That renovates the World—

This poem, which was evidently accompanied by a small gift, I take to mean either that when some difference arises, to nullify it is to make a new beginning, or that thoughtful trifles renew our world; in any case this is *benign*, irenic Nothing.[2]

There is an *icy* neutrality of Nothing, such as is found in Wallace Stevens's poem "The Snow Man": "One must have a mind of winter," he begins, and have been cold a long time, to behold the junipers shagged with ice and not to think of any misery in the sound of the wind, the sound heard by the snow man, who is "the listener, who listens in the snow, And nothing himself, beholds Nothing that is not there and the nothing that is."[3]

The snow man refutes the pathetic fallacy, the notion that there is feeling worth fellow feeling in nature, but even more the poem expresses the inherent nihilism of an absolute nominalism. This post-theological nominalism sees individuals as radically separate particulars connected neither by the substantial bonds of universality nor by a common Creator; so viewed they attain the hard-edged clarity of items unenmeshed in pathos. This nominalism comes out even more definitively in Stevens's poem "The Course of a Particular":

> Today the leaves cry, hanging on branches swept by wind,
> Yet the nothingness of winter becomes a little less.
> It is still full of icy shades and shapen snow.
>
> .   .   .
>
> The leaves cry. It is not a cry of divine attention,
>
> .   .   .
>
> It is the cry of leaves that do not transcend themselves.

And at the *somber* end of the nothing spectrum there is Shakespeare's *King Lear*, a play full of no, nothing, never, naught. The tone is set near the beginning:

Lear.   . . . what can you say to draw
              A third more opulent than your sisters? Speak.
Cordelia.   Nothing, my lord.
Lear.   Nothing?
Cordelia.   Nothing.
Lear.   Nothing will come of nothing. Speak again.

This rash, spoiled, headstrong old man—the devilishness of his bad daughters and the obstinacy of his good one are surely much his doing—is uttering here, not for the last time, and without reflection, the great formula of the Epicureans:

> Nothing comes from nothing; nothing can return to nothing.
> *Gigni de nihilo nihilum, in nihilum nil posse reverti.*

His clever daughter Goneril, complaining of Lear's unruly retinue, puts two and two together and refers to their "epicurism and lust."[4] The dark truth is that Lear is an—unwitting and incomplete—Epicurean, not so much because he wants to give up the world's business for the undisturbed life of pleasure that the Epicureans favor, but because he believes in nothing behind or beyond this life.

But are the real Epicureans and their poets rightly called nihilists devoted to the nothingness of things, and do they take Nothing as their principle? Where are they on the spectrum of Nothing? They are, I would say, semi-nihilists, as is the ancient school of Atomists from which they derive.

Their two cosmological principles—not grounding but constituting principles—are hard, impenetrable corpuscles and the Empty, the Void. The Void is very insufficiently described as empty space. We have many ways of speaking about the Outside: as a receptacle containing trace elements of physical constructions (Plato), as a cosmos of the places proper to each body (Aristotle), as an extended substance that contains bodies in geometric form (Descartes), as a form of our sensibility (Kant), as a field of geometric configurations effecting masses (modern physicists). The Void is unlike any of these. It is a potent but incoherent notion: a true nothing that is a constituent of a world, a container that is not occupied by its contents, an infinity that harbors configured collections—and once again, for the Epicureans, a nothing that abets the primary parallel fall into the abyss and the random swerve of atoms that makes their agglomeration possible. It is an attempt to yoke the emptiest no-thing with the densest things to make a world, while giving priority to the Void, which is not nothingness but *the* Nothing, the world scene. And both these principles are ungenerated and indestructible.[5]

The early Atomists, the so-called Physicists, had, it seems, the sober scientist's cheerful interest in establishing the constituents of the world and of showing how bodies could move within it. But in the writings of Epicurus and Lucretius their physical explanations begin to have the harsh cast of modern nihilism. "Nothing from nothing" now loses its neutral mundanity and begins to have a hortatory—supposedly comforting—tone, since it is used to remove the fear of the gods and the terror of death. For if the nature of things can be explained physically, the gods are shown to be idle, superfluous wraiths and the soul an epiphenomenon. Here begins a nihilistic tradition of allaying the dismal by the more dismal—human vulnerability by divine impotence and mortal anxiety by a promise of annihilation. And indeed, it is hard not to hear—as so often in talk of Nothing—the principle as saying: From the Nothing of the world comes the nothingness of human life.[6] That "nothing from nothing" is a powerful attack on divinity, at least on a creator god, is shown by the opposite principle of Christianity; Thomas Aquinas quotes a gloss on *Genesis* 1:1: "To create is to make something out of nothing," and such creation is attributed to God.[7]

One last reference is to the most vivid description of the life-diminishing horror that can overcome the Western sensibility before the Nothing that the East faces so serenely: The crucial event in E. M. Forster's *A Passage to India* is a visit the English party undertakes to the Mararbar Caves as guests of their young Indian friend Aziz, with disastrous results for all, but especially for him. Here is how these caves affect Mrs. Moore, the wise woman of the book:

> What had spoken to her in that scoured-out cavity of the granite? What dwelt in the first of the caves? Something very old and very small. Before time, it was before space also. Something snub-nosed, incapable of generosity—the undying worm itself. Since hearing its voice, she had not entertained one large thought. . . . Visions are supposed to entail profundity, but—Wait till you get one, dear reader![8]

1. That was a very quick look at the range that Nothing covers in life, poetry, and physics. But, of course, it is in philosophy that most thought is expended on Nothing. I shall, then, somehow or other talk philosophically about Nothing in the remaining sections.

2. In the Eastern tradition that is the West's great counterpart, in Buddhism, Nothing, Void, Emptiness, is an experience to be attained, a serene and even blissful state to be entered. And in one of the most respected Buddhist schools the way to Nothing is recognizable as dialectical. This *nihilismus hilaris*, to coin a Latin phrase, this blithe nihilism, is the illuminating counterpart of our own harsh apprehension of Nothing, our *horror vacui*. So the second section

will be an attempt to bring on the scene Nagarjuna's "Middle Way," a way of annihilating thinking by thinking.

3. Western nihilism always comes with the bitter taste of a confrontation, whatever the disclaimers may be. I will set out briefly the way we come on Nothing with Kant's aid, and how Bergson shows its precedence over Being.

4. A brief characterization is given of the modern movement known as Nihilism through the character of its first proponents, its God-replacing willfulness, the unintended nihilism of Hegel and the implicit nihilism of Wittgenstein.

5. I consider the profound part Nothing plays among the philosophers of Existence, particularly Heidegger, for whom Nothing makes an epiphany in the mood of anxiety in which it "naughts," with profound effects on metaphysics.

6. Finally, in the sixth section, I will try to convey why the end that happens to everyone and is experienced by no one, Death, is often referred to as Nothing, first distinguishing mortal nothing from nonexistence here and now, and from half-existence, Hades; I then articulate the Nothing of Death itself and the cold comfort offered by Kantian immortality as contrasted with Socrates' daily death; I end with a personal postscript.

2. NOTHINGNESS AS ATTAINMENT: THE EAST

The few paragraphs following are more a mention than a treatment, since the subject is so very alien to me.

The nihilism of the West is abysmal; even as a liberation its exhilaration is strenuous, desperate. This anxiety before nothingness might even be said to yield a negative definition of the Western tradition: it is the way of thought that cannot face Nothing without a shudder. But this feature really stands out and becomes remarkable, at least to me, only in confrontation with another possibility, the one found in the other great tradition with which we share the globe of the spirit. The anxious nihilism of the West has an illuminating counterpart in the serene nihilism of the East as taught by certain schools of Buddhism.

I am, however, unable to do much more than allude to its existence, for the flat reason that I cannot really grasp its teachings. The cause is double: The Eastern adepts of this tradition to whom we might look for an initiation seem to become enmeshed in the terminology of Western ontology whose resonances escape them, so that they render the wisdom of the East as a sort of shoddy contrarian metaphysics. But the real bar is that the wisdom itself seems to be less a doctrine for the understanding than a practice for the spirit, an all-absorbing meditative discipline that most of us have no realizable intention of following, certainly not I.[9]

It seems to me an interesting question how "being a practice" differs from "being beyond speech." There is in the West a powerful strain of rising—by means of dialectic—beyond the *logos*, that is, of reasoning oneself by means of articulated reasons beyond reasoning speech. Parmenides' goddess tries to talk him out of discerning speech. Plato thinks of dialectic as a preparation for a sudden illumination in which the intellect loses its cognitive distance from Being and closes with it in wordless unity.[10]

The difference must, I think, be in the kind of culmination achieved. In the Platonic tradition the end is, for want of a better word, positive and in accord, so to speak, with the way of reaching it which is always primarily positive. For even the negations of Western dialectic are always secondary to an initially affirming speech and tend toward a positive finding. The attainment of Nothing in the Eastern tradition I will briefly set out is, on the other hand, reached by a dialectic that aims at ultimate negation. But negative results in speech require an abnegatory frame of mind, a self-denying discipline that aims from the beginning at ultimate denial. To follow the way of intentional thought, thought that intends an object and is articulated in speech, is always to come on Being of some sort and on its categories; natural speech is the platform from which such thinking takes off, for in such speech both the affirmations and the negations determine *Something*. Hence it would seem that to reach *Nothing* a *second* effort is required, the effort *not* to conceive and categorize. And indeed scholars who try to present the teaching of the most accessible Eastern nihilist schools to the Western understanding dwell on the necessity for overcoming all the distinctions of the intellect, be it discursive or intuitive. Yet they try to convey that this abrogating effort is not itself a further act of the intellect, and not just one more positive effort but an overcoming of all effort, and that it is akin to what we call an experience rather than to an intellectual position. One way to put it in our terms is that, if we have ruled that negation makes beings determinate and sets them off from each other, then a further negation, not of this or that delimitation but of all determining negation together, abolishes everything we call an entity. This abolition leaves the world, so to speak, full of Nothingness, a Nothing that is a fullness, since all is merged into one "formless, boundless" void.[11]

It would therefore seem (and the modern interpreters of the Buddhist sages surely wish to leave this impression) that this Eastern wisdom exceeds the most ultimate, encompassing thought of the West by one crucial step. In our tradition there are certainly apprehensions that rise "beyond Being," and some that so come on Nothing.[12] But I think it is a general truth that this Nothing is so named as transcending every kind and degree of Being and as being the source, ground or encompassment of all Being, to be thoughtfully faced by us, at best in awe, but characteristically in anxiety. And all that is just what the Nothing of the East is not: "It is free from thought and anxiety"; it is not to be effortfully faced but entered through detachment; it is not a ground but the whole in a new aspect. The step beyond Western transcendence appears to be the negation of all determining negation itself. That is why interpreters deny that this Buddhism is well described as nihilism—because that term carries the connotations of the awefulness of Nothing in the West. So we must let the term apply only literally.

Nagarjuna is the name of the sage (the term "philosopher" is one of those words that ought to have a Western connotation too distinctive to be usable)[13] who is the patriarch of that Buddhist school that is most accessible insofar as it approaches Nothing dialectically, that is, through orderly refutation. It refutes *all* possible *pairs* articulating what there is:[14] that something is (which is the worldly truth of ordinary people) *and* that it is not; that it both is and is not *and* that it neither is nor is not. These refutations effectively block a Hegelian synthesis in which the affirmation of Being and Nothing yields a new position, Becoming (p. 164). But they are still enmeshed in dualities and are still worldly truth. A further negation, a sort of hypernegation, is necessary, whose effect is not that of Western double negation such as leads back to a positive, but that of erasing opposition itself, the Either-or and Neither-nor. When that step is taken—no longer, it seems, by thinking, but by meditation— the initiate reenters or rather merges with a world that is now empty of all positions, oppositions, discriminations, and fixities; it is a world of pure, unconceived so-ness. And of course this condition of enlightenment, in which the sage reaches the highest truth, can no longer be called an attainment, for there is nothing to be attained.[15]

3. NIHILISM AS CONFRONTATION: THE WEST

While a half-comprehending Westerner can only have the merest intimations of the allurement this Buddhist Nothing has for its adept, there is nothing concealed about the "anxiety, nausea, or panic" that the thought of nothingness induces in the West. Even the "nullophile metaphysicians" do not deny, indeed they embrace, its harsh severity.[16]

Since nihilism in the weak sense is the doctrinal affirmation of *nihil*, Nothing, a brief account of how and when we find it and how we manage to talk about it should come first.

(a) Kant does something wonderful: In the *Critique of Pure Reason*, under the heading of "Nothing," he tabulates the four ways we can get at Nothing, how it can come into our consciousness. The table is determined by his organization of human knowledge into conceptual thinking, sensible intuiting, and the objects toward which they are directed. These factors yield four Nothings, opposed as pairs in the figure of a diamond. The highest and lowest points are:

1. An empty concept without object; this Nothing is a mere being of reason, an idea, which is neither possible nor impossible and cannot be exemplified in experience, like forces of nature that are freely invented.
4. An empty object without concept; this is a "negative nothing," an "unthing" or monster *(Unding)*, a self-contradictory nothing corresponding to an impossible concept, like a two-sided rectilinear figure.

The opposed Nothings in between are on the same horizontal level:

2. An empty object of a concept; a "privative nothing," a concept of a deficient object, like a shadow.
3. An empty intuition without an object, an "imaginary entity," a mere form without substance, like pure space and time, which are the forms for intuiting objects but are not themselves objects.

These are the structures of consciousness that we may call "Nothing" in definite ways—they are not nonexistents, properly conceived and intuited objects that happen not to be positable as here and now, but the way of undoing objects in general; for Nothing and its opposite Something are the highest divisions of Kantian philosophy.[17]

Here is what is most striking in Kant's table. It has no place for *nihil absolutum*, for *the* Nothing. All the nothings are particular deficiencies, relative to human experience, to the emptiness of thinking or intuiting. There is a reason for this absence.

In a pre-Critical essay Kant had tried to prove the impossibility of annulling all existence simply.[18] The proof has a certain stupefying simplicity: The possibility of a thing can be annulled formally by the self-contradiction of its concept, for an unthinkable object is an impossible object. But there is no inner contradiction in its material annulment, if it was not posited to begin with—that nothing should exist seems thinkable. "That, however, through which all the material, all the data for possibility, is annulled, also negates possibility itself." And that is what happens if all existence is annulled—all possibility is also gone: ["If all possibility is annulled, the impossible supervenes, and that is itself impossible."] Hence it is simply impossible that "nothing at all exists."

In the *Critique of Pure Reason* the attempt to prove that "nothing simply" is impossible is in effect dropped as beyond our experience. Kant's earlier proof illuminates the assumption that is impermissible from the Critical point of view. The sentence of the proof that I have put in square brackets is only implicit in Kant's argument, but it is crucial. "Possibility" is a *thought*, the thought of the conceptual or material *positability* of Something, that is, our ability to say of it: *it is*. So possibility perishes in absolute Nothing. Were there a point of view from *Nothing*, it might be that possible and impossible perish together. But from our point of view as positing *subjects*, it is possibility that is annulled, and when possibility goes there is only impossibility, a remaindered impossibility, so to speak. But what is thus impossible, even only as the survivor of the annulment of its positive opposite, is *really impossible*. So Nothing is a real impossibility.

A curious argument, but not evidently refutable on its own terms! In fact it underlies the *Critique*, though no longer as an argument. It is everywhere the teaching of the *Critique* that we cannot exceed our own subjectivity and its experience, and that therefore the Nothing beyond its limits is inaccessible to us.[19] Indeed the argument itself sounds tautologous in the Critical context: In experience we *always* come on *something* empirically experienceable, and so the Nothings we come on are only specific discrepancies between the concepts of experience and its sensory material.

The great question that agitates those who reflect philosophically on Nothing is: Why is there Something rather than Nothing? (p. 186). It can, it seems to me, be taken in three senses. 1. One sense is this: What makes us so sure that Something *is*, rather than Nothing? To that question Kant answers, as anyone will who starts with the human subject: I am on the scene as an experiencing human being, and what I experience according to the rules of cognition is *ipso facto* existence.[20] The other two senses are deep and unruly: 2. How can we account for the accepted fact that there is Something and not Nothing if we are unwilling simply to posit the eternity of all Being or, alternately, the operation of a hyperbeing that creates Something out of Nothing? 3. Might we not even surmise that Nothing has endured the coming of Something, that it was perhaps even the ground of Being, and that as such it makes itself known to us in its own, nearly unsayable mode? This third question shifts the mystery of the world's existence from Being to Nothing, and that is the one to be taken up in the third section.

Meanwhile, there is something more to be said about the way ultimate Nothing comes to have meaning for us. Western philosophy has been bound to Being, its lesser sibling Nonbeing, and its incestuous child by Nonbeing, Becoming (to overdo the metaphor a little). Absolute Nothing, Nothing absolved, that is, from all relation to Being, does not, to my knowledge, figure in the metaphysics that approaches truth through speech.[21]

(b) But in the imaginative and meditative groping of amateurs Nothing does figure, and there it is, in a sense, before Being—it underlies Being on the mental stage. Bergson thinks it worthwhile to inquire into the causes of this fact, that is, the absence of Nothing in philosophy and its primacy in prephilosophical reflection. For Nothing "is often the hidden spring, the invisible mover of philosophical thinking."[22] He discovers, from self-inspection, that existence appears as a *conquest* over Nothing. Thus Nothing is more original, has priority. Why do we feel, before we think it out, that "the full is an embroidery on the canvas of the void"? As amateurs of reflection we begin, he says, by suppressing all perceptions so as to experience nothing, the void. We next try to do away with consciousness itself, and so we enter on a regression in which an imaginary self always arises behind the extinguished self: "I see myself annihilated only if I have already resuscitated myself by an act that is positive, however involuntary and unconscious." Each suppressed self is an imagined object external to the observing self. So we swing back and forth between a vision of an outer and an inner self. There will come a point when our mind is equidistant from both: We no longer perceive the one and not yet the other. Here the image of Nothing is formed, unstable and not fit "to oppose to Being, and put before or beneath Being." Bergson is right, at least in my experience: To *imagine* Nothing is a hopeless attempt not to imagine, but people do, on occasion, make it.

The philosophers, however, he goes on, are commonly said to represent Nothing to themselves not as an image but as an idea. Yet the mental process is not very different. An idea is a presence in the mind. The attempt to annihilate it, to create an idea void, is once again forced to go from the full to the full: "The conception of a void arises here when consciousness, lagging behind itself, remains attached to the recollection of an old state though another state is already present." The idea-void can be analyzed "into two positive elements: the idea . . . of a substitution, and the feeling . . . of a desire or a regret." Therefore "the idea of the absolute Nothing, in the sense of the annihilation of everything, is a self-destructive idea, a pseudo-idea, a mere word."

But we—as logicians and philosophers—screen this fact from ourselves by the other fact that we can "write in the margin of our thought the 'not'." We can annihilate everything mentally by negation. We mistakenly believe that affirmation and negation are symmetrical, whereas in fact negation is only an "affirmation of the second degree." Bergson means that affirmations bear on objects, while negations bear only on judgments. So logical negations do not have the power to nullify anything but opinions—as was surmised earlier in this book (p. 39).

Why, when all approaches to Nothing are so wrong-headed, do we persist in thinking (as Bergson has claimed) that it comes before or underlies things? It is, he says, because of a feeling arising from our social, practical nature. We are made to act; all action arises from a dissatisfaction, a felt absence; we proceed from nothing to something. And then we transfer this order of precedence to our speculation. Thus is implanted the idea that Reality fills a prior void and that Nothing, as absence of everything, preexists all things "in right if not in fact."

This seems to me an ingenious and occasionally true psychological account of how existence comes to be thought of as occupying territory wrested from Nothing. But it cannot be the whole or even an altogether plausible account. For one thing, a felt absence is nothing like Nothing—like absolute Nothing, that is—for desire is the most vibrant of lacks (p. xi). For another, it is odd that those philosophers, ancient and modern, who have the most specific interest in the practical life show the least need to give Nothing a place of precedence. Yet further, the movement that called itself Nihilism was very much oriented toward social practice, yet its direction was not to conquer Nothing *by* existence, but to introduce Nothingness *into* existence.

4. NIHILISM AS A MODERN MOVEMENT

These nihilists, who, after all, called themselves "nothingists," cannot well be absent in a chapter on Nothing. Perhaps insofar as their devotion to Nothing was not so much from thought as by will, they belong rather to the first chapter, which dealt with willful naysaying. But insofar as they adhered to an ideology, that is, a thought package, they had some sort of relation to a theory of nothingness, and belong to this last chapter on absolute naysaying.

(a) The arch-nihilist, the hero of the Russian Nihilist movement, which was the earliest and most distinctively generational nihilism, was not a man but a character in a novel. Moreover, his nihilism is as much or more a disposition than a doctrine. Yevgeny Vassilich Bazarov of Turgenev's *Fathers and Sons* says of himself to his admiring young friend Arkady Kissanov:

> "Principles don't exist in general—you haven't grasped that!—but there are instincts. Everything depends on them."
> "How so?"
> "Like this. Take me, for example: I have a negative disposition. I find it pleasant to negate, my brain's built that way—and that's that!"

Nonetheless, Barzanov wants to benefit society, and judges, consonant with his nature, that the total annihilation of all social institutions as utterly corrupt is what is now beneficial. What is to follow is a void; he believes in nothing and it is not his, the nihilistic revolutionary's, business to have a positive program. Bazarov is doubly a negator: of the world and of himself. Yet his unbendingly principled hate even onto self-destruction is contradicted by isolated acts of kindness; the "Satanic arrogance" and self-sufficiency of his large-gauged egotism is contradicted by his vulnerability to a woman's love; and the cold voyeurism of his scientific dissections is contradicted by his physician's desire to cure. He is a miserably self-negating yet dominatingly fascinating hero.[23]

Bazarov is introduced to Arkady's family as a "nihilist." "A nihilist," says his good-hearted father, "that comes from the Latin word *nihil*, nothing, so far as I can tell; it must mean a person—who acknowledges nothing." Arkady's uncle, Pavel, who sets himself against Bazarov from the beginning, concludes the ensuing family discussion: "Yes. First there were Hegelists and now nihilists. Let's see how you'll manage to exist in a void, in a vacuum."

Pavel's thumbnail history of movements contains a truth: I ended the last chapter with the suggestion that a nihilism is lurking in Hegel's system. The young Russian nihilists who followed Bazarov's example are really more devoted to the practical nothingness of this world than the metaphysical Nothing behind it, and the story of these antisocial intellectuals' dreams of reforming society for ordinary humanity does not belong in this book. But before it became a social movement (and after it ceased to be that) there was an intellectual and a subsequent emotional nihilism—not so much a movement that sweeps people along as a tendency that insinuates itself into opinions as an unexpected presence.

To my mind thought is, whenever it comes into its own, not moved by the pressures of invasive circumambient opinion but by the ways of its own aboriginal realm. Nonetheless if true thinking is independent of trends, the problems from which thinkers take their departure are usually given by the world of their existence. And in solving the intellectual problems set for them philosophers undergo a fate analogous in reverse to that which dogs practical problem solvers: As the worldly solutions of reformers often have unintended practical consequences, so the intellectual solutions of speculative philosophy often later reveal unintended foundations. In a word, the nihilistic strain of modern philosophy is not *at first* a conscious call on the depth of Nothing to account for the nothingness of existence; quite the contrary.

(b) The history of the nihilism that preceded the revolutionary movement called Nihilism is set out very persuasively by Michael Gillespie.[24] We usually think of nihilism as Nietzsche put it: a catastrophic weakening of the human will, which is now no longer capable of bringing forth a plenitude of divinities; the ensuing Death of God, of the Crucified who died for the pity of mankind, leads to a world in which "everything is permitted," and so nothing has any demonstrable worth. Nietzsche follows Schopenhauer, who in the vein of the Romantics sees a demonic will, a will to nothingness underlying this God-bereft world. But he opposes to Schopenhauer's weak and man-diminishing individual human will, such as produces bourgeois banality and despair and nihilism, the call for a strong will, the will to power and to self-overcoming and life; he names its deity "Dionysus."

Gillespie argues that Nietzsche himself did not understand that the Dionysian will too, the supposed antidote for the nihilism of the resentful and pity-bartering human herd, belonged to a Romantic tradition that has a deep and identifiable root in an unconsciously nihilistic philosophical, and ultimately even theological tradition—in short that Dionysus himself is nihilistic. That is to say that from its earliest beginnings modernity itself has an inbuilt nihilistic strain. This strain is not all there is to modernity, and in fact its true antidote is modern liberalism. This liberalism may indeed lead to relativism and banality, but it does *not* lead to the nihilism of political terror.

Now what is this deep root of modern nihilism? It is the evolution of the idea of God's will as absolute and the subsequent devolution of this will from God to man. In the nominalism of late medieval Christianity an omnipotent God is conceived who is in no way restrained by reason or nature. God becomes merely, transrationally, even capriciously willful. Natural science can cast loose and rely on its own nondivine laws and forces, but human beings need protection from the power of so demonic a god. Now Descartes found a way of turning this god into a benevolent guarantor of reason and science by showing that God is not malicious. But the argument was made at the expense of God's reality; he has become a mere representation of human thinking. The human being, on the other hand, is shown to be godlike. For though it is not omniscient, it does know one thing for certain: that it thinks. And, since for Descartes to think is to will, and man's will, like God's, is infinite, human freedom can be absolute. For Rousseau the divinization of man becomes more radical and more explicit: Man's will is free to capriciousness. Kant tries to overcome a newly apparent antinomy between the freedom that defines the rational will and the laws of nature constituted by rational cognition through delimiting the two realms of reason, subject and nature, against each other and leaving them each independent. This solution introduces an unintelligible duality into human beings. Fichte tries to resolve this dilemma by positing only the willful self, the subject, and allowing nature to spring from this self by self-alienation, so that the not-self appears as an objective world, an Other. His contemporary, Jacobi, would call Fichte's idealism a nihilism, because there is no truth or being beyond the self's consciousness. But this is the nihilism of the self-potentiating will, the will that comes to dominate the dreams of the Romantics in demonic form. Even Hegel, Gillespie points out, a great opponent of Romanticism, could not free himself from its spell. Gillespie's understanding of modernity (including postmodernity) as being in one aspect a nihilism is completely compelling: Anyone who reads in Ockham or in the writings of the earliest scientists and scientist-philosophers must sense that human willfulness plays a powerful role in their apparently very positive writing. What is missing in them and in most of their intellectual descendants is the clear apprehension that infinite, *absolute willfulness is next to nihilism.* For if the will is everything, nothing is what it is except by human fiat—which is to say that existence is founded on Nothing and is affected by nothingness.

(c) Even Hegel: Right in this book, in which Hegel's dialectic negativity is given prominence as the principle of conceptual life, the suspicion arose that a nihilism, not intended as such, might be lurking at the very beginning of thought (p. 164). Here is a telling passage:

Becoming in respect to essence, its reflecting movement, is therefore the *movement from nothing to nothing and thus back to itself.* Transiting or becoming therefore cancels itself *(hebt sich auf)* in its transiting; the other, which comes into being in this transiting, is not the nonbeing of a being but the nothing of a nothing: And this, to be the negation of a nothing is what constitutes being.[25]

The reader may recall that the very first movement of Hegelian dialectical negativity was that from Being to Nothing and the next resulted in their unity as Becoming. The passage above is much further on in the developmental logic of the Absolute, the whole concept. It comes from the second part, where Being is superseded by Essence. In the Doctrine of Being all the conceptual moments presented themselves immediately to us and independently from each other. Essence is mediated Being, which means that all its stages are pairs of related concepts, mediated by reflection and dependent on each other: For Essence is indissolubly related to the Unessential, to illusion-appearance or "show" *(Schein)*. The reflecting motion, the coming into being of the moments and their correlates is not an alternation but a mutual mirroring, in which the abstract Nothingnesses of either moment taken independently are reflexively related (Hegel writes *Reflexion*) so as to bring about a new, two-sided Being: essence-and-appearance. Thus one might indeed say that this new and more differentiated Being called Essence, which came to be by the negation of a Nothing, lies between two Nothings. And its negative origin is not from the outside, by the opposition of another moment to which it responds negatively, but Essence *itself* is only insofar as it negates itself.

Why is this unwitting nihilism? But first, why is it nihilism at all? Hegel himself says about Fichte's philosophy that

the infinity or the abyss of the Nothing in which all Being sinks away . . . must characterize the infinite pain . . . on which is based the religion of modernity, the feeling: "God himself is dead" as a moment.[26]

So far this is recognizably nihilistic in mood. But then Hegel goes on: "but also as no more than a moment"; philosophy must be tough enough to celebrate a "speculative Good Friday," to take the death of God seriously enough so as to make possible a resurrection of the highest totality under the shape of "the gladdest freedom." And so nihilism "rebounds upon itself and reconstitutes itself as the most comprehensive order." For the nihilism is absorbed within the Absolute Idea, and Fichte's ultimate nihilism is but a stage in Hegel's system, precisely that of Essence.[27]

In some strict sense of the word Hegel is a nihilist, because Nothing is the conceptual diameter within whose poles Being arises. But then again it is Being—in the form of the Absolute whole, within which all its defeated shapes are resurrected and recollected—which is the end, and that end is not nihilism, but its utmost opposite, a philosophy of absolutely actualized Being. So one might say that Hegel is a *momentary nihilist.*

Is it unwitting nihilism? Yes and no. Hegel fully acknowledges that the primacy of Nothing is merely temporary and that the pervasive power of negativity is in the service of actuality; thus he is not willingly a nihilist. And yet he is not as innocent of nihilism as are, say, those ancient philosophers who thought that Nonbeing and Negation were to be found in the diversity of beings and the naysaying power of human speech respectively (p. 142), that is, *within* Being, and that *beyond* Being there was either a principle yet more potent than Being such as the Good or the One or—but here they simply and wisely abstained from any mention of an alternative whatsoever. The ancients were, it seems, capable of leaving the inconceivable strictly alone. Hegel's nihilism is perched, in false security, on a slippery slope.[28]

(d) As there was Western nihilism before Nietzsche, in fact at the beginning of the modern West, so it can be found in philosophy long after nihilism as a revolutionary movement had disappeared. In his book on nihilism[29] Rosen starts with Nietzsche, and explicates "the problem of nihilism as implicit in human nature." Where Gillespie dwells on human willfulness as the basis of nihilism, Rosen sees nihilism as the self-annihilation of speech. (The two analyses are not at odds, if one considers this use of speech to be willful.) To combat the notion that nihilism is "a literary neurosis imported from continental Europe," and to show that it is primarily a theoretical and only secondarily an ethical and cultural phenomenon, Rosen first takes on Wittgenstein, that paragon of "Anglo-Saxon sobriety." He shows that "Wittgenstein and his progeny are nihilists because they cannot distinguish speech from silence."

For it makes no difference what we say. It makes no difference because if, as the later Wittgenstein says (p. 45), speech becomes meaningful only in a context of gamelike rules and conventions and as a "form of life," then we can never get beyond these and never receive a sensible answer when we query a conventional usage or conventionalism itself.

Wittgenstein's nihilism is wholly implicit, not only in the sense of coming to the surface only in a critical exposure, but also in not being based on an explicit principle of Nothing. While Rosen is persuasive about Wittgenstein, we might wonder why not every theory is vulnerable to the charge, since self-destruction lurks in every human construction. I suppose the distinguishing mark of nihilistic unviability is just that willfulness is so close to the surface of the doctrine.

If Wittgenstein is an implicit post-Nietzschean nihilist, Heidegger might be called an abjuring nihilist, for he denies his nihilism—which is by far the deepest of the speculative Western nihilisms that I know of.[30]

5. EXISTENTIAL NIHILISM:
THE NOTHING THAT "NAUGHTS"

The reader will have to put up with some curious locutions; Heidegger's willful neologisms, to which German gladly lends itself, go directly into English only by misshaping it. The heading above means that this Nothing has a power of its own—not of setting at naught *(Vernichten)* but of Naughting *(nichten*: the verb exists no more in German than in English).

A second *caveat lector* is in order. Heidegger will implicate Nothing in the account of Being. Yet the way Nothing comes to us, comes over us, is through a mood *(Stimmung*: literally, "tuning" or "attunement"). It is a very specific and yet in no way a "mere" mood, Anxiety *(Angst)*, often translated as "dread."[31] The pull to psychology is very strong here—to take what is meant to be an onto-logical inquiry, a search for Being, as a psycho-logical observation, an interpretative description of one human feeling. It takes an effort, worth the making, to exercise that much praised "principle of charity" in reading Heideggerian texts, and to refrain from deflating his account by understanding it as merely an exquisite kind of psychology with an ontological signature.[32]

One text preeminently speaks of Nothing, the essay "What is Metaphysics?"[33] Earlier in this book the question was raised whether the naysayings and negations of ordinary speech arise from a specifically human capacity only or from something in the constitution of the world. Heidegger will answer unequivocally: neither from the one nor the other, but from a transcendent Nothing. The title of this chapter is: "The Absolute Opposite: *Nothing,*" and so far this description has served to separate Nothing simply from nothingness in the world. But Heidegger will show its limitations, for the inner-worldly nothingness that I distinguished from *nihil absolutum* will be interpreted as an epiphany of Nothing itself. I cannot think of another text where Nothing actually *functions.*

Here is my understanding of the teaching which answers the question that gives "What Is Metaphysics?" its title.

(a) Heidegger begins the epiphany of Nothing with a denigrating representation of the *positive* sciences, including formal logic. "Positive," a term he introduced in the edition of 1949, here means: concerned only with all the beings *(das Seiende)*, with what is given and at hand (which is just what would *ordinarily* be called existence). The sciences, formal, human, and natural, treat all that is with egalitarian interest, and are constitutionally indifferent to what is *not* given, to the Nothing. The exposition in chapter 3 of this book certainly confirms the hostility of formal logic to nonexistence.

To be sure, the question concerning Nothing is "self-consuming," formally self-contradictory, for just to frame it is to speak of Nothing as a this or that, a being. Moreover, to mere reason Nothing is the negation of the totality of beings simply. Now since negation is considered as a mental act, within positive science Nothing must appear as just a species of logical negation.

Yet it might be the other way around. Perhaps negation is possible only because of a Nothing that is more originative than the "not" of negation. Perhaps mental negation is dependent on the Nothing.

Since there is no formal access to the Nothing, we must see if it might not be given to us in advance, in just the way that any pursuable question anticipates its object. And since it is the totality of beings that is invalidated by Nothing, we must see if there is not a mode in which all beings are brought to naught for us. But it will not do to turn these beings collectively into a mere thought and then to negate that. That gives us an ideal, an imaginary nothing, deceptively identical with genuine Nothing only in its lack of differentiation. (Recall, as an illuminating contrast, that ancient Nonbeing is precisely the source of difference, p. 141.)

(b) The required anticipation is to be found in certain fundamental "moods" in which the attunements of a human existence to its world are revealed. Heidegger briefly mentions boredom and joy,[34] but he dwells on anxiety *(Angst)*, a dread that is about nothing in particular; and that he interprets as a manifestation—*not* an apprehension—of Nothing. The description of anxiety in "What is Metaphysics?" is a moving example of existential phenomenology, the descriptive analysis of human phenomena (much more so than is the presentation of the same mood in *Being and Time*). The condition of Anxiety is a very rare but devastatingly revealing event. In it we are pervaded by a spellbound calm, a sense of the bared unhomey uncanniness *(Unheimlichkeit)* of the world. All beings together distance themselves from us, and in this very removal oppress us. Beings slip away and leave us suspended, so that we too slip away from ourselves as human beings among beings. Only our pure existence, our being there *(Dasein)* remains. Anxiety reveals Nothing.

(c) So here we have hold of an event that anticipates the object—which is not an object—of our question. All beings have become untenable, but not as having been annihilated or negated. And so we discover the essence of Nothing. It is the nihilation or Naughting *(Nichtung)* of beings; it is not our work, for "Nothing naughts on its own," nor a particular occurrence of some sort, but a unique Event. And so it reveals beings in their full alienness and otherness. "In the clear night of anxiety's Nothing," beings come into the open, and show that they are and are *not* Nothing. And this Nothing is not an explanation of beings in their totality, but the antecedent condition of their possibility. (It is the same, Heidegger says in the edition of 1949, as the source of all beings, Being, *Sein.*) Thus the human being, in the existential mood of anxiety, transcends what is within its world to come into relation with the ground of its world. Genuine human existence means "being projected into the Nothing:" for the naughting of Nothing brings the human being face to face with all beings by repelling them. Heidegger adds cryptically that there is no self-hood or freedom without the original manifesting of Nothing.

But how can it be that so fundamental a condition should reveal itself to us so rarely? It is because although Nothing naughts continually it belongs to its meaning that it is our aversion to it which makes daily life possible. Nonetheless it is continually operative in our ordinary negation. As was said in the beginning: the "not" of negation could not occur if our thinking were not looking ahead to the Nothing. For how could thinking produce a "not" out of itself if there were not already something negatable? Nor is logical negation the only evidence of Nothing; there is the harshness of opposition, the violence of loathing, the pain of refusal—each a more abysmal "naughting" than mere negation.

(d) Any or no cause can awaken anxiety and show that man is the transcending "placeholder" of Nothing. It is a mood of the courageous, beyond contrast with ordinary joy or enjoyment. The consideration of this transcending mood leads to the metaphysics of the title. Metaphysics is the inquiry that goes beyond all beings so as to regain them as a whole. The chief expression of classical metaphysics concerning Nothing is the ambiguous proposition "From nothing comes nothing." Though often cited (p. 171), it fails to incite an inquiry into Nothing itself. In Christianity the denial of the proposition and its replacement by "Something comes out of Nothing" leads to a God who must be in intimate relation to Nothing, for it is that out of which he creates. But again, Nothing itself is not an object of inquiry in Christian theology. For in ancient and in Christian metaphysics Being is taken for granted.

"Every being insofar as it is a being is made out of Nothing"—that is the new expression concerning Nothing, the new direction of inquiry, that Heidegger proposes as the new answer to the question "What is metaphysics?"

The essay "What Is Metaphysics?" itself ends with a question—"the basic question of metaphysics"—that Heidegger cites repeatedly:[35]

> Why are beings at all and not rather Nothing?
> *Warum ist überhaupt Seiendes und nicht vielmehr Nichts?*

It occurs again in the later introduction to the essay. Here Heidegger explains that the question is now not asked in pursuit of a Supreme Being, of a first cause of actual beings. Since for Heidegger the question is no longer metaphysical in the classical modern sense—the "imperturbable" sense that Being is evident and can go without saying—it does not preconceive No-thing as a being, a sort of Anti-being. For if it did, since Being always has the right of way, the Nothing in question would drop out of sight, because it simply looks too much like Being. This interpretation explains, I think, why the ancient metaphysicians—who asked "What is Being?"—never asked "the basic question of metaphysics."

Heidegger's answer is nothing like as explicit as were those given by his predecessors. One might suppose that it ought to run like this: "But all the beings together *are* Nothing, and Nothing is everywhere revealed to us in anxiety—your question was based on blind priorities and false oppositions." That would, however, be articulating too much. The question was not meant to be answered in words but to be engaged with in thought; it requires of us openness to the Nothing.

Heidegger's account of Nothing—one might call it an *oudenology* (from Greek *ouden*, Nothing), just as people now write of *meontology* (from Greek *me on*, Nonbeing)—is not the last. But those that followed during the rest of the bygone century were written under its aegis.[36]

∞ ∞ ∞

Now the question must arise what to think of all this. One way to think it out is within Heidegger's framework: Is the phenomenon of fundamental anxiety rightly interpreted—Is the levering of a human experience into a metaphysical revelation acceptable? Is the "naughting" of Nothing a comprehensible notion or a wordplay? These questions are not for this book but for a book on Heidegger.

There is, however, another way: to ask not in Heidegger's terms but in our own whether the experience of nothingness, the sudden sense of no longer being at home in the world, of facing a collection of mutely indifferent beings, stems from a passing indisposition of the mind or intimates a truth worth recollecting when we are again well spun into the cocoon of worldly activity.

I think the latter. But what is coming at us in these existential depressions may not be an intimation of our ground, the Being of all beings, that, since it cannot be grasped as *a* being, must be conjured with as *the* Nothing. It may instead be a sudden recognition that all our trust in our conjectures and all our brave functioning is much ado about nothing. This occasional cracking open of the cocoon of life may be more a salutary reminder that we know only that we know nothing than the revelation of Nothing as the background of our existence. Socrates' modest knowledge of the "nothing" that his knowledge comes to then serves to clear the way to discovering those hypotheses which we might trust to give our speech meaning and our actions rightness.

Moreover, the ultimate question of metaphysics, "Why is there something and not rather nothing?" need not even necessarily mean "nothing at all," *nil absolutum*—total Nothing. The plenum of the sensory world and the plenitude of the thought world could be altogether surrounded by an ocean of Nothing and our own little lives be rounded by a sleep. The serpent might be right when he says

That the universe is nothing but a defect
In the purity of Non-being!

*Que l'univers n'est q'un defaut
Dans la purité du Non-être!*[37]

Then our question should rather be: "How can so small a spot of Being maintain itself on the vast plain of Nothing?" And perhaps this encompassing Nothing irrupts into our world not *only* to wreak on it the varieties of nothing-ness we encounter but also to permit us to say that *not* which determines dif-ference and repels error—perhaps Nothing as neighbor to Something ceases to be absolute Nothing and becomes biddable Nothing. We may muse in these directions, but I think we will not get far by thinking in that way. The day-by-day forgetfulness of *that* overwhelmingly huge Nothing seems to me to be the sound-minded counterpart to the steady remembrance of the other, lower-case nothing, the apprehension of our ignorance, which is the launching pad of our receptive and trustful inquiries.

6. NOTHING AS INESCAPABLE END: DEATH

My guess is that the question which most incessantly agitates human beings when disposition or circumstance *drives* them to reflection is this: Is death something or nothing? Is it a passage point or a moment of utter finality?

In what follows I pass over Christian and a fortiori over other beliefs con-cerning an afterlife. When the survival of the human being after secular death is a matter of faith, the tenor of the inquiry is altogether different: The fear of death is then not a fear of nothingness but of punishment: "Since I sin every day without repenting, fear of death distresses me. For in hell there is no re-demption." And the hope is of eternal, individual, even bodily life in para-dise.[38] Death to a Christian is, one might say, only as a double negation: the annihilator is annihilated, as in Donne's sonnet: "death, thou shalt die."[39] So also in Luther's Easter song set by Bach, "Christ lay in the Bonds of Death": Christ has removed sin and therefore death: "Thus nothing *(nichts)* remains but death's mere form"—all voices cease across a beat after *nichts*, and the allegro turns into a measure and a half of adagio on death's emptiness;[40] death is a powerless nothing no longer to be feared.

Pagan and post-Christian writing on death is full of death as nothing, though its nothingness is by no means always a comfort. It might be the can-celing summation of a life-total, the advent of a purifying annihilation, the moment of no return, an inexorable evanescence, a negation of temporal being, a culmination of life's nothingness. Think of rich Croesus, who recalls on his burning pyre Solon's advice not to call himself happy until the very end of life—a most peculiarly momentary form of happiness, since nothing is promised beyond. Think of sanctified Oedipus who, called from out of a silence, is simply annihilated: "The man was nowhere present anymore." Or think of bereaved Lear's lament for Cordelia, "Thou'lt come no more, / Never, never, never, never, never!"—that most astonishing line of inverted iambs, which is but the last of his cries invoking nothingness.[41]

To and for whom is death said to be nothing or a nothing? For each separate mortal, death-bound human being, both *within* life and *beyond* it. Death, it is claimed, is nothing *to* us in this life, and has nothing *for* us afterwards. The Epicureans and their poet Lucretius phrased the sentiment in this often cited way:

> Death, then, is nothing to us.

This dubiously cheery pagan teaching has a double meaning: Death ought to be nothing to us now because, while we are, it is not, and it is nothing for us to fear for later, because when *it* will be, *we* will be nothing.[42] As it has a double meaning, so it gives a double-edged comfort, for it is just this nothingness that human beings by nature fear. How the nothing of death presents itself to us and with what kind of argumentation death is acknowledged or denied I will sketch out in the final pages. Here I should say once more that Nothing is not Nonbeing. For the latter is, even as its opposite, a relative to Being, while Nothing is beyond both Being and Nonbeing, just a blank.

The nothingness of death might be schematically set out in three types: Nothing simply, Nonexistence here and now, and Attenuated or Semi-Existence elsewhere. I leave the first of these to last, since it has elicited the most by way of philosophical writing.

(a) Whatever one's faith, in the tradition within which this book is written, it is generally accepted that the dead no longer exist in the sense of nonexistence established before: *not being here and now* in extended space and secular time (p. 79). The Hebrew Bible has a spare and vivid way of putting it: "And all the days of Enoch were three hundred sixty and five years. And Enoch walked with God, *and he was not*; for God took him."[43]

It is this nonexistence of those who have died that is most poignantly felt right after death: There is, so to speak, a black silhouette in the places where once there was a person or a place; life washes its colors over the outline, the shadow becomes transparent and faded; then memory succeeds as the locus of absent presence:

> There is a house that is no more a house
> Upon a farm that is no more a farm
> And in a town that is no more a town.[44]

This negative too becomes blurred and occasional until only sudden sporadic mental images rise up to testify to a former existence—those and perhaps some anecdotes and catalogue entries. Nonexistence is not, however, inactuality: It is often just when the ripples of primary memory have run off that the influence of the life that has gone out of existence begins to exert itself, especially if it was a life of works; it is then that this human existence is revived in fixed public memorial images, pictorial or written.

Our belief in the nonexistence of the dead is by no means universal. In the realm of the Incas, for example, the dead came onto the living scene in the body. Prescott describes the presence of the mummified royal ancestors at the accession of the Inca Manco and how "each ghostly form took its seat at the banquet-table attended by its living retinue."[45]

(b) There is also a state *between* existence and nothingness. Just as a corpse has for a little while an uncanny resemblance to the human being that has ceased to exist, so in Homer's House of Hades, a place on, not under this earth, at its end where flows the river Oceanus, the departed soul is a shadow, a diminished image, a "little form" *(eidolon)* of the human being. The souls, these mere shaped breaths of the dead, are thus significantly also called corpses *(nekroi)*. These "unmindful" dead long to drink blood so that they may speak, touch or see each other and the living (except for the seer Teiresias "who, being blind on earth, sees more than all the rest in hell")—the "eaters of bread" *(brotoi,* the Greek word for "mortals") want to become drinkers of blood here. They live in throngs and tribes, yet incommunicado, alone, and newsless. They are mere self-less phantoms—though a hero like Heracles, whose *eidolon* is in Hades, can be *himself* with the gods on Olympus. This House of Hades is a dim and joyless country, particularly for that quickest of heroes, Achilles, who utters those poignant lines to Odysseus:

> Do not speak to me consolingly of death, shining Odysseus.
> I would rather *be* upon the earth as a serf of another,
> Even of a man without an estate who has not much livelihood,
> Than to be lord over all the corpses that have died off.

Achilles longs to escape even into the lowliest existence from the semi-existence of death. Yet this semi-existence of the Elysian fields with its voiceless shades is so darkly vivid that it is again invoked for the dead soldiers of a war less than a century in our past:

> Down some cold field in a world unspoken
> the young men are walking together, slim and tall,
> and though they laugh to one another, silence is not broken;
> there is no sound however clear they call.[46]

(c) Both as the final Nothing that life comes to and insofar as that Nothing informs the passage from birth to death and drives us to thoughts of the nature of Nothing and of our eventual nothingness—death in that aspect has, as I have said, given rise to the most focused, not merely meditative but severely analytic, thinking.

That human life eventuates between not yet and no more is not news. That death is built into biological life, that the end is one anchor of the arc of life that culminates—which the Greeks called the *acme*, the prime of life—before declining in prolonged maturity is a truism whose truth impinges on us only sporadically and rarely in so oppressive a way:

> O, can I not forget that I am living?
> How shall I reconcile the two conditions:
> Living, and yet—to die?[47]

In fact, there seems to commentators on contemporary life to be a deplorable gulf between our general knowledge that everyone dies and our consciousness of our own death. Thus Freud says that we have a tendency to cast death aside and eliminate it from life, and so we make life as pallid "as a shallow kind of American flirtation," of which nothing will come. And indeed many observers of the scene are hardest on the Americans, who by losing themselves in the motoric optimism of technological tinkering hide death from view so as to obliterate its psychic presence from consciousness.[48]

It is this impression—that in modern times people evade the thought of their mortality—that inspired the various attempts to draw death back into life as a power. The most complex and weighty analysis of human death of this sort is that of Heidegger in *Being and Time*.[49] To understand death as the meaning of human existence is to forego the ways of tranquilization by which "one" *(man)*, anyone, no one, forces human existence away from death and flees in the face of it. Death must not be seen from the outside as a certainty externally acknowledged and a fact empirically observed—"one" dies, not I myself; nor as an end of an entity, an end that is as yet outstanding and deferred to an unknown later time—not yet, and so unacknowledged as a possibility borne in every moment (253 ff.); nor, above all, must death be seen as a mere actuality that conceals its character as *the* ultimate human possibility—for "higher than actuality stands possibility" (38).

Heidegger says that his own analysis of death is not to be taken as forestalling decisions about immortality such as we make for the purpose of ordinary living or as are ordinarily conveyed in homilies on how to face death (248). But the candid reader might wonder whether the interpretation of death about to be sketched does not in fact foreclose ordinary faith in the immortality of the soul.[50]

Heidegger delineates death in sum by the following determinations: *"Death as the end of human existence* [Dasein: "the being that is there, that exists"] *is the ownmost possibility of human existence, non-relational, certain, and as such indeterminate and not to be overtaken. Death* as the end of *human being* is the Being of this being *toward* its end" (258 ff.). Authentic existence is Being-toward-death *(Sein zum Tode*, 251). What the preposition "toward" *(zum)* signifies is the human being's acknowledgment of death as ever impending, ever of the future *(Zukunft)*—its own inalienable finitude. That a human being understands the impending possibility of its death turns this possibility into a potentiality, its very own capability for being: It is the power to persist in that frame of mind which is open to the threat arising from the human being's very own, most isolating possibility. It is the same existential mood described above (p. 185), only now focused on oneself: anxiety *(Angst)*. It is the frame of mind in which the human being finds itself *"before* the Nothing of the possible impossibility of its [own] existence" (266). Authentic existence goes on in the face of its own coming *nothingness.* Its frame of mind is a futural and an anticipatory, a passionate and a disillusioned "freedom toward death." This anticipation is not an expectation, for an expectation merely awaits an actualization, while *"The nearest nearness of being-toward-death as a possibility is as far away from an actuality as possible"* (262). The genuinely existing human being is not awaiting the actual advent of Nothing but daily facing its possibility—here (by sleight of language, as it seems to me) interpreted as a potentiality or a capability.

Levinas speaks of this Being-toward-death as "a supreme lucidity and hence a supreme virility." Heidegger himself terms it a "fantastic imposition" on ordinary existence. It was cited here only because it is the most impressive drawing down of death as Nothing into daily life.[51]

(d) Most reflective rational writing about death deals, however, with the question of the soul's survival after somatic death, which is to say, with its immortality, and it offers cold comfort. The issue is whether there is some reasoning by which we can persuade ourselves that we do not come to nothing. Such arguments are far removed from "Those shadowy recollections" through which

> Our Souls have sight of that immortal sea
>   Which brought us hither,
>   Can in a moment travel thither
> And see the Children sport upon the shore,
> And hear the mighty waters rolling evermore.[52]

They are instead intended to be rationally compelling trains of thought concerning either personal survival and demise or our attitude toward death, whatever it may bring. I began with the bitter antidote to the fear of death offered by the Epicureans. The Stoics offer a more agnostic comfort:

You embarked, you made a voyage, you have arrived at the far shore. Now step ashore. If you land in a new life, there will be gods enough for you . . . if you step into nothing, a condition without consciousness, you will still be free of the constraints of your earthly body, of pain and pleasure.[53]

Now here is a curious fact: The more extended and systematic the arguments get, the less they are reflections on the issue and the more they are exercises in method. The most prominent example is Kant's dialectical treatment of the soul in the *Critique of Pure Reason*.[54] "Dialectical" here means that paralogisms, fallacies of deductive reasoning, are revealed in all the arguments that might support the soul's immortality: that it is a substance, that it is simple, that it is a unity, that it has a relation to spatial objects. As substance it is the absolute, that is, the self-sufficient *subject* of our thinking; as a simple substance it is *incorporeal*; as a unity the soul has the numerical identity, the self-identity of a *person*; as being interrelated with bodies in space it is the principle of *animality*, of life. The first three taken together yield the spirituality of the soul; life as determined by spirituality yields the concept of immortality (B 403).

The arguments that can be given for these four factors which together yield the immortality of the soul are all fallacies of the same kind. All assume that we can intuit, that is, experience, the ground of our thinking, the "I" of "I think," and Kant's book is devoted to showing the impossibility of intuiting nonsensory being. Hence there is no "doctrine of the soul," no "rational psychology" (B 421 ff.). To be sure, as moral beings we are entitled to *hope* for, are even required to *postulate,* a future life (e.g., B 24). But in comparison with the conviction of reason a postulate of immortality, that is to say a want supplied because it *demands* its own fulfillment, is cold comfort. And on reading the section on paralogisms, this thought obtrudes itself: that it says nothing at all about the matter itself—Does or does not the human being come to nothing at the end of life? Kant's dialectic only shows that rational inferences—either way, though he reviews only the case *for* immortality—are on his terms unwarranted. And this deflection from the *what* of the issue to the *how* of proof runs forward to contemporary treatments[55] and backward to *the* great work on the immortality of the soul in antiquity, Plato's *Phaedo*.

Kant calls the argument from simplicity the "Achilles of all dialectical inferences" (A 351) because it seems most powerful and no mere sophism. He reviews Mendelssohn's *Phaedo*, which argues the immortality of the soul on the basis that a simple being has no way to cease existing (B 413 f.). The incomposite character of the soul is, of course, an element of one of Socrates' arguments in the ancient *Phaedo* (78 b ff.): The soul belongs among those invisible beings that are selfsame and is therefore incomposite and so indestructible. I won't detail this and the other arguments here, but simply say that they are one and all as unconvincing as are their rational critiques—on this at least there is much agreement. In Hume's elegant phrase, these arguments *"admit of no answer and produce no conviction."*[56]

(e) What then is Socrates up to on this his last day on earth? He makes the astounding assertion that it is the philosopher's part to practice dying off and being dead (64 a). The many sage writers who take up this teaching mollify us by giving it this softer sense: Philosophy is a preparation for the day of death.[57] Thus Socrates is even on his last day preparing for the time of sunset when he must die, and he is comforting the boys who are spending the remaining hours with him in prison through proving by hook or crook that neither he nor they will in fact die—surely a somewhat dissonant way to prepare for death.

But this is in fact all a venerable misapprehension. Socrates does not occupy himself just with "dying off" but with *being dead* (*tethnanai*: perfect tense!)—all his mature life. This day of the hemlock is no more the day of his death than any other. What is this philosopher's daily death? It is just that intense, thoughtful concentration on questions concerning the sources of knowledge, the nature of opposition, the passages of becoming, the stability of beings, the workings of cause, the character of numbers, and above all, the participation of things in forms and of the forms in each other—in sum, the Socratic and Platonic questions. These are the very elements of dialectic that Socrates sets out for his young followers, in the guise appropriate to his last day, as arguments about immortality, and so he keeps the boys suspended between serene absorption and anxious sorrow, between smiles of insight and tears of bereavement.[58] These notoriously unpersuasive arguments for the immortality of the soul are highly effective exercises in dialectic set for the young of that day and of the future.

I am persuaded that Socrates knows himself to be perfectly ignorant of what will happen to him at sundown. He had said as much on the day when he was condemned to death:

> For being dead is one of two things. It is either to be as nothing, so that the dead man has no sensation, none, of anything. Or it turns out to be, as people say, a certain changeover and emigration for the soul from this place hence to another place. . . . But now is the hour for going away, for me to my dying, for you to your living. Which of us goes to the better thing—that is obscure to everyone but the god.[59]

(f) I cannot resist a personal postscript. So much reading about death tends for a time to vacate the mind of all opinions and to misplace all the apprehensions of the soul. Yet eventually one thought does seem to emerge, strong and vivid, from the indifferent welter: *No one*, not anybody, has any knowledge, any knowledge at all about death as a *fait accompli*. There is plenty to be said about the abysmal fear of death and the dismal process of dying, but nothing about the hereafter. So far the skeptics, gentle or harsh, seem to have the edge, except that they appear, at least in their hearts, to push past their own agnosticism to infer from "we know nothing" that "there is nothing to know"—yet one more paralogism. Knowing nothing in respect to death really means being totally ignorant, and it is worth a great deal to allow oneself to be flooded by a feeling for this fact. It means saying "Halt!" to Hamlet at the very beginning of his meditation on dying by his own hand.[60] For the question he poses, "To be or not to be?" assumes more than he can know, that to die is not to be.

That "death is not an event in life" nor "a fact of the world," that we have no experience of it, that it is "something unimaginable, something properly unthinkable," that "what we imagine and think about it are only negations," that it is "The undiscover'd country from whose bourn / No traveller returns"[61]—these are truths one reads over and over, but to read is one thing and to take in another.

For this ignorance is unlike any other, more blunt, more final. Death—our own death—is not a fact of the world, and yet it is some sort of fact—or anti-fact. It is accessible only by negations, and yet it is not reachable by a *via negativa* such as serves theology—for there is a vast difference between our hindered attempts to reach the incomprehensible and this block of sheer unknowing. About the brute unknown we cannot even frame questions, for a question is a desire shaped into an envelope, the outline of the answer wished for. Is it even clear that we *want* to know death?

This we know: *that* we will die. Thinkers concerned with human existence, with being here and now, make much of this stark and unilluminating fact. But in the absence of knowledge about the hereafter, we can have no good judgment whether the consciousness of our finitude should devalue or intensify our lifespan, make of it a negligible interlude or an invaluably small window of opportunity. Moreover,

> death, a necessary end,
> will come when it will come,

and though we know that we will die, most of us, most of the time, do not know when. They say, in a mood of levity, that a hanging wonderfully concentrates the mind. There are indeed searing accounts from life and literature of those select human beings for whom their death has acquired a date certain or who have come within a few tens of heartbeats of being dead. The sudden confrontation of death, which ought, by the gift of Prometheus, just to be a futural possibility, tears the fabric of normalcy as a present certainty:

> But here all final hope, with which it is ten times easier to die, is removed *for certain*; here there is a sentence, and in the very fact that there is certainly no escape from it all the horrible suffering lies, and there is no suffering on earth greater than this.[62]

And, of course, there are those many who are marked by disease for certain death in the foreseeable future, though the exact day is not fixed. Whether their sayings are reflective, considerate, brave or desperate, they are testimony of being in an embarrassed situation, of being forced to face what human beings are not meant to see: their immediate end. They know the solemnity of the event, and they are a little ashamed at how keenly ordinary and banally life-bound their thoughts are.

But why should they be ashamed? If by a miracle they survive, why shouldn't they try to regain ordinariness, just because they have been shaken to the depths? Why shouldn't they struggle back into that forgetfulness of death which its uncertain advent renders feasible; why shouldn't they spin an opaque cocoon of busy life about themselves? The lesson from facing a death that has a date seems to be that our capacity for "being towards death" as an ultimate possibility owes more to the uncertainty of its advent than to the "virility" of our mood.

That is not to say that I should not think on death, perhaps even do as Prospero:

> retire me to my Milan, where
> Every third thought shall be my grave.[63]

For musing *moderately* on one's death is not unreposeful: to see that it is time to acquire less than one gives away, that it is unnecessary to knock together yet another bookcase, that it is permissible now to turn from managing the world to contemplating it. And it is also tonic. There is a Nahuatl poet, Nezahualcoyotl, lord of Texcoco, whose every *second* thought is of death, but of such a sort as to make life more vivid:

> I, Nezahualcoyotl, ask this:
> Is it true one really lives on the earth?
> Not forever on earth,
> only a little while here.
> Though it be jade it falls apart,
> Though it be gold it wears away,
> Though it be quetzal plumage it is torn asunder.
> Not forever on earth,
> only a little while here.

But then he adds to the answer:

> At last my heart knows it:
> I hear a song,
> I contemplate a flower,
> May they never fade![64]

Well, it is one thing to think serenely of one's own death, indefinitely though ever decreasingly far off and to indulge in that not entirely unpleasant prospective nostalgia in which the world seems hauntingly desolate because we ourselves are missing in it. But if our own death is not a real fact of life, it is quite another thing to outlive others. It is most false that we have no experience of others' death and that *their* death is not a fact of *our* life. Stoics, ancient and latter-day, make arguments why another's death should not move us, but they seem to me for the most part more obtuse than sage. To me it seems a matter of making distinctions. A child's death has no consolation to those who loved it, a mature man's or woman's death is a disaster—not only because existence is curtailed for them, but because of all the existence that *we* the living lose and miss out on: all the infinitely enchanting morphology of growth we look forward to in a child, all the expectation of companionship and of practical dependency we repose in an adult.

But who can acutely mourn the death of the very old? Could they themselves? It makes sense that the thought of their own death should be a grief to those who have not lived long enough or well enough. The body, however, has a word to say in this matter. As warm-blooded animals we age; age is what happens to us, insofar as nothing more drastic has happened. The body becomes increasingly vulnerable, the soul less sensitive, and the mind, if no less acute, yet less tensed. *If we are lucky* it all happens in sync, and we die the one true natural death, which is not death at all but evanescence. To rebel against this quietus is the part of the survivor, not the death bound, and what the son in Dylan Thomas's poem demands of his father is that he should feel a survivor's grief:

> Do not go gentle into that good night,
> Old age should burn and rave at close of day;
> Rage, rage against the dying of the light.[65]

Not so, especially since the thought of everlasting life on the hither side of death, of survival *before* death, of the inability to die, is surely the most desolating thought of any: to have no way out, ever.[66]

"My *death*" is thus *not* a fact or an experience of my life, though it *is* a fact for others, as their death is a fact for me. My *dying*, on the other hand, *is* an experience and a fact both for me and for others, though the fact differs as direct and derivative experience, suffering and sympathy, always do differ. But above all, the *expectation* of my death *is* an experience for me. And my point has been that it cannot be an obligation we have to our proper humanity to think strenuous and dominating thoughts about it, to be cowed by calls to authenticity, or to be ashamed of the apparently evasive triviality of our meditations. To me, our somatic duty towards our finitude is summarized in the first of Socrates' last acts.[67] He ends the conversation to go and wash so as "not to give the women the trouble of bathing a corpse"; in other words, he leaves so as to cause the least posthumous trouble. And our psychic duty is to think enough about the possibilities of death, however shapeless, so as not to be utterly stupefied by surprise before any eventuality—even though it is Nothing that may eventuate.

But the proper exercise of this posthumous imagination, a *playful* imagination, depends, it seems to me, on the deep conviction that we know nothing, not whether death is a terminus or a translation, not whether it is a relief from all debts or the final moment of retribution. This bone-deep ignorance is very unlike the understanding of the paralogisms of rational psychology and their calculating readmission of a self-awarded hope. It is instead a more positive freedom: an—occasional—openness to deliverances of faith or intimations of the imagination or surmises of paradise—or at least to the surging sense that we have as humans, the sense of having a being "in excess" of our animated body.[68]

But for the purposes of daily life, I hold with the example of Socrates, with what I think of as his orthogonal mode of living:[69] horizontally forward to the one death that takes us out of time, but also vertically outward to a daily absorption in the timeless aspects of things. Of course, doing likewise—that's yet another matter.

NOTES

1. Donne, 489, from a sermon preached at Spital on April 22, 1622. The quotation above is from Byron, "Don Juan" (1819), VII vi.

"Beingness" barely makes it into the *Oxford English Dictionary,* while "nothingness" is quite copiously represented—mostly because of its derogatory meaning. In Greek, on the other hand, nothingness, worthlessness *(oudenia)* is rare, while beingness *(ousia)* has a large dictionary entry; the reason is the same as for English but in reverse: *ousia* has many cheerful worldly uses, not least of all "real estate."

This is the place to note that the unintending Father of Nonbeing, Parmenides, who seems to have coined its Greek term *to me on,* uses "nothing," *meden,* in one crucial fragment (6, 2). Those interpreters who understand him to mean by Being "reality," the world of things, might refer to this line, for No-*thing* is indeed the opposite of Some-*thing.* I think that in 6, 4 "nothing" *(ouden)* is introduced for the sake of the wordplay. He speaks of the "mortals who know nothing [adjective]"; the ironic alternative reading is "the mortals who know not-being [noun]," i.e., who utter negations.

2. Dickinson 1883, p. 1077, no. 1563. I take Nothing to be a noun because it is capitalized. As a pronoun "nothing" is, of course, the vocable for making light of things ("It's nothing") or for being evasive (the standard answer to the question "What are you doing?" of kids up to no good); "nothing" can also be the silhouette of an unfulfilled expectation ("I looked but saw nothing"). There is a plethora of ways that "nothing" enters lightly into life; there is even competitive nothingness:

A rabbi, entering the synagogue, sees a sunbeam with its dancing motes. He falls to his knees and abases himself before God: "O Lord, I am nothing before you who can make such a dancing ray." In comes the cantor, and he too falls to his knees and joins the rabbi in saying that he is nothing before the Lord. In comes the shammes, the synagogue servant, and he also goes down on his knees and declares that he is nothing before the Lord. So the cantor, pointing his chin at the shammes, says to the rabbi: "Look who thinks he's nothing!"

The fact that "nothing" is both pronoun and noun leads to endless punning. It is already found in Parmenides (note 1); it may be somewhere behind Socrates' protestations that he knows nothing; and it is bound to happen to someone writing on Nothing: "What are you working on these days?" "Nothing." "Well, you needed a vacation." Such wordplay is not mere silliness, since it suggests a great question: Is that pronominal "nothing" which occurs so lightly within our daily speech in fact an intimation of a nominal "Nothing" which stands ominously behind our world (p. 185)?

3. "The Snow Man" is dated 1921. Note that in the last line "nothing" occurs as pronoun and again as noun. "The Course of a Particular" is dated 1950.

Since nominalism is one of the philosophical positions adopted by those for whom disillusionment is a warrant of truth, this might be the moment to insert a note on the relation of nihilim to truth telling. Jaspers 1919, 289, speaking as a psychologist of worldviews, points out that the human will to truthfulness and genuineness may tend toward nihilism: As Nietzsche puts it, the fanatical belief that "everything is false" is an insight "of truthfulness grown to maturity," under the tutelage of that same Christianity it then turns against. Adorno, 379, however, speaks of faith in nothingness as the insipid "palliative of a proud mind content to see through the whole swindle."

Of course, as grace too eagerly strained after closes itself off, so truth too fanatically pursued flees before the purist contrarianism of the fanatically honest—a tribe that takes pride in shivering in the metaphysical cold.

4. Lear's first utterance of the formula is at 1.1.84. At 1.4.123 ff. there is more nothing talk:

> Kent.   This is nothing, Fool.
> Fool.   Then 'tis like the breath of an unfeed lawyer, you gave me nothing
>   for't.—
>   Can you make no use of nothing, nuncle?
> Lear.   Why, no, boy; nothing can be made out of nothing.

The Latin epigram in the text is by Persius, III 83.

5. The description of the void *(inane)* and the atoms comes from Lucretius I 329 ff., II 216 ff. The suggestion that the void is not occupied by bodies but is an opposing principle comes from Bailey's commentary, 2:653. The law of *nihil ex nihilo* is discussed on p. 624 f., where Epicurus' originals, from which Lucretius worked, are cited, chiefly the *Letter to Herodotus*, para. 38. Aristotle cites the principle as common to all the "Physicists" in *Metaphysics* 1062 b; in *Physics* 213 a ff. he gives an extended critique of the void *(kenon)*.

6. See notes 1 and 2 for the double sense of "nothing."

7. *Summa Theologia*, question XLV, first article, 433. In the Jewish tradition Genesis 1:1 is interpreted as Creation from nothing, that is to say, the *tohuwabohu*, the pri-

mal chaos, is the unformed material that God prepared for himself as a first creation. Augustine puts it neatly: This unshaped primal matter was "not entirely nothing" (*Confessions* XII iii). This first stuff, formless and dark, is not at all like Aristotelian material *(hyle),* which is a purely relational, ideal potentiality.

8. 1924, chap. 23.

There are some lines from the poem "1959" by Gregory Corso that reach in a desolately lilting way to the limit of the sense of nothingness-within-life:

> There is no us, there is no world, there is no universe,
> there is no life, no death, no nothing—all is meaningless.

"No nothing" is, of course, a colloquial way of saying "not anything." And yet "no nothing" is here less than nothing, a rejection of the comfort of even this empty category.

In contrast, there is the elevating sense of nothingness felt by Prince Andrey Bolkonsky as he lies wounded and close to death on the battlefield of Austerlitz (*War and Peace* III xix). He says to himself: "There is nothing, nothing certain but the nothingness of all that is comprehensible to us, and the grandeur of something incomprehensible but more important!"

9. To give examples of terms used to circumscribe the "Emptiness" that is to be attained according to certain Buddhist teachings: Universal Reality, Original Nature, Ultimate Essence (Chung-Yuan, 5). Each of these phrases has a highly specifiable and different technical meaning in the West, and all together they make a muddle, not a lucid whole; I leave out of account that each of them, insofar as it has a reference, denotes an entity and not a nothing, void, or emptiness. To be sure, the fullness of emptiness seems to be part of the doctrine, but that plenitude cannot be entity-like.

Although the philosophemes of frisky logicians tend to be more witty than wise, Raymond Smullyan seems to me to have well encapsulated the difference between West and East. In speaking of the class of those propositions that are "equivalent to their own negations," he says, "The Western point of view is that the class of all such propositions is empty. The Eastern point of view is that this class is empty if and only if it isn't" (Barrow, 197). I think he means that self-contradiction yields the blankness of Nonsense for Western logicians, while for Eastern sages it is the way to the plenitude of Nothing.

I ought to say here that I hold contingency, not principle, responsible for the inaccessibility of the great alternative to the tradition native to me. "Had we but world enough and time" we could, I believe, come to inhabit any civilization as near natives. The difficulty lies, I am persuaded, in mere mundanities, such as limitations of clock time and local involvement, not in any major mysteries such as Time and Culture (understood as occult forces).

10. Plato, *Seventh Letter* 341 c ff.

11. Tao-hsiu in Chung-Yuan, 6. The next quotation below in the text is the continuation. Here it plainly appears that the Buddhist Nothing is in no way like Nonbeing, since it is neither subordinate to Being nor derived from it by negation, as Abe points out (142–143).

12. Examples: In antiquity, the Good in Plato's *Republic* is "beyond Being" (509 b); the One is Plotinus' systematic assimilation of the Good in the *Enneads*, and he says of it: Because nothing is in it, therefore all things [proceed] from it" (V 2, 1). In

the late Middle Ages, Nicholas of Cusa says in his dialogue *On the Hidden God* (para. 9–10) that God is described so negatively by the Christian to his heathen interlocutor that the latter is impelled to ask, "Then Nothing is God?" and is told, "He is not the Nothing, since this Nothing has the *name* Nothing" and God is not nameable; yet he is not Something. See also note 21. In modernity, Nothing plays a transcendent role for Heidegger.

13. In a loose sense the word "philosopher," "lover of wisdom," is *commonly* used of a *person* who has wise sagacity; its most distinctive sense, the literal Greek meaning, in which the emphasis is on "lover," on someone who longs for but has *not* attained wisdom, also reaches into modernity. The most technical meaning of the *activity*, on the other hand, that of "first philosophy" or the study of Being, has been transformed but still resonates.

14. This negative dialectic *seems* readily reminiscent of Plato's *Parmenides*, but it is worlds apart in effect. To be sure, Parmenides is *exercising* young Socrates in an apparently self-abrogating dialectic involving the fundamental terms of first philosophy. But the penultimate conclusion, the one that goes with the last hypothesis and comes just before the summary of contradictions apparently established, says: "If the one is not, there is nothing" (166 c). And this seems to me to be the beginning of Socrates' lifelong project: to find oneness and—implicitly—to defeat nothingness.

15. The Indian sage Nagarjuna is assigned a date from A.D. 150–250. He was the founder of a school called "The Middle Path," whose writings, translated from Sanskrit, became part of the Chinese and Tibetan Buddhist tradition and are still studied.

The "Middle Path" *(Madhyamika)* itself refers to the mode of refutation that we might think of as a radical denial of the Law of Contradiction: When one assertion is refuted, its opposite is immediately also refuted, thus blocking both extremes. In his work on the Middle Path Nagarjuna sets out eight negations that simultaneously deny terms that parallel, in part, aspects of the Aristotelian categories of being. They are rendered in translation as generation and destruction, continuation and interruption, unity and plurality, arriving and departing.

There are many terms associated with Nagarjuna's teaching whose meaning is not available to me since they are not amenable to essential definition. However, here are two chief ones: *sunyata*, "void, emptiness, nothing," which also signifies fullness or in Western terms "Absolute Reality," namely insofar as it is *tathata*, unconceptualized suchness or so-ness.

Nirvana, a nearly undeterminable word, which in some contexts means personal annihilation, that is, exit from the cycle of birth and death, is in the school of the Middle Way one of two extremes and therefore part of the lesser worldly truth. See Chan, 352–369; Chung-Yuan, 4–9; Hanh, 105–125; Jaspers 1966, 416–433.

16. The quotations are from the hilarious encyclopedia entry "Nothing," by P. L. Heath 1967, 524–525, pointed out to me by my colleague Carl Page, the only intentionally funny entry I've ever come across—and on a subject that is nothing to laugh about!

17. Kant 1786, B 346–349.

18. 1763, paras. 2–4. Having shown that existence is necessary, Kant concludes that there is a necessary existent, God. The demonstration was meant to replace all other ontological proofs (p. 176).

19. See Kant 1786, B 545.

20. In respect to the subject's own existence, Kant does not differ so very much from Descartes. To be sure, while Descartes finds warrant for his own being in the fact there is thinking and that an "I" controls it, Kant finds assurance of his own existence in the experience of an existing world (Kant 1786, B 274 ff.). What they have in common is the thought that cognitive activity is in fact the warrant of being or existence.

21. It does figure in mystic thought. For example, Eckhart says, "If I say: God is *a Being (ein Sein),* it is not true; he is rather a being-exceeding *(überseiendes)* Being and a being-exceeding Nothingness *(Nichtsein)!*" (Sermon 42, 353). Eckhart was accused in Article 26 of the Bull of Pope John XXII (A.D. 1329, 453) of teaching that "all creatures are pure Nothing; I do not say that they are something inferior or anything at all, but that they are a pure Nothing."

A medieval predecessor is the Christian Neoplatonist Erigena, who says in *On the Division of Nature* III 5 (A.D. 862) that God is Nothing, where "Nothing" signifies the negation and absence of all being and substance that is created and "the excellence of divine superessentiality."

22. Bergson, chap. 4, pp. 296–324. Bergson actually undertakes his inquiry about the way Nothing comes to be prior to Being for us in order to show that a metaphysics which reaches Being only by passing through Nothing will tend to endow Being with logical rather than psychological or physical existence. The reason is that only logical principles (of which identity is an example) will seem self-sufficient enough to conquer Nonexistence. But such logically obtained existence seems to him undesirable, particularly in respect to free will. Consequently he aims to show that the idea of Nothing is a pseudo-idea to begin with.

23. Turgenev, chaps. 5, 10, 21. The character of Bazarov is analyzed by Gillespie, 145–156. He shows that Bazarov, who proclaims himself an anti-Romantic and sneers at the ordinary motions of the human soul as romantic, is himself a Romantic. He is a "Romantic of Realism," in Turgenev's own phrase, compounded of Hamlet, Faust, and Byron's Manfred (as pridefully devilish a miscreant as is to be found in Romantic literature). What relates the nihilists to the Romantics is the self-apotheosis of the elect and the attraction to a demonic negativity—in sum, their will to limitlessness. Stavrogin, the Christ-Devil of Dostoyevsky's *Demons* (1872), is the most complex of these excruciated souls.

Shattuck 1996, 232 ff., details the reasons why Sade belongs to this tribe and is by some recent authors understood—and admired!—as the most audacious and original of nihilists: the most radical perverter of nature and the ultimate transgressor of norms. But, he points out, this Sadistic nihilism is parasitic. It depends on positive virtue to make its excesses properly "naughty" (281).

24. Gillespie 1995, i–xxiv. In the introduction to *Nihilism before Nietzsche*, he gives the outline of his argument, which my exposition largely follows. These points are then fleshed out chapter by chapter, and they constitute a definitively stated theory of one aspect of modernity. The liberal antithesis and answer is scattered through the text. The outcome of Gillespie's understanding is that at the end of modernity we find ourselves, once its hidden foundation in the deification of human will has been exposed, again face to face with the "dark God," the unaccountable Ockhamite god, "that modernity was constructed to restrain." It is obvious to me that this confrontation has

everything to do with the question: "How should I live?" and that such analyses of modernity are by no means academic exercises.

25. Hegel 1812a, bk. 2, sec. 1, chap. 1 c: "Reflection." In Hegel 1830b, 112, the parallel phrase "negation of the negative" has been substituted. See note 22 in chapter 5 for an exposition.

26. The quotation is from Hegel 1803, 432–433. It comes from a section entitled *Fichtesche Philosophie*. Note the dictum "God is dead," usually ascribed to Nietzsche, but clearly anticipated by Hegel. For the long theological tradition of the death of God, see Balthasar, 49 ff. The last quotation is from Gillespie, 117.

27. The relation of Fichte's philosophy to the Doctrine of Essence in the Hegelian logic is signaled by the term cited above, "reflection-philosophy"; Essence is characterized by the reflection of each pair of essential concepts into each other. Moreover, the doctrine takes up the same laws of thought with which Fichte begins (p. 40).

28. This is Gillespie's judgment as well, 120.

29. Rosen 1969. The quotations are from the preface to *Nihilism* and 17. The arguments for Wittgenstein's nihilism, which are, of course, meant as a critique, are much more detailed than is my capsule version.

30. Vattimo, 118 ff., considers whether, against the letter of Heidegger's text, he might be called a nihilist. He shows that if nihilism is understood in Heidegger's own terms as that process by which in the end "there is nothing left of Being" as such (Heidegger 1961, vol. 2, "The Eternal Return of the Same"), Heidegger is indeed himself a nihilist.

Sheehan 1999 treats of this question as it is answered in Heidegger's letter to Ernst Jünger published in 1955 as "The Question of Being." Since I am leaving the later writings out of account in the text of this chapter, I will summarize briefly Sheehan's very clear account. The danger of nihilism issues from this: "Insofar as the essence of entities entails their presence to human cognition and will, it also entails that they are disposed to be picked up and used" (296), to be reshaped "technically" as artifacts. There is no way around this human relation to things. It shows itself historically in modern nihilism, but this nihilism is made possible by the inescapable and essential *nihil* (312). This *nihil* is that enabling power which makes entities accessible to us as intelligible or as usable. It is a "nothing" because it hides itself; from our perspective it is not an entity or the beingness of entities: it is an *Ereignis*, an eventuating appropriation (the German word commonly means "event." Sheehan translates "appropriation," in Heidegger's spirit, but etymologically the *eig* part has to do with "eye," i.e., what comes to sight, not with "making one's own"). This nihilism is not to be overcome, and, when its essence is entered into, even "the desire to overcome nihilism becomes null and void" (*Letter to Jünger* in Sheehan, 284). There is then no hope for the overcoming (*Überwindung*) of the *nihil*; instead there must be acceptance (*Verwindung*, 281).

It bears noting that Heidegger became a Nazi functionary because he thought that National Socialism was an antidote to the burgeoning *historical* nihilisms of the times. When this proved to be something of a mistake, he adopted the view of acceptance. I am all for learning from experience, but there appears to me to be intellectual improbity in *this* shift. *Metaphysical* nihilism, on the other hand, does seem to be, as the discussion in the text below shows, an insuperable aspect of human existence, though even then acceptance is not the only available position. Philipse, in the section "Deciphering Deep History" (272–276), does a delicate job of matching motives and metaphysics in Heidegger's views of nihilism.

In view of Gillespie's analysis of nihilism as a hypertrophy of the will, it is interesting that Löwith, in his account of the fascination Heidegger exercised on his students (of whom he himself had been one) ends with the words that Heidegger "far exceeded all other university professors in the intensity of philosophical willing" (225).

Löwith supplies a history of literary and philosophical nihilism after Nietzsche; see especially 192–208.

31. Kierkegaard anticipates Heidegger in *The Concept of Dread*, for example: "Nothing! But what effect has—nothing? It evokes dread." But this relation of Nothing to dread is not thematic for him.

32. Bollnow 1941, 24–29, recognizes this problem but elevates its terms. Instead of mere psychology he speaks of "philosophical anthropology" (the interpretation of the observed variety of human feelings and actions regarded as expressing a unitary humanity) and he shows that Heidegger's ontological answer to such a semi-empirical anthropology, the "analysis of (human) existence," is not so easily distinguished from the approach it is meant to deepen.

33. I have made use of the translation by Hull and Crick with Broch's lucid "Account" (Heidegger 1929c) and of an unpublished translation with copious and thoughtful notes by Miles Groth (1995). The essay "What Is Metaphysics?" (1929) went through five editions. It is surrounded by a postscript (1943; revised in 1949) and an introduction (1949), neither of which make Nothing their theme. Both are printed in Heidegger 1929c.

34. "Joy" is derogated in its very definition, as occurring in the present presence of a loved person. Recall that the present is the most inauthentic of times, and presence the most concealing of conditions for Heidegger. So he drops this rare reference to a positive mood immediately. On the other hand, in *The Fundamental Concepts of Metaphysics* (1929b) he devotes roughly a hundred pages (para. 18–41) to an analysis of "profound," that is, existentially significant, boredom; such "*Boredom springs from the temporality of Dasein.*" It comes about when we live wholly in the present and bring time to a stand; this standing now "forms an emptiness that irrupts against the background of everything that is happening." It binds us to itself and "holds us in limbo" (para. 26, 127). In "What Is Metaphysics?" however, boredom is not analyzed temporally; instead it is said to "reveal being as a whole."

How are these two analyses connected? In *Being and Time* (para. 69), it is primordial time, temporality, that is the condition for the possibility of the world, of that Nothing which is the ground of all somethings. Thus the world is the *nihil originarium*, the originary Nothing (Heidegger 1928, para. 12, 210). But the same might in fact be said of primordial time itself (Motzkin, 111–112). *This* is the bridge between *Being and Time* and "What Is Metaphysics?"

35. At the end of the introduction of 1949 to "What Is Metaphysics?" Heidegger makes good an omission by crediting Leibniz with the formulation of the question, which is to be found in his *Principles of Nature and Grace Based on Reason* (1714). Heidegger's point is, however, that he himself has given the question a wholly different sense, for it is no longer directed, as it was for Leibniz, to a causative God. What is more, he has in fact intimated a new answer, as is shown above.

The question thus appears at the end of the introduction and also at the end of the essay itself. And as it ends "What Is Metaphysics?" so it heads the *Introduction to Metaphysics* (1935). It occurs, furthermore, in the essay "Of the Essence of the Ground" (1929a, 115) and in *Nietzsche* (1961, 2:246 ff.). This last reference is again a Heideggerian interpretation of Leibniz's answer to his own question: Since the question implies that Nothing is simpler and easier than Something, there must be a "principle of sufficient reason" that names the incipient essence of that which somehow makes an "uprising" *(Aufstand)* against Nothing. Thus every being is a groundingly founding ground *(gründiger Grund)*. It must have the character of *wanting* itself *(mögen)* and *being able* to be itself *(vermögen)*.

The question is treated at greatest length in the *Introduction to Metaphysics*, where Heidegger says that it is the widest, deepest, and most original of all questions and that its asking is itself an event (lecture 1). For, he says at the end of his course: "To go expressly to the boundary of Nothing in the *question* concerning Being, and to include this Nothing in the question about Being is . . . the first and only fruitful step toward a genuine overcoming of nihilism" (lecture 4, 4; see note 30). For Kant's answer, which is ontological but not theological, see p. 175.

36. Thus Sartre, in *Being and Nothing* (pt. 1, chap. 1: "The Problem of Nothingness") continues the inquiry into Nothing. His terms are Heideggerian, but his understanding is not. He asks three questions that Heidegger has left unanswered: How exactly is human existence constituted so as to have in itself the ability to transcend into Nothing? And reciprocally, how is Nothing constituted so as to descend into the world? And more fundamentally: How can this genuine Nothingness have the power to do anything, to "nihilate" (the English for the French for the German *nichten*, "to naught"), unless it is a kind of being? For he agrees with Heidegger that negation in the world "derives its foundation from Nothingness."

He concludes that "the *Being by which Nothingness comes to the world must be its own Nothingness*," and he asks "in what delicate, exquisite region of Being" we shall encounter it. This Being is Man. For a human being as questioner detaches himself in a double movement from the thing questioned. He nihilates *it* in the sense of making it a neutral thing, a thing possibly to be denied, and he nihilates *himself* in wrenching himself from the positive order of things so as to bring out of himself a possible negation: Nothingness so introduced "makes the world iridescent" and disengages the questioner from Being. All sorts of "negateds" *(négatités)* arise this way. One, in the world of objects, is the image, which posits its object as absent or not existing (see Brann 1991, 131–138). Another is time, which is the subjective condition of every negation; the human being carries Nothingness in itself "as the *nothing* which separates its present from its past." The human being is separated from its past by nothingness precisely because (1) there is *no* obstacle, *nothing* to be overcome, since the present flows continuously into the past and the past is always there, and yet, (2) it has *nihilated* its past, since it is no longer what it was. Hence the human being can issue denials to the world because it carries nothingness within itself, as a structure of consciousness. Thus Sartre recalls Nothing back *into* Being, albeit human Being.

Mainly under the influence of deconstruction and other postmodernisms, Nothing, nothingness, and negativity are currently running riot in theology, literary theory and criticism as well as the arts: See, for example, *Negation and Theology* (Scharlemann, ed.) and *Languages of the Unsayable* (Budick and Iser, eds.)

37. Valéry, "Ébauche d'un serpent."

38. The quotation is from the Office of the Dead: "*Peccantem me quotidie et non poenitentem timor mortis conturbat me. Quia in inferno nulla est redemptio.*" Thomas Aquinas, as always clear and definitive, shows how paradise is the abode of the corporeal human being (*Summa Theologica*, question 102, vol. I, 944 ff.).

39. John Donne, Holy Sonnets, no. 10: "Death Be Not Proud." See Jüngel 1990 for Christ's death as *mors mortis: per mortem suam mortem momordit*, "by his death he devoured death itself."

40. Bach, *Cantata No. 4* (1708, 52). Below I will consider rational argumentation concerning the survival of the soul, but this is the place to mention an argument against eternal life by Bernard Williams: that it would get boring (in Feldman, 821). This argument leaves out of account that tedium and tiredness afflict the mortal body, but that timeless dwelling before God, were it possible, could not conceivably be boring; even in *this* life one gets bored mostly either by a defect in one's attention or in the thing attended to. Moreover, for a foretaste of the exhilarating festivities of Heaven, listen to the triumphal march-by of the heavenly forces after the defeat of Lucifer the Reviler as depicted in Bach's *Cantata* Fragment, no. 50, "Now is the Salvation and the Strength and the Realm and the Might" (Revelation 12:10). No, if there *is* eternal life, it isn't boring.

There is also a non-Christian, Hegelian understanding of death as a double negation, that set out by Feuerbach in his spirited *Thoughts on Death and Immortality*, 165: "Death is no positive negation, but a negation that negates itself, a negation that is itself empty and nothing. Death is itself the death of death. As it ends life, it ends itself; it dies because of its own worthlessness and meaninglessness."

Feuerbach contrasts the double negation of death with a real or actual negation "that robs reality only from a determinate reality and not from reality itself," that allows reality to continue because it cancels certain properties without canceling the sphere of the real altogether: "A negation that takes everything is itself nothing."

41. Herodotus *The Persian Wars* I 32, 86; Sophocles *Oedipus at Colonus* 1649; Aristotle *Nichomachean Ethics* 1100 a 10. The quotation is from Shakespeare, *King Lear* 5.3.308 (on the assumption that it is his daughter and not the Fool he is mourning, *Variorum*, 345).

42. Lucretius III 830: *nil igitur mors est ad nos*; translated directly from Epicurus' *Principal Doctrines* (ii): *ho thanatos ouden pros hemas*. The theme is often repeated by Lucretius and had become a commonplace (see Lucretius, vol. II, 1135).

Levinas, 41, criticizes the truism because it ignores the paradox of death, which is its futurality for us—that it is *never* now but *always* in the future and so ungraspable.

43. Genesis 5:23–24; see Cassuto, 285, for the recurrent locution.

44. Robert Frost, "Directive," 216. The effect of no-longer-there is, of course, particularly strong when the living entity was one fixed in place. On the St. John's College campus there stood, until October 1999, a tulip poplar known as the city's Liberty Tree because the Sons of Liberty of Annapolis held their revolutionary meetings under it in the 1770s. It fell victim to Hurricane Floyd. Tree experts said that it might be as much as a hundred years older than Columbus's arrival in America in 1492. The subsequent nonexistence of this largest and longest-lived being on campus was near visible.

45. Prescott 1847, bk. III, chap. IX. Manco, invested in 1534, was Pizarro's crea-

ture. The American historian Prescott, incomparable for the beauty of his style and the width of his sympathy—only compare the respectfully serious treatment he accords the repellently alien Mexican and Peruvian religious practices to Gibbon's smooth superciliousness toward the Christianity of his own tradition—draws a vivid picture of this miserable epilogue to the Inca empire. The posthumous somatic existence of the ancestors (as well as other aspects of both Inca and Aztec religion) kept reminding the Christian conquerors of the Christian belief in the resurrection of the body; the first generation of Conquistador priests evolved a theory of Inca practices as a demonic aping of true religion (MacCormick, 91 and passim) that took the indigenous religion with fatal seriousness.

The invaders burned what mummies they found. But, one may speculate, the terrestrial existence of the dead with all the attendance they require is in any case an insupportable burden once a population becomes impoverished or, on the contrary, begins to increase.

The Inca practice is often compared to the Egyptian mummification of the pharaohs; in my context the great difference is that these were entombed in pyramids or hills out of sight, while the honored Inca dead belonged among the living. Scheler, 14, describes (I cannot judge how accurately) the nonsomatic existence of the dead among the Japanese of older generations—their real existence, felt and experienced, though not of the body.

46. Odysseus's "descent" to Hades comes in book XI of the *Odyssey*; Achilles speaks the lines at 488–491.

The poem by Humbert Wolfe (1885–1940) is entitled "The Soldier." Its last stanza is:

> Down some cold field in a world uncharted
> the young seek each other with questioning eyes.
> They question each other, the young, the golden-hearted,
> of the world that they were robbed of in their quiet paradise.

I found it quoted in Bernières, front. The observation about Tiresias occurs in Browne, "Hydrotaphia," 145.

47. The lines are from Harold Monro's "Living," 513. Jonas, 88 ff., speaks of "the ever-present *potential* for death of everything alive, concurrent with the life process itself" and specifies how this potential is progressively realized. Scheler, 24–25, speaks of dying as an act of living. There are many such observations, some related to the "stages of man," which include a final decline into death, others to the continual replacement of the body that is implied in metabolism.

48. Freud in Fingarette, 149, 151, from "Thoughts for the Times on War and Death." Mihm gives a bibliography of recent monographs on the treatment of physical death in America, a rollickingly macabre subject. For a review of various continental attitudes to death, see Binswanger, "Liebe und Tod," 167 ff.

Here is testimony to the gulf between death as an external phenomenon and as one's own experience: In the *Macmillan Encyclopedia of Philosophy* (1967) "Death" and "My Death" are separate entries. In the latter the utter difference between knowing about death and knowing death is emphasized (Edwards, 416 ff.).

49. The analysis of death here briefly sketched comes from *Being and Time*, para. 46–53, pp. 235–267. (The references in the text are to the German pagination, which

is standard.) Later Heidegger changed his perspective on death, but his mode then was no longer analytic; see Arendt, *Willing,* 192 f.

It is beyond this book to enter into the question whether Heidegger's view of death is a novel sort of Romanticism. In any case, the Continental-Romantic love affair with death is passed over here as having more to do with *Lust* (in the German sense of "longing") than with death.

50. Heidegger regularly employs a mode—it would seem devious in ordinary circumstances—in which derogatory words are used on the level of primordial or "ontological" analysis but their denigrating meaning is denied on the common or "ontic" level (e.g., fallenness and inauthenticity). Indeed, Heidegger himself seems to require that an ontic apprehension of his ontological analysis be possible; see note 51.

51. Levinas, 40. Heidegger, 266; he goes on to say that to make this imposition meaningful it is necessary to show that ordinary existence has a corresponding potentiality for being (also 166).

Since there is no requirement of virility on me, I may confess that Heidegger's analysis of death does not speak to me, except to acquaint me with the mystifying fact that depth and verity may be totally divergent. Nor does this way of being seem lucid to me; on the contrary, it leaves one of the more urgent questions of life—What should I *now* do?—doubly opaque: once because Heidegger lets the answer remain perfectly indeterminate and again because it is unclear whether a person in that authentic frame of mind could act at all. In other words, it remains an unanswered question whether we *can* confront Nothing as a prelude to action.

52. William Wordsworth, "Ode: Intimations of Immortality," lines 165–169.

53. Marcus Aurelius, *Meditations,* in Fingarette, 160. A contemporary argument in the Stoic vein tries to show by close conceptual analysis that death is no evil for the dyee: Seddon, 145–159. It is admitted that it *is* an evil for the survivors. Beginning with Wittgenstein's saying that "Death is not an event of life. One does not live to experience death" (*Tractatus* 6.4311), Seddon argues, in sum, that "being an evil," the value judgment that something is unpleasant, must be made by the person whose death is at issue. But he is the very one who can have no (unpleasant) experience of it. Thus the fear of death is irrational (152). The logic here is quite irrefutable and the conclusion is perfectly impotent. It is true that only the dead are experienced judges of death, but why should inexperience keep us from dark conjectures?

54. The Paralogisms of the Transcendental Dialectic run from B 399–432 (1786) in the second edition, in which Kant had tightened up the argument by removing A 348–405 (1781), the very pages containing the detailed discussion of the four topics of rational psychology that I have referred to in the text.

55. An extended and acute critique of the concept "survival after death" is to be found in Rosenberg, 30 ff. *Thinking Clearly about Death* is presented as a case study in analytic philosophy, an "exercise in logic and lexicography" (3, 91). It is heavily methodological, working particularly the analytic thesis that ordinary language is logically illusionistic. Several of the arguments thus exploded are versions of those put forward in the *Phaedo* (93 ff.) and are also shown up in the *Critique.*

56. For example, Hartle says that Socrates' demonstrations are not very good (20) and that "Socrates is carefully and deliberately, although secretly, unweaving the arguments for immortality" (57). The quotation is from Hume 1758, sec. XII, pt. I, n. 1.

57. Among them Cicero, and Montaigne quoting him at the head of his essay "To Philosophize Is to Learn to Die."

58. When I was translating the *Phaedo* with my two colleagues, we became more and more aware (1) how well Plato's style conveys the oscillating mood of the dialogue (there are, after all, people not so silently weeping in the background as the interlocutors in the foreground are distracted from their sorrow by Socrates' playfulness), and (2) how compendious an introduction to Platonic dialectic the arguments are, quite apart from their pretended purpose (see *Plato's Phaedo*, trans. Brann, Kalkavage, Salem, 1 ff.).

Desmond, 36, has coined an apt phrase for this living philosophic absorption in Being; he calls it the "*posthumous mind.*" Wittgenstein says something that on the face of it *appears* to jibe with Socrates' meaning: "If by eternity is understood not infinite temporal duration but non-temporality, then he lives eternally who lives in the present" (*Tractatus* 6.4311). If one lives collectedly, unscattered through time, one goes out of time. But to become Socratic, Wittgenstein's saying would need an addition: "if one lives collectedly and *contemplatively.*"

59. *Apology* 29 a. The quotation is from 40 c and 42.

60. I cannot believe Dr. Johnson's reading of this line, which has Hamlet pondering the possibility of losing his life if he resists the King (*Variorum Edition*, 205, on III i 56). Of course Hamlet soon amends his assumption that to die is no longer to be—the sleep of death may after all be a nightmare. Prospero throws doubt even on Hamlet's "To be," for life itself may not have the solidity of full being:

> . . . We are such stuff
> As dreams are made on, and our little life
> Is rounded with a sleep. Sir, I am vexed. (*Tempest* 4.1.156–158)

61. Quotations in order: Wittgenstein, *Tractatus* 6.4311; Jaspers 1919, 261; *Hamlet* 3.1.79. The quotation several paragraphs below is from Caesar's speech in *Julius Caesar* 2.2.36.

62. See Aeschylus, *Prometheus Bound* l.250: "I stopped mortals from knowing their death-date *(moron).*"

Fyodor Dostoyevsky, *The Idiot*, pt. I, chap. 2, and again in chap. 5. Prince Myshkin, who is the speaker in both episodes, is reporting the author's own experience as a political prisoner condemned to death but reprieved at the last moment. Prince Pierre Bezuhov also has such an experience in Tolstoy's *War and Peace* (pt. 12, chap. 11). There is a whole literature of prison letters of men condemned to execution by the Nazis (e.g., those written to his wife by Helmuth von Moltke in 1945 and a book to which Thomas Mann wrote the introduction [1954], *Farewell Letters of European Fighters of the Resistance*; they were all very young).

63. Shakespeare, *The Tempest* 5.1.310–311.

64. Léon-Portilla, 241, 243. In the *Conquest of Mexico* (I, vi), Prescott paints an unforgettable picture of this remarkable poet–prince who lived before the ascendancy of Aztec Mexico; he died in 1472.

65. Dylan Thomas, "Do Not Go Gentle into That Good Night," 1952.

66. It is usual to cite Swift's "Immortals," the *struldbruggs* of *Gulliver's Travels* (III), who live on and on with all "the infirmities of old men," and with "the dreadful prospect of never dying." They were not only opinionative, peevish, covetous, morose,

vain, talkative, but uncapable of friendship, and dead to all natural affection." I can't imagine how it would be much different if they were arrested in midlife. There is a children's story by Natalie Babbitt, *Tuck Everlasting* (1975), which conveys subtly the infinite melancholy of terrestrial immortality.

67. *Phaedo* 115 a. His very last act is to compose his features as a somatic proof to his friends of his serenity in the face of death; see *Plato's Phaedo*, 23, note.

68. Scheler, 47. Scheler's essay on death and afterlife is a keen and unprejudiced analysis of death in modern life, together with Améry's book on suicide the most illuminating reading on mortality, apart from the *Phaedo,* that I have come across.

Améry has, so to speak, the most lively apprehension of death as Nothing, since he had attempted to take his life before the writing of *On Suicide* and succeeded soon thereafter. In particular, he understands the difference between death as Nothing and as Nonbeing (12): "'Death is nothing, a nothing, a negativity,' as I have written elsewhere (*On Aging*). Still, whether to 'flee' into a region that does not exist or to seize upon something that has no being and therefore is not the 'nothing' . . . but simply 'not,' are two different kinds of things."

Améry distinguishes between the metaphorical twilight that characterizes the passive answering of death's call, be it fearful or brave, from the anticipatory "first word" spoken by suicides or potential suicides. This word is against the logic of life that balances every something only with something other—Being with Nonbeing, in the terms of this book. The antireason of suicides instead puts the Nothing of life in an equation with the Nothing of death. The Nothing of his life comes home to a human being in an *échec* (41, 81), the experience of defeat, of the ruin of his life. Voluntary death, the *"privilege of the human"* (43), is the answer: The decision once made, time is compressed; it ticks, and ticks on two levels, the ever denser nucleus of past times remembered and the ever diminishing moments before time turns into nontime (85 ff.; cf. Brann 1999, 206). Voluntary death frees its perpetrator *from* the *échecs*, the nothingnesses of life, not to go somewhere else but for the ultimate freedom of coming *to* nothing (128).

69. This "orthogonal" view of human time, in which a forward flux becomes a sort of baseline for the moments of escape from time—Wittgenstein says that "for life in the present there is no death" (*Notebooks* 6/7/16)—is set out in Brann, *What, Then, Is Time?* 122 ff. (Augustine), 134 ff. (Husserl).

Conclusion

What, Then, Is Naysaying?

The question that underlies this book—Is there something that all sorts of nay-saying have in common?—seems to me to fall apart into three sections:

1. What is the best way to speak of the naysaying that *we* do? We say *no* and *not*, rejecting by a gesture of recoil or repulsion what advances upon us and rebuffing by a judgment of denial or negation what is proposed to us. How are these negating actions and words most tellingly described? Is nay-doing and nay-saying in principle reactive, posterior to a positive proposal or proposition? Is negation inherently responsive?

2. Is *no, not, non-* only an activity of thought, found exclusively in the thinking and speaking of a rational soul? Or is there, besides the nay-saying of persons, a non-being of things, be they objects of thought or of nature? Is there Nonbeing or Nonexistence or even Nothing?

3. If there are nonbeings and nothings, by what powers of the soul do we get hold of them? Is it the negating capacity of thinking, its active negativity alone, that manages to grasp negative being, or are there also internal capacities for experiencing nonexistence? It has been the driving surmise of this last book in the trilogy on imagination, time, and naysaying, that the images of our imagination and the phases of internal time are indeed inner experiences of *not* and *non-*. How does that actually work out?

1. THE POSITION OF NAYSAYING

It is as plain as seeing can make it that the gesture *No!* is made from a defensive position, from behind the bulwarks guarding the center of a world—my own. It seems to me that the naysaying of speech, the negative judgment, the uttered *not* that refuses presumptions or forfends falsehood, is similarly issued from a personal position to an outside approach.

Most people think, going reasonably by first impressions, that the positive is the original position and the negative is a response. Position and opposition are not rooted in the same realm. The positive position is situated in the world of nature and fact; it expresses the way things are and rides on what goes without saying. The positive is the place we occupy to begin with; it is what a positive proposition expresses quite naturally. The negative is opposite; it is a reaction of thought uttered in words.

But on a first reflection it may appear that propositional naysaying is as much an entrenchment and as independent a position as affirmation. The most forceful *not*, the *not* of the contradictory judgment, is not always a responsive refusal of a proposal from another thinking being. Very often—who knows what the proportions are?—it occurs in an initial discrimination, in rational acts of distinguishing and dividing. To think is often initially to discern the fissures in the field to which we apply our attention and to pry them apart: "this and not this." Yet even when naysaying is not willful self-assertion or refusal of falsity, it is powerfully perspectival. It affirms what is positioned close to me as a center of care and a focus of attention, and it consigns all the rest to infinite reaches of undifferentiated negation, the *not* of negating judgments and the *non-* of negated things. Ordinary and not particularly self-conscious distinction-making thus appears self-centered and perspectival from its beginning, as positive as assertion.

An old way to express this aspect of naysaying is to call that which it names *not-being,* and by a more descriptive name, *otherness.* Not-being is named in merely mute opposition to being, otherness has a certain independent pathos; it expresses the alien place assigned to the negative: not here, not now, not this. All the activities of determining, defining, delineating seem to circle the wagons about a preferred positive place and repel the negative to the edge or margins, though they depend on negation.

Yet a second reflection may, however, place us after all in the opposite camp. We *can* shift our point of view to the territory of the Other and see ourselves as the other's other in human affairs, though it requires of us a passionate revision of our human nature. For ordinarily negation trails the scent of denigration.

Even to cast loose from perspectival naysaying in the realm of reason requires a passionately dispassionate self-levitation. It is accomplished most remarkably in symbolic logic, where the first element, the proposition symbolized as p, is completely opaque with respect to internal logical quality, and the negative operator is really only a quality flipper: apply it twice and the proposition with a negative prefix will have the same truth value as had plain p. In my terms, logic is positionally neutral—not from empathy but from abstraction for the love of lucidity.

But allowing for these and similar arduous exceptions, affirming thought and positive proposition do seem to issue from the place where we just happen to find ourselves, while negation marks a place as consciously maintained. Naysaying can be described as distinction making with perspective. The positive might be our natural position, but with the negative we *assert* the priority and preeminence of our own place.

This discerning, distinguishing, dividing that we do so effortlessly in daily life and more laboriously in searching thought is an activity of cutting, of cutting in two—dicho-tomy. Almost all the originating activities of negating thought are describable in terms that have the prefix *di-, dis-, dia- dy-*. They mean "asunder," "apart," "through," but the root sense is "two." And it does seem to be true that a good many of the motions of the mind can be described in dyadic terms: the dialectic that moves back and forth through the polar distance of logical opposition, the differentiation that specifies the hither from the other class, the dissent of temperamental contradiction. Collections and overviews and direct insights are of course also modes of thinking, but the discerning of divisions prepares most thoughtful conclusions.

From the very beginning of the search into the nature of things in the West, Tables of Opposites were devised to show how the world is organized so as to be amenable to the distinguishing functions of thinking. Does the study of naysaying yield evidence that it is not only rational speech which is dyadic? Besides Naysaying *is* there Nonbeing?

2. THE NEGATION OF BEING

Are there negative objects, not just as targets of discerning and denigrating judgments, but objects in themselves and inherently negative or affected with nullity? And if there are inherently negative things do they belong to the intellectual or the natural world or both? Are the old Tables of Opposites a guide in listing not merely contraries but contraries opposed as positive and negative, meant in the moral sense: right:left (sinister); straight:crooked; light:dark; square:oblong; and quite outright, good:bad?

It might be best to begin with the most extreme opposite to the positive Something: Nothing. Besides the casual positivity of life, the formal indifference of logic and the negativity of distinction-making, is there a position of thought right within the negative, an aboriginal naysaying, speaking from the absolute Nothing itself? When I ask, Is there such naysaying? I merely mean, It is comprehensible?—for it is certainly an existent human phenomenon. Nihilists do mean to speak not from the territory of the Other, that is, from Nonbeing, but from the Nothing beyond all Being and Existence.

The positive worm in the negative apple of nihilism is the nihilist. The purity of blank nothingness is always tainted by the dogged consciousness of the thinker. At least this is so in the philosophical West, where the tradition of thinking is indefeasibly assertive; in the sage East, where thinking is ascetic, the feat of self-removal, of the thinker's transit into Nothing by ceasing to make distinctions altogether is thought to be attainable.

For us the way to Nothing, that is the way to deciding whether there is Nothing, seems to be twofold. One is through the sense of nothingness that negates existence itself, a mood ranging from crude disaffection to subtle anxiety, in which "Naught" has invaded existence and manifested itself as its core. The other is the way of negation in thought, a radical *via negativa* that disqualifies all Being to achieve some sort of representation of a Nothing beyond Being. Depending on the spirit of this subtractive thinking, whether it is analogical or literal, the end thought will be God or Nothing or both in one. So I think we must say that Nothing is somehow thinkable because—and I know no other way to put it—thinking has not only its proper objects, the positive and its related negative, but also improper objects, which can be entertained for something of the same reason that we can reflect on thinking itself: If thinking can turn on itself it can also outstrip itself. We can, I think, think the thought: There might be Nothing—"might be" in the sense of "could have been" *and* in the sense of "may now be beyond our apprehensible world."

In the baldest and most extreme opposition to the Nothing beyond is Existence here and now before me. In this realm the question concerning negative being is: Are there nonexistences? I think this great problem of logicians and preoccupation of poets arises because of the way existence comes to us, namely through our senses. To think Nothing is not not to think, but to sense nothing is indeed not to sense, for the unstimulated sense organ is inactive. Nonexistence is by its very meaning incapable of activating the senses, and cannot appear to us. So how do we come to conceive of it, to conceive of an existent, a particular object of the senses, which is *not*? I think we cannot help making a problem of nonexistence because we do somehow experience it.

A fairly impersonal experience is that of Void. The spatial void is, to be sure, a piece of conceptual confusion and physical impossibility. It is a confused notion because it is impossible to specify how a total spatial void differs from a mere intellectual void, that is, from Absolute Nothing. It is a physical impossibility because its being physical implies that there are bodies in motion within it, and that means that it is configured through and through by fields of force. Yet we can experience diminishing degrees of every quality attached to existence and get from this diminution a strong sense of the ultimate dequalification and voiding of all existence—an imaginable if not a thinkable condition. But this would be the negation of existence altogether; there are also individual negative existents to be considered.

I discern three kinds of nonexistents: what is distant from us, out of sight though present somewhere in the world—absence; what once was before us but is now gone from the world—past; what never was or perhaps could never be but has assumed a habitation and a name—fiction. These are not improperly called *nonexistents*, because they are somehow visible and somehow audible and even somehow tangible—even fragrant or odorous. It is not non-sense to say that they have every aspect of existents except existence, which is why they are *non*-existent.

It is also the reason why they can occur among existent things. While they belong to the same family of things that appear as do existent things, they are not subject to the law that prohibits two bodies from being in the same place. They take their place in the world without displacing its original inhabitants. What I am describing is that translucently black silhouette that appears within the external world after absence, death, destruction have removed a local part of it. I shall try to say how these experiences come about below.

Besides the nonexistents that respond to our sense of what is missing, of seeking without finding, wanting without getting, there are also declines and falls from existence, right in the world around us, that we experience as a sort of nonexistence. Take, for example, the reflection of a willow tree that appears in a pond. Take the numerous things and people in the world without that are not what they appear to be. All these are on occasion experienced as negations of existence, right in among existents.

This last group, fallen existences, particularly raises the question whether it is our way of experience or the nature of things that provides the *not* or *non*-here. One might ask oneself whether the willow has cause to decry its reflection as having a lesser or negated existence, and this would not be a totally extravagant cogitation if the point was to figure for ourselves a world in which there were inherently privative existences. A reflection need not be less sharp or less brilliant than its original or appear as any sort of lapse in the sensory continuum; could the continuum of existents on the other hand manifest gradations that the layman's senses can interpret and polarities that the physicist's imagination can model? Could whatever it is that has made nature amenable to human discernment have implanted some sort of naysaying into nature itself? Without venturing even a guess about the how, it seems to me at least thinkable that there is inherent nonexistence in nature to which natural images and other, more arcane natural oppositions bear witness.

Nothing and nonexistence are negations along the same spectrum, the spectrum of reality. For Nothing is the negation of any thing whatsoever, and non-existence is the negation of some particular thing that might be real in the sense of being here and now. Is there also Nonbeing, an object of thought in the realm of intelligible beings?

Consider falsity, falsehood and fiction, the intentional or unintentional saying of "the thing which is not." Is that kind of masked naysaying about what is inherently false, inherently not what it pretends to be? Could it be that to think and speak falsely is indeed to have reached something in itself false, something with the *non*- built in? Are we alone the lords of lies or is there, right within the realm of thought, temptation to saying what is not the case? Is naysaying elicited by Nonbeing?

Those philosophers who leave room for Nonbeing in the realm of intelligible beings consider it the source of negativity in our thinking and speaking. That is to say, the motor of our oppositional discriminations is not in some inherent negativity of our thinking but in the object of our thought. It is Nonbeing that makes it possible for us to engage in the perspectival denials I have described above: "this, which near is near (and probably dear) to me, and not-this, which is away from me." Thus Nonbeing functions as otherness, so that the *not* in our negative propositions is a response to the *non-* of Nonbeing. And that means that our naysaying has more in it of contrariety than of contradiction, of reference to diversity than of absolute denial. That version of Nonbeing in which it plays the part of the Other might be called horizontal Nonbeing, because it means that all beings are on the same level; they are all each others' other and indifferently diverse. Nonbeing as otherness is the universal relativity, the relativity of even the most selfsame, stable beings of thought.

But there is also in this schema a vertical Nonbeing—just that responsible cause of falseness of all sorts broached above. This Nonbeing is not objectified relativity but has in it something of absolute inferiority, of defective or deficient Being. Its *non-* is that meant in the speech of denigration, that is, in the derogatory denial which seems to fit certain objects insofar as we analyze them in thought: images, fictions, lies, mistakes. Thus Nonbeing, too, is conceivable as the negative object of distinction-making speech.

3. THE NAY AND YEA OF IMAGINATION AND TIME

In the middle of our human constitution there is a fieldlike capacity for experiencing nonexistence. Its deliverances are neither the viewless, pictureless thoughts of Nonbeing that we entertain in the intellect when we analyze the nature of images nor the visual and auditory impressions that come to us through the organs of sense as we open ourselves to the appearances of the external world. They are neither the presences of thought nor the presentations of sense, yet compounded of both: *re*-presentations structured by the distinctions of thought and filled with the echoes of sense. They are the internal images of the imagination.

The external world appears to us as full of missing objects and deprived beings, although neither nonexistence nor privative being shows up immediately in the continuum of mere sensory appearances, which is unrent by lacunae and not disconcerted by defects. Yet the pathos of nonexistence or deficient existence affects us—probably more powerfully than anything else in our lives. How do we experience nonexistence?

Nonexistence seems to me to turn up in the world in four ways: as absences through distance, as bygones in time, as visual images or verbal fictions, as fallings-off from an ideal or norm. We apprehend these through the projections of our imagination: We insert the image of distant friends into our daily rounds; we see the outlines of a tree that's been taken down written into the blue sky; we cast the images of our desire onto canvas or into words; we hold a picture of what ought to be against what does exist. With these projections we defeat the desolating spatial variations and temporal variability of the world, for to experience nonexistence is also to experience a kind of worldly existence—existence with a negative prefix. Against the fair objection that this is conceptual double talk there is this defense: That is how it is for us—we experience quasi-existence, a vivid kind of nonexistence, directly, though internally.

Whether the external world itself harbors inexistence is perhaps undecidable. There are views by which the world that we experience through the senses, the world of existent reality, is in itself and as a whole mere appearance, more a nonbeing than a being. However that may be, we are schooled in the absences *within* existence by an internal capacity. Behind the projections and as their source stand the inward experiences of our *imagination*. The images of the imagination make absence present; they bring before us the distant, the wished for, the bygone as presences in the present.

The rational analysis of these inward phenomena cannot get around the terms Being, Nonbeing and their mingling: Any image, an image in general, is and is *not* what it represents. The *memory* in particular holds images ordered by temporal markers into sequences of "was," "is" and "might be," of which fixed "was" and fluid "might be" are *not* in existence—and thus arises *time*. The imaginative image, the fictive image that can be projected outward but is more often entertained inwardly, the image of what never was and hardly ever could be, lacks reality, that is to say, it does not have the more solid, massive properties of thinghood; it is in part a nonbeing.

It was because the internal images that make an imaginative and a temporal life possible proved to have a negative element in their constitution that an inquiry into negation seemed called for in the first place. Negation has then seemed to be: the human capability for feeling and saying *no*, for having negative objectives in thought and expressing them in sentences qualified by *not*, for entertaining negative objects of sense and thought such as Nonexistence and Nonbeing, for the conceptual motion of dialectical negativity, and finally, for the feel of nothingness and the apprehension of Nothing.

The most matter of course kind of naysaying now appeared to be describable as perspectival distinction-making, a differentiation between what belongs to the naysayer and what is other. Yet reason and reflection could levitate itself above this point of view into more global, objective, neutral positions, those taken in logic and philosophy. At the same time some denials were ineradicably denigrations, recognitions of a hierarchy among beings or existents, insofar as they are infected by Nonexistence or privation.

The most intimately familiar among such mixed beings are the images of the imagination. An image is compounded of nay and yea. It is *not* what it imagines and yet, somehow it *is*. The imagination, which is the capacity for having images, must therefore be thought of as having a negative and a positive aspect. Positively it is, first, the internal "space" that harbors colorless figures of pure mathematics and vivid figures of fiction, paradigms of ideality and dreams for the rectification of reality, quasi-visible models of discursive thinking and figurative representations of the viewless objects of thought. And it is also, as memory, the place where are held fast the shapes of things that no longer are and where are prefigured the things that are not yet. In short, it is in the imagination that appearances are held and time passes. But negatively it is the place of unreal things and evanescent nows.

The question then is this: Imagination and time seem to lie, in the imagined topography of the soul, between the negativity of thinking and the positivity of sensing. Is the naysaying of thought and speech recognizably related to the yea, and particularly the nay, which appear to lie in the constitution of the representations that arise in the imagination and in memory? Of course I have phrased the question prejudicially—I am looking to find a commonality.

The ability we have to live longitudinally around the now point, preserving what no longer is and projecting what might be, and the related capacity to experience nonentities as vivid appearances in a timeless present, seem to mirror the two features of naysaying delineated above: One is the "horizontal" negation that, beginning with the perspective of the naysayer, rises to a panoramic view from which every other is an other's other and every positive is also a negative. The other is its complement, a "vertical," hierarchical negation of Being revealed in Nonbeing and nonexistence, in the thinkable and sensible nonentities.

The first, level dimension of discursive, distinction-making thinking, which is always passing from this to *not* this, from here to *not* here, seems to be mirrored in the passages of *time*; in fact I surmise that it underlies and enters into our internal sense of time. The second, hierarchical dimension of direct—if you like, intuitive—thought has before it beings and their subordinate reflections, nonbeings, nonexistents, nothings; it meets the deliverances of the senses on the inward plain of the *imagination*. There, I conjecture, the thought structure of Nonbeing mates with existence-voided sensation to produce inward images. It is in these images at the center of our human being that all the ways of naysaying come together to deliver us from the brute positivity of existence without consigning us to the blank nothingness of oblivion.

Bibliography

Abbot, Edwin. 1884. *Flatland: A Romance of Many Dimensions.*

Abe, Masao. 1992. "Reply." In *Negation and Theology,* ed. Robert P. Scharlemann. Charlottesville: University Press of Virginia.

Adorno, Theodor W. [1966] 1995. *Negative Dialectics,* trans. E. B. Ashton. New York: Continuum.

Aeschylus. *Prometheus Bound.*

Allen, R. E., and David J. Furley, eds. 1975. *Studies in Presocratic Philosophy II.* London: Routledge & Kegan Paul.

Améry, Jean. [1976] 1999. *On Suicide: A Discourse on Voluntary Death,* trans. John D. Barlow. Bloomington: Indiana University Press.

Anscombe, G. E. M. 1959. *An Introduction to Wittgenstein's* Tractatus. London: Hutchinson University Library.

Anselm, St. [c. 1070a] 1951. *Proslogium; Monologium; An Appendix in Behalf of the Fool by Gaunilon;* and *Cur Deus Homo,* trans. Sidney Norton Deane. La Salle, Ill.: Open Court.

———. [c. 1010b] 1965. *Proslogion.* With *A Reply on Behalf of the Fool* by Gaunilo and *The Author's Reply to Gaunilo,* trans. M. J. Charlesworth. Oxford: Oxford University Press. With Latin text.

———. [c. 1100] 1976. "On the Fall of the Devil." In *Anselm of Canterbury.* Toronto: Edwin Mellen.

Arendt, Hannah. [1971] 1978. *The Life of the Mind.* Vol. 1, *Thinking.* New York: Harcourt Brace Jovanovich.

———. 1971. *The Life of the Mind.* Vol. 2, *Willing.* New York: Harcourt Brace Jovanovich.

Aristotle. [4th. cent. B.C.] *Categories.*

———. *Metaphysics.*

———. *On Interpretation.*

———. *On the Motion of Animals.*

———. 1991. *On Rhetoric: A Theory of Civic Discourse,* trans. George A. Kennedy. Oxford: Oxford University Press.

219

————. *Prior Analytics.*

Auerbach, Erich. [1946] 1957. *Mimesis: The Representation of Reality in Western Literature,* trans. Willard Trask. Garden City, N.Y.: Doubleday Anchor.

Austin, J. L. 1956. "A Plea for Excuses." *Proceedings of the Aristotelian Society* 57: 1–30.

————. [1950] 1964. "Truth." In *Truth,* ed. George Pitcher. Englewood Cliffs, N.J.: Prentice-Hall.

Bach, Johann Sebastian. [c. 1708] 1967. *Cantata No. 4: Christ lag in Todesbanden,* ed. Gerhard Herz. New York: Norton.

Balthasar, Hans Urs von. [1970] 1993. *Mysterium Paschale: The Mystery of Easter,* trans. Aidan Nichols. Grand Rapids, Mich.: Eerdmans.

Barnes, Annette. 1997. *Seeing through Self-Deception.* Cambridge: Cambridge University Press.

Barnes, Jonathan. 1982. *The Presocratic Philosophers.* London: Routledge.

Barrow, John D. 1998. *Impossibility: The Limits of Science and the Science of Limits.* Oxford: Oxford University Press.

Belnap, Nuel D., and Thomas B. Steel. 1976. *The Logic of Questions and Answers.* New Haven, Conn.: Yale University Press.

Bergson, Henri. [1907] 1944. *Creative Evolution,* trans. Arthur Mitchell. New York: Modern Library.

Bernières, Louis de. 1994. *Corelli's Mandolin.* New York: Vintage.

Binswanger, Ludwig. 1962. *Grundformen und Erkenntnis menschlichen Daseins.* 4th ed. Munich: Ernst Reinhardt Verlag.

Boethius. [c. 505] 1997. "On Division." In *Logic and the Philosophy of Language: The Cambridge Translations of Medieval Philosophical Texts,* ed. Norman Kretzmann and Eleanor Stump. Cambridge: Cambridge University Press.

Bok, Sissela. [1978] 1980. *Lying: Moral Choice in Public and Private Life.* London: Quartet.

————. [1983] 1989. *Secrets: On the Ethics of Concealment and Revelation.* New York: Vintage.

Bollnow, Otto Friedrich. [1941] 1968. *Das Wesen der Stimmungen.* Frankfurt: Vittorio Klostermann.

Booth, Stephen. 1998. *Precious Nonsense: The Gettysburg Address, Ben Jonson's Epitaphs on His Children, and* Twelfth Night. Berkeley: University of California Press.

Bosanquet, Bernard. [1888] 1931. *Logic: Or the Morphology of Knowledge.* London: Oxford University Press. 2d ed., 1911.

Bradley, F. H. [1883] 1950. *The Principles of Logic.* London: Oxford University Press. 2d ed., 1922.

Brann, Eva. 1991. *The World of the Imagination: Sum and Substance.* Lanham, Md.: Rowman & Littlefield.

————. [1992] 1997a. "The Second Power of Questions." In *The Past-Present: Selected Writings of Eva Brann,* ed. Pamela Kraus, 167–189. Annapolis, Md.: St. John's College Press.

————. [1993] 1997b. "Telling Lies." In *The Past-Present: Selected Writings of Eva Brann,* ed. Pamela Kraus, 311–325. Annapolis, Md.: St. John's College Press.

————. 1997. "Plato's Theory of Ideas" *The Past-Present: Selected Writings of Eva Brann,* ed. Pamela Kraus, Annapolis, Md.: St. John's College Press.

————. 1999. *What, Then, Is Time?* Lanham, Md.: Rowman & Littlefield.

Brecht, Bertolt. [c. 1930] 1967. "Die Neinsager" (The Naysayers). In *Gesammelte Werke*, 2:623–630. Frankfurt: Suhrkamp Verlag.

Brentano, Franz. 1874. "The Distinction between Mental and Physical Phenomena." In *Psychology from an Empirical Point of View*. Vol. 1, bk. 2, chap. 1.

Brown, Roger. 1973. *A First Language: The Early Stages*. Cambridge: Harvard University Press.

Browne, Sir Thomas. [1658] 1968. "Hydrotaphia: Urne-Burial." In *Sir Thomas Browne: Selected Writings*, ed. Sir Geoffrey Keynes. Chicago: University of Chicago Press.

Budick, Sanford, and Wolfgang Iser. 1996. *Languages of the Unsayable: The Play of Negativity in Literature and Literary Theory*. Stanford, Calif.: Stanford University Press.

Burke, Kenneth. 1945. *A Grammar of Motives*. Berkeley: University of California Press.

Burnet, John. [1892] 1961. *Early Greek Philosophy*. Cleveland, Ohio: Meridian.

Burton, Robert. [1621] 1967. *The Anatomy of Melancholy*. 3 vols. New York: Everyman's Library.

Carroll, Lewis. [1865] 1960. *The Annotated Alice:* Alice's Adventures in Wonderland *and* Through the Looking Glass, annotated by Martin Gardner. New York: Clarkson N. Potter.

———. [1874] 1962. *The Annotated Snark*, ed. Martin Gardner. New York: Simon & Schuster.

———. [1896] 1958. *Symbolic Logic and the Game of Logic*. 4th ed. New York: Dover.

Cartwright, Richard L. 1960. "Negative Existentials." *Journal of Philosophy* 57 (September–October): 629–639.

Carus, Paul. [1900] 1991. *The History of the Devil and the Idea of Evil*. La Salle, Ill.: Open Court.

Casati, Robert, and Achille C. Varzi. 1994. *Holes and Other Superficialities*. Cambridge: MIT Press.

Cassuto, Umberto. [1944] 1961. *A Commentary on the Book of Genesis*, trans. Israel Abrahams. Jerusalem: Magnes.

Chan, Wing-tsit, trans. 1963. "The Philosophy of Emptiness: Chi-tsang of the Three-Treatise School." In *A Source Book of Chinese Philosophy*, chap. 22. Princeton, N.J.: Princeton University Press.

Chaucer, Geoffrey. [1387–1400] 1989. *The Canterbury Tales*, ed. V. A. Kolve and Glending Olson. London: Norton.

Chisholm, Roderick M., ed. 1960. *Realism and the Background of Phenomenology*. Atascadero, Calif.: Ridgeview.

Chung-Yuan, Chang, trans. 1969. *Original Teachings of Ch'an Buddhism*. New York: Pantheon.

Cohen, Hermann. [1914] 1922. *Logik der reinen Erkenntnis*. Berlin: Bruno Cassirer Verlag.

Collingwood, R. G. 1940. *An Essay on Metaphysics*. Oxford: Clarendon.

Coleridge, Samuel Taylor. 1817. *Biographia Literaria*.

Crittenden, Charles. 1991. *Unreality: The Metaphysics of Fictional Objects*. Ithaca, N.Y.: Cornell University Press.

Curd, Patricia. 1998. *The Legacy of Parmenides: Eleatic Monism and Later Presocratic Thought*. Princeton, N.J.: Princeton University Press.

Curme, George O. [1931] 1977. *A Grammar of the English Language*. Vol. 2, *Syntax*. Essex, Conn.: Verbatim.

Currie, Gregory. 1990. *The Nature of Fiction*. Cambridge: Cambridge University Press.

Curtius, Robert. [1948] 1963. *Europäische Literatur und lateinisches Mittelalter*. 4th ed. Bern: Francke Verlag.

Darwin, Charles. 1872. *The Expression of the Emotions in Man and Animals*. Chicago: University of Chicago Press, 1965.

Desmond, William. 1995. *Being and the Between*. Albany: State University of New York Press.

Descartes, René. 1641. *Meditations on First Philosophy*.

Dewey, John. 1938. *Logic and the Theory of Inquiry*. New York: Henry Holt.

Dickinson, Emily. [1883] 1955. *The Poems of Emily Dickinson*, ed. Thomas H. Johnson. Cambridge, Mass.: Belknap.

Diehls, Hermann, ed. 1954. *Die Fragmente der Vorsokratiker: Griechisch und Deutsch*, ed. Walther Kranz. 7th ed. Vol. 1. Berlin: Weidmannsche Verlagsbuchhandlung.

Donne, John. [1590s–] 1952. *The Complete Poetry and Selected Prose*, ed. Charles M. Coffin. New York: Modern Library.

Donnellan, Keith S. [1974] 1977. "Speaking of Nothing." In *Naming, Necessity, and Natural Kinds*, ed. Stephen P. Schwartz. Ithaca, N.Y.: Cornell University Press.

Eck, Marcel. [1965] 1970. *Lies and Truth*, trans. Bernard Murchland. New York: Macmillan.

Eckhart, Johannes. [c. 1300] 1978. *Meister Eckhardt: Deutsche Predigten und Tractate*, trans. Joseph Quint. Munich: Carl Hanser Verlag.

Edwards, Paul. 1967. "My Death." In *The Encyclopedia of Philosophy*. New York: Macmillan.

Ende, Michael. [1973] 1997. *The Neverending Story*, trans. Ralph Manheim. New York: Puffin. I prefer to translate the title as *The Endless Story*.

Feldman, Fred. 1998. "Death." In *Routledge Encyclopedia of Philosophy*. London: Routledge.

Feuerbach, Ludwig. [1830] 1980. *Thoughts on Death and Immortality*, trans. James A. Massey. Berkeley: University of California Press.

Fichte, Johann Gottlieb. 1794. *Grundlage der gesammten Wissenschaftslehre* (Foundations of the Whole Doctrine of Knowledge).

Findlay, J. N. 1962. *Hegel: A Re-examination*. New York: Collier.

———. 1963. *Meinong's Theory of Objects and Values*. Oxford: Clarendon.

Fingarette, Herbert. 1996. *Death: Philosophical Soundings*. La Salle, Ill.: Open Court.

Forster, E. M. 1924. *A Passage to India*. New York: Harcourt, Brace and World.

Fränkel, Hermann. [1955] 1975. "Studies in Parmenides." In *Studies in Presocratic Philosophy II*, ed. R. E. Allen and David J. Furley. London: Routledge & Kegan Paul.

Frege, Gottlob. [1919] 1970. "Negation." In *Translations from the Philosophical Writings of Gottlob Frege*, ed. Peter Geach and Max Black. Oxford: Basil Blackwell.

Freud, Sigmund. [1925] 1963. "Negation." In *General Psychological Theory: Papers on Metapsychology*, ed. Philip Rieff. New York: Macmillan.

Fried, Charles. [1978] 1993. "The Evil of Lying." In *Vice and Virtue in Everyday Life: Introductory Readings in Ethics*, ed. Christina Sommers and Fred Sommers. Fort Worth, Tex.: Harcourt Brace College Publishers.

Friedländer, Paul. [1954] 1958. *Plato.* New York: Pantheon.

Frisk, Hjalmar. 1960. *Griechisches Etymologisches Wörterbuch.* Heidelberg: Carl Winter.

Fritz, Kurt von. [1945] 1974. "*Nous, Noein*, and Their Derivation in Pre-Socratic Philosophy." In *The Pre-Socratics: A Collection of Critical Essays*, ed. Alexander P. D. Mourelatos. Garden City, N.Y.: Anchor.

Frost, Robert. [1947] 1973. "Directive." In *The Norton Anthology of Modern Poetry*, ed. Richard Ellmann and Robert O'Clair. New York: Norton.

Furth, Montgomery. [1971] 1974. "Elements of Eleatic Ontology." In *The Pre-Socratics: A Collection of Critical Essays*, ed. Alexander P. D. Mourelatos. Garden City, N.Y.: Anchor.

Gale, Richard M. 1976. *Negation and Non-Being.* Monograph 10. *American Philosophical Quarterly.* Oxford: Basil Blackwell.

Gallagher, Shaun. 1998. *The Inordinance of Time.* Evanston, Ill.: Northwestern University Press.

Gallop, David. 1984. *Parmenides of Elea: Fragments, a Text, and Translation.* Toronto: University of Toronto Press.

Gardiner, Patrick. [1969] 1980. "Error, Faith, and Self-Deception." In *The Philosophy of Mind*, ed. Jonathan Glover. Oxford: Oxford University Press.

Gebauer, Gunter, and Christoph Wulf, eds. 1995. *Mimesis: Culture—Art—Society*, trans. Don Reneau. Berkeley: University of California Press.

Genz, Henning. 1994. *Nothingness: The Science of Empty Space*, trans. Karin Heusch. Reading, Mass.: Perseus.

Gillespie, Michael Allen. 1995. *Nihilism Before Nietzsche.* Chicago: University of Chicago Press.

Goethe, Johann Wolfgang von. 1797. *Faust: Part One of the Tragedy.*

Goodman, Nelson. 1976. *Languages of Art: An Approach to a Theory of Symbols.* Indianapolis, Ind.: Hackett.

Graham, A. C. 1989. *Disputers of the Tao: Philosophical Argument in Ancient China.* La Salle, Ill.: Open Court.

Graves, Robert. [1948] 1959. *The White Goddess.* New York: Vintage.

Grayling, A. C. 1982. *An Introduction to Philosophical Logic.* Sussex: Harvester.

Greville, Fulke. [1633] 1870. *The Works in Verse and Prose Complete*, ed. Rev. Alexander B. Grosal. Private circulation.

Grossman, Reinhardt. 1974. *Meinong.* London: Routledge & Kegan Paul.

Grudin, Robert. 1991. "The Cretan Saieth: 'All Cretans are Liars.'" *Hellas* 2, no. 1: 78–92.

Hanh, Thich Nhat. [1974] 1995. *Zen Keys.* New York: Doubleday.

Hardwick, Elizabeth. 1984. "Bartleby in Manhattan." In *Bartleby in Manhattan and Other Essays.* New York: Vintage.

Harris, Errol E. 1983. *An Interpretation of the Logic of Hegel.* Lanham, Md.: University Press of America.

Harrison, Bernhard. 1993. "Imagined Worlds and the Real One: Plato, Wittgenstein, and Mimesis." *Philosophy and Literature* 17: 26–46.

Hartle, Ann. 1986. *Death and the Disinterested Spectator: An Inquiry into the Nature of Philosophy.* Albany: State University of New York Press.

Hartmann, Nicolai. [1909] 1965. *Platos Logik des Seins.* Berlin: Walter de Gruyter.

Hartshorne, Charles. 1965. *Anselm's Discovery: A Re-examination of the Ontological Proof for God's Existence.* La Salle, Ill.: Open Court.

Hausdorff, Felix. [1937] 1962. *Set Theory,* trans. John R. Aumann et al. New York: Chelsea.

Heath, P. L. 1967. "Nothing." In *The Encyclopedia of Philosophy,* ed. Paul Edwards. New York: Macmillan.

Heath, Thomas L., trans., ed., comm. [1925] 1956. *The Thirteen Books of Euclid's Elements.* 2d ed. New York: Dover.

Hegel, G. W. F. [1803] 1970. *Werke 2: Jenaer Schriften* (1801–1807), ed. Eva Moldenhauer and Karl Markus Michel. Frankfurt: Suhrkamp Verlag.

———. [1807] 1952. *Phänomenologie des Geistes,* ed. Johannes Hoffmeister. *Philosophische Bibliothek.* Hamburg: Felix Meiner.

———. [1812a] 1951. *Wissenschaft der Logik,* ed. Georg Lasson. *Philosophische Bibliothek.* Leipzig: Felix Meiner.

———. [1812b] 1989. *Hegel's Science of Logic,* trans. A. K. Miller. Atlantic Highlands, N.J.: Humanities.

———. 1820s. *Lectures on the History of Philosophy.*

———. [1830a] 1959. *Enzyklopädie der philosophischen Wissenschaften im Grundrisse,* ed. Friedhelm Nicolin and Otto Pöggeler. *Philosophische Bibliothek.* Hamburg: Felix Meiner.

———. [1830b] 1965. *The Logic of Hegel Translated from The Encyclopaedia of the Philosophical Sciences,* trans. William Wallace. Oxford: Oxford University Press.

Heidegger, Martin. [1924] 1992. *Platon: Sophistes.* Vol. 19, ed. Ingeborg Schüssler. Frankfurt: Vittorio Klostermann.

———. [1925–1926] 1976. *Logik: Die Frage nach der Wahrheit.* Frankfurt: Vittorio Klostermann.

———. [1927a] 1988. *The Basic Problems of Phenomenology,* trans. Albert Hofstadter. Bloomington: Indiana University Press.

———. [1927b] 1962. *Being and Time,* trans. John Macquarrie and Edward Robinson. New York: Harper & Row.

———. [1928] 1992. *The Metaphysical Foundations of Logic,* trans. Michael Heim. Bloomington: Indiana University Press.

———. [1929a] 1969. *The Essence of Reasons* [Vom Wesen des Grundes], trans. Terence Malick. Evanston: Northwestern University Press.

———. [1929b] 1995. *The Fundamental Concepts of Metaphysics: World, Finitude, Solitude,* trans. William McNeill and Nicholas Walker. Bloomington: Indiana University Press.

———. [1929c] 1949. "What Is Metaphysics?" trans. R. F. C. Hull and Alan Crick. In *Existence and Being.* Chicago: Henry Regnery. With an introduction by Werner Brock.

———. [1935] 1958. *Einführung in die Metaphysik.* Tübingen: Max Niemeyer Verlag.

———. [1942] 1998. *Parmenides,* trans. André Schuwer and Richard Rojcewicz. Bloomington: Indiana University Press.

————. 1961. *Nietzsche.* Pfullingen: Neske.

Heiss, Robert. 1932. *Logik des Widerspruchs.* Berlin: Walter de Gruyter.

Herodotus. [450–430 B.C.] *The Histories.*

Hintikka, Jaakko. 1969. "On the Logic of Perception." In *Models for Modalities.* Boston: Reidel.

Hiż, Henry, ed. 1979. *Questions.* Boston: Reidel.

Hofstadter, Douglas R. 1980. *Gödel, Escher, Bach: An Eternal Golden Braid.* New York: Vintage.

Holy Bible: Authorized Version [King James], ed. Rev. C. F. Scofield. 1917. New York: Oxford University Press.

Homer. [8th cent. B.C.] *The Iliad, The Odyssey.*

Hopkins, Burt C. 1999. *Phenomenology: Japanese and American Perspectives.* Dortrecht: Kluwer Academic Publishers.

Howell, Robert. 1998. "Fiction, Semantics of." In *Routledge Encyclopedia of Philosophy,* ed. Edward Craig. Vol. 3. London: Routledge.

Howland, Jacob. 1998. *The Paradox of Political Philosophy: Socrates' Philosophic Trial.* Lanham, Md.: Rowman & Littlefield.

Hume, David. 1739. *A Treatise of Human Nature.*

————. 1758. *An Enquiry Concerning Human Understanding.*

Inwood, Michael. 1992. *A Hegel Dictionary.* Oxford: Blackwell.

James, William. [1896–1906] 1963. *Pragmatism and Other Essays.* New York: Washington Square.

Jaspers, Karl. [1919] 1960. *Psychologie der Weltanschauungen.* Berlin: Springer-Verlag.

————. [1957] 1966. "Nagarjuna." In *The Great Philosophers.* London: Rupert Hart-Davis.

Jay, Martin. 1993. *Downcast Eyes: The Denigration of Vision in Twentieth Century French Thought.* Berkeley: University of California Press.

Jespersen, Otto. [1922] 1954. *Language: Its Nature, Development, and Origin.* London: George Allen & Unwin.

————. [1924] 1958. *The Philosophy of Grammar.* London: George Allen & Unwin.

Johnson-Laird, P. N. 1983. *Mental Models: Towards a Cognitive Science of Language, Inference, and Consciousness.* Cambridge: Harvard University Press.

Jonas, Hans. [1962–1993] 1996. *Mortality and Morality: A Search for the Good after Auschwitz,* ed. Lawrence Vogel. Evanston, Ill.: Northwestern University Press.

Jüngel, Eberhard. 1990. *Theological Writings II,* trans. and ed. J. B. Webster. Edinburgh: Clark.

Kainz, Howard P. 1976. *Hegel's* Phenomenology. Pt. 1, *Analysis and Commentary.* Tuscaloosa: University of Alabama Press.

Kamke, E. [1928] 1950. *Theory of Sets,* trans. F. Bagemihl. New York: Dover.

Kant, Immanuel. 1763a. "An Attempt to Introduce the Concept of Negative Numbers into Philosophy."

————. 1763b. "The Only Possible Argumentative Ground for a Demonstration of God's Existence."

————. 1781 (A, 1st ed.). *Critique of Pure Reason.*

————. 1786 (B, 2nd ed.). *Critique of Pure Reason.*

————. 1783. *Prolegomena to Any Future Metaphysics.*

———. 1790. *Critique of Judgment.*

Kaufman, Walter, trans. and ed. 1965. *Hegel, Texts and Commentary.* Garden City, N.Y.: Anchor.

Kearney, Richard. 1988. *The Wake of Imagination: Toward a Postmodern Culture.* Minneapolis: University of Minnesota Press.

Keats, John. [1816–1820] 1952. *The Letters of John Keats,* ed. Maurice Forman. London: Oxford University Press.

Kierkegaard, Søren. [1841] 1966. *The Concept of Irony, With Constant Reference to Socrates,* trans. Lee M. Capel. London: Collins.

———. 1844a. *Philosophical Fragments, or A Fragment of Philosophy.*

———. 1844b. *The Concept of Dread.*

Kingsley, Peter. 1999. *In the Dark Places of Wisdom.* Inverness, Calif.: Golden Sufi Center.

Kirk, G. S., and J. E. Raven. 1963. *The Presocratic Philosophers.* Cambridge: Cambridge University Press.

Kleene, Stephen C. 1952. *Introduction to Metamathematics.* Princeton: D. Van Nostrand, 1964.

Klein, Jacob. [1934–1936] 1992. *Greek Mathematical Thought and the Origin of Algebra,* trans. Eva Brann. New York: Dover.

Klima, Edward S., and Ursula Bellugi-Klima. 1966. "Syntactic Regularities in the Speech of Children." In *Psycholinguistics Papers,* ed. J. Lyons and R. J. Wales. Edinburgh: Edinburgh University Press.

Kneale, William. [1936] 1949. "Is Existence a Predicate?" In *Readings in Philosophical Analysis,* ed. Herbert Feigl and Wilfred Sellars. New York: Appleton-Century-Crofts.

Kneale, William, and Martha Kneale. [1962] 1978. *The Development of Logic.* Oxford: Clarendon.

Knight, Deborah. 1997. "Does Tom Think Squire Allworthy Is Real?" *Philosophy and Literature* 21: 433–443.

Kojève, Alexandre. [1947] 1969. *Introduction to the Reading of Hegel: Lectures on the Phenomenology of the Spirit,* ed. Allan Bloom, trans. James H. Nichols. New York: Basic. Assembled by Raymond Queneau.

Kretzmann, Norman, and Eleanor Stump. 1997. *Logic and the Philosophy of Language: The Cambridge Translations of Medieval Philosophical Texts.* Cambridge: Cambridge University Press.

Kristeva, Julia. [1974] 1984. *Revolution in Poetic Language,* trans. Margaret Waller. New York: Columbia University Press.

Ladusaw, William A. 1996. "Negative Concord and 'Mode of Judgment.'" In *Negation: A Notion in Focus,* ed. Henrich Wansing. New York: Walter de Gruyter.

Lamarque, Peter. 1996. *Fictional Points of View.* Ithaca, N.Y.: Cornell University Press.

———. 1998. "Fictional Entities." In *Routledge Encyclopedia of Philosophy,* ed. Edward Craig. London: Routledge.

Lambert, Karel. 1983. *Meinong and the Principle of Independence: Its Place in Meinong's Theory of Objects and Its Significance in Contemporary Logic.* Cambridge: Cambridge University Press.

Langer, Susanne K. 1937. *An Introduction to Symbolic Logic.* New York: Dover, 1953.

Lavoisier, Antoine. 1789. *Treatise on the Elements of Chemistry.*

Lawson, Hilary. 1985. *Reflexivity: The Post-Modern Predicament.* La Salle, Ill.: Open Court.

Leiber, Justin. 1993. *Paradoxes.* Newburyport, Mass.: Focus.

L'Engle, Madeleine. 1973. *A Wind in the Door.* New York: Dell.

Léon-Portilla, Miguel, ed. 1980. *Native Mesoamerican Spirituality.* New York: Paulist.

Levinas, Emmanuel. [1946] 1989. "Time and the Other." In *The Levinas Reader,* ed. Seán Hand. Oxford: Basil Blackwell.

Lewis, David. 1978. "Truth in Fiction." *American Philosophical Quarterly* 15: 37–46.

Linsky, Leonard. 1967. *Referring.* Atlantic Highlands, N.J.: Humanities, 1984.

Lloyd, G. E. R. 1966. *Polarity and Analogy: Two Types of Argumentation in Early Greek Thought.* Cambridge: Cambridge University Press.

Lotz, J. B. 1967. "Transcendentals." In *New Catholic Encyclopedia.* New York: Mc-Graw-Hill.

Löwith, Karl. [1983] 1995. *Martin Heidegger and European Nihilism,* trans. Gary Steiner. New York: Columbia University Press.

Lucretius. 1963. *Titi Lucreti Cari:* De Rerum Natura *Libri Sex.* Vol. 2, ed. Cyril Bailey. Oxford: Clarendon.

Lyons, John. [1970] 1984. *Noam Chomsky.* New York: Penguin.

———. [1977] 1994. *Semantics.* Cambridge: Cambridge University Press.

MacCormick, Sabine. 1991. *Religion in the Andes: Vision and Imagination in Early Colonial Peru.* Princeton, N.J.: Princeton University Press.

MacDonald, Scott. 1991. "The Metaphysics of Goodness and the Doctrine of the Transcendentals." In *Being and Goodness: The Concept of the Good in Metaphysics and Philosophical Theology,* ed. Scott MacDonald. Ithaca, N.Y.: Cornell University Press.

Mallik, Basanta Kumar. 1940. *The Real and the Negative.* London: George Allen & Unwin.

Manchester, Peter. 1979. "Parmenides and the Need for Eternity." *Monist* 62, no. 1: 81–106.

Mann, Thomas. [1954] 1956. "Abschiedsbriefe europäischer Freiheitskämpfer." In *Altes und Neues.* Frankfurt: S. Fischer.

Maritain, Jacques. 1937. *Formal Logic,* trans. Imelda Choquette. New York: Sheed & Ward.

Martin, Robert L., ed. 1978. *The Paradox of the Liar.* Atascadero, Calif.: Ridgeway.

Maurer, Daphne, and Charles Maurer. 1988. *The World of the Newborn.* New York: Basic.

McGinn, Bernard. 1994. *Antichrist: Two Thousand Years of the Human Fascination with Evil.* San Francisco: HarperCollins.

Meinong, Alexius. [1889] 1929. "Phantasie-Vorstellung und Phantasie: Abhandlung IV." In *Gesammelte Abhandlungen.* Vol 1. Leipzig: Johann Ambrosius Barth. This volume was edited by Meinong's students.

———. [1904] 1960. "The Theory of Objects," trans. Isaac Levi, D. B. Terrell, and Roderick M. Chisholm. In *Realism and the Background of Phenomenology,* ed. Roderick Chisholm. Atascadero, Calif.: Ridgeview.

———. [1910] 1983. *On Assumptions,* trans. James Heanue. Berkeley: University of California Press.

Melville, Herman. 1853. *Bartleby, the Scrivener.*

Mihm, Stephen. 2000. "The Dead." *Lingua Franca,* December–January, 26–28.

Mikolajczak, Michael, ed. 1997. *Logos* 1, no. 1.

Miller, George A., and Philip N. Johnson-Laird. 1976. *Language and Perception.* Cambridge: Harvard University Press.

Milton, John. 1667. *Paradise Lost.*

Moltke, Helmut James von. [1939–1945] 1990. *Letters to Freya,* trans. Beate Ruhm von Oppen. New York: Knopf.

Monro, Harold. "Living." In *Immortal Poems of the English Language,* ed. Oscar Williams. New York: Washington Square, 1952.

Montaigne, Michel. 1580. *Essays.*

Moore, G. E. [1936] 1965. "Is Existence a Predicate?" In *Logic and Language,* ed. Anthony Flew. Garden City, N.Y.: Anchor.

———. [1910–1911] 1953. *Some Main Problems in Philosophy.* London: Allen & Unwin.

More, Thomas. [1516] 1965. *Utopia: The Complete Works of Sir Thomas More.* Vol. 4, ed. Edward Surtz, S. J., and J. H. Hexter. New Haven, Conn.: Yale University Press.

Morris, Desmond, et al. 1980. *Gestures: Their Origins and Distribution.* New York: Stein & Day.

Motzkin, Gabriel. 1996. "Heidegger's Transcendent Nothing." In *Languages of the Unsayable: The Play of Negativity in Literature and Literary Theory,* ed. Sanford Budick and Wolfgang Iser. Stanford, Calif.: Stanford University Press.

Mounce, H. O. 1981. *Wittgenstein's* Tractatus*: An Introduction.* Chicago: University of Chicago Press.

Mourelatos, Alexander P. D. [1970] 1974. "The Deceptive Words of Parmenides' 'Doxa.'" In *The Pre-Socratics: A Collection of Critical Essays.* Garden City, N.Y.: Anchor.

Mourelatos, Alexander P. D., ed. 1974. *The Pre-Socratics: A Collection of Critical Essays.* Garden City, N.Y.: Anchor.

Mure, G. R. G. 1940. *An Introduction to Hegel.* Oxford: Clarendon.

Nabokov, Vladimir. 1972. *Transparent Things.* New York: Vintage, 1989.

Nicholas of Cusa. 1444. *On the Hidden God.*

Nogales, Patti D. 1999. *Metaphorically Speaking.* Stanford, Calif.: CSLI Publications.

O'Brien, Denis. 1996. "Plotinus on Matter and Evil." In *The Cambridge Companion to Plotinus,* ed. Lloyd P. Gerson. Cambridge: Cambridge University Press.

Ockham. [c. 1320] 1957. *Philosophical Writings,* ed. Philotheus Boehner. Edinburgh: Thomas Nelson.

Ogden, C. K., and I. A. Richards. 1923. *The Meaning of Meaning: A Study of the Influence of Language upon Thought and of the Science of Symbolism.* New York: Harcourt Brace Jovanovich.

Ong, Walter J., S. J. 1958. *Ramus: Method, and the Decay of Dialogue.* Cambridge: Harvard University Press.

Owen, G. E. L. 1966. "Plato and Parmenides on the Timeless Present." In *The Pre-Socratics: A Collection of Critical Essays,* ed. Alexander P. D. Mourelatos. Garden City, N.Y.: Anchor.

Oxford Dictionary of English Etymology, ed. C. T. Onions. Oxford: Clarendon, 1966.

Panofsky, Erwin. 1924. *Idea: A Concept in Art Theory,* trans. Joseph Peake. Columbia: University of South Carolina Press, 1968.

Parsons, Terence. 1980. *Nonexistent Objects.* New Haven, Conn.: Yale University Press.

Pears, D. F., and James Thompson. 1963. "Is Existence a Predicate?" In *Philosophical Logic,* ed. P. F. Strawson. Oxford: Oxford University Press, 1967.

Peirce, Charles S. [1867–1893] 1992. *The Essential Peirce: Selected Philosophical Writings,* ed. N. Hauser and C. Klosel. Vol. 1. Bloomington: Indiana University Press.

Pelletier, Francis Jeffry. 1990. *Parmenides, Plato, and the Semantics of Not-Being.* Chicago: University of Chicago Press.

Philipse, Herman. 1998. *Heidegger's Philosophy of Being: A Critical Interpretation.* Princeton, N.J.: Princeton University Press.

Piaget, Jean. [1928] 1969. *Judgment and Reasoning in the Child.* London: Routledge & Kegan Paul.

Pitcher, George, ed. 1964. *Truth.* Englewood Cliffs, N.J.: Prentice-Hall.

Plantinga, Alvin. 1974. *The Nature of Necessity.* Oxford: Clarendon.

Plato. [c. 385 B.C.] 1998. *Plato's Phaedo,* trans. Eva Brann, Peter Kalkavage, and Eric Salem. Newburyport, Mass.: Focus.

———. *The Republic.*

———. 1996. *Plato's Sophist or the Professor of Wisdom,* trans. Eva Brann, Peter Kalkavage, and Eric Salem. Newburyport, Mass.: Focus.

Plotinus. 255–270 *Enneads.*

———. c. 265 "Concerning What Are and Whence Come Bad Things" *Ennead* 1.8.

Prescott, William H. 1843. *History of the Conquest of Mexico.*

———. 1847. *History of the Conquest of Peru.*

Prior, A. N. 1967. "Existence." In *Encyclopedia of Philosophy,* ed. Paul Edwards. New York: Macmillan.

Quine, Willard Van Orman. 1950. *Methods of Logic.* 3d ed. New York: Holt, Rinehart & Winston, 1972.

———. [1953] 1980. "On What There Is." In *From a Logical Point of View: Nine Logico-philosophical Essays.* Cambridge: Harvard University Press.

Récanati, François. 1979. "Pragmatic Paradoxes," trans. Bettina Bergo. *Graduate Faculty Philosophy Journal* 17: 289–298.

Reinhardt, Karl. 1959. *Parmenides und die Geschichte der griechischen Philosophie.* 2d ed. Frankfurt: Vittorio Klostermann.

Ricoeur, Paul. 1967. *The Symbolism of Evil,* trans. Emerson Buchanan. Boston: Beacon, 1969.

Rosen, Stanley. 1969. *Nihilism: A Philosophical Essay.* New Haven, Conn.: Yale University Press.

———. 1980. *The Limits of Analysis.* New York: Basic Books, Inc.

———. 1983. *Plato's Sophist: The Drama of Original and Image.* New Haven, Conn.: Yale University Press.

———. 1988. "Much Ado about Nothing." In *The Quarrel Between Philosophy and Poetry.* London: Routledge.

Rosenberg, Jay F. 1998. *Thinking Clearly about Death.* 2d ed. Indianapolis, Ind.: Hackett.

Russell, Bertrand. 1903. *The Principles of Mathematics.* London: George Allen & Unwin, 1956.

———. [1904] 1973. "Meinong's Theory of Complexes and Assumptions." In Essays in Analysis, ed. Douglas Lackey. New York: George Braziller.

———. [1905a] 1973. "The Existential Import of Propositions." In *Essays in Analysis*, ed. Douglas Lackey. New York: George Braziller.

———. [1905b] 1973. Review of *Untersuchungen zur Gegenstandstheorie und Psychologie,* by A. Meinong. In *Essays in Analysis*, ed. Douglas Lackey. New York: George Braziller.

———. [1905c] 1973. "On Denoting." In *Essays in Analysis*, ed. Douglas Lackey. New York: George Braziller.

———. 1907. Review of A. Meinong, "Über die Stellung der Gegenstandstheorie im System der Wissenschaften." In *Essays in Analysis*, ed. Douglas Lackey. New York: George Braziller.

———. [1918] 1956. "The Philosophy of Logical Atomism." In *Logic and Knowledge, Essays 1901–1950*, ed. R. C. Marsh. London: Allen & Unwin.

———. [1919] 1956. *Introduction to Mathematical Philosophy.* London: George Allen & Unwin.

———. [1957] 1973. "Mr. Strawson on Referring." In *Essays in Analysis*, ed. Douglas Lackey. New York: George Braziller.

———. 1973. *Essays in Analysis,* ed. Douglas Lackey. New York: George Braziller.

Sartre, Jean-Paul. [1943] 1956. *Being and Nothing: A Phenomenological Essay on Ontology,* trans. Hazel Barnes. New York: Pocket Books.

Scharlemann, Robert P., ed. 1992. *Negation and Theology.* Charlottesville: University Press of Virginia.

Scheler, Max. [1912–1916] 1957. "Tod und Fortleben." In *Schriften aus dem Nachlass.* Vol. 1, *Zur Ethik und Erkenntnislehre.* Bern: Franke Verlag.

Schopenhauer, Arthur. 1819. *The World as Will and Representation.*

Schwartz, Joseph, ed. *Renascence* 37, no. 3 (Spring 1985).

Searle, John R. 1983. *Intentionality: An Essay in the Philosophy of Mind.* Cambridge: Cambridge University Press.

Seddon, Keith. 1987. *Time: A Philosophical Treatment.* London: Croon Helm.

Shakespeare, William. 1593. *Sonnets.*

———. [1600] 1964. *Much Ado about Nothing: A New Variorum Edition.* New York: Dover.

———. [1605] 1963. *King Lear: A New Variorum Edition.* New York: Dover.

Shattuck, Roger. 1996. "The Divine Marquis." In *Forbidden Knowledge: From Prometheus to Pornography,* chap. 7. San Diego, Calif.: Harcourt, Brace.

Sheehan, Thomas. 1999. "Nihilism: Heidegger/Jünger/Aristotle." In *Phenomenology: Japanese and American Perspectives*, ed. Burt C. Hopkins. Boston: Kluwer Academic Publishers.

Shepard, Odell. [1956] 1979. *The Lore of the Unicorn.* New York: Harper & Row.

Smith, David Eugene. [1923] 1958. *History of Mathematics.* Vol. 2. New York: Dover.

———. [1929] 1959. *A Source Book in Mathematics.* New York: Dover.

Sokolowski, Robert. 1978. *Presence and Absence: A Philosophical Investigation of Language and Being*. Bloomington: Indiana University Press.

――――. 1979. "Making Distinctions." *Review of Metaphysics* 32: 639–676.

Sophocles. *Oedipus at Colonus*.

Spitz, René A. 1957. *No and Yes: On the Genesis of Human Communication*. New York: International Universities Press.

――――. 1965. *The First Year of Life: A Psychoanalytic Study of Normal and Deviant Development of Object Relations*. New York: International Universities Press.

Spock, Benjamin. 1968. *Baby and Child Care*. Rev. ed. New York: Pocket Books.

Stace, W. T. 1923. *The Philosophy of Hegel: A Systematic Exposition*. New York: Dover, 1955.

Stebbing, L. Susan. [1931] 1961. *A Modern Introduction to Logic*. New York: Harper & Brothers.

Stelzner, Werner. 1996. "Negation and Relevance." In *Negation: A Notion in Focus,* ed. Henrich Wansing. New York: Walter de Gruyter.

Stevens, Wallace. [1915–1955] 1972. *The Palm at the End of the Mind: Selected Poems*, ed. Holly Stevens. New York: Vintage.

Strawson, P. F. [1950] 1956. "On Referring." In *Essays in Conceptual Analysis*, ed. Anthony Flew. London: Macmillan.

Swift, Jonathan. 1726. *Gulliver's Travels into Several Remote Nations of the World*.

Tarán, Leonardo. 1965. *Parmenides: A Text with Translation, Commentary, and Critical Essays*. Princeton, N.J.: Princeton University Press.

Tashlin, Frank. 1946. *The Bear That Wasn't*.

Thomas Aquinas. [1256–1272] 1945. *Summa Theologica*. In *Basic Writings of Saint Thomas Aquinas,* ed. Anton C. Pegis. New York: Random House.

――――. [1266–1272] 1961. *Commentary on the* Metaphysics *of Aristotle*, trans. John P. Rowan. Chicago: Henry Regnery, 1961.

Thomas Aquinas and Cajetan. [1496] 1962. *Aristotle:* On Interpretation, *Commentary*, trans. Jean T. Oesterle. Milwaukee, Wis.: Marquette University Press.

Turgenev, Ivan. 1861. *Fathers and Sons*.

Ueberweg, Friedrich. [1862] 1885. *A History of Philosophy from Thales to the Present Time*, trans. George S. Morris. London: Hodder & Stoughton.

Umphrey, Stewart. 1988. "The Meinongian-Anti-Meinongian Dispute Reviewed: A Reply to Dejnozka and Butchvarov," *Grazer Philosophische Studien* 32: 169–179.

――――. 2000. *Complexity*. Unpublished.

Valéry, Paul. 1922. "Ébauche d'un serpent." In *Charmes ou poèmes*.

Vattimo, Gianni. [1985] 1991. *The End of Modernity*, trans. John R. Snyder. Baltimore, Md.: Johns Hopkins University Press.

Waismann, Friedrich. [1951] 1959. *Introduction to Mathematical Thinking: The Formulation of Concepts in Modern Mathematics*. New York: Harper & Brothers.

Walde, A., and J. B. Hoffmann. 1938. *Lateinisches etymologisches Wörterbuch*. 3d ed. Heidelberg: Carl Winter.

Wallace, W. A. 1967. "Thing." In *New Catholic Encyclopedia*. New York: McGraw-Hill.

Wansing, Heinrich, ed. 1996. *Negation: A Notion in Focus*. Perspectives in Analytical Philosophy. New York: Walter de Gruyter.

Watkins, Calvert. 1992. "Indo-European Roots Appendix." In *The American Heritage Dictionary.* Boston: Houghton Mifflin.

Weidemann, Hermann. [1979] 1983. "'*Socrates Est'/'There Is No Such Thing as Pegasus*': Thomas Aquinas and W. Van Orman Quine on the Logic of Singular Existence Statements." In *Contemporary German Philosophy,* ed. Darrel E. Christensen et al. 3d ed. University Park: Pennsylvania State University Press.

Westphal, Jonathan, and Carl Levenson, eds. 1993. *Life and Death.* Indianapolis, Ind.: Hackett.

Whitehead, Alfred North, and Bertrand Russell. [1913] 1962. *Principia Mathematica to *56.* Cambridge: Cambridge University Press.

Wilder, Raymond L. 1964. *Introduction to the Foundations of Mathematics.* New York: Wiley.

Wilson, John Cook. [1926] 1969. *Statement and Inference.* Oxford: Clarendon.

Witt, Charlotte. 1989. *Substance and Essence in Aristotle: An Interpretation of* Metaphysics VII–IX. Ithaca, N.Y.: Cornell University Press.

Wittgenstein, Ludwig. [1914–1916] 1961. *Notebooks 1914–1916.* Oxford: Blackwell.

———. [1921] 1961. *Tractatus Logico-philosophicus,* trans. D. F. Pears and B. F. McGuiness. London: Routledge & Kegan Paul. With an introduction by Bertrand Russell. Facing German and English.

———. [1933–1935] 1965. *The Blue and Brown Books: Preliminary Studies for the "Philosophical Investigations."* New York: Harper & Row.

———. [1945–1949] 1957. *Philosophical Investigations,* trans. G. E. M. Anscombe. New York: Macmillan. Facing German and English.

Wordsworth, William. 1807. "Ode: Intimations of Immortality from Recollections of Early Childhood." In *The Norton Anthology of Poetry,* ed. Alexander W. Allison et al. New York: Norton, 1983.

Zwarts, Frans. 1996. "A Hierarchy of Negative Expressions." In *Negation: A Notion in Focus,* ed. Henrich Wansing. New York: Walter de Gruyter.

Index

About the Author

Eva Brann began her working life at the American excavations of the Athenian marketplace, studying a particularly exuberant period in early Attic pottery. In 1957 she left archaeology to become a tutor at St. John's College in Annapolis, Maryland, where she has taught ever since, except for seven years' service as dean (1990–97).

This is her third book with Rowman & Littlefield, and the last of a trilogy dealing with three central human capacities. *The World of the Imagination* (1991) is about our ability to make the absent present. *What, Then, Is Time?* (1999) is about our ability to live with what is no longer or not yet. And now *The Ways of Naysaying* deals with our ability to focus on something to which we deny existence, reality, or being.